The Mortal Messiah
From Bethlehem to Calvary
Book III

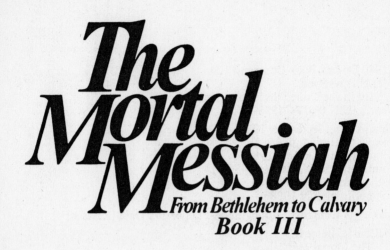

The Mortal Messiah

From Bethlehem to Calvary
Book III

Bruce R. McConkie

Deseret Book Company
Salt Lake City, Utah
1980

©1980 Deseret Book Company
All rights reserved
Printed in the United States of America
Vol. 3, ISBN 0-87747-825-2

First printing September 1980
Second printing April 1982
Third printing October 1983
Fourth printing November 1986
Fifth printing July 1987
Sixth printing July 1988

Library of Congress Cataloging-in-Publication Data (Revised)

McConkie, Bruce R.
　　The Mortal Messiah.

　　Includes index.
　　1. Jesus Christ—Biography.　2. Christian
biography—Palestine.　3. Judaism—History—Post-
exilic period, 586 B.C.-210 A.D.　I. Title.
BT301.2.M16　　　232.9'01　　　79-19606
ISBN 0-87747-784-1

THE MESSIANIC TRILOGY

The forerunner of this work is *The Promised Messiah: The First Coming of Christ*, which deals with the Messianic Prophecies. This work, *The Mortal Messiah: From Bethlehem to Calvary*, is a Life of Christ published in four books. This is Book III.

BOOK III

Section VII   The Galilean Ministry Reaches Its Peak
Section VIII   The Later Judean Ministry
Section IX   The Perean Ministry
Section X   From the Anointing to the Royal Reign

The other books on the Life of Christ are published separately as follows:

BOOK I

Section I   A Root Out of Dry Ground
Section II   Jesus' Years of Preparation
Section III   Jesus' Early Judean Ministry

BOOK II

Section IV   Jesus Begins the Great Galilean Ministry
Section V   The Twelve, The Sermon on the Mount, and Rising Pharisaic Opposition
Section VI   The Continuing Galilean Ministry

BOOK IV

Section XI   The Paschal Feast, The Private Prayers and Sermons, and Gethsemane
Section XII   The Trials, The Cross, and The Tomb
Section XIII   He Riseth; He Ministereth; He Ascendeth

The concluding work in this whole series will be *The Millennial Messiah: The Second Coming of the Son of Man.*

ABBREVIATIONS

Scriptural references are abbreviated in a standard and self-identifying way. Other books are cited by author and title except for the following:

Commentary I   Bruce R. McConkie, *Doctrinal New Testament Commentary*. Vol. 1, *The Gospels*. Bookcraft, 1965.

Edersheim   Alfred Edersheim, *The Life and Times of Jesus the Messiah*. 1883.

Farrar   F. W. Farrar, *The Life of Christ*. London: Cassell & Co., Ltd., 1874.

Geikie   Cunningham Geikie, *The Life and Words of Christ*. 1886.

Hymns   *Hymns, The Church of Jesus Christ of Latter-day Saints*. 1948.

JST   Joseph Smith Translation (Inspired Version) of the Bible.

Mormon Doctrine   Bruce R. McConkie, *Mormon Doctrine*, 2nd ed. Bookcraft, 1966.

Sketches   Alfred Edersheim, *Sketches of Jewish Social Life in the Days of Christ*. 1876.

Talmage   James E. Talmage, *Jesus the Christ*. 1915.

Teachings   Joseph Fielding Smith, comp., *Teachings of the Prophet Joseph Smith*. 1938.

Temple   Alfred Edersheim, *The Temple: Its Ministry and Services As They Were at the Time of Jesus Christ*.

CONTENTS

SECTION VII

THE GALILEAN MINISTRY REACHES ITS PEAK

Chapter 60

THE LOST SHEEP AMONG THE HEATHEN 5
A Day of Deepening Opposition 5
Ministering Among the Heathen 8
The Miraculous Healings in Decapolis 13
Jesus Feeds the Four Thousand 16

Chapter 61

THE LEAVEN OF THE PHARISEES AND
SADDUCEES 21
False Ministers Seek Signs 22
Beware of the Leaven of Evil Men 25
Jesus Restores Sight by Stages 28

Chapter 62

"THE TESTIMONY OF OUR LORD" 31
'I Am the Son of Man' 31
"Thou Art the Christ" 33
"The Keys of the Kingdom of Heaven" 36

Chapter 63

GOD'S SON—A SUFFERING SERVANT 43
"The Messiah Shall Die and Rise Again" 43

Losing One's Life to Save It 47
The Second Coming—A Day of Rewards 50

Chapter 64

THE TRANSFIGURATION 53
Peter, James, and John Receive the Keys
of the Kingdom 53
Elohim, the Shekinah, and the Son 59
Elias of the Restoration 63

Chapter 65

FROM SUNSHINE TO SHADOW 69
The Healing of the Demoniac Youth 69
Jesus Foretells His Death and Resurrection ... 74
The Miraculous Payment of the Temple Tribute 76

Chapter 66

THE DISCOURSE ON MEEKNESS AND
HUMILITY 79
On Becoming as a Little Child 79
On Casting Sinners Out of the Church 83

Chapter 67

DISCOURSES ON FORGIVENESS AND THE
SEALING POWER 89
On Forgiving One Another 89
On the Sealing Power 91
On Faith and Unity 93
Parable of the Unmerciful Servant 94

Chapter 68

JESUS SENDS FORTH THE SEVENTY 99
Seventies: Their Position and Power 99
Jesus Appoints Other Seventy 101
The Seventy: Their Charge and Commission ... 103
The Damning Doom of Disbelief 106
The Mortal Messiah Leaves Galilee 111

SECTION VIII
THE LATER JUDEAN MINISTRY

Chapter 69

JESUS MINISTERS AT THE FEAST OF
TABERNACLES 121
He Preaches the Gospel at the Feast 121
The Sinless One Acclaims His Divine Sonship . 127

Chapter 70

LIVING WATER FOR ALL MEN 133
"Come Ye to the Waters" 133
"Never Man Spake Like This Man" 136
The Woman Taken in Adultery 140

Chapter 71

MESSIAH—THE LIGHT OF THE WORLD 146
"I Am the Light of the World" 146
The Pharisees Reject the Light 149
'Believe in Me, or Die in Your Sins' 153

Chapter 72

ABRAHAM'S SEED 156
  "The Truth Shall Make You Free" 157
  Who Are the Children of Abraham? 160
  'Before Abraham Was I Jehovah' 166

Chapter 73

JESUS SPEAKS OF SPIRITUAL THINGS 171
  The Seventies Report on Their Apostleship 171
  Christ Is the Father and the Son 173
  Parable of the Good Samaritan 175
  A Familial Scene 180

Chapter 74

THE WONDROUS WORD POURS
FORTH 185
  Parable of the Friend at Midnight 185
  He Ministers in Judea as in Galilee 189
  Parable of the Rich Fool 190
  Parable of the Barren Fig Tree 193

Chapter 75

THE MAN BORN BLIND 198
  The Miracle—One Born Blind Is Healed 198
  *The Testing of the Miracle—Pharisaic
    Contention* 202
  *The Purpose of the Miracle: Jesus Acclaims
    His Divinity* 206

Chapter 76

THE GOOD SHEPHERD 210
  Jesus Is the Good Shepherd 210

The Good Shepherd Has Power over Death 215
Jesus Says: "I Am the Son of God" 217

SECTION IX

THE PEREAN MINISTRY

Chapter 77

SACRIFICE AND SALVATION 227
More Sabbath Healings 227
Parable of the Wedding Guests 232
Parable of the Great Supper 233
Will Many or Few Be Saved? 237
Sacrifice Prepares Disciples for Salvation 239

Chapter 78

THE LOST SHEEP, COIN, AND SON 244
Parable of the Lost Sheep 244
Parable of the Lost Coin 247
Parable of the Prodigal Son 248

Chapter 79

THE TWO PECULIAR PARABLES 254
Parable of the Unjust Steward 254
The Law and the Prophets Testify of Christ 257
Parable of Lazarus and the Rich Man 260
Parable of the Unprofitable Servant 264

Chapter 80

THE RAISING OF LAZARUS 268
The Message That Lazarus Is Sick 268

"Lazarus, Come Forth" 273
The Sanhedrin Plots Jesus' Death 281

Chapter 81

MORE HEALINGS, PARABLES, AND SERMONS .. 283
Jesus Cleanses Ten Lepers 283
The Discourse on the Kingdom of God 286
Parable of the Unjust Judge 287
Parable of the Pharisee and the Publican 289
The Discourse on Marriage and Divorce 291

Chapter 82

GAINING ETERNAL LIFE 298
Little Children Shall Be Saved 298
Riches and Eternal Life 300
Riches and Rewards in the Day of Regeneration 305
Parable of the Laborers in the Vineyard 307

Chapter 83

JOURNEYING TOWARD THE CROSS 311
The Coming Baptism of Blood 311
The Healing of Zaccheus and of Bartimeus 315
Parable of the Pounds 318

SECTION X

FROM THE ANOINTING TO THE ROYAL REIGN

Chapter 84

"HOSANNA TO THE SON OF DAVID" 331
Mary Anoints Jesus at Simon's Supper 331
Jesus Enters Jerusalem as King Messiah 337

Chapter 85

JESUS—ONE HAVING AUTHORITY 344
He Curseth a Barren Fig Tree 344
Jesus Cleanseth the Temple the Second Time .. 348
*Jesus Confoundeth the Jews on the
Question of Authority* 350

Chapter 86

THREE PARABLES TO THE JEWS 357
Parable of the Two Sons 357
Parable of the Wicked Husbandmen 359
Parable of the Marriage of the King's Son 364

Chapter 87

THE JEWS PROVOKE, TEMPT, AND REJECT
JESUS 369
Render unto God and Caesar Their Own 369
Jesus Teaches the Law of Eternal Marriage ... 374
"The First and Great Commandment" 381
"What Think Ye of Christ?" 385

Chapter 88

THE GREAT DENUNCIATION 388
Jesus Speaks with the Voice of Vengeance 389
*The Eight Woes Against the Scribes and
Pharisees* 394
*Jewish Accountability for the Sins of
Their Ancestors* 402

Chapter 89

JESUS' FINAL TEACHING IN THE TEMPLE 407
He Laments over Doomed Jerusalem 407

The Widow's Mite 409
Jesus Offers Salvation to the Gentiles 411
"Who Is This Son of Man?" 415

Chapter 90

THE OLIVET DISCOURSE: JERUSALEM
AND THE TEMPLE 421

"Your House Is Left unto You Desolate" 422
The Dispensation of Persecution and
Martyrdom 424
Jerusalem and the Abomination of Desolation . 429

Chapter 91

THE OLIVET DISCOURSE: THE LAST DAYS 436

Universal Apostasy Before the Second Coming . 436
An Era of Restoration Before the Second
Coming 438
Desolations Precede the Second Coming 440
Gentile Fulness Ends Before the Second
Coming 441

Chapter 92

THE OLIVET DISCOURSE: THE SECOND
COMING 446

The Abomination of Desolation at the
Second Coming 446
The Glories Attending Our Lord's Return 448
When Will the Son of Man Come? 453
"Who May Abide the Day of His Coming 455
Watch, Pray, Take Heed, Be Ready! 457

Chapter 93

THE OLIVET DISCOURSE: PARABLES AND
THE JUDGMENT 464
  Parable of the Ten Virgins 464
  Parable of the Talents 468
  Christ Shall Sit in Judgment at His Coming ... 473

INDEX 477

SECTION VII

THE GALILEAN MINISTRY REACHES ITS PEAK

THE GALILEAN MINISTRY REACHES ITS PEAK

Thou art the Christ,
the Son of the living God.
(Matt. 16:16.)
This is my beloved Son,
in whom I am well pleased;
hear ye him.
(Matt. 17:5.)

Jesus our Lord, in whose mortal life we so much rejoice, now comes to a day of deepening opposition, even in Galilee.

He departs thence to visit the lost sheep among the heathen. In the coasts of Tyre and Sidon and throughout Decapolis his voice is heard, his miracles abound, and he feeds the four thousand.

He is challenged to show a sign from heaven, a sign of the sort the Messiah of Jewish expectation should show.

He warns his disciples of the leaven of the Pharisees and Sadducees.

Then in the coasts of Caesarea Philippi, Peter makes the great confession, with which all the disciples accord.

Jesus promises to give Peter the keys of the kingdom of heaven. Then upon Mount Hermon those keys are conferred upon Peter, James, and John. Shortly thereafter all of the

Twelve receive them and have power, thus, to bind and loose both on earth and in heaven.

Over and over again he who came to die speaks of being delivered into the hands of evil men, and of his death in Jerusalem, and of his rising again the third day.

On the Holy Mount, Jesus and the chosen three are transfigured. Moses and Elias minister unto them.

There on the heights of Hermon, Peter, James, and John see the wonders of eternity, including the transfiguration of the earth.

The Shekinah returns to Israel. Even the Father visits the Son and testifies: *"This is my beloved Son, in whom I am well pleased; hear ye him."*

Jesus foretells the coming of Elias of the Restoration.

He begins the descent from the Mountain of Glory to the Valley of Humiliation and Death.

In the valley, he heals the demoniac youth, and he provides, miraculously, the temple-tax for himself and for Peter.

He discourses on meekness, on humility, on the salvation of children, on forgiveness, and on the sealing power. And he gives the parable of the unmerciful servant.

Then, from among his Galilean friends, he chooses the Seventy to stand with the Twelve, in bearing witness of his holy name in all the world.

And so closes his Galilean ministry—a ministry of preaching and healings and miracles and keys and powers and authorities and visions and heavenly confirmation of his divine Sonship.

As God's Son he goes to Jerusalem to do the thing for which he came into the world.

Chapter 60

THE LOST SHEEP AMONG THE HEATHEN

From the rising of the sun
even unto the going down of the same
my name shall be great
among the Gentiles;
and in every place incense shall be offered
unto my name, and a pure offering:
for my name shall be great
among the heathen,
saith the Lord of hosts.
(Mal. 1:11.)

A Day of Deepening Opposition
(Matthew 15:21; John 7:1)

Lucifer is now loosing his legions to fight the Lord of Life. Heretofore opposition to him has centered mainly in the scribal-sectarian ministers, in the rabid Rabbinists, in the Sanhedrists, in the religious rulers and leaders of the people—all of whose crafts are endangered by the New Order. Among the peasant people, among the Galilean multitudes, among the common folk—whose thoughts, however, are greatly influenced by their leaders—there has been a division of opinion. Some have followed him gladly. He has been rejected twice by his own at Nazareth. There are those who believe he is the Messiah, and others who accept the Pharisaic sophistry that he is Satan Incarnate and casteth out devils and worketh miracles by the power of Beelzebub.

The foul murder by Antipas of the blessed Baptist has left the people in an excitable state. Herod was seeking Jesus to do to him what he did to John.[1] It was in the midst of this popular excitement that Jesus and the Twelve sought refuge from persecution and surcease from toil by sailing to the area of Bethsaida-Julias. In the green and solitary fields near that city—now famed forever for what took place there—Jesus fed the five thousand, and there was a brief, dazzling tide of popular acclaim that sought to force an earthly crown upon that head destined only, while on earth, to wear a crown of thorns.

Then came the sermon on the bread of life, which winnowed the chaff from the wheat and cleared the threshing floor of those who sought only the loaves and fishes and who chose not to eat the Bread that came down from heaven.

Next came the spies and scribes from the Sanhedrin—renewed in their persecuting zeal by the enthusiasm and emotion of their Passover worship—to confront him on the issue of the traditions of the elders.

And at this point Jesus himself declared war. His acts and those of his disciples in eating with unwashen hands—and many such like things—had no defense except that the traditions were evil, false, and base, and would lead men to hell. And he said so, plainly, clearly, emphatically.

"But the craft and violence of the half-heathen Antipas, was a slight evil compared with the hatred which glowed ever more intensely in the breasts of the Rabbis and priests of Jerusalem, and in those of the Pharisees, and other disciples of the schools, scattered over the country. The demands of Jesus were far beyond the mere summons of the Baptist, to prepare for a new and better time. He required immediate submission to a new Theocracy. He excited the fury of the dominant party, not like the Baptist, by isolated bursts of denunciation, but by working quietly, as a King in His own kingdom, which, while in the world, was something far higher. Hence, the feeling against Him was very different from the partial, cautious, and intermittent hatred of the Baptist. The hierarchy and the Rabbis, as the centre of that which, with all its corruptions, was the only true religion on earth as yet, felt themselves compromised directly and fatally by Him, and could not maintain themselves as they were, if He were tolerated. The whole spiritual power of Israel was thus arrayed against Him; a force slowly created by the possession, for ages, of the grandest religious truths known to the ancient world, and by the pride of a long and incomparably sublime national history. It had been assailed in the past, at long intervals, from without, but in recent years it had been for the first time attacked from within, by the Baptist, and now felt itself still more dangerously assaulted by this Galilean. To crush such an apparently insignificant opponent—a peasant of Nazareth, rising, singly and unsupported, against a power so colossal—seemed easy; nor could it be fancied more difficult to scatter and destroy His small band of followers, as yet, mostly, despised peasants." (Geikie, pp. 532-33.)

Now the war is open and fierce; opposition against him has spread out among the Galilean and Judean multitudes; and it is the people and the nation, not alone their religious leaders, who wield the sword. Lucifer's legions are fighting the saints on all fronts, and the warfare will not cease until the cross of crucifixion becomes the weapon of death; or, rather, until the great dragon himself, along with the false prophets who carry his banner, are cast into the bottomless pit.

Jesus is still in need of the rest he sought when he and his disciples set sail from Capernaum to the site where the five thousand Passover pilgrims were fed. The fires of political unrest, fanned by the Herodians, and the fires of religious hatred, fanned by the scribes and rulers from Jerusalem, are everywhere ablaze. Lest the fiery holocaust burn the scarcely built house of faith that he is building in the hearts of men, he must withdraw from Galilee and go far to the north, into Phoenicia. As to the opposition in Judea, which has been intense for a long time, John says: "After these things Jesus walked in Galilee: for he would not walk in Jewry, because the Jews sought to kill him." And as to the opposition now burning even in Galilee, Matthew says: "Then Jesus went thence, and departed into the coasts of Tyre and Sidon."

Tyre and Sidon! Cities of abominations, cities of wickedness, cities like Sodom and Gomorrah! They were Canaanitish, heathen, pagan cities, the home of the worship of Baal and Ashtoreth. Ashtoreth, whose worship Jezebel had imposed on Israel, was the goddess of sensual love; she was worshipped as a sacred prostitute and a divine courtesan, if such words may be used without committing blasphemy. For millenniums the Canaanitish worship had been lewd, lascivious, and immoral. Prostitute goddesses were the order of the age, and their devotees sought to be like those upon whose altars they offered their sacrifices. Such was the area into which the holy party now traveled to continue those labors which collectively are known as the Father's business.

Ministering Among the Heathen
(Mark 7:24-30; JST, Mark 7:22-23, 26-27; Matthew 15:22-28)

Whether Jesus entered Tyre and Sidon proper we do not know, only that he was in the area or region. It was not his practice to seek out Gentiles as such to hear his voice, though there would have been many Jews in the cities themselves. In Jesus' day Tyre, the larger of the two cities, was probably more populous than Jerusalem, and it would appear that he remained two or three months in the area before going on to Decapolis and his ministry in the cities there.

We have heretofore shown that the Gospels contain only selected sayings and doings of Jesus. Of the months he spent in the borders of Tyre and Sidon, like the period he spent visiting all of the cities and towns of Judea in the early Judean ministry, we know very little. It is inherent in the very nature of things that he taught the gospel, testified of his own divine Sonship, and worked miracles. Such words and deeds as have come down to us of any parts of his mortal ministry have been recorded by the Gospel authors, as guided by the Holy Spirit, to preserve the specific teachings intended for us by an all-wise Providence.

Once we have learned how and under what circumstances certain miracles are wrought, for instance, there is no compelling need to record numerous similar illustrations. Generally speaking our evangelist friends have selected matters to record that we need to know about and that, taken as a whole, give us the knowledge and understanding we need in order to follow him whose words and deeds should guide our lives.

As pertaining to the ministerial service here involved, this selection concerns a Syro-Phoenician woman. Mark, who gained his knowledge from Peter, begins the account by saying that when Jesus came "into the borders of Tyre and Sidon," he "entered into a house, and would that no man should come unto him. But he could not deny them; for he had compassion upon all men." Two things are apparent from this: first, that even here the Lord Jesus failed to find the rest he sought; and second, that the disciples, being present and aware of all that transpired, saw in our Lord's acts a reaffirmation of his compassion for all men, not for the house of Israel only.

Phoenicia, or Syria, lies to the north of Galilee and extends from the Mediterranean Sea to the river Jordan. It is ruled by Rome. Tyre and Sidon, about twenty miles apart, are on the seashore. Between them is Zarephath (Sarepta), where dwelt the widow whose son Elijah raised from death. Somewhere in this region now dwelt a Gentile woman of faith who believed that Jesus was the Messiah, the one by whom salvation comes. How she gained her testimony and how many other true believers, either Jews or Gentiles, there were in the area we do not know; perhaps there were whole congregations, and Jesus was visiting them as he ministered among those who were surrounded by pagans and heathens.

This we do know, the "woman of Canaan" came out of "the coasts of Tyre and Sidon" and, finding Jesus, cried out: "Have mercy on me, O Lord, thou son of David; my daughter is grievously vexed with a devil." Matthew says: "But he answered her not a word."

Mark says she was a Greek and a Syro-Phoenician by nation. She would thus be a subject of Rome. Accordingly, she was a Canaanite by birth, a Greek by ancestry, a Syro-Phoenician by political allegiance, and thus also a subject of the empire ruled by Rome. In other words, she was a Gentile of the Gentiles, a pure Gentile, who could claim no descent whatever from Abraham; in whose veins flowed none of the believing blood of Jacob; and who was outside the royal lineage and could not be classed, in any sense, as one of the chosen people. This we must know to envision what here transpired.

Her pleas fell on deaf ears. Jesus, compassionate and merciful as none other has ever been, would not even speak to her, let alone reward her faith and heal her daughter, as he had been doing in like cases in all Israel for more than two years. Her importunings must have been extended and repetitious, both to Jesus and to the Twelve, for the disciples, knowing that on occasions *he* had healed Gentiles, though he had instructed *them* to go only to the lost sheep of Israel in their ministries, "came and besought him, saying, Send her away; for she crieth after us." Implicit in this request is the plea, 'Grant her petition, let her daughter be healed,' as is evident from Jesus' reply, not to the woman but to the Twelve: "I am not sent but unto the lost sheep of the house of Israel."

Jesus is declining not only to heal, but even to give a courteous response, to a Gentile woman who has faith, for no other reason than the fact that she is a Gentile and not an Israelite. Sectarian commentators—not knowing the plans

and purposes of the Lord; having no knowledge of preexistence and foreordination; incapable of explaining why
and how a just God can show mercy and compassion to one
person and deny it to another, and how he can "make one
vessel unto honour, and another unto dishonour" (Rom.
9)—sectarian commentators almost go wild devising reasons
and explanations to justify the course here pursued by the
Compassionate One.

In reality he is doing only what he has always done. In all
the earth he chose only Noah and his family to enter the ark;
upon all the rest of mankind—men, women, and children—
he sent the flood to sweep them into a watery grave. In all of
Chaldea he chose only Abraham of Ur to be his friend;
upon the others he poured out wrath. In all of Sodom and
the cities of the plains he chose only Lot and his wife and
two daughters to be saved; upon the masses of people he
rained fire and brimstone, destruction and death. Out of
Egypt he called only the seed of Jacob, leaving millions of
Pharaoh's minions to temporal and spiritual ruin. And so it
has always been: the Canaanites and Hittites and Philistines
he destroyed, to make room for his people. Assyria and
Babylon and Greece were all denied the blessings of his law.
The word was sent to Israel, and to Israel only.

Why? Because the house of Israel is composed of the
spirits from preexistence who there developed a talent for
spirituality, and who are therefore entitled to the blessings of
heaven in this life on a preferential basis. All men, in due
course, either in this life or in the spirit world, will be offered
the blessings of salvation. But there is an eternal system of
priorities; there is a law of election, a doctrine of foreordination; and Israel is entitled to the blessings of the holy word
ahead of their Gentile fellows. During his lifetime Jesus took
the gospel and its blessings, with isolated exceptions, to his
kinsmen in Israel; after his resurrection he will send his
apostolic witnesses to all men, irrespective of creed or race or
ancestry. The Lord Jehovah—Jesus in the flesh—is simply
conforming to the eternal law of gospel priorities that he and

11

his Father ordained from before the foundations of the world, and such a limited exception to the eternal provisions of the eternal law as may properly be made is about to be shown forth.

By combining the accounts of Matthew and Mark we are led to believe that the importunings of our Gentile friend began before Jesus entered the house, that they were made both to him and to his disciples, and that his refusal even to converse with her was in the open for all men to see. Then, after he sought seclusion in the house, she yet entered—we can suppose she insisted upon so doing—and fell at his feet importuning and worshipping. "Lord, help me," she pled, as "she besought him that he would cast forth the devil out of her daughter." It was as though she had made the suffering of her daughter her own sorrow, even as He would do who came to bear the griefs and carry the sorrows of all men on conditions of repentance.

No longer could Jesus remain silent, but even now his spoken words carried little hope to the sorrowing mother. "Let the children of the kingdom first be filled," he said— 'Let the gospel and its blessings go in this day to the Jews; it is the right and privilege of the chosen seed first to hear the message'—"for it is not meet to take the children's bread, and to cast it unto the dogs."

"But not all the snows of her native Lebanon could quench the fire of love that was burning on the altar of her heart, and prompt as an echo came forth the glorious answer" (Farrar, p. 367): "Yes, Lord; thou sayest truly, yet the dogs under the table eat of the children's crumbs."

How common it was among the Jews to refer to those without—to the Gentiles—as dogs. The Jews were the children of the kingdom, as they supposed; the heathen, none of whom were more accursed than the Canaanites, were the dogs who growled and sniveled and snapped at those within. But here the reference is more particularly to the little dogs, the household pets, who, though still Gentile

12

dogs, yet fed themselves with such cast-off food as fell from the Jewish table.

"O woman, great is thy faith: be it unto thee even as thou wilt," Jesus said. "And her daughter was made whole from that very hour." The woman of Canaan triumphed; hers were not only the crumbs, but she ate of the children's bread; by faith she was adopted into the house of Israel. At Jesus' invitation she now came from without and joined those within. She was no longer a Gentile; she was now a daughter of Abraham.[2]

"For this saying go thy way," Jesus said, "the devil is gone out of thy daughter. And when she was come to her house, she found the devil gone out, and her daughter laid upon the bed."

The Miraculous Healings in Decapolis
(Mark 7:31-37; Matthew 15:29-31)

From the heathen lands of Tyre and Sidon to the semi-pagan lands of Decapolis is a long, wearisome route. His work finished among the pagans of the Syro-Phoenician area, Jesus and his loyal friends now travel by an unnamed ministerial circuit to that area of ten cities located south and east of the Sea of Galilee. The Decapolis, or confederacy of ten cities, whose identities are only partially known,[3] was wedged between the tetrarchies of Philip and Antipas. These were free Greek cities subject only to the governor of Syria. Anciently this part of the promised land fell primarily to Gad and Manasseh, but since the Babylonian exile it had been the habitat primarily of Gentile peoples who worshipped idols and devils.[4]

As the holy party made their way to their new fields of labor, we cannot doubt that they preached and healed and baptized in the cities and villages en route. Divine voices, fired with a zeal borne of the Spirit, are wont to speak forth on every available occasion; the worth of souls is great, and the holy word must be sounded in every ear. Our next recorded miracle of wonder and healing, however, is the giving of speech and hearing to a deaf and speech-impeded man. Jesus and his power were not unknown among the pagans and Jewish people of Decapolis. Nor would the accounts of his miracles in Gennesaret and Capernaum and all Galilee be unknown to them. News of this sort traveled rapidly by word of mouth; it was spoken everywhere by the tongues of believers and belittlers alike.

It comes as no surprise, then, to see them bring to Jesus "one that was deaf, and had an impediment in his speech." Their plea is that our Lord will heal him by the laying on of hands, a request showing that they knew both of his power to heal and of the procedure he used in healing.

Whether Jesus did in fact bless this afflicted man by the laying on of hands is not recorded; he was at liberty to follow such formalities as he chose, as also are his servants who perform miracles in his name and by his power. Elijah stretched himself three times upon the dead body of the widow's son as he pled with the Lord that the child's soul might return, which it then did. When Elisha raised a child from death, he lay upon the child so that their eyes and mouths and hands touched, and after much struggling in the Spirit, life came again into the dead body. Naaman was required to immerse himself seven times in Jordan before his leprous flesh became again as the flesh of a child. And so it goes; such formalities and rituals are followed as will increase the faith of the person, or even of the prophet in whose hands is found the power of God. The Urim and Thummim itself is an instrument that increases the faith of the seer who is privileged to use it for holy purposes.

Mark, who alone preserves the account of this miracle, records these four things that Jesus did, and for each of them we can see a valid reason and an intelligent purpose:

1. He took him aside, away from the multitude. This was not to be a public but a private healing, and after it was performed, those privy to the miraculous happening were charged to keep the knowledge within themselves. For some

special and unspecified reason this miracle should not have been published to the world.[5] Our Lord's counsel, however, went unheeded, and the event was published abroad, to the astonishment of the people, who acclaimed: "He hath done all things well: he maketh both the deaf to hear, and the dumb to speak."

2. He put his own fingers into the deaf ears. Since the man could not hear, this act substituted for a vocal exhortation. It testified to ears unable to hear the spoken word that by faith the hearing obstruction would be pierced.

3. He spit and placed his own saliva on the man's tongue. Such was a practice commonly believed by the Rabbis and the Jews to have healing virtue; it thus encouraged the man to believe—or, rather, increased his faith—that his tongue would be loosed and his fluency restored.

4. Jesus looked up to heaven, signifying that the healing would come by the power of the Father; then "he sighed," and he said: "Ephphatha, that is, Be opened." From this we know that he was speaking the Aramaic of the day.

"St. Mark preserves for us the sigh, and the uplifted glance, as He spoke the one word, 'Ephphatha! Be opened!' Here again it is not revealed to us what were the immediate influences which saddened His spirit. He may have sighed in pity for the man; He may have sighed in pity for the race; He may have sighed for all the sins that degrade and all the sufferings which torture; but certainly He sighed in a spirit of deep tenderness and compassion, and certainly that sigh ascended like an infinite intercession into the ears of the Lord God of Hosts." (Farrar, p. 371.)[6]

Jesus, Matthew tells us, "went up into a mountain, and sat down there." Hearing of this miracle, knowing of other wondrous things attributed to him, and, no doubt, having heard him speak words of infinite wisdom in their hearing, "great multitudes came unto him, having with them those that were lame, blind, dumb, maimed, and many others, and cast them down at Jesus' feet; and he healed them."

Were there Gentiles as well as Jews among those restored

to health and vigor? The people of the area were made up of both cultures; and, as we have seen, in the case of the Syro-Phoenician woman who pled for the crumbs that fall from Israel's table, the compassion of the Great Healer, following great faith, extends beyond the children of the kingdom and takes in the Gentiles who are without. Matthew says simply: "The multitude wondered, when they saw the dumb to speak, the maimed to be whole, the lame to walk, and the blind to see: and they glorified the God of Israel." It is, thus, the same thing we have seen before in Galilee where Israel dwelt. The new dimension here is not *what* was done, but *those* upon whom the blessings were showered.

"Let us try to realize the scene. They have heard of Him as the wonder-worker, these heathens in the land so near to, and yet so far from, Israel; and they have brought to Him 'the lame, blind, dumb, maimed, and many others,' and laid them at His feet. Oh, what wonder! All disease vanishes in [the] presence of Heaven's Own Life Incarnate. Tongues long weighted are loosed, limbs maimed or bent by disease are restored to health, the lame are stretched straight; the film of disease and the paralysis of nerve-impotence pass from eyes long insensible to the light. It is a new era—Israel conquers the heathen world, not by force, but by love; not by outward means, but by the manifestation of life-power from above. Truly, this is the Messianic conquest and reign: 'and they glorified the God of Israel.' " (Edersheim 2:46.)

Jesus Feeds the Four Thousand
(Mark 8:1-10; JST, Mark 8:3, 6-7; Matthew 15:32-39; JST, Matthew 15:34)

Jesus has now been in the Decapolis area for some time, preaching, healing, declaring his own divine Sonship, giving his apostolic witnesses time to mingle among the people and do in their own right the same things the Chief Apostle is doing. As to the actual time period involved, we can only speculate; certainly it involved weeks and may have been a month or even two. It is the summer of A.D. 29. We know the

16

places he went and certain of the things he said and did, but not how long he stayed in each place. During this season, from spring through autumn, he was in the region of Tyre and Sidon, the area of the Decapolis, back again in Galilee, in the region of Caesarea Philippi (where Peter bore his witness), and at Mount Hermon (where the transfiguration occurred). Now he is about to climax his ministry in the Decapolis area and return to Galilee.

We are about to see the Giver of Manna spread another table in the wilderness—not for all Israel as they dwelt in the deserts, awaiting the trumpet call to cross the famous river and enter their promised land; not for the Passover pilgrims, symbolical of all Israel, as they wended their way to the Paschal feast in the Holy City, but a table in the wilderness where Jews and Gentiles, as brethren in the new kingdom, will first feast upon his word and then eat the multiplying loaves and fishes together. Jesus is about to feed four thousand men, besides women and children, with seven loaves and a few small fishes.

This miracle and the prior one near Bethsaida-Julias have much in common, but also some major and vital differences. Who knows, for that matter, whether the Giver of Manna may not have fed many multitudes during his mortal ministry, multitudes who had faith to be fed and for whom he multiplied such provisions as were available. It may be that the inspired authors preserved only these two accounts so that we may know the basic foundation on which all such miracles rest, as well as the distinctive message proclaimed by each of these.

Here in Decapolis we are nearing the climax of our Lord's ministry among a semi-heathen people. He has now done what he did at Bethsaida-Julias: he has taught the plan of salvation; testified of his own divinity; invited all men to come unto him and be saved; performed many mighty miracles; and been accepted and glorified as the God of Israel. There is a spirit of faith and devotion and true worship among the people. Those about to partake of his bounty have been with him for three days in a wilderness area; many of them have traveled great distances from their home cities, and such provisions as they may have brought with them have long since been exhausted.

"I have compassion on the multitude, because they have now been with me three days, and have nothing to eat: And if I send them away fasting to their own houses, they will faint by the way: for divers of them came from far," Jesus said. "From whence can a man satisfy these men with bread here in the wilderness?" his disciples responded.

"They knew that there was in Him no prodigality of the supernatural, no lavish and needless exercise of miraculous power. Many and many a time had they been with multitudes before, and yet on one occasion only [of which we know] had he fed them; and moreover, after He had done so, He had most sternly rebuked those who came to Him in expectation of a repeated offer of such gifts, and had uttered a discourse so searching and strange that it alienated from Him many even of His friends. For them to suggest to Him a repetition of the feeding of the five thousand would be a presumption which their ever-deepening reverence forbade, and forbade more than ever as they recalled how persistently He had refused to work a sign, such as this was, at the bidding of others.

"But no sooner had He given them the signal of His intention, than with perfect faith they became His ready ministers. They seated the multitude on the ground, and distributed to them the miraculous multiplication of the seven loaves and the few small fishes; and, this time unbidden, they gathered the fragments that remained, and with them filled a large basket of rope seven times, after the multitude—four thousand in number, besides women and children—had eaten and were filled. And then kindly, and with no exhibition on the part of the populace of that spurious excitement which had marked the former miracle, the Lord and His Apostles joined in sending away the rejoicing and grateful throng." (Farrar, pp. 371-73.)[7]

When Jesus fed the five thousand, he was dealing with Jews and Jews alone; with those who kept the law of Moses; with a people who expected their Messiah to feed them temporal bread in the deserts of mortality; with brethren en route to Jerusalem to participate in those sacrifices which testified of the atoning sacrifice of the Lamb of God. Thereafter they sought to make him king, and he preached to them the sermon on the bread of life, with the deliberate intention of winnowing the chaff from the wheat.

Here in Decapolis the symbolism is quite different. Both Jews and Gentiles surround the sacred board; the table set in the wilderness is not for Israel only, but for all mankind. Here is the prefiguring of the Gentile harvest, the harvest scheduled to begin when he sends the apostles into all the world to preach the gospel to every creature. Here is the prefiguring of that day when the gospel will go to all mankind and there will truly be one God and one Shepherd over all the earth.

After this miracle and the witness it bore, the Decapolis ministry ended. Jesus and his associates returned by ship to Magdala, or as Mark says, "the parts of Dalmanutha," which must have been an area on the western side of the lake, there to continue his light-giving ministry among those who sat in darkness. Our next view of him, however, will be in Capernaum, when he again discourses about signs.

All things, as we would expect, are going forward as foreordained and designed; the work is being done as decreed by Him who governeth all things by his own omnipotent power. Jesus, the Son, is representing his Father, as that Holy Being designed, intended, and expected. The Father's business is well managed by the Son. And blessed be his holy name forever.

NOTES

1. "Rumours of possible action against Him by Antipas increased the difficulty of the situation. Every one knew that He and many of His followers had come from the school of the Baptist, whom Antipas had just murdered, and it was evident that His aim was more or

19

less similiar to John's, though His acts were more wonderful. Hence speculation was rife respecting Him. Was He the promised Elias? or, at least, Jeremiah, risen from the dead? or was He some special prophet sent from God? Many, indeed, were questioning if He might not even be the Messiah, and were willing to accept Him as such, if He would only head a national revolt, in alliance with the Rabbis and priests, against the Romans. To Antipas His appearance was doubly alarming, for it seemed as if the fancied revolutionary movement of John had broken out afresh more fiercely than ever, and superstition, working in an uneasy conscience, easily saw in Him a resurrection of the murdered Baptist, endowed, now, with the awful power of the eternal world from which He had returned. A second murder seemed needed to make the first effective, and to avoid this additional danger Jesus for a time sought concealment." (Geikie, p. 532.)

2. "As many as receive this Gospel shall be called after thy name," Jehovah said to Abraham, "and shall be accounted thy seed, and shall rise up and bless thee, as their father." (Abr. 2:10.)

3. It is not known whether the cities of the Decapolis either actually or always numbered ten. Names that have come down to us include Gerasa, Gadara, Hippos, Pella, Gergesa, Scythopolis (the ancient Bethshean), and Philadelphia.

4. "This extensive 'Ten Cities' district was essentially heathen territory. Their ancient monuments show, in which of them Zeus, Astarte, and Athene, or else Artemis, Hercules, Dionysos, Demeter, or other Grecian divinities, were worshipped." (Edersheim 2:44-45.)

5. "On some occasions a knowledge of healing miracles may engender faith, on others it fosters unbelief and persecution. Accordingly, Jesus sought either to advertise or keep secret his miraculous healings, depending upon the needs of the ministry at the particular time and place. On a previous occasion, when he was leaving this very region, he had commanded the man out of whom a legion of devils was cast to publish the miracle through all Decapolis. But now, sojourning, for a season in the area, the Master Healer sought to keep secret the dramatic nature of this particular miracle." (*Commentary* 1:373.)

6. Farrar's footnote to this passage reads: "It [the sigh] was not drawn from Him," says Luther, "on account of the single tongue and ears of this poor man; but it is a common sigh over all tongues and ears, yea, over all hearts, bodies, and souls, and over all men, from Adam to his last descendant." (Farrar, p. 371.)

7. "They knew full well the miraculous creative powers of the Master whom they followed. The question as here put is rather an expression of their own inability to feed such a multitude with the scanty provisions at hand. We may suppose also that in their subservient position as followers of him who exceeds all men in power and might, they modestly and properly left to their Lord the decision as to what should be done. It is evident that Jesus did not deem it necessary to test their faith, as he had done before, by saying, 'They need not depart; give ye them to eat'; this time he simply asked what provisions were at hand and gave directions as to their distribution." (*Commentary* 1:376.)

Chapter 61

THE LEAVEN OF THE PHARISEES AND SADDUCEES

If there arise among you a prophet,
or a dreamer of dreams,
and giveth thee a sign or a wonder,
And the sign or the wonder come to pass,
whereof he spake unto thee,
saying, Let us go after other gods,
which thou hast not known,
and let us serve them;
Thou shalt not hearken unto the words
of that prophet, or that dreamer of dreams:
for the Lord your God proveth you,
to know whether ye love the Lord your God
with all your heart and with all your soul.
Ye shall walk after the Lord your God,
and fear him, and keep his commandments,
and obey his voice, and ye shall serve him,
and cleave unto him.
And that prophet, or that dreamer of dreams,
shall be put to death;
because he hath spoken to turn you away
from the Lord your God,

which brought you out of the land of Egypt,
and redeemed you out of the house of bondage,
to thrust thee out of the way
which the Lord thy God commanded thee
to walk in. So shalt thou put
the evil away from the midst of thee.
(Deut. 13:1-5.)

False Ministers Seek Signs
(Matthew 16:1-4; JST, Matthew 16:2-3; Mark 8:11-12; JST, Mark 8:12)

We have somewhat more to say about signs, sign-seekers, and the state of the souls of those whose hearts are centered on such portents. We have heretofore heard Jesus—it was in Capernaum, his own city—utterly defeat and discomfit certain of the scribes and of the Pharisees who demanded that he show them a sign from heaven. (Book 2, chap. 48.) The only sign for them, he then testified, was the sign of Jonah, the sign of his own resurrection, the sign of the glory and triumph of that kingdom which is not of this world.

That former dialogue created a division among the people. Those who believed and understood the truth from heaven as it fell from the lips of Jesus knew full well that signs of the sort sought by the scribes would do nothing but demean the One called upon to give them. True prophets— least of all earth's Chief Prophet—do not go about calling down fire from heaven, turning rivers upstream, or drying up seas, to prove their prophetic powers. Those whose hearts were hardened remained darkened in mind and spirit and continued to whine that he did his miracles by the power of Beelzebub—the lord of idolatrous worship—because he did not produce the heavenly display of fire and power that they said they would accept as a sign. They had learned by experience that however contrary to the true order their demand for a supernatural display might be, it would have the effect of prejudicing many people against him.[1]

22

This time the challenge is hurled not only by certain scribes and Pharisees, but by the Pharisees and the Sadducees combined, by the united power of all the rulers of the people. "Every section of the ruling classes—the Pharisees, formidable from their religious weight among the people; the Sadducees, few in number, but powerful from wealth and position; the Herodians, representing the influence of the Romans, and of their nominees the tetrarchs; the scribes and lawyers, bringing to bear the authority of their orthodoxy and their learning—were all united against Him in one firm phalanx of conspiracy and opposition, and were determined above all things to hinder His preaching, and to alienate from Him, as far as was practicable, the affections of the people among whom most of His mighty works were done." (Farrar, p. 375.)[2]

Their reasoning was persuasive; however false their premises, their arguments had the effect of destroying the influence of Jesus. If he gave no sign from heaven—which it was generally believed the Messiah would do—then he could not be the Messiah, and it must be true that his miracles were wrought by Satan's power. If, on the other hand, he did give a sign from heaven, of the sort Rabbi Eliezer would have given,[3] he was still a false prophet and worthy of death because his teachings did not conform to the Rabbinical standards. Had not Jehovah said by the mouth of Moses that if a prophet gave a sign or wonder that came to pass, the prophet nevertheless should be put to death, if his teachings controverted their system of revealed religion? (Deut. 13:1-5.) And surely everyone knew—it was common knowledge, and no proof need be offered—that the teachings of the Man of Nazareth were false because they contradicted what Moses said as interpreted by the scribes and Rabbis. This matter of demanding a sign from heaven, they reasoned, was truly the way to destroy this Galilean peasant who had attended none of their schools and certainly was not learned in Rabbinic lore.

But suppose, just suppose, he had given them a sign?

23

What then? Would it have proved the truth and divinity of his work? "If He had granted their request, what purpose would have been furthered? It is not the influence of external forces, but it is the germinal principle of life within, which makes the good seed to grow; nor can the hard heart be converted, or the stubborn unbelief removed, by portents and prodigies, but by inward humility, and the grace of God stealing downward like the dew of heaven, in silence and unseen. What would have ensued had the sign been vouchsafed? By its actual eye-witnesses it would have been attributed to demoniac agency; by those to whom it was reported it would have been explained away; by those of the next generation it would have been denied as an invention, or evaporated into a myth." (Farrar, pp. 375-76.)[4]

The demand that their Messiah prove his claim to divine Sonship by showing a sign from heaven has now been made again. His answer: The signs of the times are everywhere to be seen; they abound on every hand; all men are bound to interpret them correctly and to prepare for the storms ahead. "When it is evening ye say, The weather is fair, for the sky is red; and in the morning ye say The weather is foul today; for the sky is red and lowering." 'Ye hear me speak words of eternal truth whose verity is attested by the power of the Spirit. Ye hear my witnesses that God is my Father. Ye see me cast out devils, cleanse lepers, and raise the dead. Ye know that I have stilled storms, walked on water, and multiplied a few loaves and fishes to feed thousands. If I say I am the Son of God, and I then do all these wondrous works, can my words be other than true? What more do you want in the way of a sign?' "O hypocrites! ye can discern the face of the sky; but ye cannot tell the signs of the times."[5] Then came the biting denunciation:

A wicked and adulterous generation seeketh after a sign; and there shall no sign be given unto it, but the sign of the prophet Jonas.

"The only sign to Nineveh was Jonah's solemn warning of near judgment, and his call to repentance—and the only

24

sign now . . . was the warning cry of judgment and the loving call to repentance." (Edersheim 2:70.)

With this Jesus left his detractors, going by boat from Magdala toward the coast of Bethsaida-Julias, en route to the coasts of Caesarea Philippi where Peter will make his great confession.

Beware of the Leaven of Evil Men
(Matthew 16:5-12; JST, Matthew 16:8-9; Mark 8:13-21; JST, Mark 8:16)

Jesus came from the semiheathen region of the Decapolis to the Israelite area of Magdala. "For some time He had been absent from home. He had been sought out with trustful faith in the regions of Tyre and Sidon. He had been welcomed with ready gratitude in heathen Decapolis; here, at home, He was met with the flaunt of triumphant opposition, under the guise of hypocritical zeal." In Decapolis the multitudes believed his words, rejoiced in his miracles, ate of the loaves and fishes provided by his providence, and glorified him as the God of Israel. Back among his own he found "all the self-satisfied hypocrisies of a decadent religion drawn up in array to stop His path!" (Farrar, p. 376.) There among his own he was assailed by the rulers of the people, who, under the guise of demanding a sign from heaven, proclaimed their utter disbelief in and complete rejection of his Messianic claims.

Thus the issue was squarely set. It is the doctrine of the Almighty that Jesus Christ is the Son of the living God; that salvation comes by him and him alone; that he has abolished death and brought life and immortality to light through the gospel; and that all men everywhere must believe in him, repent of their sins, be baptized in water, receive the gift of the Holy Ghost, and work the works of righteousness, or they can in nowise enter into the kingdom of God.

It was the doctrine of the Pharisees—and all who joined

with them in opposing Jesus[6]—that salvation came by the law of Moses alone; that the man Jesus was a deluded fanatic without divine power; that he was a rabble-rouser, an anarchist, a subverter of all that was great and good in their traditions; that he was a blasphemer worthy of death; that he performed miracles by the power of the prince of devils, yea, that he was even Beelzebub Incarnate; and that he should be rejected, cast out, and stoned to death as one who prophesied falsely and led the people away from their ancient moorings.

And so Jesus, after deriding the sign-seekers as wicked and adulterous, chose to leave them and minister and heal among other people. Thanks to their darkened minds, their perverted consciences, and their stony hearts, he would go elsewhere to preach. "He did not press His mercies on those who rejected them. As in after days His nation were suffered to prefer their robber and their murderer to the Lord of Life, so now the Galileans were suffered to keep their Pharisees and lose their Christ." (Farrar, pp. 376-77.) He and his disciples set sail, leaving Magdala for the area of Bethsaida-Julias on the north and east of the sacred sea.

Their departure was made in haste, and the disciples failed to take food for their sustenance. Apparently after they landed at their destination, Jesus—ever anxious to strengthen them spiritually; concerned lest any of them be tainted in any degree by the damning doctrine of his enemies; and using their failure to bring bread as a teaching aid—took occasion to raise a warning voice. "Take heed and beware of the leaven of the Pharisees and of the Sadducees," he said. Mark tells us that he also warned them against "the leaven of Herod."

Those same disciples, at Jacob's Well, had missed the true meaning of his statement that he had meat to eat that they knew not of. But a short time back the metaphors about eating the bread which came down from heaven had failed to find quick and easy lodgment in their souls; and yet in the future they would miss the deep meaning of the expression about Lazarus sleeping and needing to be awakened. At this stage of their spiritual development, metaphors seemed to give them some trouble. They therefore "reasoned among themselves, saying, He said this because we have taken no bread."

Jesus, perceiving how foolish and spiritually immature they were, responded with a severe and stern rebuke. "O ye of little faith, why reason ye among yourselves, because ye have brought no bread?" he said. "Perceive ye not yet, neither understand? have ye your heart yet hardened? Having eyes, see ye not? and having ears, hear ye not? and do ye not remember? When I brake the five loaves among five thousand, how many baskets full of fragments took ye up? They say unto him, Twelve. And when the seven among four thousand, how many baskets full of fragments took ye up? And they said, Seven. And he said unto them, How is it that ye do not understand?" "How is it that ye do not understand that I spake it not to you concerning bread, that ye should beware of the leaven of the Pharisees and of the Sadducees?"

Only then, after such a rebuke, was Matthew able to conclude: "Then understood they how that he bade them not beware of the leaven of bread, but of the doctrine of the Pharisees and of the Sadducees." And, of course, of the Herodians and every other sect, party, cult, or denomination, for all such are not of God, and have not the fulness of the gospel, which alone sets forth the doctrine of God.

"Leaven was one of the very commonest types of sin, and especially of insidious and subterranean sin." (Farrar, p. 379.) Leaven—the fermenting, defiling, contaminating influence of those who opposed him! Leaven—the debasing, damning doctrines of those who would one day cause his death! Leaven—the views and feelings of those who were anti-Christ and who sought to keep others from accepting him as their Messiah and Deliverer! The leaven of the Pharisees, Sadducees, Herodians, scribes—of all who believed and preached false doctrine—such leaven was evil.

They must beware lest they be tainted in the slightest degree.[7]

Jesus Restores Sight by Stages
(Mark 8:22-26)

Every miracle is unique; no two are alike. Two blind men have their eyes opened by divine power, and each wondrous deed is as different from the other as are the two recipients of the heavensent goodness. Those few of Jesus' miracles which are recorded in any sort of detail were selected from the many by the spirit of inspiration; such accounts preserve for us patterns and types of miraculous acts, with a view to encouraging us—whatever our disabled or diseased condition may be—to ourselves rely on Him by whose power miracles are wrought, and to seek to gain an outpouring of his goodness and grace in our own lives.

Further, all healings do not happen instantaneously; the prophetic fingers do not always snap and cause a prostrate sufferer to leap from his pallet as though by magic. A sightless one may be sent to wash the spittle and clay from his eyes in the pool of Siloam; a leper may be required to immerse seven times in Jordan; a suffering soul may be tested to the full before hearing the blessed words: "Be it unto thee according to thy faith." It is no less a miracle when shattered bones weld themselves together gradually than when they reform in an instant. A withered arm that attains its proper and perfect frame through a growth process may be an exhibition of as great a miracle as one that bursts suddenly into being. And so we come to the miracle at hand, the only New Testament instance of a person being healed by stages.

Jesus is in Bethsaida-Julias. A blind man is brought to him. For reasons that are not recited, Jesus chooses not to perform a miracle in the city; perhaps the idolatrous infidels of this Gentile city are not even worthy to see a wonder wrought on one whose faith and works warrant such divine intervention in his behalf. "All that we can dimly see is

Christ's dislike and avoidance of these heathenish Herodian towns, with their spurious and tainted Hellenism, their tampering with idolatry, and even their very names commemorating, as was the case with Bethsaida-Julias, some of the most contemptible of the human race." (Farrar, pp. 380-81.)[8]

Rather, Jesus began a series of acts, each of which was designed to increase faith in the heart of the sightless one. First he led the blind man by the hand out of town; then he spat in his eyes, an act that was a well-known Jewish remedy for diseases of the eye; and then he performed the gospel ordinance of the laying on of hands. We cannot doubt that words of encouragement and exhortation and healing were spoken as he performed the ministerial service that is usually incident to the laying on of hands.

After this Jesus asked the man "if he saw ought." His reply: "I see men as trees, walking." Then the initial miracle was added upon. "He put his hands again upon his eyes, and made him look up: and he was restored, and saw every man clearly." Then Jesus sent the man away—not back into Bethsaida-Julias, but to his own house. "Neither go into the town, nor tell it to any in the town," Jesus said.

"Certainly the manner in which this healing took place teaches that men should seek the Lord's healing grace with all their strength and faith, though such is sufficient for a partial cure only, following the receipt of which, however, they may then gain the added assurance and faith to be made whole and well every whit. Men also are often healed of their spiritual maladies by degrees, step by step as they get their lives in harmony with the plans and purposes of Diety." (*Commentary* 1:379-80.)

NOTES

1. "They had already found by experience that the one most effectual weapon to discredit His mission and undermine His influence was the demand of a sign—above all, a sign from heaven. If He were indeed the Messiah, why should He not give them bread from heaven as Moses, they said, had done? where were Samuel's thunder and Elijah's

flame? why should not the sun be darkened, and the moon turned into blood, and the stars of heaven be shaken? why should not some fiery pillar glide before them to victory, or the burst of some stormy *Bath Kol* ratify His words?" (Farrar, p. 375.)

As to the meaning of the *Bath Kol* here named, and also as illustrative of the kind of signs sought, we take these words from Edersheim: "As regards 'a sign from heaven,' it is said that Rabbi Eliezer, when his teaching was challenged, successively appealed to certain 'signs.' First, a locust-tree moved at his bidding one hundred, or, according to some, four hundred cubits. Next, the channels of water were made to flow backwards; then the walls of the Academy leaned forward, and were only arrested at the bidding of another Rabbi. Lastly, Eliezer exclaimed: 'If the Law is as I teach, let it be proved from heaven!' when a voice fell from the sky (the *Bath Qol*): 'What have ye to do with Rabbi Eliezer, for the Halakhah is as he teaches?' " (Edersheim 2:69.)

2. In a footnote to this passage, Farrar notes a comparison of "the sects of the Jews to modern schools of thought." It is: Pharisees as pietists; Essenes as mystics; Sadducees as rationalists; Herodians as political clubs and the like; Zealots as radicals; and Samaritans as schismatics—all of this points up to the truism that Lucifer repeats himself, generation after generation, as he seeks to destroy the souls of men.

3. See footnote 1 above.

4. There is a striking parallel between the demands of the ancient Pharisees that Jesus show them a sign, and the demands of modern Pharisees that the Latter-day Saints produce the gold plates from which the Book of Mormon was translated, and the Urim and Thummim used in the translation process. Such, of course, is not the Lord's way of proving the truth and divinity of his work. With reference to this latter-day demand, the Lord said to Joseph Smith: "If they will not believe my words, they would not believe you, my servant Joseph, if it were possible that you should show them all these things which I have committed unto you. Oh, this unbelieving and stiffnecked generation—mine anger is kindled against them. . . . But this generation shall have my word through you." (D&C 5:7-8, 10.)

5. In like manner, worldly people today fail to discern the signs of our times; fail to see that the coming forth of the Book of Mormon and the restoration of the gospel, for instance, are signs certifying that the coming of the Son of Man is near; fail to understand that the wars and plagues and wickedness of our day are preparatory to that great confrontation between good and evil which will usher in the Second Coming. And much, much more. See *Mormon Doctrine,* 2nd ed., pp. 715-34.

6. "Strange bedfellows these—Sadducees and Pharisees, bitter religious enemies of each other, now uniting in an unholy alliance to fight Jesus and his doctrines. But such is ever the case with the various branches of the devil's Church. One thing always unites warring sects of religionists—their common fear and hatred of the pure truths of salvation. Sects of modern Christendom fight each other on nearly all fronts save one—on that they unite to oppose Joseph Smith and the gospel restored through his instrumentality." (*Commentary* 1:378.)

7. Similarly: Beware the leaven of the modern sects of Christendom—sects so near in one sense to salvation, and yet so far away in the eternal sense—sects that believe false doctrines. Beware of the leaven of the Baptists, that belief in Christ without more brings a spiritual rebirth. Beware of the leaven of the Lutherans, that men are justified by faith alone, without works of righteousness. Beware the leaven of all the sects and cults, for among them the fulness of the everlasting gospel is not found.

8. In his footnote to this passage, Farrar says: "Herod Philip had named his renovated capital in honor of Julia, the abandoned daughter of the Emperor Augustus."

Chapter 62

THE TESTIMONY OF OUR LORD

Ye are blessed,
for the testimony which ye have borne
is recorded in heaven for the angels
to look upon; and they rejoice over you,
and your sins are forgiven you.
(D&C 62:3.)[1]

'I Am the Son of Man'
(Matthew 16:13; Mark 8:27; Luke 9:18; JST, Luke 9:18)

Jesus is now constrained to hold a testimony meeting with the disciples. He himself opens with prayer, names the subject for discussion, and invites any of those present who so desire to bear witness of what God, by the power of the Holy Ghost, has revealed to them. Whether others than the Twelve were present is not stated. On previous missionary journeys mention has been made of the presence of Mary Magdalene and other women, possibly wives of some of the apostles. Whatever the attendance on this occasion, we are sure it was only a select and favored few who were present to hear the witnesses borne and to feel the Spirit about to be poured out upon them.

The need for this meeting was real. The intimate friends

of the Master had been subject to severe trials of their faith in the days just past, and Jesus now planned for them some sacred moments of spiritual uplift. There had been disaffection and falling away when, though urged by thousands of his Israelite kin, he refused to step forth as King-Messiah and wear their proffered crown.

The winnowing effect of his bread of life sermon had blown Israelitish chaff to the four winds. His confrontation with the united leaders of the people, when they challenged him to show a sign from heaven—a sign of the sort the Jewish-Messiah was expected to show—had weakened his influence with many people. Multitudes who once basked in the light of his presence had now gone back to their wallowing in the mire of ritualistic Judaism. Jesus was now virtually an outcast and an escapee from Galilee, from Antipas, who had slain John, and from the people who no longer savored his sermons and believed his doctrines. Was it not true, they reasoned, that his miracles, as the Rabbis said, were done by the power of the devil? Indeed, so severe were the circumstances and so widespread the falling away that he had even felt constrained to warn his closest friends against the leaven of the Jewish leaders. In these dark and dire days, what was more natural than to assemble his friends around him for a period of spiritual refreshment?

Jesus himself bore the first testimony of his own divinity on this memorable occasion. Luke introduces his account by saying: "As he went alone with his disciples to pray, he asked them, saying, Who say the people that I am?" Matthew records the query as "Whom do men say that I the Son of man am?" What other things he may have said by way of introduction we do not know; perhaps it suffices to understand what he meant by saying, 'I am the Son of Man,' a designation he so frequently applied to himself.

To his Jewish disciples—who knew that the Almighty was their Father in heaven; who knew that God was a personal being in whose image man is created; who knew that Deity was a holy man—to his Jewish disciples, to say 'I am the Son of Man' meant 'I am the Son of God.' The two name-titles are and were totally synonymous. The Son of Man and the Son of God are one and the same because the *Man* involved is *God;* they are simply two designations of the same exalted person. From earliest times, speaking of the Father of us all, holy writ has testified: "In the language of Adam, Man of Holiness is his name, and the name of his Only Begotten is the Son of Man, even Jesus Christ, a righteous Judge, who shall come in the meridian of time." (Moses 6:57.)[2]

As we ponder the profound and deep import of Jesus' declaration that he is the Son of Man and therefore the Son of God, we must remind ourselves anew of the single most important truth in all eternity. It is that God himself, the Supreme Being, the maker, upholder, and preserver of all things, the creator of the universe, our Eternal Father, is a glorified and perfected man.[3] A knowledge of this truth is the beginning of all spiritual progression. This truth is the foundation upon which the whole plan of salvation rests. God himself, the Father of us all, ordained and established the plan of salvation to enable us, his children, to advance and progress and become like him. Salvation consists in becoming as God is. He is a holy man—Man of Holiness is his name—and his beloved Son is the Son of Man of Holiness, or, as Jesus now expresses it, *The Son of Man.*

"Thou Art the Christ"
(Matthew 16:14-16; Mark 8:28-29; JST, Mark 8:31; Luke 9:19-20; JST, Luke 9:19-20)

Our Lord has now testified to these favored few that he is the Son of God—a witness he has borne to many people in many places on many occasions. It is, as it were, a new and an everlasting testimony—*new* each time its burning fire sinks into a human heart; *everlasting* because it is always borne by Gods, angels, and men, whenever receptive hearers can be assembled to hear an inspired voice.

To Joseph and Mary the *Lad of Twelve* spoke of being about his Father's business; to the Passover throngs the *Cleanser of the Temple* spoke of his Messiahship and the death and resurrection that would attend it; to Nicodemus the *Teacher sent from God* spoke of his coming crucifixion and identified himself as the Only Begotten Son of God; to the woman of Samaria the *Weary Traveler* testified, "I who speak unto thee am the Messias"; to his own in Nazareth the *Promised Messiah* acclaimed that in him were the Messianic prophecies fulfilled; to the messengers who came from John, *Jesus* said his miracles and his teachings bore record that he was the promised one who should come; to the throngs in Capernaum the *Bread from Heaven* taught that men must eat his flesh and drink his blood to be saved; to thousands upon thousands of the house of Israel, in all the cities of Judea and Galilee and beyond, the *Preacher,* the *Healer,* the *Witness of Truth* preached the gospel of the kingdom, which is that men are saved through his atoning sacrifice; on occasions without number, the *son of Mary,* in plain words and in clear similitudes, taught that he was the *Son of God.*

It comes as no surprise, then, here in the coast of Caesarea Philippi, for his disciples to hear him say what they have heard him say before: *'I am the Son of that Holy Man who is God!'* It is the same witness he has always borne; it is a testimony that burns with heavenly fire in their hearts; it is a simple truth that they believe in their souls. As we shall see shortly, they did not as yet envision in full how and in what manner their holy Messiah would accomplish his work and bring life and immortality to light through his gospel. But they knew who he said he was, and they believed the witness he bore of himself.

What then of the question he now asked: "Whom do men say that I am?" It is as though he said: 'My words and my works bear testimony of my divine commission. If men do not accept me as the Son of God, how do they explain these things? Who do they suppose that I am? Am I a devil, as the Pharisees say? How do they explain me and my words if I am not the Son of Man?' Such ever is the dilemma facing unbelievers. How can the work prosper so gloriously if it be not true!

That these same questions tormented the minds of many people is clear from the response of the disciples. The human mind cries out for an explanation of the divine wonders everywhere to be seen. "Some say that thou art John the Baptist; some, Elias; and others, Jeremias, or one of the prophets" is the response; and it is a reply that shows how false and foolish Jewish traditions were, and how far those who believed them would go to avoid accepting revealed truth.

Antipas, who slew John—fearful, superstitious, with a sin-laden conscience, and exhibiting a touch of the madness and mental derangement that tortured the body and tormented the soul of his evil father—Antipas saw in Jesus the slain Baptist risen from death. Others, also darkened in mind and spirit, adopted the overcredulous superstitions of their depraved ruler, and this in spite of the fact Jesus and John were contemporaries. Such a way to account for Jesus and his works seems wholly incredible to us.

Some said he was Elias, who was to come and restore all things, according to one of their scriptures, which we no longer have; or he was Elijah, who was to return before the great and dreadful day of the Lord. Some also had thought that John the Baptist was one or the other of these prophets.

Others thought Jesus was Jeremiah, around whom Jewish tradition had spun a wondrous web of supernatural foolishness. They believed that this ancient prophet—he was ministering in Israel when Lehi left Jerusalem—had hidden the ark in a cave on Mount Nebo when their capital city was overrun by Nebuchadnezzar; that he had called Abraham, Isaac, Jacob, and Moses from their tombs to wail with him over the destruction of the temple; and that he and Elijah would prepare the way before the Messiah by returning the ark and the Urim and Thummim to the Holy of Holies.

And yet others supposed our Lord was this or that

ancient prophet returned again. There is never agreement among those who believe false doctrine; it matters not to their master what they believe so long as they do not believe the truth. And we can suppose there was a reservoir of rumors and a mountain of explanations relative to Jesus and his works.

"But whom say ye that I am?" he asks. It matters not what carnal men may think. The things of God are known only by the power of the Spirit. Where Christ and his gospel are concerned, the only witness of worth comes from his disciples. Thus Peter—for himself, for the Twelve, for the little group there assembled, for all truth believers in all ages— gives answer: *"Thou art the Christ, the Son of the living God."* 'As thou hast said, Lord, thou art the Son of Man; thou art the Messiah; thou art the One of whom Moses and the prophets spoke; thou art the Son of God.'

Peter thus speaks that which they all believe and of which they all are sure. He confesses the Lord Jesus with his lips. No doubt he then said more than is recorded, and no doubt others bore like witness on this same occasion. But as for Peter, he is only repeating what he has said before. It is not a new testimony, simply a reaffirmation of that which has long been in his heart and which has often fallen from his lips. One of the most fluent and fervent of these prior testimonies of Peter was the one we heard following the sermon on the bread of life. As others dissembled, as the loaves-and-fishes disciples departed from the Living Bread, Peter testified—and it is the equal of his great Messianic confession here beyond the borders of Israel—

Lord . . . thou hast the words of eternal life. And we believe and are sure that thou art that Christ, the Son of the living God. (John 6:68-69.)

"The Keys of the Kingdom of Heaven"
(Matthew 16:17-20; Mark 8:30)

"The Son of the living God." An awesome thought; in itself a solemn sermon; wonder of wonders, miracle of mira-

cles: that God should have a son! The Almighty, the First Great Cause, the Supreme Being, the Creator of all things from the beginning—God the Eternal Father begets a son! That holy Man, who is omnipotent and omniscient, who sits enthroned in eternal glory—the maker, preserver, and upholder of all things, before whom all things bow in humble reverence—that holy being, who is immortal and eternal, the Supreme God, fathers a son after the manner of the flesh. An immortal Man—glorified and exalted, having a body of flesh and bones—sires a son in mortality, a son who has a body of flesh and blood.

"The Son of the living God." Such a thing transcends human comprehension. How can it be, and if it is, how can such a truth be known? We are not dealing here with physical facts or chemical formulas; we are not solving geometric theorems or learning the principles of astronomy. That which pertains to God is in the realm of the Spirit. God stands revealed or he remains forever unknown. And if he has a son, such an awesome reality can only be known in the same way—by revelation.

"No man can say [know] that Jesus is the Lord, but by the Holy Ghost," Paul says. (1 Cor. 12:3.) "The testimony of our Lord"—of which Paul says we ought not be "ashamed" (2 Tim. 1:8)—what is it? It is to know by revelation that the man Jesus is the Son of Man. The Holy Ghost is a revelator whose mission is to bear witness of the Father and the Son. "To some it is given by the Holy Ghost to know that Jesus Christ is the Son of God." (D&C 46:13.) "I am thy fellowservant, and of thy brethren that have the testimony of Jesus," was the angelic word to John, "for the testimony of Jesus is the spirit of prophecy." (Rev. 19:10.) And so Peter, who is one of the prophets, proclaims his testimony: "Thou art the Christ, the Son of the living God." To this Jesus can give but one answer:

> *Blessed art thou, Simon Bar-jona: for flesh and blood hath not revealed it unto thee, but my Father which is in heaven.*

37

All who bear testimony by the power of the Holy Ghost are blessed; their inspired utterances are recorded in heaven for the angels—their fellowservants—to look upon. Peter is thus blessed. In contrast to Christ, who is the Son of God, Peter is the son of Jonah. Though he is blessed, he is as other men, born of a mortal father. There is only one whose Father was immortal, and Jesus maintains that distinction in dealing even with his intimate friends whom he is training to be his apostolic witnesses.

Mortal though Peter is, his testimony has come to him by revelation—not from reason, not by logic, not from man, but by revelation from the Father by the power of the Holy Ghost. It is a true testimony.

And I say also unto thee, That thou art Peter, and upon this rock I will build my church; and the gates of hell shall not prevail against it.

Yet again Jesus reaffirms the difference between himself and his disciples. He calls Peter, Simon Bar-jona, Simon the son—not of God as He was, but of Jonah; Simon, who is called Peter, is distinguished from Jesus, who is called Christ.[4]

And having thus testified again of his divine Sonship, Jesus promises that upon the rock of revealed truth, the rock of revelation, the rock of personal testimony received by the power of the Holy Ghost—upon this rock he will build his church.[5] And thus it has ever been. Whenever God speaks and men hear; whenever there is revelation by the power of the Holy Ghost; whenever men enjoy the gift of the Holy Ghost—then they have the true church. And where any of these things are not, there the true church is not. And further, as long as the true saints walk in this light of heaven, the gates of hell do not and cannot prevail against them. Thus, in thought content, Jesus acclaims:

'Blessed art thou Peter, for thy unwearying devotion to my cause and for the testimony which thou hast borne of my divine Sonship; and this testimony was not revealed to thee by mortal man, but it came by revelation from my Father, by the power of the Holy Ghost. And now Peter, my chief apostle, know this: It is upon this very rock of revelation that I have built up my Church in all ages past, and upon which I will build and perfect it in this your day; for after I have ascended to my Father, ye and your brethren and all the worthy saints shall receive the gift of the Holy Ghost, so that you may receive revelation from me and learn all things that are expedient for you to know concerning the building up and rolling forth of my kingdom.' (*Commentary* 1:386.)[6]

And I will give unto thee the keys of the kingdom of heaven: and whatsoever thou shalt bind on earth shall be bound in heaven: and whatsoever thou shalt loose on earth shall be loosed in heaven.

"The kingdom of heaven": the kingdom of God on earth; the Church of Jesus Christ organized among men; the earthly kingdom designed to prepare men for the heavenly kingdom of the Father—such is the meaning of the language of our Lord.

"The keys of the kingdom": the governing, controlling, regulating power over the Church or kingdom; the instrumentality that opens the door to the receipt of peace in this life and eternal life in the world to come—such is what Jesus meant by keys.

Since the earthly church, which is a kingdom, prepares men for the heavenly kingdom, which is in the celestial world, it follows that what is bound on earth is bound in heaven, and what is loosed on earth is loosed in heaven. If the Lord's legal administrators baptize repentant and worthy souls on earth, that baptism is binding in heaven and admits the faithful to celestial rest. If those legal administrators seal a worthy and faithful man to a worthy and faithful woman in the everlasting covenant of marriage, that marriage is binding in heaven and the blessed recipients of so great a bounty come forth in the resurrection as husband and wife and enter into eternal glory. And if the Lord's lawfully empowered servants, acting in his name and with his authorization, sever sinners from among the saints and turn them over

39

to the buffetings of Satan on earth, all that might have been theirs is loosed in heaven, and they shall fail to gain what might have been theirs. It matters not whether the binding or loosing is done by the mouth of the Lord himself or by his servants who do and say what he directs. "Whether by mine own voice or by the voice of my servants, it is the same," he says. (D&C 1:38.)

Strange as these expressions about binding and loosing may seem to an apostate Christendom, they were understood by the Jewish disciples to whom Jesus then spoke. "No other terms were in more constant use in Rabbinic Canon-Law than those of 'binding' and 'loosing.' . . . In regard to some of their earthly decrees, they were wont to say that 'the Sanhedrin above' confirmed what 'the Sanhedrin beneath' had done. But the words of Christ, as they avoided the foolish conceit of His contemporaries, left it not doubtful, but conveyed the assurance that, under the guidance of the Holy Ghost, whatsoever they bound or loosed on earth would be bound or loosed in heaven." (Edersheim 2:85.)[7]

That Jesus, after hearing the witness of Peter and perhaps of others, charged them all "that they should tell no man that he was Jesus, the Christ" is not strange in the light of the historical circumstances. This very witness of his divine Sonship had been borne in congregations without number by him and his disciples for some two and a half years. Now, however, the opposition was so great, the hatred so intense, the desire to hinder the work so well organized, that it seemed the course of wisdom, for the moment, not to hold him forth as the Messiah. He had many things yet to accomplish before Jewish Sanhedrists turned him over to Roman soldiers to drive nails in his hands and feet and hurl a spear into his side.

NOTES

1. The relationship between the bearing of testimony by the power of the Holy Ghost and the forgiveness of sins illustrates a glorious gospel truth. It is that whenever faithful saints gain the companionship of the Holy Spirit, they are clean and pure before the Lord,

for the Spirit will not dwell in an unclean tabernacle. Hence, they thereby receive a remission of those sins committed after baptism.

This same eternal verity is illustrated in the ordinance of administering to the sick. A faithful saint who is anointed with oil has the promise that "the prayer of faith shall save the sick, and the Lord shall raise him up; and if he have committed sins, they shall be forgiven him." (James 5:14-15.) The reasoning of the ancient apostle James, in this instance, is that since the miracle of healing comes by the power of the Holy Ghost, the sick person is healed not only physically but spiritually, for the Spirit who comes to heal will not dwell in a spiritually unclean tabernacle.

2. "Behold, I am God; Man of Holiness is my name; Man of Counsel is my name; and Endless and Eternal is my name, also." (Moses 7:35.)

3. These words from the King Follett Sermon, delivered by the Prophet Joseph Smith, are the high point of Latter-day Saint doctrine on the points here involved: "God himself was once as we are now, and is an exalted man, and sits enthroned in yonder heavens! That is the great secret. If the veil were rent today, and the great God who holds this world in its orbit, and who upholds all worlds and all things by his power, was to make himself visible,—I say, if you were to see him today, you would see him like a man in form—like yourselves in all the person, image, and very form as a man; for Adam was created in the very fashion, image and likeness of God, and received instruction from, and walked, talked and conversed with him, as one man talks and communes with another.

"In order to understand the subject of the dead, for [the] consolation of those who mourn for the loss of their friends, it is necessary we should understand the character and being of God and how he came to be so; for I am going to tell you how God came to be God. We have imagined and supposed that God was God from all eternity. I will refute that idea, and take away the veil, so that you may see.

"These are incomprehensible ideas to some, but they are simple. It is the first principle of the Gospel to know for a certainty the Character of God, and to know that we may converse with him as one man converses with another, and that he was once a man like us; yea, that God himself, the Father of us all, dwelt on an earth, the same as Jesus Christ himself did." (*Teachings*, pp. 345-46.)

4. This same distinction between the Almighty and his servants was also carefully set forth by the spirit Jesus, before his mortal birth, when he gave the keys of the kingdom to Nephi the son of Helaman. "Blessed art thou, Nephi, for those things which thou hast done," the Lord said. "Behold, thou art Nephi, and I am God. . . . ye shall have power over this people. . . . Whatsoever ye shall seal on earth shall be sealed in heaven; and whatsoever ye shall loose on earth shall be loosed in heaven." (Hel. 10:4, 6-7.) The same heavensent power is, of course, in the true Church today. (D&C 132:46-47.)

5. "What rock? Revelation." (*Teachings*, p. 274.) So said the inspired seer of latter days. Edersheim, without the light of latter-day revelation, reached a somewhat similar conclusion. "Perhaps it might be expressed in this somewhat clumsy paraphrase," he said: " 'Thou art Peter (Petros)—a Stone or Rock—and upon this Petra—the Rock, the Petrine—will I found My Church.' " Thus, he reasons, the Church is to be built on "the Petrine in Peter: the heaven-given faith which manifested itself in his confession." That is, Christ "would build His Church on the Petrine in Peter—on his faith and confession." This is akin to saying that the rock is revelation; it is the heavensent faith, the Spirit-borne testimony, the revealed truth—the fact that God speaks by the power of the Spirit to mortal man.

"Nor would the term 'Church' sound strange in Jewish ears," our learned friend continues. "The same Greek word, as the equivalent of the Hebrew *Qahal*, 'convocation,' 'the called,' occurs in the LXX rendering of the Old Testament, and in 'the Wisdom of the Son of Sirach' and was apparently in familiar use at the time. In Hebrew use it referred to Israel, not in their national but in their religious unity. As here employed, it would convey the prophecy, that His disciples would in the future be joined together in a religious unity; that this religious unity or 'Church' would be a building of which Christ was the Builder; that it would be founded on 'the Petrine' of heaven-taught faith and confession; and that this religious unity, this Church, was not only intended for a time, like a school of thought, but would last beyond death and the disembodied state: that, alike as regarded Christ and

His Church—'the gates of Hades shall not prevail against it.' " (Edersheim 2:83-84.)

Farrar, also without the benefit of latter-day revelation, reaches the same general conclusion, which he climaxes by quoting these words of Origen: "If *any one* thus confess, when flesh and blood have not revealed it unto him, but our Father in heaven, *he,* too, shall obtain the promised blessings; as the letter of the Gospel saith indeed to the great St. Peter, but as its spirit teacheth to every man who hath become like what that great Peter was." (Farrar, p. 386.)

6. "The gates of hell are the entrances to the benighted realms of the damned where the wicked go to await the day when they shall come forth in the resurrection of damnation. Those beckoning gates prevail against all who pass through them. But those who obey the laws and ordinances of the gospel have the promise that the gates of hell shall not prevail against them. In this instance, Jesus is telling Peter that the gates of hell shall never prevail against the rock of revelation; that is, as long as the saints are living in righteousness so as to receive revelation from heaven, they will avoid the gates of hell and the Church itself will remain pure, undefiled, and secure against every evil. But when, because of iniquity, revelation ceases, then the gates of hell prevail against the people and also against the organization of which they are members.

"Similarly, the Lord, by revelation, has said in our day: 'Open your mouths and they shall be filled, saying: Repent, repent, and prepare ye the way of the Lord, and make his paths straight; for the kingdom of heaven is at hand; Yea, repent and be baptized, every one of you, for a remission of your sins; yea, be baptized even by water, and then cometh the baptism of fire and of the Holy Ghost. Behold, verily, verily, I say unto you, this is my gospel; and remember that they shall have faith in me or they can in nowise be saved; And upon this rock I will build my church; yea, upon this rock ye are built, and if ye continue, the gates of hell shall not prevail against you.' " (*Commentary* 1:388-89.)

7. Of the Catholic view of the text in question, Farrar uses these aptly chosen words: "Were it not a matter of history, it would have been deemed incredible that on so imaginary a foundation should have been rested the fantastic claim that abnormal power should be conceded to the bishops of a Church which almost certainly St. Peter did not found, and in a city in which there is no indisputable proof that he ever set foot. The immense arrogancies of sacerdotalism; the disgraceful abuses of the confessional; the imaginary power of absolving from oaths; the ambitious assumption of a right to crush and control the civil power; the extravagant usurpation of infallibility in wielding the dangerous weapons of anathema and excommunication; the colossal tyrannies of the Popedom, and the detestable cruelties of the Inquisition—all these abominations are, we may hope, henceforth and for ever, things of the past." (Farrar, p. 385.)

Chapter 63

GOD'S SON—
A SUFFERING SERVANT

Surely he hath borne our griefs,
and carried our sorrows:
yet we did esteem him stricken,
smitten of God, and afflicted.
But he was wounded for our transgressions,
he was bruised for our iniquities. . . .
He was oppressed, and he was afflicted. . . .
For the transgression of my people
was he stricken. . . .
Yet it pleased the Lord to bruise him:
he hath put him to grief. . . .
He shall see of the travail of his soul,
. . . for he shall bear their iniquities.
(Isa. 53:4-11.)

The Messiah Shall Die and Rise Again
(Matthew 16:21-23; Mark 8:31-33; Luke 9:21-22; JST, Luke 9:21)

We have seen Peter—like a giant redwood in the forest of the world—standing on the mountain height; receiving revelation from the Revelator; testifying of the divine Sonship; gaining a blessed benediction from the lips of Him whom he loved.

The revelation: 'Thou art the Messiah; thou art the Son of Man; thou art the Son of the living God.'

The divine benediction: 'Blessed art thou, Simon. Thy testimony has come to thee from the Father by the power of the Spirit; it is recorded in heaven, and the angels rejoice over it.'

The yet future promise of power and dominion and glory: 'Thine are the keys. Thou shalt preside over the earthly kingdom, and the true Sanhedrin in heaven shall be bound by thy decisions on earth.'

Peter and the favored few who surround the person of Him whom they all now know to be the Messiah have received the testimony of Jesus. They know, in a way and by means beyond their mortal powers to explain, that Mary's son had God for his Father. Jesus now plans to build on this foundation of revealed truth and to expound to them in plainness some of the mysteries of that new kingdom to which their testimonies bind them. New converts, having testimonies, are soon tested with new and deep doctrines that often do not accord with their preconceived notions about religion and salvation. From the mesas of exultation, where testimonies flourish, they are often led through the lowlands of despair, where deep doctrines test their allegiance. Having gained glory on the mountains of praise, they must prove their worthiness in the valleys of rebuke.

The witness has been borne as to *who* Jesus is; now he must teach them *what* he is destined to do to fulfill his life's mission. First, "he must go unto Jerusalem." His great Galilean ministry is drawing to a close; he has visited and preached and healed in every village and city, time and again. He has proclaimed in Galilee, from one end to the other, the everlasting word; his voice has been heard in all of the adjacent coasts, in Phoenicia (the Roman province of Syria), and in Decapolis, and through the tetrarchy of Herod Philip. And his own, if so they may be called, have rejected him. The gladsome acceptance with which his ministry began in his homeland has turned into a Satan-guided rejection. The leaven of the scribes and Pharisees has turned the populace against him. He will live in Galilee for another month or six weeks, two months at the most, and will then go to Jerusalem.

Jerusalem, the Holy City! There "the Son of man must suffer many things, and be rejected of the elders, and of the chief priests, and scribes, and be killed, and after three days rise again." Such now became the burden of his teachings. Galilee was the land of his miracles and preaching for most of his ministry; Judea, the land of his sorrow and suffering; in it was found the valley of the shadow of death. He had ministered among the rude peasants of Galilee, whose dialect and dress were ridiculed by the conceited and self-righteous in Judea, but he must now go up to the religious capital of the world to confront the leaders; to rebuke the rulers; to cleanse the temple again; to finish his work; and, finally, to die where so many of the prophets had been slain.

This announcement of his destined death and his assured resurrection was no new doctrine. Among the Jews there were some who waited for a Messiah who would be a suffering servant. Isaiah's words about One who would be smitten and afflicted, wounded and slain, were part of their prophetic library. And Jesus himself had, during his whole ministry, made frequent allusion to his future demise and his coming forth in a newness of resurrected life. He had spoken openly of the bridegroom being taken from the children of the bridechamber; of the Son of Man spending three days in the earth, as Jonah spent a like period in the whale's belly; of the raising up of the temple of his body after three days; of the Son of Man being lifted up, even as Moses lifted up the serpent in the wilderness; and of the need to eat his flesh as the living bread in order to inherit eternal life—all referring to his atoning sacrifice, death, burial, and resurrection.[1]

The doctrine is not new nor the concept strange. But now, coupled with the testimonies of Peter and the others of the divine Sonship, which give it a new dimension, and because of its apparent nearness—he "must go unto Jerusalem" *for that very purpose*—Jesus' teaching causes a tide of fear to rise up in the hearts of the disciples. It is one thing to have a general awareness that death will overtake us at some future time, and quite another to come face to face, suddenly and unexpectedly, with the destroyer's sword.

"Then Peter took him"—apparently aside from the others—"and began to rebuke him, saying, Be it far from thee, Lord: this shall not be unto thee." Or better: 'God forbid; this shall certainly not happen to thee.' Or: 'God forbid it; God be merciful to thee and keep this evil far from thee.' Peter is appealing, as had Lucifer before, to the human element in Christ's nature. 'Lord, this cannot be; you must prevent it by thy divine power. Thy kingdom cannot prosper if evil men afflict and slay its King. Such indignities must not fall upon thee, of all men.'

Temptation from the lips of a faithful friend and confidant is even worse than from the mouth of the arch-tempter himself. Are not a man's worst foes they of his own household when they seek to dissuade him from the course of duty and right? Do not his friends, who love him best, become his worst enemies, when they seek to drag him down from heights of self-sacrifice to the vulgar, the conventional, the comfortable?[2] To Lucifer Jesus had said, "Get thee behind me, Satan"; can he say less to the same allurement when it is proposed by the one whom he has just praised for the verity of his testimony? The answer comes like lightning, in a blazing flash of indignant fire:

Get thee behind me, Satan: thou art an offence unto me: for thou savourest not the things that be of God, but those that be of men.

"This thy mere carnal and human view—this attempt to dissuade me from my 'baptism of death'—is a sin against the purposes of God. Peter was to learn—would that the Church which professes to have inherited from him its exclusive and superhuman claims had also learnt in time!—that he was far indeed from being infallible—that he was capable of falling, aye, and with scarcely a moment's intermission, from heights of divine insight into depths of most earthly folly." (Farrar, p. 388.)

Losing One's Life to Save It
(Matthew 16:24-26; JST, Matthew 16:26-29; Mark 8:34-37; JST, Mark 8:37-38; Luke 9:23-25; JST, Luke 9:24-25)

Jesus, whom they acclaim as King-Messiah, shall die. He shall lose his life to save it. He shall suffer many things of the Rabbinic rulers, and finally be slain, that he may rise again the third day. He shall lay down his life in his Father's cause that he may take it up in eternal glory and then receive an everlasting inheritance in the kingdom that is prepared.

Horrible thought? So Peter presumed, for he saw only the cross and not the crown; he looked only upon the loss of the Lord to the earthly kingdom and not upon the eternal blessings that would flow to all men through the atonement. Accordingly, to his sorrow—with the piercing sword of righteous indignation—he was rebuked by the Lord. And then, before the thunder of Christ's words ceased to roll in his tingling ears, the Master Teacher "called the people unto him with his disciples," that all might hear his further words on the death, the demise, yet to descend—not on the Lord Jesus only, but also on Peter and those who accepted the burdens of full discipleship.

The servants shall be as their Lord. If they suffer with him, they shall also be with him when men shall sorrow no more and all tears shall cease. If they lay down their lives in his cause, they shall take them up again in immortal glory and receive that eternal life which he came to prepare. Jesus has now taught his disciples—and angelic ministrants before an open tomb shall remind them that he did so—Jesus has now taught those who believe on his name that he, the mighty Messiah, shall, after suffering many things, be slain in Jerusalem. But such is only the beginning of sorrow, if sorrow it is. True disciples also must be prepared and willing to lay down their own lives in his cause, for his name's sake. He shall come forth, the firstfruits of them that sleep, to re-

47

ceive all power in heaven and on earth; and if his disciples expect to come forth and inherit eternal life, they must be prepared to suffer and die with him. His death is but the beginning; Peter, who dreaded to see Jesus suffer and die, must himself also step forward and be martyred.

Whosoever will come after me, let him deny himself, and take up his cross, and follow me.

And now for a man to take up his cross, is to deny himself all ungodliness, and every worldly lust, and keep my commandments.

Break not my commandments for to save your lives; for whosoever will save his life in this world, shall lose it in the world to come.

'Come Peter; come James; come John; come all ye saints who seek salvation—come. Take up your cross; take it up daily and follow me. Your cross is to overcome the lusts of the flesh—all ungodliness—and to keep my commandments. Your cross is to bear the burdens placed on the backs of the saints. Your cross is to keep my commandments, and, if I will it, to lay down your lives even as I shall permit evil men to slay me. I shall carry my cross; if you are to be with me, you must carry yours. And whosoever will lose his life in this world, for my sake, shall find it in the world to come. Therefore, forsake the world, and save your souls.'

For whosoever will save his life, shall lose it; or whosoever will save his life, shall be willing to lay it down for my sake; and if he is not willing to lay it down for my sake, he shall lose it.

But whosoever shall be willing to lose his life for my sake, and the gospel's, the same shall save it.

Here indeed is strong doctrine. Jesus the Lord shall suffer before he enters into his glory. "Ought not Christ to have suffered these things, and to enter into his glory?" he shall ask two disciples on the Emmaus road. (Luke 24:26.) Truly, he shall do the will of the Father and withhold nothing, not even his own life. And so it must be with all who are his.

Though they do not court martyrdom, some shall be so honored, and all must be willing, if need be, so to die. "For he who is not able to abide the law of a celestial kingdom cannot abide a celestial glory." (D&C 88:22.) It is the law of heaven and the royal road to eternal life.[3]

Therefore, forsake the world, and save your souls; for what is a man profited, if he shall gain the whole world, and lose his own soul? Or what shall a man give in exchange for his soul?

For what doth it profit a man if he gain the whole world, and yet he receive him not whom God hath ordained, and he lose his own soul, and he himself be a castaway?

"What value is to be placed on a human soul? How can we determine its worth? Two things will give some indication of the priceless value of the souls of men: (1) What these souls have cost up to this point—the labor, material, and struggle that has gone into their creation and development; and (2) The effective use to which they can be put—the benefits that result when souls fill the full measure of their creation and take their rightful place in the eternal scheme of things.

"To use these standards of judgment it is necessary to view human souls in their relationship to the eternal plan of creation, progression, and salvation. Souls had their beginning, as conscious identities, when they were born as the spirit offspring of Deity. There then followed an infinitely long period of training, schooling, and preparation, so that these spirits might go on and attain their exaltation. 'God himself,' as the Prophet Joseph Smith expressed it, 'finding he was in the midst of spirits and glory, because he was more intelligent, saw proper to institute laws whereby the rest could have a privilege to advance like himself.'

"As part of this schooling process this earth was created; spirits were given temporal bodies; gospel dispensations were vouchsafed to men; prophets were sent forth to labor and preach; oftentimes they were persecuted, tormented, and slain; and even the Son of God taught and served among mortals, climaxing his ministry by suffering beyond mortal endurance in working out the infinite and eternal atonement. All this is included in the price already paid toward the purchase of human souls.

"Such of these souls as keep all the commandments shall attain eternal life. They shall go on to exaltation and glory in all things, becoming like the Father, begetting spirit off-spring, creating worlds without number, and forever and endlessly rolling forth the eternal purposes of the Infinite God.

"How much is a human soul worth? No man can say, no tongue can tell, no mind can comprehend it. How apt, then, is Jesus' illustration. If a man—even if such a thing were possible—should gain the whole world, and lose his soul in the process, the acquired wealth would be slight indeed as compared to the value of his own soul.

"It is because of their understanding of this doctrine of the worth of souls that our Lord's ministers go forth with all the energy and capacity they have to labor in the vineyard, pleading with men to repent and save their souls, that they may have eventual eternal joy in the Father's kingdom." (*Commentary* 1:393-94.)

The Second Coming—A Day of Rewards
(*Matthew 16:27-28; Mark 8:38; 9:1; JST, Mark 8:40-44; Luke 9:26-27; JST, Luke 9:26-27*)

If ever there was a sermon showing that men do not live for this life only; if ever the saints were taught that the rewards for righteous works are reserved for a life to come; if ever the scant worth of worldliness was weighed in the balance and found wanting—such is found in Jesus' counsel that his disciples, his saints, must take up their cross, forsake the world, keep the commandments, and be willing to die martyrs' deaths, if they are to gain eternal life.

Eternal life: what is it and when shall its glories and

blessing rest upon the saints? It is full salvation; it is an inheritance in the highest heaven; it is exaltation. It is to sit down with Abraham, Isaac, and Jacob in the kingdom of God, to go no more out. It is the greatest of all the gifts of God, for it is to be like God, to inherit, receive, and possess as he does. It is to be a joint-heir with Christ of all the glory of his Father's kingdom. And it shall come to the faithful in that day when the Son of Man comes to make up his jewels. It is gained when those who so inherit come forth in the resurrection of the just.

For the Son of Man shall come in the glory of his Father with his angels; and then he shall reward every man according to his works.

The Second Coming is a day of judgment, a day of rewards, a day of vengeance for the wicked, a day of glory and honor for the righteous. It is a day for which all men prepare by the lives that they live. Those who live as becometh saints shall be as their Lord; those who walk in carnal paths shall be cast out. (*Commentary* 1:396.)

Therefore deny yourselves of these, and be not ashamed of me. Whosoever shall be ashamed of me, and of my words, in this adulterous and sinful generation, of him also shall the Son of Man be ashamed, when he cometh in the glory of his Father with the holy angels.

And they shall not have part in that resurrection when he cometh. For verily I say unto you, That he shall come; and he that layeth down his life for my sake and the gospel's, shall come with him, and shall be clothed with his glory in the cloud, on the right hand of the Son of Man.

This, then, is the promised day. The martyrs, who lost their lives here, shall find their lives there. With Him they shall reign in eternal glory. What matter our momentary sorrows and sufferings—even though they be unto death—if we gain eternal life in the coming day? In that day "he shall come in his own kingdom, clothed in the glory of his Father, with the holy angels," and those on his right hand shall be in glory even as he is.

There be some standing here, which shall not taste of death, till they see the Son of Man coming in his kingdom.

Enoch and his whole city were translated, taken up bodily into heaven without tasting death. There they served and labored with bodies of flesh and bones, bodies quickened by the power of the Spirit, until that blessed day when they were with Christ in his resurrection. Then, in the twinkling of an eye, they were changed and became immortal in the full sense of the word. So it was also with Moses and Elijah, who were taken up bodily into heaven for reasons that will be manifest on the Mount of Transfiguration. They too were with the Lord Jesus in his resurrection. (D&C 133:54-55.)

Of those here promised that they should "not taste of death" until the Second Coming, we have no knowledge except that the Beloved John was one of them, as shall hereafter be noted. The others are not named, nor has the Lord revealed their whereabouts or ministries to us in this dispensation.[4] Manifestly, there are many things that we do not know; but those things of which we have knowledge are sufficient to enable us to gain eternal life with the ancients if we, in our day, will live as they did in theirs.

NOTES

1. This summary is taken from *Commentary* 1:391.

2. These questions are framed from expressions made by Farrar in footnote 5, p. 388, who also quotes Stier as saying: "Those whose intentions towards us are the best, are the most dangerous to us when their intentions are merely human."

3. "And whoso layeth down his life in my cause, for my name's sake, shall find it again, even life eternal. Therefore, be not afraid of your enemies, for I have decreed in my heart, saith the Lord, that I will prove you in all things, whether you will abide in my covenant, even unto death, that you may be found worthy. For if ye will not abide in my covenant ye are not worthy of me." (D&C 98:13-15.)

4. It may be that they are the ones of whom our revelation says: "I will that all men shall repent, for all are under sin, except those which I have reserved unto myself, holy men that ye know not of." (D&C 49:8.)

Chapter 64

THE TRANSFIGURATION

For we have not followed cunningly devised fables,
when we made known unto you the power
and coming of our Lord Jesus Christ,
but were eyewitnesses of his majesty.
For he received from God the Father
honour and glory, when there came
such a voice to him from the excellent glory,
This is my beloved Son,
in whom I am well pleased.
And this voice which came from heaven we heard,
when we were with him in the holy mount.
(2 Pet. 1:16-18.)
And the Word was made flesh,
and dwelt among us,
(and we beheld his glory,
the glory as of the only begotten of the Father,)
full of grace and truth. (John 1:14.)

Peter, James, and John Receive
the Keys of the Kingdom
(*Matthew 17:1-3; Mark 9:2-4; JST, Mark 9:1-3; Luke 9:28-32;*
JST, Luke 9:28-32)

Our Synoptic authors make brief mention of—in reality
it is scarcely more than an allusion to—what happened on

the heights of Hermon when they and Jesus spent a sacred night enwrapped in the visions of eternity. This blessed night was one of those seeric periods when the mysteries of the kingdom, "which surpass all understanding," are shown forth to souls who are in tune with the Infinite. So marvelous are such revealed truths that it is "not lawful for man to utter" them, "Neither is man capable to make them known, for they are only to be seen and understood by the power of the Holy Spirit." They are reserved by the Lord for those prophets and seers who, "while in the flesh," are yet able "to bear his presence in the world of glory." (D&C 76:114-118.)

In the providences of the Lord the saints know some things that the world does not know about the spiritual outpouring of divine grace that fell on the Mount of Transfiguration. But even latter-day revelation does not set forth the full account, and until men attain a higher state of spiritual understanding than they now enjoy, they will continue to see through a glass darkly and to know only in part the visionary experiences of the presiding officers of the meridian Church. That which is known, however, singles out this night as one of the most important and glorious in the lives of those who saw within the veil and who heard the voices of the heavenly participants.

Near Caesarea Philippi, Peter—a mortal man: impetuous, bold, highly spiritual—had borne a heavensent testimony, one revealed by the power of the Holy Ghost, of the divine Sonship of Christ. Then Jesus, of whom Simon testified, promised to give his chief apostle the keys of the kingdom, including the power to bind and loose on earth and in heaven. After this, Jesus taught them of his coming death and resurrection.

Now on the Mount of Transfiguration, a heavenly voice—that of the Almighty Father who is visiting his Son on planet earth—bears holy witness of the same divine Sonship. And now Jesus and angelic visitants, who do his bidding, join in conferring upon Peter, James, and John the promised keys of the kingdom with their sealing powers.

And these angelic ministrants—fellowservants of the apostles, who like their mortal friends need the blessings of the coming atonement—also speak with Jesus of his coming death and resurrection. The bearing of testimony, the use of the keys of the kingdom, the reality of the atonement—all these are operative on both sides of the veil. Both men on earth and the angels of God in heaven are saved and blessed by the same eternal laws.

From the great confession until Jesus took Peter, James, and John "into a high mountain apart by themselves" was either six or eight days, depending upon whether the day of the confession and the day of travel up the mountain slopes are counted. There is no record of the teachings of that week, but they must have centered around the sad and shocking announcement of the nearness of the death of their Messiah. We do know that the three apostles "asked him many questions concerning his sayings," as they journeyed up what Peter later called "the holy mount."[1] No doubt Jesus, by his answers, prepared them for the spiritual experiences ahead.

After they arrived at a proper and solitary place where they would be undisturbed in their worship and prayer, Luke tells us that Jesus prayed and that the apostles "were heavy with sleep." We are left to conclude that while they slept, even as it would be in Gethsemane, Jesus' prayers ascended to his Father, and—we say it reverently—he received such comfort and reassurance as he needed. Though he were a Son yet learned he obedience by the things which he suffered; and in Gethsemane itself he was strengthened by angelic assistance.

At the proper time the three chief apostles—the First Presidency of the Church—awoke; the time for their participation in the two-realm wonders of that night was at hand. They beheld their beloved Lord in prayer. We can suppose his petitions ascended up on high for himself and for the three spiritual giants who were about to receive the keys of the kingdom and view the wonders of eternity.

From the slivers of knowledge preserved for us in the New Testament of what then transpired, and from the allusions to the spiritual experiences then vouchsafed to those mortals, we can reconstruct the hallowed happenings somewhat along this line: "It was the evening hour when He ascended, and as He climbed the hill-slope with those three chosen witnesses—'The Sons of Thunder and the Man of Rock'—doubtless a solemn gladness dilated His soul; a sense not only of the heavenly calm which that solitary communion with His Heavenly Father would breathe upon the spirit, but still more than this, a sense that He would be supported for the coming hour by ministrations not of earth, and illuminated with a light which needed no aid from sun or moon or stars. He went up to be prepared for death, and He took His three Apostles with Him that, haply, having seen His glory—the glory of the only Begotten of the Father, full of grace and truth—their hearts might be fortified, their faith strengthened, to gaze unshaken on the shameful insults and unspeakable humiliation of the cross.

"There, then, He knelt and prayed, and as He prayed He was elevated far above the toil and misery of the world which had rejected Him. He was transfigured before them, and His countenance shone as the sun, and His garments became white as the dazzling snow-fields above them. He was enwrapped in such an aureole of glistering brilliance—His whole presence breathed so divine a radiance—that the light, the snow, the lightning are the only things to which the Evangelist can compare that celestial lustre." (Farrar, pp. 394-95.)

The apostles "were eyewitnesses of his majesty." (2 Pet. 1:16.) "And his raiment became shining, exceeding white, as snow; so white as no fuller on earth could whiten them." He himself "was transfigured before them."[2] Nor is this all. Peter, James, and John, as the powers of heaven fell upon them, were also transfigured and tasted themselves of the heavenly gifts.[3]

Then our apostolic friends, quickened by the power of

the Spirit—their souls attuned to the infinite; their spirit eyes wide open; their spirit ears unstopped—saw two men, Moses and Elijah, "who appeared in glory, and spake of his death, and also his resurrection, which he should accomplish in Jerusalem." *Moses,* whose very name is the personification of the law, the law of Jehovah, the law by which all Israel lived; *Elijah,* the prophetic defender of that law, the one whose name personified all the prophets; these two, both of whom were translated and taken up into heaven without tasting death, now discussed with their Lord that infinite and eternal atoning sacrifice by which their translated bodies would gain full immortality and yet shine forth with celestial glory. John the Baptist, a spirit personage whose mortal ministry completed what Moses had begun, was also present, rejoicing with his fellow laborers over the atonement about to be wrought.

Hear, O ye heavens, and give ear, O earth; let mortal men and angelic ministrants join hands; let all who belong to the family of the Father, whether on earth or in heaven, rejoice in the great atonement. By it redemption comes; by it the dead are raised; by it eternal life is gained. Truly, there is nothing of greater concern to men and angels than the "decease which he should accomplish at Jerusalem."

At this point, the angelic witness of the atoning sacrifice having been borne by Moses and Elijah, and no doubt by John the Baptist also—the two men from ancient Israel, having retained their physical bodies so they might confer priestly authority upon mortals—these two joined with Jesus in conferring upon Peter, James, and John the keys of the kingdom.[4] Moses conferred the keys of the gathering of Israel, Elijah the keys of the sealing power, so that whatever they bound or loosed on earth would be bound or loosed in heaven. Jesus himself gave them all else that they needed to preside over his earthly kingdom; to lead all men to eternal salvation in the mansions on high; to send the gospel to the ends of the earth; and to seal men up unto eternal life in the kingdom of his Father.[5] Truly Peter, James, and John, while on this holy mount, received their endowments and were empowered from on high to do all things for the building up and rolling forward of the Lord's work in their day and dispensation. (*Commentary* 1:399-404.) "Peter says that while there, they 'received from God the Father honour and glory,' seemingly bearing out this conclusion. It also appears that it was while on the mount that they received the more sure word of prophecy, it then being revealed to them that they were sealed up unto eternal life." (*Commentary* 1:400; 2 Pet. 1:16-19; D&C 131:5.)

Next came the great vision of the transfiguration of the earth; at least we cannot suppose it came earlier in the great spiritual outpourings of this night of nights. How many prophets have been blessed with such seeric foresight of the millennial state of this lowly orb we do not know. Perhaps Enoch, who saw the day when the earth should rest, when the New Jerusalem should come down from God out of heaven to men on earth, and who saw the Son of Man dwell a second time among men. (Moses 7:58-65.) Perhaps Isaiah, who spoke so much of the great age of restoration, and who wrote so plainly about the new heaven and the new earth, when "the wolf and the lamb shall feed together, and the lion shall eat straw like the bullock," and when "there shall be no more thence an infant of days, nor an old man that hath not filled his days: for the child shall die an hundred years old." (Isa. 65:17-25.)

But however much others may have known, the Lord himself, there on Mount Hermon, as part of the wonders of eternity then opened to the view of mortal men, showed unto the Three the transfiguration of the earth. We ourselves are not prepared to see or understand what then transpired. As of now we know only that those who come forth in the resurrection of the just "shall receive an inheritance upon the earth when the day of transfiguration shall come; When the earth shall be transfigured, even according to the pattern which was shown unto mine apostles upon the mount"—the Lord who was on the mount is speaking these words to Joseph Smith in August of 1831—"of which account the fulness ye have not yet received." (D&C 63:20-21.) How many things there are that we have not yet received because we have not attained the spiritual stature of the ancients to whom they were once revealed!

Elohim, the Shekinah, and the Son
(Matthew 17:4-9; JST, Matthew 17:5; Mark 9:5-10; JST, Mark 9:6; Luke 9:33-36; JST, Luke 9:33, 36)

At some time that night on the holy mount something happened—we know not what—that caused Peter to make an inappropriate statement about the practice followed by Israel at the Feast of Tabernacles, the practice of dwelling and worshipping in booths or tabernacles made of wattled boughs. Perhaps amid all the glory and wonder of that night shouts of hosanna and praise, like those that came from worshipful lips at Tabernacle Time, came from the united voices of Christ's servants on both sides of the veil. How could they have contained their joy as they came to understand the infinite scope of the infinite atonement soon to be made by the Infinite One, or as the visions of eternity, including the millennial destiny of the earth, rolled before their spiritually opened eyes? Or perhaps, amid the glory and wonder of it all, Peter sought simply to restrain the departure of those ancient ones whom all the faithful revered so highly. What is more natural than for spiritually endowed mortals, having gained the fellowship of heavenly beings, to desire to prolong that divine association? Whatever the cause, Peter, speaking impetuously, as was his nature, said: "Lord, it is good for us to be here"—and truly it was—"if thou wilt, let us make here three tabernacles; one for thee, and one for Moses, and one for Elias."

"As the splendid vision began to fade—as the majestic visitants were about to be separated from their Lord, as their Lord Himself passed with them into the overshadowing brightness—Peter, anxious to delay their presence, amazed, startled, transported, not knowing what he said—not knowing that Calvary would be a spectacle infinitely more transcendent than Hermon—not knowing that the Law and the Prophets were now [that is, soon would be] fulfilled—not fully knowing that his Lord was unspeakably greater than the Prophet of Sinai and the Avenger of Carmel," made the quoted statement which we, for want of full knowledge, cannot understand. "But it was not for Peter to construct the universe for his personal satisfaction. He had to learn the meaning of Golgotha no less than that of Hermon. Not in cloud of glory or chariot of fire was Jesus to pass away from them, but with arms outstretched in agony upon the accursed tree; not between Moses and Elias, but between two thieves, who 'were crucified with Him, on either side one.'" (Farrar, p. 396.)

All else of that night's wonders was but preliminary to what now was destined to be. Had they seen their Lord transfigured before them, his face and clothes shining as the sun in his strength? Had the Personifier of the Law and the Symbol of the Prophets—both holy men who were taken up into heaven without tasting death—conferred keys and powers upon their fellow servants? Had they seen in vision the transfigured earth in its millennial glory? Had their eyes and ears and souls been opened to understand the infinite and eternal import of the death and resurrection soon to be in Jerusalem? Had there been other spiritual outpourings of like magnitude and import? Truly all this was so. And yet now, on this foundation, the Father himself, the Almighty Elohim, that Holy Being who is the source of all things and all men, the Father himself is about to manifest himself to mortals.

The ancient Shekinah, the luminous cloud, the visible manifestation of the Divine Presence; the bright and flashing glory that rested upon Sinai when Jehovah conversed face to face with the man Moses; the divine brilliance out of which anciently a voice spoke from between the cherubim in the Holy of Holies—the Shekinah came down from heaven to shield the face and form of God from his earthbound creations.

Elohim was there in the cloud. That he was seen by the Son we cannot doubt. Whether our Lord's three companions saw within the veil we do not say. We do know that even now those who have been sealed up unto eternal life, whose calling and election has been made sure, have the privilege of receiving the Second Comforter; and that this Comforter "is no more nor less than the Lord Jesus Christ Himself," who then appears to them "from time to time"; and that "He will manifest the Father," and "they will take up their abode" with him, and the visions of heaven will be opened unto them. (*Teachings,* pp. 150-51.) Let each man determine for himself what happened there on the slopes of Mount Hermon in the summer or autumn of A.D. 29. All that is preserved for us in the New Testament account is that while Peter yet spake of making the three tabernacles for Moses, Elias, and Jesus, "behold, a bright cloud overshadowed them: and behold a voice out of the cloud, which said,

This is my beloved Son, in whom I am well pleased; hear ye him.

Thus, once again the Divine Voice—the Father of us all; the one above all others whose right it is to command obedience and invite worship of himself—affirmed the eternal truth that Christ is the Son; that salvation comes by the Son; that all men must honor the Son and believe his words; that the only approved course for all men of all races in all ages is: "Hear ye him!" To say more about this, at this point, would but detract from the glorious simplicity of this great truth upon which salvation rests.

Hearing the Divine Voice, the three disciples fell on their faces "and were sore afraid." Thereupon Jesus touched them and in tender solicitude said simply, "Arise, and be not afraid." They did so, and "when they had looked round about with great astonishment, they saw no man any more, save Jesus only, with themselves. And immediately they departed."

As they came down the mountain, Jesus said, "Tell the vision to no man, until the Son of man be risen again from the dead." The wonders they had seen could not then lawfully be uttered even to the others of the Twelve, nor could they be understood by any without the enlightening power of the Holy Ghost. After the resurrection of their Lord, after the day of Pentecost when the promised enlightening gift would be given, it would be time enough to tell even those spiritual giants with whom they and Jesus associated on such intimate terms.

Mark, at this point, says they questioned "one with another what the rising from the dead should mean." Their questions could not have been about the reality of the resurrection; nor about its universal nature; nor about the fact Jesus would die and rise again the third day. All this Jesus has already taught them in plainness. In recent weeks his own decease, and his own rising as the firstfruits of them that sleep, has been the burden of his teachings. He has spoken openly and plainly about his own death and resurrection. They know what the resurrection as such is, and in fact have just seen in vision the resurrection that will usher in the millennial day, when the earth itself shall be transfigured. And they know what Jesus said at the Feast of the Passover: that all who are in their graves shall hear the voice of the Son of God and come forth, either in the resurrection of the just or that of the unjust.

It is true that there were many false doctrines taught by the Rabbis about the resurrection. "Current Jewish theology" abounded in conflicting views and unresolved problems in this field. There was no basic agreement among the Rabbis on any major points. "They had heard from some of the preachers in the synagogues, that Israel alone would rise; from others, that the resurrection would include godly heathen also, who had kept the seven commands given to the sons of Noah; from some, that all the heathen outside the holy land would be raised, but only to shame and everlasting contempt before Israel; while still others maintained, that neither the Samaritans, nor the great mass of their own nation, who did not observe the precepts of the Rabbis, would have part in the resurrection. But if there was confusion as to who should rise again, there was still more contradiction between what they had always heard before, of the occasion and time of the resurrection. . . . They had been trained to believe that all Israel would be gathered from the four quarters of the earth at the coming of the Messiah, and that the dead would be raised immediately after. . . . They had always, moreover, heard the synagogue preachers say that the holy dead, when thus raised, were to take part in the kingdom of the Messiah, at Jerusalem, and once more become fellowcitizens with the living." (Geikie, pp. 561-62.) For that matter, the Sadducees did not believe in any resurrection at all.

But none of this could have had any bearing on the questioning discussions the three disciples had among themselves. Their questions must have been the kind any believing disciples would have asked in similar circumstances: When will the resurrection be? How will it be brought to pass? With what body will we arise? Where do resurrected beings dwell? Does the family unit continue among them? And so forth. And like questions can be heard to this day in the congregations of the saints.

We know of one other subject discussed by Jesus and the Chosen Three as they descended the slopes of Hermon—that of Elias and the Restoration—and of this we shall now make more particular mention as we see the Son of Man begin the journey from sunshine into shadow, from the Mount of Transfiguration to the Valley of Humiliation and Death.

Elias of the Restoration
(Matthew 17:10-13; JST, Matthew 17:10-14; Mark 9:11-13;
JST, Mark 9:10-11)

Elias—that figure of ancient renown about whom the world knows so little; whose mission is to bring to pass the restoration of all things before the great and dreadful day of the Lord—who is he and when shall he minister among men?

The Chosen Three, but hours before, had seen and conversed with translated Elias, who is Elijah, and with translated Moses, and from them and from Christ received the keys of the kingdom of heaven. These two ancient worthies had now departed to realms unknown without revealing themselves to the people generally. Further, they had come *after*—nearly three years after—the Messiah had commenced his ministry, not *before* as the scribes taught and as their scriptures testified. How could this be?

Nor had this vanishing and evanescent Elias, who had ministered in glory on Hermon's slopes, done any of the things he was expected to do. According to Jewish legend and scribal teaching, Elias was to come "three days before the coming of the Messiah." Then, they taught, "he will stand and weep and lament on the hills of Israel, over the desolate and forsaken land, till his voice is heard through the world." Further, "he will then cry to the mountains, 'Peace and blessing come into the world, peace and blessing come into the world! '—'Salvation cometh, salvation cometh!' " Then, he will "gather all the scattered sons of Jacob, and restore all things in Israel as in ancient times." He will "turn the hearts of all Israel to receive the Messiah gladly." (Geikie, p. 562.) Further, "the Jewish expectation" of the coming of Elias was so "well known" that "a thing of unknown ownership" might "be kept by the finder 'till the coming of Elias.' He was to restore to the Jews the pot of manna, the rod of Aaron," and so forth, and his coming generally was to be "a time of restoration." (Farrar, p. 397, footnote 2.) Indeed, at the Feast of the Passover it was customary to set an extra place at the table for Elias should he then choose to come and commence his legendary labors.

There had been no hint of any of this on the part of the now invisible being who had talked not of the life and temporal triumph of their Messiah, but of his sorrows and sufferings and death. Were all of the Rabbinic traditions and all of the scribal teachings wrong? To Jesus they said, "Why then say the scribes that Elias must first come?"

Jesus' companions knew that John the Baptist—whose spirit body they had seen on the holy mount—as Gabriel promised, had come before the Lord "in the spirit and power of Elias, to turn the hearts of the fathers to the children, and the disobedient to the wisdom of the just; to make ready a people prepared for the Lord." (Luke 1:17.) They knew that when the Jews sent priests and Levites from Jerusalem to ask John, "Who art thou? . . . Art thou Elias?" the Son of Zacharias had said "he was Elias," but that he was "not that Elias who was to restore all things." They knew that John, speaking of Christ, had then testified: "He is that prophet, even Elias, who, coming after me, is preferred before me, whose shoe's latchet I am not worthy to unloose, or whose place I am not able to fill." (JST, John 1:20-28.) They also knew that when John, imprisoned by Antipas in Machaerus, had sent messengers to Jesus, that they might learn for themselves of his divine Sonship, Jesus had said of John: "If ye will receive it, this is Elias, which was for to come." (Matt. 11:14.)

Clearly, they knew of John's mission as an Elias, as a forerunner, as one appointed to prepare the way, as the one who would prepare a people for the Lord. Yet, learning line upon line and precept upon precept, as the Lord's servants always do, there were still unanswered questions about that Elias who was to restore all things. And well might this have been, for the great restoration was not for their day, as they would learn on the Mount of Olives, after Christ's resurrection, when, still not fully advised in the premises, they will ask: "Lord, wilt thou at this time restore again the kingdom to Israel?" Then they will be told that the great restoration is not for their time; the return of Elias to restore all things is destined to occur in the last days, before the Second Coming of the Son of Man. (Acts 1:6-8.)

For their present edification, Jesus chose to teach them

that Elias the Forerunner was one thing, Elias of the Restoration another. The one had already come; the ministry of the other lay ahead. "Elias truly shall first come, and restore all things, as the prophets have written," Jesus said. Peter, learning his doctrine from the Lord, will later testify to all Israel that all the holy prophets "since the world began" have spoken of the latter-day "times of restitution." (Acts 3:19-21.) But now, Jesus continues:

And again I say unto you that Elias has come already, concerning whom it is written, Behold, I will send my messenger, and he shall prepare the way before me; and they knew him not, and have done unto him, whatsoever they listed. Likewise shall the Son of Man suffer of them.

But I say unto you, Who is Elias? Behold, this is Elias, whom I sent to prepare the way before me.

Such is the Lord's own testimony of the one whose voice, crying in the wilderness of sin and evil, called out to fallen Israel: 'Prepare ye the way of the Lord; make his paths straight; come unto him; repent; be baptized for the remission of your sins; live righteously and be ready to be numbered among his people, for the time is at hand.'

As we are aware, each Gospel author recorded fragments only of much longer conversations. In this instance Mark gives us this account:

Elias verily cometh first, and prepareth all things; and teacheth you of the prophets; how it is written of the Son of Man, that he must suffer many things, and be set at naught.

Again I say unto you, That Elias is indeed come, but they have done unto him whatsoever they listed; and even as it is written of him; and he bore record of me, and they received him not. Verily this was Elias.

John's work was well done; his mortal ministry was over; the way had been prepared for the Coming One. Elias had first come; he had come before the face of Him in whose hand is all power. But Elias also would yet come to restore all things; and so the inspired account attests: "Then the disciples understood that he spake unto them of John the Baptist, and also of another who should come and restore all things, as it is written by the prophets."6

NOTES

1. There can be little doubt that the Mount of Transfiguration is Mount Hermon, north of Caesarea Philippi, though Mount Tabor in the south of Galilee has been so considered by many. In the sixth century three churches were erected on Mount Tabor to commemorate Peter's desire to erect three tabernacles on "the holy mount." Jesus and his party are known to have been near Caesarea Philippi the week before, and Mark expressly says they did not return to Galilee until after the Transfiguration. (Mark 9:30.)

2. Something akin to this, though lesser in degree, happened to Moses. After spending forty days and nights with the Lord in the mountain, "the skin of his face shone," and he had to wear a veil when he talked with the children of Israel. (Ex. 34:28-35.)

3. Such also has been the case with many prophets in many ages when they have seen the wonders of eternity. "I was transfigured before him," Moses says as he recounts how he beheld God with his "spiritual eyes." (Moses 1:11.) "They were caught up into heaven, and saw and heard unspeakable things," the Nephite record says of the three Nephite disciples, the three who were comparable in the New World to Peter, James, and John in the Old World. "And it was forbidden them that they should utter; neither was it given unto them power that they could utter the things which they saw and heard; And whether they were in the body or out of the body, they could not tell; for it did seem unto them like a transfiguration of them, that they were changed from this body of flesh into an immortal state, that they could behold the things of God." (3 Ne. 28:13-15.) As to the transfiguration of Peter, James, and John, the Prophet Joseph Smith says: "The Savior, Moses, and Elias, gave the keys to Peter, James, and John, on the mount, when they were transfigured before him." (*Teachings*, p. 158.)

4. Moses and Elijah were translated—taken into heaven with physical bodies—so they could return, with their bodies, to confer keys upon Peter, James, and John on the Mount of Transfiguration. Of these two ancient prophets, President Joseph Fielding Smith says: "They had a mission to perform, and it had to be performed before the crucifixion of the Son of God, and it could not be done in the spirit. They had to have tangible bodies. Christ is the first fruits of the resurrection; therefore if any former prophets had a work to perform preparatory to the mission of the Son of God, or to the dispensation of the meridian of times, it was essential that they be preserved to fulfill that mission in the flesh. For that reason Moses disappeared from among the people and was taken up into the mountain, and the people thought he was buried by the Lord. The Lord preserved him, so that he could come at the proper time and restore his keys, on the heads of Peter, James, and John, who stood at the head of the dispensation of the meridian of time. (Deut. 34:5-6; Alma 45:18-19.) He reserved Elijah from death that he might also come and bestow his keys upon the heads of Peter, James, and John and prepare them for their ministry.

"But, one says, the Lord could have waited until after his resurrection, and then they could have done it. It is quite evident, due to the fact that it did so occur, that it had to be done before; and there was a reason. There may have been other reasons, but that is one reason why Moses and Elijah did not suffer death in the flesh, like other men do.

"After the resurrection of Christ, of course, they passed through death and the resurrection, and then as resurrected beings came to fulfill a mission of like import in the dispensation of the fulness of time. (D&C 110:11-16; 133:54-55.)" (*Doctrines of Salvation* 2:110-111.)

The concept here presented ties in with and is related to the pronouncements in section 129 of the Doctrine and Covenants about mortals being able to feel the bodies of resurrected persons but not the bodies of spirit beings.

5. When Peter, James, and John came to Joseph Smith and Oliver Cowdery in May or June of 1829, they conferred upon their mortal fellow laborers the Melchizedek Priesthood, including the holy apostleship, and "the keys of [the] kingdom, and a dispensation of the gospel for the last times." (D&C 27:12-13.) Of this divine conferral of power, the Prophet Joseph Smith said: "The voice of Peter, James, and John in the wilderness between Harmony, Susquehanna county, and Colesville, Broome county, on the Susquehanna river, declaring themselves as possessing the keys of the kingdom, and of the dispensation of the fulness of times!" (D&C 128:20.) That mortal men might receive again all that was possessed by their ancient counterparts, Moses and Elias and Elijah—and what others we do not know—came to Joseph Smith and Oliver Cowdery on April 3, 1836, and perhaps at other times, each conferring their "keys, and powers, and glories." (D&C 110; 128:18-21.) There may have been other messengers besides Moses and Elijah who also came to the Mount of Transfiguration, as for instance a translated person from Enoch's day, who also gave keys and authorities to the chosen heads of the dispensation of the meridian of time. We know so little—for want of spiritual preparation on our part—of what transpired on the holy mount.

6. For an analysis of the various usages of the name-title *Elias*, with particular reference to the coming of Elias of the Restoration in modern times, see *Mormon Doctrine*, 2nd ed., pp. 219-22.

Chapter 65

FROM SUNSHINE TO SHADOW[1]

And whatsoever ye shall ask the Father
in my name, which is right,
believing that ye shall receive,
behold it shall be given unto you.
(3 Ne. 18:20.)

The Healing of the Demoniac Youth
(Matthew 17:14-21; Mark 9:14-29; JST, Mark 9:15, 17-20, 23;
Luke 9:37-43)

Edersheim, in concluding his account of the Transfiguration, says: "To all ages it is like the vision of the bush burning, in which was the Presence of God. And it points us forward to that transformation, of which that of Christ was the pledge, when 'this corruptible shall put on incorruption.' As of old the beacon-fires, lighted from hill to hill, announced to them far away from Jerusalem the advent of solemn feast, so does the glory kindled on the Mount of Transfiguration shine through the darkness of the world, and tell of the Resurrection-Day.

"On Hermon the Lord and His disciples had reached the highest point in this history. Henceforth it is a descent into the Valley of Humiliation and Death! " (Edersheim 2:101.)

Elder James E. Talmage, at this same point in his analysis of the same transcendent happenings, makes this explanation: "Our Lord's descent from the holy heights of the Mount of Transfiguration was more than a physical return from greater to lesser altitudes; it was a passing from sunshine into shadow, from the effulgent glory of heaven to the mists of worldly passions and human unbelief; it was the beginning of His rapid descent into the valley of humiliation. From lofty converse with divinely-appointed ministers, from supreme communion with His Father and God, Jesus came down to a scene of disheartening confusion and a spectacle of demonized dominion before which even His apostles stood in impotent despair. To His sensitive and sinless soul the contrast must have brought superhuman anguish; even to us who read the brief account thereof it is appalling." (Talmage, p. 378.)

Farrar speaks in similar tones: "The imagination of all readers of the Gospels has been struck by the contrast—a contrast seized and immortalized forever in the great picture of Raphael—between the peace, the glory, the heavenly communion on the mountain heights, and the confusion, the rage, the unbelief, the agony which marked the first scene that met the eyes of Jesus and His Apostles on their descent to the low levels of human life." (Farrar, p. 398.)

At the foot of the holy mount, amid "the low levels of human life," Jesus and his three intimate apostles found the other members of the Quorum of the Twelve surrounded by a great multitude in the midst of an unseemly contention. His disciples were being accused, maligned, and ridiculed by the scribes, those self-exalting interpreters of the law who kept alive the traditions and legends of the past.

In their ministries the Twelve had gone forth on missions, preaching, healing, casting out devils, perhaps even raising the dead. They had done, in Jesus' name and by his will, what none others had power to achieve. But this day, though they had tried, they had failed to call down the powers of heaven to heal a poor, suffering soul. And their failure was the source of great satisfaction to the scribes. Had not multitudes forsaken the Galilean when he failed to place manna in their mouths that their bellies might bulge? Had he not failed the Messianic test when he did not show them a sign from heaven, not just a healing that could be done by Satan's power, but one of the great expected Messianic signs? How could he be their Messiah and Deliverer if he was going to die in Jerusalem? And now his disciples could work no miracles! Surely his influence was declining and soon they would be rid of this imposter who made such self-serving claims for himself!

Jesus' sudden appearance "greatly amazed" the people, though for what reason we do not know. Some have supposed that his face still shone to some extent as had Moses' when he came down from his holy mount. They all ran to him and saluted him, and he immediately assumed the part of his disciples in the contentious affray then in progress. "What question ye with them? " he asked the scribes.

There was no answer. His bearing, his dignity, their knowledge of what he had theretofore done, perhaps their fear of what he might yet do—for sinners always fear the righteous indignation that may burst forth at any time from godly souls—all these combined to lay a blanket of silence over the scribes. Nor did the disciples have opportunity to state their case. Rather, from the multitude came a certain man who said: "Master, I have brought unto thee my son, who hath a dumb spirit that is a devil; and when he seizeth him he teareth him; and he foameth, and gnasheth with his teeth, and pineth away: and I spake to thy disciples that they might cast him out; and they could not."

How sad a case is this! The boy is possessed with a devil—not an ordinary devil, though they all are evil and vicious beyond mortal comprehension, but a particularly violent and offensive follower of the father of lies. This evil spirit has imposed upon the lad all the misfortunes of lunacy, epilepsy, dumbness, atrophy, and suicidal mania. Though alive, the youth suffers a thousand deaths daily. "And I brought him to thy disciples, and they could not cure him," the father said.

71

Then Jesus, addressing himself to the disciples—whom he loved and to whom he had given power over diseases and evil spirits—and also to the multitudes in general, said: "O faithless and perverse generation, how long shall I be with you? how long shall I suffer you? bring him hither to me."

Heeding Jesus' command, they brought forth the lad. Luke says he was the man's "only child," though he must by now have been more than twelve years of age, for the account says: "And when the man saw him, immediately he was torn by the spirit; and he fell on the ground and wallowed, foaming."

Jesus seemed to be in no hurry to ease the burden and remove the sufferings imposed by the evil spirit. Perhaps, in part at least, he was letting the multitude assemble and giving them opportunity to envision how serious the affliction was. "How long a time is it since this came upon him? " Jesus inquired of the father. "When a child," came the response. "And ofttimes it hath cast him into the fire and into the water, to destroy him, but if thou canst, I ask thee to have compassion on us, and help us."

"*If thou canst*"—so importuned the father who had made the agony of his son the suffering of himself. "*If thou canst*"—there is little or no faith in such a plea, and to it Jesus does not even respond. He feels no need to tell anyone what he can or cannot do; his deeds speak for themselves.

"If thou wilt believe all things I shall say unto you, this is possible to him that believeth," he says. "*If thou wilt believe*"—that is the issue. The issue is not what Jesus can do—he is God and has all power—but what the *man* will do. All things are possible to those who have faith. This man has yet to learn the truths that will enable him to have faith. He is just beginning to believe. But no man has all faith and all assurance to begin with, and if anyone covenant in his heart to believe all that is spoken to him by the Lord or his servants, then the desired blessing will flow unto him.

In tears, the man who but moments before had knelt before Jesus pleading for mercy now cries out the twofold feelings of his heart. "I believe," and "help thou mine unbelief." And so it is with all of the Lord's suffering saints. They believe—nay, they know—that Jesus is their Lord and has all power and can do all things to bless and help them, and yet their need is for that divine assurance which will enable them to know that the divine help will be forthcoming in their case.

Having allowed time for the people to come running together, for this healing must not be done in secret, Jesus now speaks directly to the evil spirit within the man: "Thou dumb and deaf spirit, I charge thee, come out of him, and enter no more into him." There is a piercing scream; the spirit cries out; agony envelops the man; the spirit rends him; he falls to the earth as though dead; the evil spirit leaves; and many say, "He is dead." Jesus, however, takes him by the hand and lifts him up, and he arises and is delivered to his father. "And the child was cured from that very hour." That which could not be done by the disciples, to the joy of the scribes, has now been done by the Master, to their sorrow and discomfiture.

Jesus' triumph—as always—is complete. And yet his disciples are ill at ease; a feeling of failure fills their breasts. Alone in the house, they ask: "Why could not we cast him out?" The reply is clear, incisive, instructive:

> Because of your unbelief: for verily I say unto you, If ye have faith as a grain of mustard seed, ye shall say unto this mountain, Remove hence to yonder place; and it shall be removed; and nothing shall be impossible unto you.

Faith is power; by faith the worlds were made; nothing is impossible to those who have faith. If the earth itself came rolling into existence by faith, surely a mere mountain can be removed by that same power. 'Let Mount Hermon be cast into the Great Sea.' Such would not be one whit different than the brother of Jared saying "unto the mountain Zerin, Remove—and it was removed." (Ether 12:30.)[2]

However, in a less severe tone, Jesus gives this further

explanation as to the failure of the disciples. "Howbeit this kind goeth not out but by fasting and prayer," he says. Clearly there are degrees of malignity and evil powers among the demons in hell. Just as there is a heavenly hierarchy, so is there a satanic government that puts one evil spirit in charge of another; and just as there are degrees of righteousness and glory, so are there levels of lewdness and evil. And it takes greater faith to overcome greater evils. "If a man has not faith enough to do one thing," the Prophet Joseph Smith says, "he may have faith to do another: if he cannot remove a mountain, he may heal the sick." (*History of the Church* 5:355.)

And on this occasion of which we now speak, so great was the faith and so wondrous the miracle that Luke concludes: "They were all amazed at the mighty power of God."

Jesus Foretells His Death and Resurrection
(Matthew 17:22-23; Mark 9:30-32; JST, Mark 9:27; Luke 9:43-45; JST, Luke 9:44)

Our Lord, who but a few weeks ago left his Galilean homeland, seeking peace and rest in the coasts of Caesarea Philippi, is now about to return again to Capernaum, his own city. He came with a few of his intimate disciples to these northern reaches of the Holy Land to escape the scribal scrutiny and Rabbinic wrath that is now sweeping like a flood through all Galilee. He came to find rest from the throngs who scarcely allow him time to eat or sleep. Here he desired to be alone with and to teach his apostolic associates and the limited few of like spiritual stature who hold constant converse with him. And he came to be at the appointed place, on the heights of Hermon, there to meet with Moses and Elias, and there to confer upon Peter, James, and John the keys of the kingdom of heaven.

While in this half-Gentile area he has also received with approbation the testimony of Peter; has taught his intimates plainly concerning his death and resurrection; and he has cast out a particularly vicious and malignant devil from a suffering lad.

Now, however, the scribes and Rabbis have found his party and are again tempting, tormenting, and harassing them; the multitudes, aware of his presence, are again thronging about; and the day for his decease in Jerusalem is drawing near. There is time only for a brief visit in Capernaum and then he must go to the Holy City to keep the Feast of Tabernacles and do a certain few appointed and remaining deeds, there and in Judea and Perea, before the day of his demise. Thus we see him leaving the area around Caesarea Philippi and Dan, leaving the majestic mountain masses called Hermon and Lebanon, and traveling by an unusual and little-used route back to Capernaum. Mark says the blessed party "departed thence, and passed through Galilee privately." The reason: "He would not that any man should know it." The day of his public ministry in Galilee is past. His desire now is to instruct the favored few and prepare them for the coming ordeal and the burdens they must bear when it falls their lot to stand in his place and stead in taking salvation to a weary world of spiritually illiterate souls who prefer worldliness to godliness.

As they traveled, "and while they abode in Galilee," Jesus came back again to the matter that weighed most heavily upon him, the chief reason he came into the world—to die and be resurrected. "Let these sayings sink down into your hearts," he counseled as he spoke of his coming betrayal and death. As though the agonies of that hour were passing before his view, he said: "The Son of man is delivered into the hands of men, and they shall kill him; and after that he is killed, he shall rise the third day."

It was not intended that the full significance of this teaching should dawn upon all of them at this time. Such a full view of the eternal plan that centered in Him whose friends they were was reserved for a future day—a day when the women who then heard his words would weep before an open tomb and hear an angelic voice say: "He is not here,

75

but is risen: remember how he spake unto you when he was yet in Galilee, Saying, The Son of man must be delivered into the hands of sinful men, and be crucified, and the third day rise again." (Luke 24:6-7.) But for the present, as Luke expresses it, "they understood not this saying, and it was hid from them, that they perceived it not: and they feared to ask him of that saying."

The Miraculous Payment of the Temple Tribute
(Matthew 17:24-27)

Jesus and his disciples are now back in Capernaum, and a situation is about to arise that will enable him to reaffirm his divine Sonship to Peter in a miraculous way. He is about to perform an unusual and unique miracle, one like none other ever wrought by his hands. He will pay a tax he does not owe, with money he has not earned, to appease those whom he prefers not to offend. He will use his gift of seership to find the needed coin, and Peter, in the process, will have another rough edge ground off from that impetuous nature which one day, smoothed and refined to perfection, will guide the destinies of the earthly kingdom.

Those who collect the tax for the temple in Jerusalem come to Peter and ask: "Doth not your master pay tribute?" Or better: "Doth not your master pay the half-shekel?" for, properly speaking, no tribute was involved. Tribute is payable to foreign powers; this was a tax, the "half a shekel after the shekel of the sanctuary," which every Jew, who had reached the age of twenty years, paid to the Lord as a "ransom for his soul." (Ex. 30:11-16.) This was money due Jehovah; it was comparable to the tithes imposed by the Lord upon his people. Its use: the repair and upkeep of the Lord's House; payment for the public sacrifices, the scapegoats and red heifers, and the incense and the shewbread; and the payment of the Rabbis, bakers, judges, and others connected with the temple services.

To the query of the tax collectors, which apparently was

asked in good faith—for the annual tax was nearly six months in arrears, and it was the custom of the collectors to compel compliance—Peter said, "Yes." "If he had thought a moment longer—if he had known a little more—if he had even recalled his own great confession so recently given—his answer might not have come so glibly. This money was, at any rate, in its original significance, a redemption-money for the soul of each man; and how could the Redeemer, who redeemed all souls by the ransom of His life, pay this money-ransom for His own? And it was a tax for the Temple services. How, then, could it be due from Him whose own mortal body was the new spiritual Temple of the Living God? He was to enter the veil of the Holiest with the ransom of His own blood. But He paid what He did not owe, to save us from that which we owed, but could never pay." (Farrar, p. 406.)

Deservedly, when Peter entered the house—no doubt his own, for this is Capernaum—"Jesus rebukes him." "What thinkest thou Simon?" he asked, "of whom do the kings of the earth take custom or tribute? of their own children, or of strangers?" To this there is only one reply: "Of strangers." Jesus' answer: "Then are the children free."

How inconsistent for the Messiah, who is the Son of God, to pay tribute for the upkeep of his Father's House, which is also the Son's House. If even earthly princes are exempt from capitation taxes, will not the Highest free his Son from such a burden? He who came to give his own soul a ransom for all surely should not pay a ransom for his own. Should he do so, he would be withdrawing his claim to Messiahship and attesting that he was a man like other men.

Notwithstanding all this, Jesus says, "Lest we should offend them, go thou to the sea, and cast an hook, and take up the fish that first cometh up; and when thou hast opened his mouth, thou shalt find a piece of money: that take, and give unto them for me and thee."

Jesus will not raise the issue of his divine Sonship with the tax collectors. Let them consider him as a man only if they choose, though it is of note that they addressed their query not to him, but to Peter. All men, believers and nonbelievers alike, held the Master in awe. Thus he pays the tax but does it in such a manner that distinctive and divine powers are reaffirmed, not alone to Peter but to all who learn of the miracle. How could any but divine wisdom devise such a teaching situation, and how could any but divine power place the coin in the mouth of the first fish to take the hook of an impetuous Peter? Again wisdom is justified of her children.

NOTES

1. This chapter title is also the one used by Elder James E. Talmage as he begins his description of what befell our Lord after the glorious happenings on the Mount of Transfiguration.

2. "And so great was the faith of Enoch, that he led the people of God, and their enemies came to battle against them; and he spake the word of the Lord, and the earth trembled, and the mountains fled, even according to his command; and the rivers of water were turned out of their course." (Moses 7:13.)

Chapter 66

THE DISCOURSE ON MEEKNESS AND HUMILITY

Little children are whole,
for they are not capable of committing sin. . . .
Teach parents that they must repent
and be baptized, and humble themselves
as their little children,
and they shall all be saved
with their little children. . . .
I love little children with a perfect love;
and they are all alike and partakers of
salvation. . . . All little children are
alive in Christ. (See Moro. 8:5-26.)
And little children also have
eternal life. (Mosiah 15:25.)

On Becoming as a Little Child
(Matthew 18:1-5; Mark 9:33-40; JST, Mark 9:31, 34-35; Luke 9:46-50; JST, Luke 9:49-50)

During the wearisome hours of walking between the area of Caesarea Philippi and Capernaum, the disciples, no doubt out of earshot of Jesus, contended among themselves over the issue of precedence and position in the coming kingdom. Perhaps the fires of jealousy blazed forth because Jesus took only three of the Twelve with him on special occasions—into the home of Jairus when the maiden was raised from death, alone on the slopes of Hermon for what purpose the others did not even then know. Perhaps they still envisioned, to some degree, that their Messiah would be the Messiah of Jewish expectation with a court of courtiers, a cabinet of ministers, and an army of captains and generals. Who among them would serve as his prime minister, his secretary of state, the chief justice in his judiciary? Will Matthew collect the taxes, Judas keep the treasury, and the Sons of Thunder—who one day soon will speak of calling down fire from heaven upon their enemies—will they command the armies? Through it all Jesus is either not aware or takes no apparent note of the bickerings of the brethren.

But now, back in Peter's home in Capernaum, away from prying eyes and surrounded only by those whom he loves, Jesus chooses to disabuse their minds on this matter of position and rank and preferment. Even the slightest leaning toward that Pharisaic practice of seeking the highest seats in the synagogue must be corrected. The eyes of the disciples must be opened so as to see wherein true greatness lies and what manner of men they must be even to gain an inheritance in the kingdom of the saints.

"What was it that ye disputed among yourselves by the way?" he asked. There was silence, the silence of shame; none dared to answer him. As Mark says, "They held their peace, being afraid, for by the way they had disputed among themselves who was the greatest among them." Further, as they traveled by the way, there had arisen "a reasoning among them, which of them should be greatest." 'Who is the greatest among us now, and who shall reign supreme in the heavenly kingdom ahead? Who shall sit on his right hand and who on his left?' Such had been their thoughts and such their words as they had given vent to the jealousies of their hearts. "It must have been part of His humiliation and self-exinanition to bear with them," Edersheim says as he contrasts "this constant self-obtrusion, self-assertion, and low, carnal self-seeking, this Judaistic trifling," with the "utter self-abnegation and self-sacrifice of the Son of Man." (Edersheim 2:116.)[1]

Jesus then said, "If any man desire to be first, the same shall be last of all, and servant of all." Men should not seek to assign themselves to positions of preferment, in which one outranks the other, either in this world or in the world to come. True greatness consists in doing best those things which are the common lot of all mankind. Service to one's family and to his fellowmen in general—in such a course lies true greatness. It is greater to be a loving and wise father than a commanding general or a corporate executive.

At this point the disciples asked: "Who is the greatest in the kingdom of heaven?" In answer, "Jesus called a little child unto him," no doubt one of Peter's children, "and set him in the midst of them." Mark says he took the child "in his arms." With the scene thus set, Jesus said:

> *Verily I say unto you, Except ye be converted, and become as little children, ye shall not enter into the kingdom of heaven.*
> *Whosoever therefore shall humble himself as this little child, the same is greatest in the kingdom of heaven.*

Little children—holy and pure infants, scarcely out of the presence of their Eternal Father—come into this world free from any taint of sin. They are alive in Christ through the atonement, and of them, thus saith the Father: "Little children are redeemed from the foundation of the world through mine Only Begotten; Wherefore, they cannot sin, for power is not given unto Satan to tempt little children, until they begin to become accountable before me." (D&C 29:46-47.) Should they die before they partake of the sins and evils of this wicked world—being still pure and spotless; being yet qualified to dwell in that Celestial Presence whence they just came—they are thus saved in the kingdom of God.

Accountable men, to gain salvation, must become as

their little children. The refining powers of the gospel must operate in their lives. Sin and evil must be burned out of them as though by fire; they must receive the baptism of fire. They must be converted—changed from their carnal and fallen state to a state of righteousness, becoming again pure and spotless as they were in their infancy. Such is the state of those who become heirs of salvation. Then they will be "greatest in the kingdom of heaven." That is to say, all who gain salvation, which is eternal life, shall be greatest in the kingdom of heaven, "for there is no gift greater than the gift of salvation." (D&C 6:13.) All shall inherit alike in that eternal kingdom; all shall be greatest, for they shall possess, inherit, and receive all that the Father hath. Thus, Jesus continues:

Whosoever shall humble himself like one of these children, and receiveth me, ye shall receive in my name. And whosoever shall receive me, receiveth not me only, but him that sent me, even the Father.

Recently we saw Peter rebuked for his rash and intemperate views. Jesus said Peter was an offense unto him and that his doctrine was satanic, when the chief apostle tried to dissuade the Lord from following the course to crucifixion. Now the beloved John comes in for censure. Having heard the instruction that they must receive in Christ's name all who humble themselves as little children, John confesses what he and the others had done. "Master, we saw one casting out devils in thy name, and he followeth not us: and we forbad him, because he followeth not us."

"He followeth not us," or, better, as Luke has it, "He followeth not *with* us"—he was not one of the Twelve, not one of the intimate group of disciples who traveled with Jesus and his party. They were contending over precedence and rank, debating who was the greatest among them and who would be the greatest in the kingdom of heaven! And, lo, they found another member of the Church, another faithful saint of the Most High—for "there was not any man who could do a miracle in the name of Jesus save he were cleansed every whit from his iniquity" (3 Ne. 8:1)—they found another priesthood holder casting out devils as they themselves had done. Him they rebuked lest he be greater than they.

Jesus' response—harmonious with his counsel that they must receive "in his name" all who humbled themselves and came unto him, for all men are equal in his kingdom: the apostles are to be as the seventies, and the seventies as the elders—Jesus' response was: "Forbid him not: for there is no man which shall do a miracle in my name, that can lightly speak evil of me. For he that is not against us is on our part." And further, again as Luke has it, "Forbid not any" who cast out devils or do good works in the name of Jesus, for he had many faithful followers, and the more of them who exercised their priesthood and worked righteousness the better.

On Casting Sinners Out of the Church
(Matthew 18:6-11; JST, Matthew 18:9, 11;
Mark 9:41-50; JST, Mark 9:40-50)

All things have their opposites. Having spoken of the blessings awaiting those who receive his little ones in his name, Jesus now sets forth the curses that shall befall those who lead these guileless ones astray. If, as he said, "Whosoever shall give you a cup of water to drink in my name, because ye belong to Christ, verily I say unto you, he shall not lose his reward," then those who withhold water, or who give wine and vinegar to drink, as it were, shall be condemned.

"Every spirit of man was innocent in the beginning." We all started out in preexistence on an equal footing, though in due course Lucifer and one-third of the hosts of heaven rebelled. "And God having redeemed man from the fall, men became again, in their infant state, innocent before God." We all commence mortal life on an equal footing. No sin or taint attaches to any newborn infant: all are alike unto God; all leave his presence to come to earth; all are prepared to return to his presence if death overtakes them

83

before they become subject to sin. But once again, in due course, sin and evil enter their lives. "And that wicked one cometh and taketh away light and truth, through disobedience, from the children of men, because of the tradition of their fathers." Hence the Lord's command to his saints "to bring up" their "children in light and truth." (D&C 93:38-40.)

When Judas of Galilee led an insurrection, the Romans in Galilee captured some of the leaders, tied millstones around their necks, and drowned them in the sea. Such was a Roman manner of execution in the days of Augustus. To show how serious it is to bring up children in a house of iniquity—to lead them into unbelief and wickedness "because of the tradition of their fathers"—Jesus says:

But whoso shall offend one of these little ones which believe in me, it were better for him that a millstone were hanged about his neck, and that he were drowned in the depth of the sea.

Then Jesus reaches out with his words to include all his saints of whatever age: "Woe unto the world because of offences! for it must needs be that offences come, but woe to that man by whom the offence cometh!" Though the plan of salvation calls for a tempter; though man cannot be saved unless he overcomes opposition; though the Son of God must be betrayed by a traitor's kiss—yet the tempter, the opposer, the Judas, shall all suffer the wrath of God. Wo unto them.

Therefore, if thy hand offend thee, cut it off; or if thy brother offend thee and confess not and forsake not, he shall be cut off. It is better for thee to enter into life maimed, than having two hands, to go into hell.

For it is better for thee to enter into life without thy brother, than for thee and thy brother to be cast into hell; into the fire that never shall be quenched, where their worm dieth not, and the fire is not quenched.

Horrible as the prospect may be, it is better to saw off a gangrenous leg and walk through life on a wooden stump than to keep the mortified flesh and die an agonizing death. And so it is with church members who teach false doctrines and foster evil and lewd practices. "All those who preach false doctrines, and all those who commit whoredoms, and pervert the right way of the Lord, wo, wo, wo be unto them, saith the Lord God Almighty, for they shall be thrust down to hell!" (2 Ne. 28:15.)

In the course of this sermon, Jesus says: "And a man's hand is his friend, and his foot, also; and a man's eye, are they of his own household." It is better to sever evil people from the family of Christ, which is the Church, than, by retaining them in fellowship, to destroy those who otherwise would have been saved. It is better that one evil and wicked soul burn in the everlasting fires of Gehenna—where rats and worms and crawling things feast upon the garbage—which is his assured destiny in any event, than to permit him to poison the souls of others and lead them to a like damnation.

And again, if thy foot offend thee, cut it off; for he that is thy standard, by whom thou walkest, if he become a transgressor, he shall be cut off. It is better for thee, to enter halt into life, than having two feet to be cast into hell; into the fire that never shall be quenched.

Men must not pin their faith on others. Faith centers in the Lord Jesus Christ, who alone was perfect. All others fall short to one degree or another. It is the doctrine and the principles of the gospel that are true. If men—weak, struggling, sinning mortals—fail and lose their souls, so be it. Let not others in the kingdom go down to hell with them.

Therefore, let every man stand or fall, by himself, and not for another; or not trusting another.

Seek unto my Father, and it shall be done in that very moment what ye shall ask, if ye ask in faith, believing that ye shall receive.

And if thine eye which seeth for thee, him that is appointed to watch over thee to show thee light, become a transgressor and offend thee, pluck him out.

It is better for thee to enter into the kingdom of God, with one eye, than having two eyes to be cast into hell fire.

For it is better that thyself should be saved, than to be cast into hell with thy brother, where their worm dieth not, and where the fire is not quenched.

Jesus now—after teaching his disciples that salvation comes only to those who are converted and become as a little child; after showing them that true greatness, here and hereafter, is reserved for those who serve their fellowmen; after rebuking the false zeal that had forbidden others of his saints than the Twelve from casting out devils; after discoursing on the offenses that would come upon church members; and after dramatizing the need to cut off even leaders in the family and leaders in the Church who draw men astray, lest the pupil and the teacher both go down to hell—after all this (and certainly it is but a brief summary of what Jesus taught), Jesus now climaxes these teachings with a powerful illustration. It is one that only those then living in their Jewish social order could understand fully. We, however, can put ourselves in their position and view much of the brilliance and beauty of the words of the Master Teacher.

"For every one shall be salted with fire," he said. That is, "Just as salt is sprinkled over every sacrifice for its purification, so must every soul be purged by fire; by the fire, if need be, of the severest and most terrible self-sacrifice. Let this refining, purging, purifying fire of searching self-judgment and self-severity be theirs." (Farrar, p. 403.) Or, "Every member of the Church shall be tested and tried in all things, to see whether he will abide in the covenant 'even unto death,' regardless of the course taken by the other members of his family or of the Church. To gain salvation men must stand on their own feet in the gospel cause and be independent of the spiritual support of others. If some of the saints, who are themselves the salt of the earth, shall fall away, still all who inherit eternal life must remain true, having salt in themselves and enjoying peace one with another." (*Commentary* 1:421.)

"And every sacrifice shall be salted with salt," Jesus continues. That is, "No one is fit for the sacrificial fire, no one can himself be, nor offer anything as a sacrifice, unless it have been first, according to the Levitical Law, covered with salt, symbolic of the incorruptible." (Edersheim 2:121.)

But the salt must be good. For if the salt have lost his saltness, wherewith will ye season it? (the sacrifice;) therefore it must needs be that ye have salt in yourselves, and have peace one with another.

"If the salt, with which the spiritual sacrifice is to be salted for the fire, 'have lost its savour, wherewith will ye season it?' " That is, 'If ye yourselves are not purified and clean; if ye have not risen above worldly things, including your bickerings about greatness; if ye have lost the spirit of the gospel, how shall your spiritual sacrifices be purified?' "Hence, 'have salt in yourselves,' but do not let that salt be corrupted by making it an occasion of offence to others, or among yourselves, as in the dispute by the way, or in the disposition of mind that led to it, or in forbidding others to work who follow not with you, but 'be at peace among yourselves.' " (Edersheim 1:121.)[2]

To understand Jesus' next pronouncement, we yet again must turn to the Jewish theological context in which it was made; we must know "the Rabbinic teaching about the Angels." It was: "In the Jewish view, only the chiefest of the Angels were before the Face of God within the curtained Veil, or *Pargod,* while the others, ranged in different classes, stood outside and awaited his behest. The distinction which the former enjoyed was always to behold His Face, and to hear and know directly the Divine counsels and commands." (Edersheim 2:122.) Thus, we suppose with Peter's son still enfolded in his arms, Jesus said:

Take heed that ye despise not one of these little ones; for I say unto you, That in heaven their angels do always behold the face of my Father which is in heaven.

To the disciples this was more than a refutation of the Jewish concept that in the hierarchy of the angelic world only Michael and Raphael and Gabriel and the great and mighty stood in the divine presence. The words "my Father" were, of course, a renewed witness of Jesus' divine Sonship, but the whole statement was an allusion to preexistence; perhaps it was an outright teaching of that doctrine, for the words recorded may be only a small part of what Jesus then said. Truly, the spirits of all children, prior to entering the mortal body, dwell in the presence of the Father. They see his face, hear his voice, and know his teachings. What a monstrous evil it is to lead little children—born with angelic purity—into the pit of false doctrine and the mire of worldly living!

For the Son of Man is come to save that which was lost, and to call sinners to repentance; but these little ones have no need of repentance, and I will save them.

At this point Jesus gave the parable of the lost sheep with the emphasis "on keeping the sheep from getting lost, on showing how precious the sheep are, and on how reluctant the Shepherd is to lose even one." (*Commentary* 1:508.) Later, in Perea, he will give the same parable again in an expanded form and with an entirely different application. At that time he will make the scribes and Pharisees the shepherds, and it will be more appropriate for us to consider both versions together in the latter setting.

NOTES

1. When Edersheim speaks of Jesus' self-exinanition, he means that our Lord voluntarily abased himself, or, rather, emptied himself of all his divine power, or enfeebled himself by relying upon his humanity and not his Godhood, so as to be as other men and thus be tested to the full by all the trials and torments of the flesh.

2. "It is a well-known law, that every sacrifice burned on the Altar must be salted with salt. Indeed, according to the Talmud, not only every such offering, but even the wood with which the sacrificial fire was kindled, was sprinkled with salt. Salt symbolised to the Jews of that time the incorruptible and the higher. Thus, the soul was compared to the salt, and it was said concerning the dead:'Shake off the salt, and throw the flesh to the dogs.'The Bible was compared to salt; so was acuteness of intellect. Lastly, the question: 'If the salt have lost its savour, wherewith will ye season it?' seems to have been proverbial, and occurs in exactly the same words in the Talmud." (*Edersheim* 2:121-22.)

Chapter 67

DISCOURSES ON FORGIVENESS AND THE SEALING POWER

My disciples, in days of old,
sought occasion against one another
and forgave not one another in their hearts;
and for this evil they were afflicted
and sorely chastened.
Wherefore, I say unto you,
that ye ought to forgive one another;
for he that forgiveth not his brother his trespasses
standeth condemned before the Lord;
for there remaineth in him the greater sin.
(D&C 64:8-9.)

On Forgiving One Another
(Matthew 18:15-17, 21-22)

We are still with Jesus, in the blessed home of Peter, in the evil city of Capernaum, upon which dire woes rest. The Master continues to counsel our souls and to enlighten our minds. Some of us have been offended by the words and deeds of our fellow disciples, and we have not forgiven them. Our brethren in the Church—the very people with whom we should be joined together as though we were one flesh—these our brethren have trespassed against us. We hear Jesus say:

Moreover if thy brother shall trespass against thee, go and tell him his fault between thee and him alone: if he shall hear thee, thou hast gained thy brother.

The burden is not on the guilty but upon the innocent. It is the one whose hands are clean and whose conscience is clear, not the culprit, who is to start the processes of reconciliation. "It is not the sinner, the trespasser, the offender, who is to take the initiative in restoring peace and unity among brethren. If perchance he should do so, well and good. But the Lord commands the innocent person, the one without fault, the one who has been offended, to search out his brother and seek to repair the breach. Thus: If thy brother trespass against thee, wait not for him to repent and make restitution; he is already somewhat hardened in spirit because of the trespass itself; rather, go to him, extend the hand of fellowship, shower him with love, and perchance 'thou hast gained thy brother.' " (*Commentary* 1:422-23.)

"I, the Lord, will forgive whom I will forgive, but of you it is required to forgive all men; And ye ought to say in your hearts—let God judge between me and thee, and reward thee according to thy deeds." (D&C 64:10-11.)

But if he will not hear thee, then take with thee one or two more, that in the mouth of two or three witnesses every word may be established.

How much better it is if brethren settle their differences in private, apart from the courts of the land, apart even from the judicial system of the Church. If an offense is known by others they may themselves take offense also. The mere knowledge of the existence of sin may be an invitation to commit sin.

And if he shall neglect to hear them, tell it unto the church: but if he neglect to hear the church, let him be unto thee as an heathen man and a publican.

Even if a matter must be brought before the Church itself, even if it must come before the organized body of believers who comprise the earthly kingdom, it is not to come before the congregation generally. "If thy brother or sister offend thee" is the divine decree, "thou shalt take him or her between him or her and thee alone; and if he or she confess thou shalt be reconciled. And if he or she confess not thou shalt deliver him or her up unto the church, not to the members, but to the elders. And it shall be done in a meeting, and that not before the world." (D&C 42:88-89.) Thus, if all else fails, and the offense is sufficiently serious, there remains no alternative but to withdraw from the offending brother the blessings of fellowship with the saints and membership in the earthly kingdom. He must be excommunicated and dropped from the brotherhood of Christ, becoming thus as the heathen and the publican.

Peter's reaction to all this was typically Jewish. Rabbinism called upon the offender to initiate a course of reconciliation with his brother and specified that forgiveness should not be extended more than three times to any offender. His soul as yet not afire with the Holy Spirit, Peter asked a question that, as he must have then supposed, assumed a far more liberal rule than that imposed by the Rabbis. "Lord, how oft shall my brother sin against me, and I forgive him? till seven times?" Jesus answered: "I say not unto thee, Until seven times: but, Until seventy times seven," meaning there is no limit to the number of times men should forgive their brethren. Forgiveness is qualitative, not quantitative. Forgive and be forgiven, for there will be a day when the Lord shall "measure to every man according to the measure which he has measured to his fellow man." (D&C 1:10.)

On the Sealing Power
(Matthew 18:18)

Verily I say unto you, Whatsoever ye shall bind on earth shall be bound in heaven; and whatsoever ye shall loose on earth shall be loosed in heaven.

Sometime after Jesus and the Three came down from

Hermon's slopes; sometime before these words were spoken in Capernaum; on some sacred, holy, and unnamed occasion, the remainder of the Twelve, all nine of them, received the keys of the kingdom of heaven. These keys, in their nature, were the right and power of full presidency, the right and power to preside over and direct all of the affairs of the kingdom of God on earth, and the right and power to bind and loose on earth and in heaven.

How wondrous are the ways of Him of whom Isaiah said, "His name shall be called Wonderful." (Isa. 9:6.) He, on the holy mount, assisted by Moses, Elias, and possibly by others, conferred upon the First Presidency of his earthly church all of the keys and powers they needed to govern the earthly kingdom and to seal men up unto eternal life in the heavenly kingdom.

Then he and the Three—acting, we may suppose, in concert—conferred those same keys and powers upon the others, all of whom (save Judas) used them for the salvation and exaltation of their fellowmen.

How glorious is the voice we hear from heaven! Keys and sealing powers are vested in mortal hands. Mortal men can now say to their fellow mortals: "We seal thee up to come forth in the morning of the first resurrection, clothed with glory, immortality, and eternal lives; we seal thee up to pass by the angels and the gods which guard the way, so that you may enter into the fulness of the glory of Him who is in all things, and through all things, and round about all things, even God, who sitteth upon his eternal throne; we seal thee up to be a Joint-Heir with the Natural Heir, to inherit, receive and possess as he does, and to sit with him in his throne even as he sits with his Father on the Great White Throne."

The sealing power! The apostolic power possessed by Adam and all the ancients; the heavenly endowment enjoyed by Enoch and Abraham and Elijah; the power of the Great God without which man cannot ascend to heights beyond the stars! Such now is resident with *all* of the

Twelve—not with Peter only, to whom it was promised; not with the Chosen Three, who received it by angelic and divine conferral on the mount of Transfiguration, but with *all* of the Twelve.

True, keys are the right of presidency, and only one man on earth can exercise them in their eternal fulness at any one time; but all other possessors of these powers can exercise them at any time under the direction of the senior apostle of God on earth.

And so Jesus now has his Twelve—holy men who hold the keys and have the sealing power; holy men, any one of whom has power to preside over and direct all of the affairs of the Church; holy men who shall now bind and seal on both sides of the veil, and who shall retain and remit sins as seemeth good to them and to the Holy Ghost.

Be it known that now, with the conferral of these keys and powers, the Church of Jesus Christ for the Meridian of Time is duly organized and officered, and all things can now go forward as seemeth good to Him whose kingdom it is.

On Faith and Unity
(Matthew 18:19-20; JST, Matthew 18:19)

Again, I say unto you, that if two of you shall agree on earth as touching any thing that they shall ask, that they may not ask amiss, it shall be done for them, of my Father which is in heaven.

For where two or three are gathered together in my name, there am I in the midst of them.

We have almost no way of knowing the wonders and marvels that would attend the Lord's work on earth if all of those who are engaged in it were perfectly united together in the same mind and in the same judgment. "Be one; and if ye are not one ye are not mine," he says. (D&C 50:29.) Our souls can scarcely conceive of the gifts and blessings that would be showered upon each of us individually if we possessed that faith which it is within our power to receive.

"By faith all of the righteous desires of the saints can be gained. There are no limits to the power of faith; nothing is too hard for the Lord. Prayer is the mode of communication by which the petitions of the saints are presented to their Eternal Father. 'Ye must always pray unto the Father in my name,' Jesus said to the Nephites, 'And whatsoever ye shall ask the Father in my name, which is right, believing that ye shall receive, behold it shall be given unto you.' " (*Commentary* 1:427.)

Now Jesus tells the Twelve that if any two of them are united—"that they may not ask amiss"—the Father will grant their petition. And as with the Twelve so with all the saints; there is no spiritual gift or heavenly endowment available to the Twelve that will not flow, following obedience to the same law, to the least and last of the saints. Jesus, by the power of his Spirit, will always be with even two or three of his true believers.

If the saints desire to be led, guided, and preserved by the power of the Holy Ghost, let them importune the Lord in unity and faith, and their petition shall be granted. If they desire eternal life in the kingdom of God, let them ask in faith, nothing doubting, and it shall be granted. If they desire new revelations from the Lord, by the voice of his prophet, let them make their united wants known, and the Lord will loose the tongue and open the spiritual eyes of the one who presides over his earthly kingdom. Deity gives unto his people according to their desires, and his promise to the Twelve and to all his people is: "If ye are purified and cleansed from all sin, ye shall ask whatsoever you will in the name of Jesus and it shall be done." (D&C 50:29.)

Parable of the Unmerciful Servant
(Matthew 18:23-35; JST, Matthew 18:26-27)

After teaching his disciples the gospel standard that requires men to forgive one another their trespasses, and after telling Peter that, contrary to Rabbinic standards, there was no limit to the number of times brethren should forgive each other, Jesus gave the parable of the unmerciful servant. It illustrates the glorious truth that "as Deity forgives men the immeasurable debt they owe to him, so men should forgive their fellowmen the relatively slight debts incurred when brethren sin against each other." (*Commentary* 1:428.) Part of a petition to the Lord for forgiveness is the spoken or unspoken pledge to forgive, in turn, one's fellowmen.

"Therefore," that is, in the light of all I have told you about forgiveness, "is the kingdom of heaven likened unto a certain king," Jesus said, "which would take account of his servants." The kingdom of heaven here named is the Church, the Church of Jesus Christ; it is the kingdom of God on earth, the earthly kingdom that prepares men to inherit the heavenly kingdom. The King is the Lord himself—the heavenly King and the earthly King—the One who reigns supreme over all the creatures of his creating, but to whom the members of his earthly kingdom have sworn an especial and a particular allegiance. And his servants are the members of his church, perhaps more especially those members who have been called to positions of trust and responsibility. Though all his saints will be called to account for their stewardships, those who are appointed to lead and guide others have a fiduciary relationship with the King, a relationship that calls for the exercise of special trust.

"And when he had begun to reckon, one was brought unto him, which owed him ten thousand talents." Clearly this servant was a high and trusted officer in the kingdom, one of the king's ministers perhaps, one who collected revenue and cared for treasures. An attic silver talent is worth about twelve hundred dollars, a Hebrew talent nearly twice that sum, and a gold talent about twenty-five times as much. The servant's debt is thus some twelve or twenty-four or three hundred million dollars, as the case may be—a sum indicative of the infinite debt the Lord's people have, and his servants in particular owe to him.

"But forasmuch as he had not to pay, his lord commanded him to be sold, and his wife, and children, and all that he had, and payment to be made." His infinite debt, admitted and acknowledged by him, was to be paid by his own suffering, as provided in the law of Moses. (Ex. 22:3; Lev. 25:39, 47.) No endorsement of slavery is intended; the procedure for payment is simply the established order found universally in the codes of antiquity.

"And the servant besought him, saying, Lord, have patience with me, and I will pay thee all. Then the lord of that servant was moved with compassion, and loosed him, and forgave him the debt. The servant, therefore, fell down and worshipped him."

"A more accurate representation of our relation to God could not be made. We are the debtors of our heavenly King, Who has entrusted to us the administration of what is His, and which we have purloined or misused, incurring an unspeakable debt, which we can never discharge, and of which, in the course of justice, unending bondage, misery, and utter ruin would be the proper sequence. But, if in humble repentance we cast ourselves at His Feet, He is ready, in infinite compassion, not only to release us from meet punishment, but—O blessed revelation of the Gospel!—to forgive us the debt.

"It is this new relationship to God which must be the foundation and the rule for our new relationship towards our fellow-servants." (Edersheim 2:295.) "But the same servant went out," forgetting the infinite forgiveness that was his, "and found one of his fellowservants, which owed him an hundred pence"—an almost inconsequential sum, a mere pittance as it were, a thin dime as compared to millions of dollars—"and he laid hands on him, and took him by the throat, saying, Pay me that thou owest." There is no mercy here, no feeling for the sorrows and sufferings of another, just a harsh, avaricious grasping to receive the uttermost farthing that is due.

"And his fellowservant fell down at his feet, and besought him, saying, Have patience with me, and I will pay thee all"—the very words the unmerciful servant had used in his own importuning before the king. "And he would not: but went and cast him into prison, till he should pay the debt." It is always sinners who seek to imprison those who sin against them. Men whose hearts are attuned to the gospel follow instead the counsel of Paul: "Brethren, if a man be overtaken in a fault, ye which are spiritual, restore such an one in the spirit of meekness; considering thyself, lest thou also be tempted." (Gal. 6:1.)

"So when his fellowservants saw what was done, they were very sorry, and came and told unto their lord all that was done." How meet and proper it is for the saints to importune at the throne of grace for the well-being of their fellowservants!

"Then his lord, after that he had called him, said unto him, O thou wicked servant, I forgave thee all that debt, because thou desiredst me: Shouldest not thou also have had compassion on thy fellowservant, even as I had pity on thee? And his lord was wroth, and delivered him to the tormentors, till he should pay all that was due unto him." "And so it is in the dealings of the Eternal King with his servants. Sooner or later all face an enforced rendering of accounts, all are subjected to temptation, trials, and impending death, and all are rewarded with mercy or justice as their situations merit. Mercy is for the merciful; justice, retribution, and punishment fall upon those who have dealt harshly with their fellow servants. 'With what measure ye mete, it shall be measured to you again.' 'Forgive us our debts, as we forgive our debtors.' " (*Commentary* 1:429.)

"So likewise shall my heavenly Father do also unto you, if ye from your hearts forgive not every one his brother their trespasses."

"Men are indebted to God for all that they have and are—for life itself, for the probationary experiences of mortality (including some measure of food, clothing, and shelter), for redemption from death, and for the hope of eternal life in his presence. These and all other debts owed to

Deity are listed on an account that shall never be marked paid. As King Benjamin expressed it, 'In the first place, he hath created you, and granted unto you your lives, for which ye are indebted unto him. And secondly, he doth require that ye should do as he hath commanded you; for which if ye do, he doth immediately bless you; and therefore he hath paid you. And ye are still indebted unto him, and are, and will be, forever and ever.' " (Ibid.)

Chapter 68

JESUS SENDS FORTH THE SEVENTY

And the Lord said unto Moses,
Gather unto me seventy men
of the elders of Israel,
whom thou knowest to be the elders of the people,
and officers over them; ...
And I will take of the spirit which is upon thee,
and will put it upon them;
and they shall bear the burden of the people
with thee, that thou bear it not
thyself alone. (Num. 11:16-17.)

Seventies: Their Position and Power

What of seventies? Who are they, and how do they fit into the eternal scheme of things? That their mission and ministry is unknown among the cults of Christendom is one of the great evidences of the apostate darkness that engulfs those who call themselves by the name of Him who called seventies to stand as especial witnesses of that very name. As it is with apostles, so it is with seventies: where they serve and minister, there is the Church and kingdom of God on earth; and where they are not, there is no earthly kingdom of that King who is preparing subjects to dwell with him in a heavenly realm.

As it was with Moses anciently, so it was with the Prophet like unto Moses in the meridian of time. Both had their Twelve and both had their Seventy, and if we had the full scriptural accounts, it is assumed we would know that in both dispensations these officers had like powers and ministered in a like manner. We do know that the Twelve in Moses' day were chosen, one from each tribe, to rule over their brethren; that they were "the princes of Israel, heads of the house of their fathers, . . . the princes of the tribes," who in Joshua's day were called "the princes of the congregation." It was their offerings that were used to dedicate the altar in the tabernacle of the congregation, and their names are given in the Holy Record as Nahshon, Nethaneel, Eliab, Elizur, Shelumiel, Eliasaph, Elishama, Gamaliel, Abidan, Ahiezer, Pagiel, and Ahira. (Num. 7; Josh. 9:15.)

We also know that when, thereafter, Moses needed added help to bear the burdens of the ministry, he was commanded to choose from among the elders of Israel seventy men, wise men, men of renown, men whom he knew to be leaders, so that they might "bear the burden of the people" with him. We do know that this was an occasion of such moment that Jehovah himself came down, met with the Seventy, and poured out his Spirit upon them so that "they prophesied, and did not cease." This is the occasion when Eldad and Medad, the only two of the Seventy who are named, prophesied in the camp, and when Moses made his great proclamation: "Would God that all the Lord's people were prophets, and that the Lord would put his spirit upon them!" (Num. 11.) These Seventy are the ones who, with Moses, Aaron, Nadab, and Abihu, "saw the God of Israel" when he appeared in his glory and majesty, all of them becoming thereby especial witnesses of his holy name. (Ex. 24:9-11.) We suppose that the Great Sanhedrin of Jesus' day, with its seventy members and judicial powers, was but a continuation or outgrowth of this ancient administrative body.

In our dispensation the first Twelve and the first Seventy were chosen from among those tested and tried souls who had laid their all on the altar in the march of Zion's camp. Of these two great councils, both of which operate as did their ancient counterparts, our revelations say: "The twelve traveling councilors are called to be the Twelve Apostles, or special witnesses of the name of Christ in all the world. . . . The Seventy are also called to preach the gospel, and to be especial witnesses unto the Gentiles and in all the world. . . . The Twelve are a Traveling Presiding High Council, to officiate in the name of the Lord, under the direction of the Presidency of the Church, agreeable to the institution of heaven; to build up the church, and regulate all the affairs of the same in all nations, first unto the Gentiles and secondly unto the Jews. The Seventy are to act in the name of the Lord, under the direction of the Twelve or the traveling high council, in building up the church and regulating all the affairs of the same in all nations, first unto the Gentiles and then to the Jews. . . . It is the duty of the traveling high council to call upon the Seventy, when they need assistance, to fill the several calls for preaching and administering the gospel, instead of any others." (D&C 107:23-38.)

Jesus Appoints Other Seventy
(Luke 9:57-62; 10:1; Matthew 8:19-22)

Jesus now—still in Galilee, but soon to depart for Judea—is about to appoint "other seventy" and send them "two and two before his face into every city and place, whither he himself would come." They are to be heralds of salvation, chosen witnesses who step forth to prepare a people for the coming of the Lord. As John the Baptist raised his voice in doctrine and testimony to prepare all Israel for the Coming One, so the apostles and seventies, called by the one who came, now go forth to teach and testify that he has come and now ministers among them.

What say the seventies? 'Forsake your vineyards and fields; leave your nets and plows; lay down your tools. Come to the synagogue; join the congregations in the streets and at the market place. He is here; give heed to his voice; he is the Messiah of whom John testified. Salvation is in Him. You must believe his words and live his law to gain eternal life. We join our testimony with that of Peter and the Twelve. Come and hear; believe the gospel message; this is he of whom Moses and the prophets spoke. The hour is at hand. He is the Son of God.'

When Jesus chose "the first seventy" we do not know, but suppose it must have been at the time he called the Twelve or soon thereafter.[1] In our dispensation the Twelve and "the first seventy" were called in February 1835. In the Mosaic age the Twelve Princes in Israel were regulating the affairs of their tribes before the seventy elders were chosen to bear with them and with Moses the burdens of the kingdom. We are left to assume that seventies have been serving in the meridian dispensation for almost as long as have the apostles, but that only now, as the final great witness of Christ is borne in Galilee, does the account call for an announcement of their ministry. Heretofore the emphasis, properly, has been upon the Twelve, as they ministered and taught and received the keys of the kingdom. Now as the kingdom expands, the Seventy are identified, instructed, and endowed with apostolic power.

Luke tells us that before the selection of these "other seventy," Jesus spoke pointedly and plainly to three different persons about service in the kingdom. These were: the scribe who offered to follow the Master wherever he went, and who was told, "The foxes have holes, and the birds of the air have nests; but the Son of man hath not where to lay his head." Also, the reluctant disciple who, having been called to the ministry, asked if he might first go and bury his father, and who was told, "Let the dead bury their dead: but go thou and preach the kingdom of God." And finally, the delaying disciple who sought to bid farewell to loved ones at home, and who was told, "No man, having put his hand to the plough, and looking back, is fit for the kingdom of God."

We have considered these or almost identical incidents in connection with the stilling of the storm on the sea of Galilee, which is the setting in which Matthew places them. (Chapter 51, Book 2.) If, however, they were an immediate prelude to the calling of additional seventies, then the persons involved may have been among those called to this apostolate, and the events mentioned were part of the testing that prepared them for their high ministerial responsibilities. Thus, with reference to the disciple who sought to bury his father before engaging in the ministry to which he had been called, Edersheim says: "We feel morally certain, that, when Christ called this disciple to follow Him, He was fully aware that at that very moment his father lay dead. Thus, He called him not only to homelessness—for this he might have been prepared—but to set aside what alike natural feeling and the Jewish Law seemed to impose on him as the most sacred duty. . . . There are higher duties than either those of the Jewish Law, or even of natural reverence, and a higher call than that of man. No doubt Christ had here in view the near call to the Seventy—of whom this disciple was to be one—to 'go and preach the kingdom of God.' When the direct call of Christ to any work comes, . . . then every other call must give way. For, duties can never be in conflict—and this duty about the living and life must take precedence of that about death and the dead. . . . There are critical moments in our inner history, when to postpone the immediate call, is really to reject it; when to go and bury the dead—even though it were a dead father—were to die ourselves!" (Edersheim 2:133.)

The Seventy: Their Charge and Commission
(Luke 10:2-11, 16; JST, Luke 10:2, 7, 17)

These seventies—having been called of God, as was Aaron; having been ordained and set apart to their high and holy callings either by Jesus personally or by members of the Twelve, at his direction; having thus received a divine commission to stand as especial witnesses of the Holy Name—these seventies are now sent forth into the missionary service. They go forth as representatives of the Lord Jesus Christ. They stand in his place and stead in administering salvation to the children of men. Their words are his words; their acts are his acts; the heed men give to them is the heed they would have given to the Messiah himself.

He that heareth you heareth me; and he that despiseth you despiseth me; and he that despiseth me despiseth him that sent me.

What an awesome thing it is when the servants of the Lord stand before the people and teach the word of truth! It is as though the Lord himself were there, for their words, spoken by the power of the Holy Ghost, are his words. And so we now see these seventies go forth, with apostolic power, to preach Jesus Christ and him crucified. And as it had been with the Twelve, under whose direction they now served, so would it be with them.

Thus Jesus said: "The harvest truly is great, but the labourers are few: pray ye therefore the Lord of the harvest, that he would send forth labourers into his harvest." O that there were laborers enough to preach to all who will give ear. Always—except in the days of Noah, when all flesh had become corrupt before the Lord—there have been more receptive souls who would heed the message of salvation than there have been ministers to teach its truths. Those who have desires to serve God are always called into his ministry, and every missionary strives to bring souls into the kingdom so the newly found converts may in turn take the glad tidings of salvation to others of our Father's children.

"Go your ways: behold, I send you forth as lambs among wolves." 'Ye are the sheep of my fold. I, the Good Shepherd, have called you out of the deserts of the world into the sheepfold of Zion; now I send you forth among the wolves of wickedness to lead other sheep into my fold.'

"Carry neither purse, nor scrip, nor shoes."[2] 'Have faith. Rely upon your Father which is in heaven; he will care for your needs. Do not be encumbered by worldly possessions; your mission is more important than any temporal concerns.' "And salute no man by the way." 'Your mission is urgent. Be about your Father's business; do not stop by the way to make or renew personal friendships.'

"And into whatsoever house ye enter, first say, Peace be to this house. And if the son of peace be there, your peace shall rest upon it: if not, it shall turn to you again." 'You are sent forth to preach the gospel of peace; your message assures men of peace in this world and eternal life in the world to come. If those to whom you preach are worthy to hear your words, they shall find peace and rest to their souls; otherwise, the peace gained through the gospel will be yours only and will not come into their lives.'

"And into whatsoever house they receive you, remain, eating and drinking such things as they give: for the labourer is worthy of his hire. Go not from house to house. And into whatsoever city ye enter, and they receive you, eat such things as are set before you." 'Those who believe will account it a privilege to care for your needs. Their compensation is to hear my words from your lips. Seek not to be feasted and banqueted in the houses of the rich; eat the common fare of the people. Preach and receive sustenance in the homes of those who are receptive.'[3]

"And heal the sick that are therein, and say unto them, The kingdom of God is come nigh unto you." Heal the sick! These signs shall follow them that believe. Among the true saints healing miracles are always found. True ministers, endowed with power from on high, always walk in Jesus' path and do the things he did. Say to the faithful: 'You are citizens of the earthly kingdom, which is the Church, and heirs of the heavenly kingdom, which is found in celestial realms.'

"But into whatsoever city ye enter, and they receive you not, go your ways out into the streets of the same, and say,

Even the very dust of your city, which cleaveth on us, we do wipe off against you: notwithstanding be ye sure of this, that the kingdom of God is come nigh unto you."[4] Cursings as well as blessings attend the preaching of the gospel. Those who believe and obey are blessed eternally; those who harden their hearts, reject the truth, and continue to walk in worldly ways shall be damned.

The Damning Doom of Disbelief
(Luke 10:12-15; JST, Luke 10:12-16; Matthew 11:20-24)

How awful it is—how fearful and damning; how fraught with the most disastrous consequences—for men to reject the revealed truth that would save them. It is bad enough to live in spiritual darkness when the gospel sun does not shine, and to be denied the privilege of walking in the light; but it is far worse to see the sun shine, to turn away from the gospel light, and to walk willfully in the dark abyss of sin.

The seventies are now to go forth and carry the gospel light to a people who sit in darkness. The effect of their preaching will be as it is with their modern ministerial counterparts to whom the Lord says: "Verily, verily, I say unto you, they who believe not on your words, and are not baptized in water in my name, for the remission of their sins, that they may receive the Holy Ghost, shall be damned, and shall not come into my Father's kingdom where my Father and I am. And this revelation unto you, and commandment, is in force from this very hour upon all the world, and the gospel is unto all who have not received it." (D&C 84:74-75.)

And so, with reference to any city that rejected the seventies and their witness of revealed truth, Jesus said: "I say unto you, That it shall be more tolerable in the day of judgment for Sodom, than for that city. Then began he to upbraid the people in every city wherein his mighty works were done, who received him not, saying, Woe unto thee, Chorazin! Woe unto thee, Bethsaida! For if the mighty works had been done in Tyre and Sidon, which have been done in you, they would have repented, sitting in sackcloth and ashes. But it shall be more tolerable for Tyre and Sidon at the day of judgment, than for you." As to his own city, the place where he abode in the home of Peter, he acclaimed: "And thou, Capernaum, which art exalted unto heaven, shalt be brought down to hell: for if the mighty works, which have been done in thee, had been done in Sodom, it would have remained unto this day."

Matthew says these upbraiding words were spoken of "the cities wherein most of his mighty works were done, because they repented not." *Most of his mighty works!* How little we know of the mortal ministry of Jesus! We know of a blind man who was healed in Bethsaida and of a number of miracles wrought in Capernaum, but Chorazin is not so much as mentioned elsewhere in the scriptures, and if it were not for the statement here quoted we would not even know that such a city ever existed.

Tyre and Sidon were famous Gentile-Phoenician seaports, renowned for their moral decadence and spiritual degeneracy. Sodom sank to such degenerate depths in Abraham's day that the Lord rained fire and brimstone upon it and destroyed every living creature within its walls. Its very name was and is the symbol of all that is base and evil and lewd and lascivious in the world. Yet the judgment eternally destined for the inhabitants of these Gentile strongholds will be more tolerable than that of the cities of Israel that rejected their King. Truly, "it shall be more tolerable for the heathen in the day of judgment" than for houses and cities which reject the servants of the Lord. (D&C 75:18-22.) Why? Because of the eternal law that says: "For of him unto whom much is given much is required; and he who sins against the greater light shall receive the greater condemnation." (D&C 82:3.)[5]

We thus come, in our prayerful and Spirit-guided study of the one life that brought hope and life to a despairing and dying world, to the point where that One has been fully rejected by his own in Galilee. He has been rejected in Galilee of the Gentiles; in Galilee where Israelite blood had partaken of Gentile disbelief, "For they are not all Israel, which are of Israel" (Rom 9:6); in Galilee where stony hearts refused to receive his message—a message presented with such power that had it come in like manner to those centers of iniquity and immorality among the ancient heathen, the people would have believed and repented.

"Galilee had rejected Him, as Judea had rejected Him. On one side of the lake which He loved, a whole populace in unanimous deputation had besought Him to depart out of their coasts; on the other, they had vainly tried to vex His last days among them by a miserable conspiracy to frighten him into flight.

"At Nazareth, the sweet mountain village of His childish days—at Nazareth, with all its happy memories of His beloved boyhood and His mother's home—they had treated Him with such violence and outrage, that He could not visit it again. And even at Chorazin, and Capernaum, and Bethsaida—on those Edenshores of the silver lake—in the green delicious plain, whose every field He had traversed with His apostles, performing deeds of mercy, and uttering words of love—even there they loved the whited sepulchres of a Pharisaic sanctity, and the shallow traditions of a Levitical ceremonial, better than the light and the life which had been offered them by the Son of God.

"They were feeding on ashes; a deceived heart had turned them aside. On many a great city of antiquity, on Nineveh and Babylon, on Tyre and Sidon, on Sodom and Gomorrah, had fallen the wrath of God; yet even Nineveh and Babylon would have humbled their gorgeous idolatries, even Tyre and Sidon have turned from their greedy vanities, yea, even Sodom and Gomorrah would have repented from their filthy lusts, had they seen the mighty works which had been done in these little cities and villages of the Galilean sea." (Farrar, pp. 450-53.)

We must not leave this part of our account without recounting how desolation and death, in a few short years, overtook the cursed cities of Galilee. And was not this temporal doom but a type and a shadow of the spiritual fate that awaits those rebels in Israel when they shall stand before the bar of Him whose judgments are just to be judged according to the deeds done in the flesh?

'Woe unto thee Chorazin, Bethsaida, and Capernaum—cities in Israel who rejected their King! Wo unto thee!' As the Divine Voice decreed, so it was; as the heavenly judgment went forth, so the woes fell. "On all this land, and most of all on the region of it, the woe has fallen. Exquisite still in its loveliness, it is now desolate and dangerous. The birds still sing in countless myriads; the water-fowl still play on the crystal mere; the brooks flow into it from the neighbouring hills, 'filling their bosoms with pearl, and scattering their path with emeralds;' the aromatic herbs are still fragrant when the foot crushes them, and the tall oleanders fill the air with their delicate perfume as of old; but the vineyards and fruit-gardens have disappeared; the fleets and fishing-boats cease to traverse the lake; the hum of men is silent; the stream of prosperous commerce has ceased to flow.

"The very names and sites of the towns and cities are forgotten; and where they once shone bright and populous, flinging their shadows across the sunlit waters, there are now grey mounds where even the ruins are too ruinous to be distinguishable. A solitary palm-tree by one squalid street of huts, degraded and frightful beyond any, even in Palestine, still marks the site, and recalls the name of the one little town where lived that sinful penitent woman who once washed Christ's feet with her tears and wiped them with the hairs of her head.

"And the very generation which rejected Him was doomed to recall in bitter and fruitless agony these peaceful happy days of the Son of Man. Thirty years had barely elapsed when the storm of Roman invasion burst furiously over that smiling land. He who will, may read in the Jewish War of Josephus the hideous details of the slaughter which decimated the cities of Galilee, and wrung from the historian the repeated confession that 'it was certainly God who brought the Romans to punish the Galileans,' and exposed the people of city after city 'to be destroyed by their bloody enemies.'

"Immediately after the celebrated passage in which he describes the lake and plain of Gennesareth as 'the ambition of nature,' follows a description of that terrible sea-fight on these bright waters, in which the number of the slain, including those killed in the city, was six thousand five hundred. Hundreds were stabbed by the Romans or run through with poles; others tried to save their lives by diving, but if once they raised their heads were slain by darts; or if they swam to the Roman vessels had their heads or hands lopped off; while others were chased to the land and there massacred. 'One might then,' the historian continues, 'see the lake all bloody, and full of dead bodies, for not one of them escaped. And a terrible stink, and a very sad sight there was, on the following days over that country; for, as for the shores, they were full of shipwrecks and of dead bodies all swelled; and as the dead bodies were inflamed by the sun, and putrefied, they corrupted the air, insomuch that the misery was not only an object of commiseration to the Jews, but even to those that hated them, and had been the authors of the misery.'

"Of those that died amid this butchery; of those whom Vespasian immediately afterwards abandoned to brutal and treacherous massacre between Tarichea and Tiberias; of those twelve hundred 'old and useless' whom he afterwards caused to be slain in the stadium; of the six thousand whom he sent to aid Nero in his attempt to dig through the Isthmus of Athos; of the thirty thousand four hundred whom he sold as slaves—may there not have been many who in their agony and exile, in their hour of death and day of judgment, recalled Him whom they had repudiated, and remembered that the sequel of all those gracious words which had proceeded out of His lips had been the 'woe' which their obduracy called forth!" (Farrar, pp. 453-55.)[6]

The Mortal Messiah Leaves Galilee
(John 7:1-10; Luke 9:51-56)

Our Blessed Lord is now going to leave his homeland forever. He will not again in mortality gaze upon those rugged Galilean hills nor sail securely over the fish-filled waters of Gennesareth. Nazareth and Nain, Capernaum and Chorazin, Bethsaida and Magdala—cities of sin in which he has converted a few righteous souls—will not again see his face or hear his voice. Their lepers will be left to suffer and die in caves and tombs; their blind and deaf and lame shall neither see nor hear nor walk; their dead bodies shall rot and decompose in their graves, awaiting such a resurrection as they merit. But what is worse, sin-sick souls, who might have gained spiritual health and life by heeding the words of Him who came with healing in his wings, shall remain in their sins. It is a dark and dreary day. The Son of God is leaving Galilee.

Yes, the Son of God is leaving Galilee to go to Jerusalem. He will have a short ministry in Judea and Perea. Then, as the Paschal Lamb, he will be slain for the sins of the world. This will occur at the time of Passover. Now, however, it is the Feast of Tabernacles that approaches. And it is incumbent upon all the males in Palestinian Israel to appear before the Lord in his temple at Tabernacles Times. Jesus' "brethren," the other sons of Mary, say to him: "Depart hence, and go into Judea"—not as their intent should have been, that he keep the Feast of Tabernacles as required of faithful Israelites—but, "that thy disciples also may see the works that thou doest. For there is no man that doeth any thing in secret, and he himself seeketh to be known openly. If thou do these things, shew thyself to the world."

This is an ironical statement, a chiding challenge. John appends to it the explanation that "his brethren" did not "believe in him." John also tells us that Jesus was in Galilee and not in Judea "because the Jews sought to kill him." His brothers, then, those in whose veins flows the same blood bequeathed by Mary to him, are making this argument: 'If you

111

are what you claim to be, then all men should see your miracles and hear your message. We know you are one of us; we had the same parents; we grew up with you in Nazareth. But if you are really what you claim, why do you hide out here in Galilee, when you could go to Jerusalem where all Israel will be assembled to keep the Feast of Tabernacles? There before all the people and before the rulers whose position it is to judge these matters, your claims can be adjudicated. If you are the Messiah, now is the time to show it in the Temple in the Holy City.'

Jesus replies: "My time is not yet come: but your time is alway ready. The world cannot hate you; but me it hateth, because I testify of it, that the works thereof are evil. Go ye up unto this feast: I go not up yet unto this feast; for my time is not yet full come."[7]

Jesus' response means that he will determine when to go to Jerusalem. He and his party will not go with the great caravans that parade openly and ostentatiously to the festive celebration. Such a journey befits Mary's other sons; they are of the world, and they can mingle with evil men without fear; the world loves its own. But the Son of Man is hated by worldly people because he testifies of their iniquities. Let his kinsmen travel as they choose, he will yet abide in Galilee and travel to Jerusalem at a time of his own choosing and with his own associates.

But even then he will walk in a troublesome way. When the time of his own choosing came to make the journey, he "sent messengers," possibly some of the seventies, "before his face: and they went, and entered into a village of the Samaritans, to make ready for him." Apparently all he sought was the normal hospitality—food, shelter, and a place to lay his head—which by oriental standards was offered freely to all who journeyed through any part of Palestine, Samaria included. That he also would have preached to the people, teaching gospel truths and proclaiming his own divine Sonship, is implicit in the proposal of his messengers. All itinerant Rabbis preached and taught as they traveled, and all Palestinians now knew that this rare and unusual Rabbi from Nazareth preached and taught everlastingly and accompanied his words with wondrous deeds.

But, Luke tells us, the Samaritans would "not receive him, because his face was as though he would go to Jerusalem." Their hatred of all things Jewish—including this Jewish Messiah, as he was acclaimed—was so great that they withheld from him and his associates even the normal civilities of life. And we cannot but think that in this instance they were joining with the Galileans in rejecting his Messianic pronouncements. In an earlier day, as he traveled away from Jerusalem, many Samaritans received him gladly, rejoiced at his teachings, and hailed him as the Promised Messiah. Since then the wonders of his word and the might of his miracles have been made known to them; apostles and seventies have taught and testified in their streets. But now this one who many say is the Messiah is going up to Jerusalem to minister and to worship. He cannot, therefore, be the Messiah; if he were, they reasoned, he would go to Mount Gerizim, not to Jerusalem, there to worship the Father in spirit and in truth. All of this dramatizes how false beliefs, false doctrines, false forms of worship—used as they so often are, as a standard to measure the truth—cause men to reject even God himself.[8]

"And when his disciples, James and John"—two of the favored Three; two whose valiance knew no bounds; two who were called the Sons of Thunder—saw that they would not receive him, they said, "Lord, wilt thou that we command fire to come down from heaven and consume them, even as Elias did?"

That James and John should propose such a penalty for Samaritans who worshipped false gods—"Ye worship ye know not what," Jesus had once said to them (John 4:22)—is far from strange. Harsh and pitiless as it may sound in Christian ears, it was akin to much that prevailed in the Mosaic system. When King Ahaziah lay at death's door, he sent messengers to "enquire of Baal-zebub the god of Ekron" whether he should recover of his disease. The angel of the Lord, however, sent Elijah "to meet the messengers of the king of Samaria, and say unto them, Is it not because there is not a God in Israel, that ye go to enquire of Baal-zebub the god of Ekron?" Further, Elijah pronounced the divine judgment that the king should surely die. When the king, hearing this message, sought to bring Elijah before him, that prophet twice called down fire from heaven to destroy a total of 102 armed men who would have taken him. (2 Kgs. 1.)

We can suppose that James and John reasoned that these Samaritans who now rejected the true King of Israel, because they worshipped Baalzebub the god of Ekron, as it were, were guilty of as gross a crime as the Samaritans of old whose lives were taken by the fiery flames from heaven. Further, they knew that the Messiah in whose presence they then stood would, in fact, destroy all the wicked by fire at his second coming. If the God of Israel destroyed his enemies by fire in days of old, and will do so again in days to come, why not execute a like judgment upon them now? The logic, though Mosaic and rational, was contrary to the new spirit of the new age with its new gospel. Jesus' rebuke came enveloped in a fire of righteous indignation:

Ye know not what manner of spirit ye are of. For the Son of man is not come to destroy men's lives, but to save them.

How often the Lord's servants in all ages—as they are pressed by prejudices, anxieties, rebuffs, and persecutions, to curse rather than to bless—how often they must remind themselves of this eternal truth: The gospel is given to save and not to damn, "For God sent not his Son into the world to condemn the world; but that the world through him might be saved." (John 3:17.)

"And they went to another village." Had he not but recently said to the seventies that when rejected in one village or city they should go to another? And so shall it ever be until that day when the judgment is set, and the books are

114

opened, and the wicked become as stubble, and the vineyard is cleansed by fire, and the lowly Messiah comes again to reign in might, power, and dominion on earth for a thousand years.

NOTES

1. After the Seventy were called in our dispensation, the Lord empowered their presidents, who are seven in number, "to choose other seventy besides the first seventy" until there were "seven times seventy, if the labor in the vineyard of necessity requires it." (D&C 107:95-96.) The meaning of this is that there can be as many seventies as are needed to administer the affairs of the earthly kingdom and to take the message of salvation to all men.

2. "And thou shalt take no purse nor scrip, neither staves, neither two coats, for the church shall give unto thee in the very hour what thou needest for food and for raiment, and for shoes and for money, and for scrip." (D&C 24:18.)

3. "Whoso receiveth you receiveth me; and the same will feed you, and clothe you, and give you money. And he who feeds you, or clothes you, or gives you money, shall in nowise lose his reward. And he that doeth not these things is not my disciple; by this you may know my disciples." (D&C 84:89-91.)

4. "And in whatsoever place ye shall enter, and they receive you not in my name, ye shall leave a cursing instead of a blessing, by casting off the dust of your feet against them as a testimony, and cleansing your feet by the wayside." (D&C 24:15.)

5. It was on this same basis that Jehovah said to rebellious Israel: "You only have I known of all the families of the earth: therefore I will punish you for all your iniquities." (Amos 3:2.)

6. Similar judgments of God—also rained forth in the providences of Him who does all things well—rested upon that Missouri area which persecuted and ravaged and slaughtered the Latter-day Saints in the early days of this dispensation. The punishment fell upon those persecutors of the saints and rejectors of the revealed word when the Civil War battles raged in their area. God will not be mocked.

7. That these blood brothers of God's Son were later converted and numbered with the saints is a matter of consolation for them and rejoicing for us all. One of them was "James the Lord's brother" (Gal. 1:19), who ministered in the holy apostleship; another Judas, who called himself "Jude, the . . . brother of James" (Jude 1), who wrote the epistle of Jude. Two others were named Joses (Joseph) and Simon. (Matt. 13:55.)

8. In like manner, how often it is that modern Samaritans, as it were, reject the living words of the latter-day witnesses of gospel truth, because the witness borne does not conform to the false creeds of an apostate Christendom. How can the words of those Mormon elders be true when they do not even believe the Nicene Creed?

SECTION VIII

THE LATER
JUDEAN MINISTRY

THE LATER JUDEAN MINISTRY

The right way is to believe in Christ,
and deny him not;
and Christ is the Holy One of Israel;
wherefore ye must bow down before him, and
worship him with all your might, mind,
and strength, and your whole soul;
and if ye do this ye shall in nowise
be cast out. (2 Ne. 25:29.)

Our Galilean Friend—the Man from Nazareth—now returns to Judea, to minister again among those who are thirsting for his blood and devising his death.

He appears suddenly in the midst of the Feast of Tabernacles, mingles with the millions then in the Holy City, and speaks as never man spake before.

His message, then and throughout this whole Judean ministry: He is the Son of God who came into the world to do the will of the Father; all who believe in him shall be saved.

As the priests pour water from Siloam on the Great Altar, he invites all men to come to him and he will give them living water.

The woman taken in adultery is commanded: "Go, and sin no more."

Before those gigantic candelabra, fifty cubits in height, from which light goes forth from the temple, he acclaims: "I am the light of the world."

'Believe in me, or die in your sins,' he says.

To Abraham's seed comes the message: "The truth shall make you free," and 'Before Abraham, was I Jehovah.'

We hear the Seventies report on their apostleship; learn how Christ is the Father and the Son; are edified by the parable of the good Samaritan; and sit in on a familial scene in Bethany as Martha and Mary minister to the Master.

Other parables—the friend at midnight, the rich fool, the barren fig tree—salute our ears with joy.

Then we see how a man born blind is healed; how Pharisaic opposition mounts with satanic zeal; how the man is wiser than the Pharisees in council; and how Jesus says plainly he is the Son of God.

And finally—wonder of wonders—there is the matter of the Good Shepherd who giveth his life for the sheep; the Good Shepherd who has power over death; who says, again, "I am the Son of God"; and who teaches that all who believe and obey shall be gods themselves.

Truly, this later Judean ministry—with its Pharisaic opposition, its strong doctrine, its plain testimony—gives us a view of God's Son that will dwell in our hearts forever.

Chapter 69

JESUS MINISTERS AT THE FEAST OF TABERNACLES

And it shall come to pass,
that every one that is left of all the nations
which came against Jerusalem
shall even go up from year to year
to worship the King, the Lord of hosts,
and to keep the feast of tabernacles.
And it shall be, that whoso will not come up
of all the families of the earth
unto Jerusalem to worship the King,
the Lord of hosts,
even upon them shall be no rain.
(Zech. 14:16-17.)[1]

He Preaches the Gospel at the Feast
(John 7:11-17)

Never from that day, a millennium and a half before,
when Moses, the man of God, speaking for Jehovah, ordained and established the Feast of Tabernacles; never during their long and wearisome wanderings in the wilderness,
nor during the years of their joy when Jerusalem was indeed
a Zion unto them; never before, not even during the earlier
life of our Lord, when he himself worshipped before the

121

great altar and renewed his covenants to do the will of him whose Son he was—never was there such an outpouring of divine truth as we shall hear at this Feast of Tabernacles.

It is October 11, A.D. 29; four days ago, on the great day of atonement, "solemn expiation was made for the sins of all the people." (Farrar, p. 410.) It is now the Sabbath day, and seven and eight days hence—on October 17 and 18, on the great day of the feast and then on the next Sabbath or the Octave of the feast—the climax will be reached as the Hosanna Shout rends the air and as repeated eternal witness of the divine Sonship is borne. Then the Feast of Tabernacles will cease as a legally approved season of worship; then it will cease until its millennial restoration, when not only the Jews but all nations will go up to Jerusalem to worship the King, the Lord of Hosts, according to the new rituals and performances that are part of that eternal fulness which supersedes the lesser Mosaic system.

Under normal circumstances the Feast of Tabernacles is the most cosmopolitan of all the Jewish feasts. Linked with the day of atonement and coming at the time when the temple contributions are received and counted, it attracts more devout pilgrims from distant places than even the Passover or Pentecost. It also comes in the autumn, after the harvests are gathered, and when in a spirit of thanksgiving and rejoicing those who recognize the divine hand in all things are wont to praise and worship him for all he has given them.

How they love to assemble in the Holy Sanctuary "of marble, cedarwood, and gold, up there on high Moriah, symbol of the infinitely more glorious overshadowing Presence of Him, Who was the Holy One in the midst of Israel." How they rejoice in the multitude of sacrifices, including the seventy bullocks, symbolical of "the seventy nations of heathendom." How their souls are stirred by the chants of the Levites, the solemn responses of the *Hallel,* and the piercing blasts from the silver trumpets of the priests. And at night, when "the great Candelabras" are lighted in "the

Court of the Women," when the glare of the torches lights up the temple buildings, and when the "strange sound of mystic hymns and dances" rings in their ears, how their souls light up anew as they contemplate the future glory of the chosen race. Truly, "the Temple-illumination" is the light which shall "shine from out the Temple into the dark night of heathendom."

How they exult within themselves when the priests draw water from the spring of Siloam and pour it out in the holy place, "symbolical of the outpouring of the Holy Spirit," and giving to "the whole festival the name of House of Outpouring." How their voices rise in great crescendos of praise as they wave their *lulavs* and cry Hosanna, Hosanna, to God and the Lamb. And how they covenant anew to stand forever as Jews of the Jews when the solemn proclamation is made, "We are Jehovah's—our eyes are towards Jehovah." (Edersheim 2:149-50.)

Glorious as is each festive season at Tabernacle Times, this one is destined to surpass all the rest. This time the Son of God himself will come; he will announce who he is, what power he possesses, and whom he represents; and by his own voice he will tell his people and all men what they must believe and how they must live to gain celestial rest.

But he will not come at the beginning of the feast; and whether he will dwell in a booth, as the law requires, and present himself in the temple and bow to the ritualistic rules of the Rabbis, our inspired author does not tell us. We suppose that at this point in our Lord's ministry the practices of the priests and the laws of the Levites are of little concern to him. He has already declined to travel with his blood-brothers in the great Galilean caravan of pilgrims, choosing rather to journey with his disciples somewhat in secrecy.

This late arrival has the desired effect upon the people. The Galileans who preceded him have now recited in detail the wondrous works done in all their cities and villages. All Jerusalem hears again of the blind eyes that now see, the deaf ears that now hear, the lame legs that now leap, and of the lepers whose flesh has returned again to its clean and healthy state. All Jerusalem is reminded anew that storms have ceased, devils have departed, and dead corpses have walked again—all at his word. And all Jerusalem is left to ponder anew the words he has spoken and the sermons he has preached in Galilee, as these are now recited by the reputable witnesses who heard his voice.

Never in all her long history, reaching back at least to the days of Melchizedek, has Jerusalem seen such a ferment of opinion, felt such an anxiety about a doctrine, and had such a concern about a man. All people sought him. 'Where is he; when will he come; are the reports about him true; will he continue his ministry among us; is he the promised Messiah; will he deliver us from Roman bondage; is he the Son of God?'

None, however, went into the temple to preach sermons about him and his saving power; none gathered groups together in the bazaars or on the street corners to acclaim his doctrine publicly, or to trumpet his wondrous works in the ears of all men; none raised a Messianic standard and called others to enlist in the new cause—"for fear of the Jews," meaning the leaders of the people. No apostle or seventy was present to speak "openly of him." But among the people "there was much murmuring." In private conversations some were saying, "He is a good man"; others, "Nay; but he deceiveth the people." He who came not to bring peace on earth but a sword; who came to set members of the same household against each other; who came to divide families and sift the wheat from the tares—he whose gospel proclamation always divides mankind was accomplishing his purpose.

The good news of gospel grace was believed by some, rejected by others. The sifting processes were at work; the great Harvester was sifting out the hearts of men before his judgment seat. The sheep were getting ready to enter the sheepfold of the Good Shepherd, the goats to be driven out

into the wilderness of spiritual darkness. The time for the arrival of the Man was at hand.

John says: "Now about the midst of the feast"—perhaps
about the fourth or fifth day—"Jesus went up into the
temple, and taught." Without warning he was there; his arrival was then as the Second Coming will be; to the wicked
and ungodly and to all who are not waiting with anxious expectation for the promised day, it will come suddenly. On
this day, the Lord whom they sought had come suddenly to
his temple. Surely John and the other disciples were with
him to hear his words and record his doings. As to the initial
events surrounding his appearance, John, who alone records
any of the happenings at the Feast of Tabernacles, tells us
only that he came among them and "taught."

What did he teach? As to his spoken word, there is no
record presently available where it can be read. Based on the
responses that were forthcoming, and upon the questions
raised by virtue of his sayings, and upon our prior
knowledge of the general course he customarily pursued,
however, there is little doubt as to the substance and purport
of what he then said. He who is the same yesterday, today,
and forever had preached, did then preach, and everlastingly
will preach the gospel—the gospel of the kingdom; the
gospel of salvation; the fulness of the everlasting gospel. In
Galilee, in Judea, in Perea, in Phoenicia, in the Decapolis;
among the Jews and to the Gentiles—everywhere and always—Jesus preached the gospel. This gospel is that he
came into the world to work out the infinite and eternal
atonement; that he is God's Son, the Promised Messiah; and
that if men will believe in him and live his law they will be
raised not alone in immortality but unto everlasting life in
the Everlasting Presence.

How he couched the message on this occasion we know
not. He may have used parables or dramatic illustrations, or
recited eternal verities as he had done in the Sermon on the
Mount. Perhaps he drew his illustrations from the sacrificial

victims whose shed blood and burnt flesh adorned the great altar; or from the golden table whereon lay the holy bread, the bread of the Presence; or from the veil that shrouded the Holy of Holies, wherein the Shekinah, in olden times, had rested on the mercy seat between the cherubim. Whatever the words used, the thoughts expressed, and the doctrine taught, his preachments were not like those of the scribes. He spoke in his own right, with authority, and not by reciting a long concatenation of Rabbinical lore and tradition.

Consequently: "The Jews marvelled" at his teachings. Their natural queries were: "How knoweth this man letters, having never learned?" "He is no authorised Rabbi; He belongs to no recognised school; neither the followers of Hillel nor those of Shammai claim Him; He is a Nazarene; He was trained in the shop of the Galilean carpenter; how knoweth this man letters, having never learned? . . . In all ages there is a tendency to mistake erudition for learning, knowledge for wisdom; in all ages there has been a slowness to comprehend that true learning of the deepest and noblest character may co-exist with complete and utter ignorance of everything which absorbs and constitutes the learning of the schools." (Farrar, p. 413.) And so, to their misplaced queries, Jesus responds:

My doctrine is not mine, but his that sent me. If any man will do his will, he shall know of the doctrine, whether it be of God, or whether I speak of myself.

Never man spake as this Man. The Lord Jesus Christ, supreme above all, ministers among men; he who made heaven and earth and the sea and the fountains of waters; he who is the Teacher of teachers, the Preacher to preachers, the One whose very word is perfect—this Man has no doctrine of his own! He speaks only those things which are in the bosom of the Father. It is the Father's plan; it is the gospel of the Father; those who do the will of the Father— and it is the will of God that men should believe in his Son—shall know by the power of the Holy Ghost of the truth and divinity of the gospel word.[2]

The Sinless One Acclaims His Divine Sonship
(John 7:18-36; JST, John 7:24)

Jesus now speaks of himself. Having announced that he was sent of God, having said that he did not speak of himself, he now adds: "He that speaketh of himself seeketh his own glory." Why else do the orators of the world, be they ministers or politicians, pour forth their mouthings except to gain prominence and position and power for themselves? "But he that seeketh his glory that sent him," that servant who glorifies the lord who sent him, even I myself who glorify my Father, "the same is true, and no unrighteousness is in him."

There is no unrighteousness in him! He is the Sinless One! All that he has done and said is perfect, which he here states in plainness—he is defending himself—because there are those then present who are plotting his death. The supposed sin: On his last visit to Jerusalem, some eighteen months ago, at the time of the Second Passover, he healed the blind man at the pool of Bethesda on the Sabbath day. "Did not Moses give you the law"—the law that says "Thou shalt not kill"—"and yet none of you keepeth the law" because ye go "about to kill me."

Those whose guilt has thus been revealed have no recourse but to plunge wildly on in their maddened course. "Thou hast a devil: who goeth about to kill thee?" they respond. Both their blasphemous charge against him and their own self-serving attestation of false innocence, he waves aside, as he continues his own defense: "I have done one work, and ye all marvel," he says. Even now, after a year and a half, the contention still raged among them: Was he the Messiah because he opened blind eyes, or was he possessed of a devil because he violated their self-imposed Sabbath restrictions?

"Moses therefore gave unto you circumcision," he continued, "(not because it is of Moses, but of the fathers;) and ye on the sabbath day circumcise a man." Such was a

127

factual recitation of what they all knew to be true. "If a man on the sabbath day receive circumcision, that the law of Moses should not be broken; are ye angry at me, because I have made a man every whit whole on the sabbath day?"

This logic cannot be gainsaid. "On their own purely ritual and Levitical principle, . . . His word of healing had in no respect violated the Sabbath at all. . . . Moses had established, or rather re-established, the ordinance of circumcision on the eighth day, and if that eighth day happened to be a Sabbath, they without scruple sacrificed the one ordinance to the other, and in spite of the labour which it involved, performed the rite of circumcision on the Sabbath day. If the law of circumcision superseded that of the Sabbath, did not the law of Mercy? If it was right by a series of actions to inflict that wound, was it wrong by a single word to effect a total cure? If that, which was at the best but a *sign* of deliverance, could not, even on account of the Sabbath, be postponed for a single day, why was it criminal not to have postponed for the sake of the Sabbath a perfect deliverance?" (Farrar, pp. 414-15.)

Our Lord then concluded this line of reasoning with the bold counsel, nay, with the command, a command falling from divine lips: "Judge not according to your traditions, but judge righteous judgment."

Jesus spent many hours in the temple teaching; occasional sentences—those necessary to preserve the moving majesty of his life, as he went relentlessly to a martyr's doom on a Roman cross—occasional statements only have come down to us. As he spoke he was interrupted, heckled, and harassed; attempts were made to arrest him; many of his sayings were in response to the sophistries of the scribes, the ruses of the Rabbis, and the armed assaults of the temple guards. The open classroom, in which multitudes milled about and talked among themselves, was totally devoid of decorum; angry mobs mingled in the courts with believing souls; and his disciples participated in the affrays and were part of the great proselyting work then being done by earth's Chief Missionary.

Thus we now read in John's account that "some of them of Jerusalem," whose opinions had been molded by their scribes and Rabbis, asked: "Is not this he, whom they seek to kill?" It seemed incomprehensible to them that if he were Satan incarnate, as the rulers said, they would stand idly by and let him speak freely to the people. "Lo, he speaketh boldly, and they say nothing unto him. Do the rulers know indeed that this is the very Christ?"

Then, lest any think their zeal for Moses and the law had lessened, and lest any accuse them of departing from their ancient moorings, they aligned themselves against their Deliverer by saying, "Howbeit we know this man whence he is: but when Christ cometh, no man knoweth whence he is." Again their traditions led them astray; these included the teaching that the Messiah's coming would be sudden and unexpected, a view that may have arisen from Messianic utterances about the Second Coming. "Do not the Rabbis tell us," said some, "that the Messiah will be born in Bethlehem, but that He will be snatched away by spirits and tempests soon after His birth, and that when He returns the second time no one will know from whence He has come? But we know that this man comes from Nazareth. Our chief men, if they choose, may accept Him as the Messiah; we will not." (Geikie, p. 587.)

'He is a good man!' 'He is a deceiver!' The tension mounts and the division widens. Thereupon Jesus, in a loud voice that all the disputants might hear, cries out: "Ye both know me, and ye know whence I am." Our Lord—and blessed be his name—was making himself an active participant in their disputes. 'In a worldly sense you know me. You know I was born in Bethlehem; you know I am the Son who was called out of Egypt; you know I grew up in Nazareth, that I might be called a Nazarene. But in the true and eternal sense you neither know me nor from whence I came.'

And I am not come of myself, but he that sent me is true, whom ye know not. But I know him: for I am from him, and he hath sent me.

'I alone of myself do not claim to be the Messiah; I am sent by my Father. He is God, and I am his Son. His witness of me is true. Ye do not know that he is God, that he sent me, and that I came forth from him. But I know him and testify that I am the Messiah.'

At the pool of Bethesda, on the Sabbath when the impotent man, at his word, took up his bed and walked, Jesus said: "My Father worketh hitherto, and I work." On that occasion, for Sabbath violation and for blasphemy, as they supposed, the rulers sought his life. "The hostile part of the crowd rightly saw a similar claim repeated now, and with the wild fanaticism of their race in that age, proposed to lay hold of Him, and hurry Him outside the city on the instant, to stone Him, as the Law against blasphemy enjoined. But His hour had not yet come, and whether from fear of the Galileans at the feast, or from other reasons, their rage died away in words." (Geikie, p. 588.)

The long hours of teaching in the temple began to bear fruit. His words, his bearing, the spirit that attended him, the testimonies of disciples who mingled among them—perhaps also there were miracles—all softened the hearts of those who were spiritually receptive. "Many of the people believed on him," John says. "When Christ cometh," they asked, "will he do more miracles than these which this man hath done?"

With this turn of events, "the Pharisees and the chief priests sent officers to take him." He must be arrested before the spell of his presence caused the rabble to acclaim him King-Messiah as it was reported they had done near Bethsaida-Julias when he fed the five thousand. 'Unless he is silenced our craft is in danger. He defames our Sabbath; our traditions are set at naught. What will happen to our washings before we eat, our sacrifices on the great altar, the temple contributions that flow in from our people everywhere? He must be silenced!'

These temple police, warrant in hand, singled out by their distinctive dress, mingled with the multitudes, seeking opportunity to make the arrest without raising a tumult. To them in the hearing of all, Jesus said: "Yet a little while am I with you, and then I go unto him that sent me. Ye shall seek me, and shall not find me: and where I am, thither ye cannot come." The Master simply declines to be arrested; such does not accord with his needs and plan. "Your desire to take me is premature; I am to remain with you until the appointed time. Then I shall return to my Father, and we shall part company forever." 'In the troubles of the coming day ye shall seek your Deliverer, your Messiah.' But "ye shall not find me, for no unclean thing can come into my Father's kingdom. Later he will tell his repentant and faithful disciples that where he went they can come also. (John 14:1-6.)" (*Commentary* 1:444-45.)

Jesus' words—testifying that God is his Father, that he shall die and return to him whose Son he is, and that the unbelieving and rebellious shall not find place in the Divine Presence—these words refresh the hearts of the faithful and pour light into their souls. To the unbelieving among his hearers, their effect is the reverse. "Whither will he go, that we shall not find him?" they ask. The things of the Spirit are understood only by the power of the Spirit; these Jews know nothing of the Eternal Kingdom and the Father who reigns there, nor of the identity of the Son who is now on earth. "Will he go unto the dispersed among the Gentiles, and teach the Gentiles?" "What! Will he leave us to go to the scattered remnant of Israel among the Greeks? Will he leave us, the assembled and chosen people, to preach to Gentiles?" (*Commentary* 1:445.) "What manner of saying is this that he said, Ye shall seek me, and shall not find me: and where I am, thither ye cannot come?" Truly, there is no darkness as deep as spiritual darkness, and no mind as closed as one bound by the chains of a false religion.

Thus endeth, as far as the record goes, Jesus' ministry during the initial days of the Feast of Tabernacles. But all this is but the foundation for the proclamation he will make "in the last day, the great day of the feast," and for what he will say and do on the octave of the same festal season, as we are about to see.

NOTES

1. These prophetic words of Zechariah are found in a millennial setting. Their fulfillment will come after all nations have assembled at Armageddon; after "the day of the Lord cometh"; after his feet stand again "upon the mount of Olives"; after "the Lord my God shall come, and all the saints with thee"; after the Lord has become "king over all the earth," and is thus reigning in millennial splendor. Then not only the Jews but all nations shall worship him in the latter-day temple, in Jerusalem, the Holy City. (See Zech. 12 through 14.)

2. The Father, not the Son, is the author of the plan of salvation. The Father did not—as some have falsely supposed—ask for suggestions as to what he should do to save his children. Rather, the Father announced his own plan, explained its terms and provisions, including the need for a Redeemer, and then asked whom he should send to be his Son and the Redeemer. Then it was that the Lord Jesus and Lucifer made their offers, with the first being accepted and the second rejected. Thus Paul speaks of "the gospel of God . . . Concerning his Son Jesus Christ our Lord, which was made of the seed of David according to the flesh." (Rom. 1:1-3.) The gospel of the Father was adopted by the Son and is called by us the gospel of Jesus Christ, because our Lord is the one who, through his atoning sacrifice, put its terms and conditions into full operation.

Chapter 70

LIVING WATER
FOR ALL MEN

I will pour water upon him that is thirsty,
and floods upon the dry ground:
I will pour my spirit upon thy seed,
and my blessing upon thine offspring.
(Isa. 44:3.)[1]

"Come Ye to the Waters"
(John 7:37-39; JST, John 7:39)

How men long for water in a dry and thirsty land! Moses smites the rock with his rod that Israel may drink and live. Elijah abides by the brook Cherith when the heavens are sealed for three and a half years. Without water, men die.

No metaphor is more intense than that offered by the longing for water among the dwellers in the desert. As the Lord laveth the desert soil, so he rains down righteousness upon his people. As he sendeth the early and latter rains, so pools of living water spring up in the parched soil; and where there are living prophets, there streams of living water flow, streams from which men may drink and never thirst more.

When Isaiah invites men to come unto Christ and believe his gospel, his cry is: "Ho, every one that thirsteth, come ye to the waters." (Isa. 55:1.) And in the echoing call recorded by the Beloved Revelator we hear: "Come. And let him that

133

is athirst come. And whosoever will, let him take the water of life freely." (Rev. 22:17.) For our day, the day of restoration, the prophetic assurance promises: "And in the barren deserts there shall come forth pools of living water; and the parched ground shall no longer be a thirsty land." (D&C 133:29.)[2]

And when the ceremonial performances of the Feast of Tabernacles were perfected, they too were designed to depict an outpouring of divine grace upon all men of all nations, using water as the symbol of life. As Edersheim observes, this feast "points forward to that great, yet unfulfilled hope of the Church: the ingathering of Earth's nations to the Christ," including the nations of heathendom, for whom sacrifices were then offered. "This eventuality can, of course, only be realized through the outpouring of the Holy Spirit upon the Gentile nations. As we have already seen, the daily and ritualistic pouring out of the water, which gave the whole festival the name *House of Outpouring,* was understood by the Rabbis to be symbolical of the outpouring of the Holy Spirit." (Edersheim 2:156.)

Now we must describe this performance, hear the cries of Hosanna that attend it, and show how all this prepared the way for Jesus to testify that he was the source of that living water of which all men must drink to gain salvation. We must not pass over this or any of the local settings in which Jesus chose to proclaim his eternal truths, and none of them is more dramatic than that which we shall now recount.

It has been calculated that it took "not fewer than 446 priests," and an equal number of Levites, to carry out the sacrificial worship at the Feast of Tabernacles. On each of the seven days, and possibly also on the octave day, one of these sons of Aaron, after the morning sacrifice was laid on the altar, drew three *logs* of water—somewhat more than two pints—from the Pool of Siloam. Attended by throngs of worshippers who carried their palm branches, to be waved in the Hosanna Shout, this priest brought the water from the pool in a golden ewer. A solemn procession carried the "living water" to the temple; joyous blasts on the sacred trumpets heralded its arrival; and while one priest poured it into a silver basin on the western side of the altar, another poured the wine for the drink-offering into another silver basin on the eastern side.

Then came the chanting by the Levites, with responses from the people, of the Hallel, which consists of Psalms 113 through 118. At designated places the people responded with the following cries:

"Hallelu Yah" (Praise ye the Lord, from which Hebraic expression comes the designation, *Hallel*); "O then, work now salvation, Jehovah"; "O Lord, send now prosperity"; and "O give thanks to the Lord." As these expressions were made—similarly, we suppose, as is the case in the latter-day Hosanna Shout—they waved their palm branches toward the great altar.

Then followed the special sacrificial offerings for the day and the chanting, to instrumental accompaniment, of the appointed psalm. On "the last day, that great day of the feast," this was Psalm 82:5, which—perhaps not without divine irony—read: "They know not, neither will they understand; they walk on in darkness: all the foundations of the earth are out of course." This reading was attended by three threefold blasts from the priestly trumpets while all the people bowed in worship.

"In further symbolism of this Feast, as pointing to the ingathering of the heathen nations, the public services closed with a procession round the Altar by the Priests, who chanted 'O then, work now salvation, Jehovah! O Jehovah, send now prosperity.' But on 'the last, the Great Day of the Feast,' this procession of Priests made the circuit of the altar, not only once, but seven times, as if they were again compassing, but now with prayer, the Gentile Jericho which barred their possession of the promised land. Hence the seventh or last day of the Feast was also called that of 'the Great Hosannah.' As the people left the Temple, they saluted the altar with words of thanks, and on the last day of the Feast they shook off the leaves on the willow-branches round the altar, and beat their palm-branches to pieces." (Edersheim 2:159-60.)

In the light of all this, there can be little doubt as to when Jesus stood and cried: "If any man thirst, let him come unto me, and drink." "It must have been with special reference to the ceremony of the outpouring of the water, which, as we have seen, was considered the central part of the service. Moreover, all would understand that His words must refer to the Holy Spirit, since the rite was universally regarded as symbolical of His outpouring." (Edersheim 2:160.) Thus we hear Jesus say:

> He that believeth on me, as the scripture hath said, out of his belly shall flow rivers of living water.[3]

To this John appends an explanation: "But this spake he of the Spirit, which they that believe on him should receive; for the Holy Ghost was promised unto them who believe, after that Jesus was glorified."

Further, in setting the scene for the great proclamation, Edersheim continues: "The forthpouring of the water was immediately followed by the chanting of the *Hallel*. But after that there must have been a short pause to prepare for the festive sacrifices. It was then, immediately after the symbolic rite of water-pouring, immediately after the people had responded by repeating those lines from Psalm 118—given thanks, and prayed that Jehovah would send salvation and prosperity, and had shaken their *Lulavs* towards the altar, thus praising 'with heart, and mouth, and hands,' and then silence had fallen upon them—that there rose, so loud as to be heard throughout the Temple, the Voice of Jesus. He interrupted not the services, for they had for the moment ceased: He interpreted, and He fulfilled them." (Edersheim 2:160.)

"Never Man Spake Like This Man"
(John 7:40-50; 8:1)

This great Man, on this great day, at this great feast—this Man, the mightiest of all the prophets of Israel—has now discharged the preacher's responsibility to this mob-multitude who mill about in the court of the temple, a court that can contain two hundred and ten thousand souls. He has preached the doctrine given him by his Father; he has reaffirmed his own divine Sonship; he has invited all men to come unto him and to drink that living water which quenches thirst forever. Now the event rests with the hearers. At the peril of their salvation they must make their choice. 'Is he the Christ, or wait we for another?' Multitudes, multitudes, in the Valley of Decision! For them the day of the Lord has come. He has thrust in his sickle to reap among a multitude whose wickedness is great. For some, the light of heaven blazes in their hearts; as to others, even the stars withdraw their shining.

Many said, "Of a truth this is the Prophet." The Prophet, the one like unto Moses, is the Messiah, their Deliverer, though as used here it may have meant to some, not the Anointed One himself, but his forerunner. Others said, "This is the Christ," a plain, straightforward declaration that partook of part of that spirit which attended the great confession of Peter.

Yet others queried: "Shall Christ come out of Galilee? Hath not our scripture said, That Christ cometh of the seed of David, and out of the town of Bethlehem, where David was?" How marvelously adept Lucifer is at quoting scripture for his own purposes! He did it to the Master himself, when after forty days of fasting Jesus was tempted in a face-to-face confrontation with Beelzebub. At that time he was totally discomfited by Him who gave the scripture. Now the evil one quotes holy writ by the mouths of his ministers, as it were, by the mouths of those who hearken to his entice-ments. And, as far as the record shows, there was none to refute their false assertions. Of course the Seed of David was to come from the City of David, from Bethlehem, as their scriptures said; but their scriptures also said that he was to come not only from Galilee, but from Nazareth in Galilee, that he, as the prophets foretold, would be called a Naza-rene.[4]

"So there was a division among the people because of him," just as there is division in so-called Christendom today, *because of him,* because some—again at the peril of their salvation—choose to worship a Christ of one sort, some of another. And again, in the temple court, some sought to arrest him for blasphemy, that he might be stoned, as Moses in the law commanded. "But no man laid hands on him," he declining again to be arrested. And we are left to wonder, to ponder in our hearts, how many in the religious climate of today would deny his doctrines and use the processes of the law to impede his work if he again ministered personally among men. Would they do other to Christ than they do to his servants?

After this, "the chief priests and Pharisees"—members, no doubt of the Great Sanhedrin itself—demanded of the temple police, "Why have ye not brought him?" Why indeed? Could any man arrest the Son of God before his time? If no man can take his life from him so that he must lay it down of himself, can any arrest him and hail him before the council unless he wills it? He at whose word ten legions of angels wield fiery flaming swords had work yet to do. Though their orders were strict, the officers dared not make the arrest. Some of his divine words had pricked their hearts; they were words that sapped their strength and paralyzed their wills. To their military superiors they could only respond: "Never man spake like this man."

"Are ye also deceived?" asked the rulers. 'Ye sons of Levi who serve in the temple itself, have you no more sense and judgment than this rabble to whom he preaches?' "Have any of the rulers or of the Pharisees believed on him?" 'If his claims were true, would not the rulers in the Great Sanhedrin—those who sit in judgment on the people and the law—be the first to know it? Surely the wise and the learned—the scribes who interpret the law and the Pharisees who live it to the very letter—these are the ones who should judge his claims.' "But this people who knoweth not the law are cursed." 'This ignorant rabble who have not been taught in the schools of Hillel and Shammai, who have never attended a divinity school to learn how to interpret the scriptures, are led by their superstitions to ruin.'

One voice on the council, one member of the Great Sanhedrin, was raised in Jesus' defense. Nicodemus, with whom Jesus conversed by night at the time of the First Passover, asked: "Doth our law judge any man, before it hear him, and know what he doeth? " What else Nicodemus said, we do not know; it is idle to suppose his defense was limited to one sentence only. But this single sentence sufficed to cut his colleagues to the core. They knew Jehovah's charge to the judges: "Hear the causes between your brethren, and judge righteously between every man and his brother, and the stranger that is with him. Ye shall not respect persons in judgment; but ye shall hear the small as well as the great; ye shall not be afraid of the face of man, for the judgment is God's." (Deut. 1:16-17.)

There is no way to refute a right reply; the rulers fell back on their only recourse—taunts and derision. "Art thou also of Galilee? " they demanded of Nicodemus. "Search, and look: for out of Galilee ariseth no prophet." No? "Where then . . . was Gath-hepher, whence Jonah came? where Thisbe, whence Elijah came? where Elkosh, whence Nahum came? where the northern town whence Hosea came? . . . But there is no ignorance so deep as the ignorance that will not know; no blindness so incurable as the blindness which will not see. And the dogmatism of a narrow and stolid prejudice which believes itself to be theological learning is, of all others, the most ignorant and the most blind. Such was the spirit in which, ignoring the mild justice of Nicodemus, and the marvellous impression made by Jesus even on their own hostile apparitors, the majority of the Sanhedrin broke up, and went each to his own home." (Farrar, p. 421.)

"Jesus," however, "went unto the mount of Olives," and

perhaps beyond to Bethany where dwelt his friends Mary and Martha and Lazarus, whence, on the morrow, he will return to continue his teaching in the temple.

The Woman Taken in Adultery
(John 8:2-11; JST, John 8:9-11)

Early the next morning—October 18, A.D. 29, the day following "the Great Hosanna," when he had offered living water to all men—Jesus came early to the temple. Back from the quiet and peace and sweetness of the Mount of Olives, he was once again, at duty's call, amid the stench and smells and human filth of the city. When he was seated, probably in the Court of the Women, "all the people came unto him," to hear those words of eternal life which prepare men for immortal glory.

As his wondrous words flow forth, weaving themselves into the very fibers and sinews of believing souls, the scribes and Pharisees are about to confront him with one of the most devilish plots yet devised in their scheming minds. During the night a woman has been caught in the very act of adultery; they will ask him to judge her, thus forcing him to side, as they suppose, either with Moses or with Rome, where her heinous sin is involved. "The repeated instances in which, without a moment's hesitation, He foiled the crafty designs of His enemies, and in foiling them taught for ever some eternal principle of thought and action, are among the most unique and decisive proofs of His more than human wisdom; and yet not one of those gleams of sacred light which were struck from Him by collision with the malice or hate of man was brighter or more beautiful than this."[5]

"It is probable that the hilarity and abandonment of the Feast of Tabernacles, which had grown to be a kind of vintage festival, would often degenerate into acts of licence and immorality, and these would find more numerous opportunities in general disturbance of ordinary life caused by the dwelling of the whole people in their leafy booths."

"Master, this woman was taken in adultery, in the very act," taunted the scribal rulers and Pharisaic hypocrites as they, with physical persuasion, placed her in the midst of those whom Jesus was teaching. "Now Moses in the law commanded us, that such should be stoned," they said, "but what sayest thou?" This cunningly devised interrogatory was in no sense a search for guidance, nor did it raise any point with reference to an infamous act of adultery that needed a decision. Though it was the custom to consult distinguished Rabbis in cases of doubt or difficulty, this was not such a case. They knew, and everyone knew, that Moses decreed death for adulterers, both of them, the man and the woman, and that the accuser's hand should cast the first stone. This was not such a case. The guilty man was absent; the aggrieved husband was lodging no charge; and no witnesses had been summoned, that in the mouth of two or three witnesses every word might be established. Their purpose, rather, as John expresses it, was to tempt him, "that they might have to accuse him."

The character of the conniving religionists is seen perfectly in their callous use of the woman. "To subject her to the superfluous horror of this odious publicity—to drag her, fresh from the agony of detection, into the sacred precincts of the Temple—to subject this unveiled, dishevelled, terror-stricken woman to the cold and sensual curiosity of a malignant mob—to make her, with total disregard to her own sufferings, the mere passive instrument of their hatred against Jesus—and to do all this, not under the pressure of moral indignation, but in order to gratify a calculating malice—showed on their parts a cold, hard cynicism, a graceless, pitiless, barbarous brutality of heart and conscience, which could not but prove, in every particular, revolting and hateful to One who alone was infinitely tender, because He alone was infinitely pure."

These wily scribes and crafty Pharisees have done their work well. 'Master, what sayest thou of this adulteress and the penalty she should receive?' "They thought that now they had caught Him in a dilemma. They knew the divine trembling pity which had loved where others hated, and praised where others scorned, and encouraged where others crushed; and they knew how that pity had won for Him the admiration of many, the passionate devotion of not a few. They knew that a publican was among His chosen, that sinners had sat with Him at the banquet, and harlots unreproved had bathed His feet, and listened to His words. Would He then acquit this woman, and so make Himself liable to an accusation of heresy, by placing Himself in open disaccord with the sacred and fiery Law? or, on the other hand, would He belie His own compassion, and be ruthless, and condemn? And, if He did, would He not at once shock the multitude, who were touched by His tenderness, and offend the civil magistrates by making Himself liable to a charge of sedition? How could He possibly get out of the difficulty? Either alternative—heresy or treason—accusation before the Sanhedrin or delation to the Procurator—opposition to the orthodox or alienation from the many—would serve equally well their unscrupulous intentions. And one of these, they thought, *must* follow. What a happy chance this weak, guilty woman had given them! "

Thus their trap was baited; but Jesus—not deigning to respond, scarce considering their stratagem worthy of a fleeting notice—"stooped down, and with his finger wrote on the ground, as though he heard them not." Perhaps what he wrote were the words he was about to speak; perhaps the act was symbolical—a symbol of forgiveness, "a symbol that the memory of things thus written in the dust might be obliterated and forgotten." But his detractors, inattentive to what they might learn, insensitive to anything but the scheme they had so cunningly devised, continue to attack him with their repetitious question: 'What sayest thou?'

Jesus stood up. He spoke. "He that is without sin among you, let him first cast a stone at her." Those words alone sufficed. He spoke, and they knew he spoke, not of sins in general, but of the same sin—adultery—of which the woman was guilty. 'He among you that is not an adulterer, let him cast the first stone.' What saith the law of Moses? "The hands of the witnesses shall be first upon him to put him to death, and afterward the hands of all the people." (Deut. 17:7.) Jesus had read their hearts and discerned their sins. There were none fit to accuse her according to the law. "And again he stooped down, and wrote on the ground."

"The spirit which actuated these Scribes and Pharisees was not by any means the spirit of a sincere and outraged purity. In the decadence of national life, in the daily familiarity with heathen degradations, in the gradual substitution of a Levitical scrupulosity for a heartfelt religion, the morals of the nation had grown utterly corrupt. . . . Not even the Scribes and Pharisees—for all their external religiosity—had any genuine horror of an impurity with which their own lives were often stained. They saw in the accident which had put this guilty woman into their power nothing but a chance of annoying, entrapping, possibly even endangering this Prophet of Galilee, whom they already regarded as their deadliest enemy."

As Jesus pointedly ignored the evil and sinful leaders of the people, they slunk guiltily away. "Convicted by their own conscience," they went out of the temple "one by one, beginning at the eldest, even unto the last." "He had but calmly spoken a few simple words, but those words like the still small voice to Elijah at Horeb, had been more terrible than wind or earthquake. They had fallen like a spark of fire upon slumbering hearts, and lay burning there till 'the blushing, shame-faced spirit' mutinied within them. The Scribes and Pharisees stood silent and fearful; they loosed their hold upon the woman; their insolent glances, so full of guile and malice, fell guiltily to the ground. They who had unjustly inflicted, now justly felt the overwhelming anguish of an intolerable shame, while over their guilty consciences there rolled, in crash on crash of thunder, such thoughts as these:—'Therefore thou art inexcusable, O man, whosoever thou art that judgest: for wherein thou judgest another, thou condemnest thyself: for thou that judgest doest the same things. But we are sure that the judgment of God is according to truth against them which commit such things. And thinkest thou this, O man, that judgest them which do such things and doest the same, that thou shalt escape the judgment of God? Or despisest thou the riches of His goodness and forbearance, and long-suffering; not knowing that the goodness of God leadeth thee to repentance? but after thy hardness and impenitent heart treasurest up to thyself wrath against the day of wrath and revelation of the righteous judgment of God, who will render to every man according to his deeds.' (Rom. 2:1-6.) They were *'such'* as the woman they had condemned, and they dared not stay."

Permitting the sin-smitten scribes and the impure Pharisees to depart without so much as a glance, Jesus then stood up again. "Woman, where are those thine accusers? hath no man condemned thee? " he asked.

"No man, Lord," she replied. "Neither do I condemn thee; go, and sin no more. And the woman glorified God from that hour, and believed on his name." And, we cannot doubt, she repented of her sins, was washed clean in the waters of baptism, and joined herself to the true believers who through righteousness have their garments washed clean by the blood of the Lamb.

We cannot, at this point, refrain from expressing these words of sound doctrine: Jesus did not condone an adulterous act; rather, he did and does condemn those who commit any immoral act. Those guilty of sexual sins, including adultery and homosexual perversions, may repent and be saved in the kingdom of the Father. When he says here that he does not condemn this woman, his words carry two connotations: (1) He does not condemn her within the meaning of the Mosaic law where her accuser is obligated to sit in judgment and cast the first stone, and (2) he does not condemn her because she repented and became clean before him.

NOTES

1. The Targum that paraphrases this verse reads: "Behold, as the waters are poured on arid ground and spread over the dry soil, so will I give the Spirit of My Holiness on thy sons, and My blessing on thy children's children." (Edersheim 2:161.)

2. Other relevant passages say: "With joy shall ye draw water out of the wells of salvation." (Isa. 12:3.) "Thou shalt be like a watered garden, and like a spring of water, whose waters fail not." (Isa. 58:11.) "I will even make a way in the wilderness, and rivers in the desert. . . . Because I give waters in the wilderness, and rivers in the desert, to give drink to my people, my chosen." (Isa. 43:19-20.) Heretofore also we have heard Jesus speak of giving "living water" to the Samaritan woman, and of the fact that those who believe in him shall never thirst more. (John 4:10-14; 6:35.)

3. "There is no single Old Testament passage which promises that living waters shall flow from the disciples to others. Jesus is either quoting a prophecy which has not been preserved for us or he is combining such statements as those found in Isaiah 44:3, 55:1, and 58:11, in such a way as to give an interpretive rendition of them." (*Commentary* 1:446.) There is also a possibility he was adapting the prophecy in Ezekiel 47:1 through a play on the Hebrew word translated "threshold" and speaking of the living water coming therefrom. Compare Zechariah 14:8 and Revelation 22:1.

4. An interesting sidelight on Matthew's quotation that Jesus would be called a Nazarene because he dwelt in Nazareth (Matt. 2:23) is that Nazarene (*Netzer* in Hebrew) has the same root word as Branch. The Nazarene was the promised Branch. (Isa. 11:1; Jer. 23:5; 33:15; Zech. 3:8.)

5. This quotation and the balance of those in this subsection, "The Woman Taken in Adultery," are found in Farrar, chapter 40, pages 422-31. In this chapter, as Edersheim comments, Archdeacon Farrar has written "some of his most pictorial pages." (Edersheim 2:163, footnote 1.)

Chapter 71

MESSIAH—THE LIGHT OF THE WORLD

In me shall all mankind have light,
and that eternally, even they who shall believe
on my name. (Ether 3:14.)[1]
Behold I am the light;
I have set an example for you. . . .
Behold I am the light which ye shall hold up—
that which ye have seen me do.
(3 Ne. 18:16, 24.)[2]

"I Am the Light of the World"
(John 8:12)

Few of our Lord's bold utterances had such an effect on his Jewish hearers as did his claim to Messiahship by saying he was the Light of the World. Heretofore he has named himself as the Bread of Life, which if men eat they shall never hunger more. Only yesterday he offered living water to all who thirst for spiritual drink. His present claim to be the Light—the Example, Guide, Archetype, Model—the Perfect Pattern for all men, this claim surpasses in some respects all of the other Messianic symbolisms he has applied to himself.

To envision its meaning and effect upon his Jewish hearers, we must realize two things that they knew: (1) their

146

Messianic prophecies spoke plainly of a Deliverer who would bring light to Israel and—note it well—to all nations; and (2) those fonts of Jewish wisdom, the scribes and Rabbis, taught that the Messiah would be the Light of men.

What Jesus will now do is apply the Messianic prophecies and the Rabbinic teachings to himself. It is not the doctrinal principle that is at stake—there is universal agreement on that; it is the application of what the prophets and the Rabbis have said to the person of this Man from Galilee who has now come into Judea to say to the Jews what he has been saying all along to his Galilean compatriots.

Indeed, how could the Promised Messiah come to declare glad tidings to the meek, to preach the gospel to the poor, to free men from the bondage of sin, without bringing light into the world? How could the Holy One of Israel— who is sinless and perfect, and who is the same everlastingly—come into mortality without remaining as the Sinless One and therefore being a light and an example to all men? If the Great Jehovah—the Lord Omnipotent, who was and is from all eternity—was destined to make flesh his tabernacle, how could he do other than bring with him the effulgent light and glory which dwelt in his person?

With reference to his eternal status as the Lord Jehovah, the prophetic word abounds in such statements as: "The Lord is my light and my salvation." (Ps. 27:1.) "O send out thy light and thy truth: let them lead me." (Ps. 43:3.) "God is the Lord, which hath shewed us light." (Ps. 118:27.) "Thy word is a lamp unto my feet, and a light unto my path." (Ps. 119:105.) None can doubt that the Jewish Jehovah who led their fathers was himself the source of light and truth for all.

With reference to his future Messianic ministry, his ministry among mortals as the Son of God, it is written: "I will also give thee for a light to the Gentiles, that thou mayest be my salvation unto the end of the earth." (Isa. 49:6.) Of the kingdom he shall set up the prophetic word is: "And the Gentiles shall come to thy light, and kings to the brightness of thy rising." (Isa. 60:3.) And of his personal ministry among men, a ministry in the Gentile-infested lands of Zebulun and Naphtali, Isaiah says: "The people that walked in darkness have seen a great light: they that dwell in the land of the shadow of death, upon them hath the light shined." (Isa. 9:2.) And so the saintly Simeon, having long waited for the Consolation of Israel to come—while holding the Child in his arms in Jehovah's house, and while speaking as the Holy Ghost gave him utterance—this devout and righteous man acclaimed Mary's Son as "a light to lighten the Gentiles, and the glory of thy people Israel." (Luke 2:32.)

The teachings of the Rabbis, naming their Messiah as the great light-bearer to the world, are summarized in these words: In the Midrash we are told that, "while commonly windows were made wide within and narrow without, it was the opposite in the Temple of Solomon, because the light, issuing from the Sanctuary was to lighten that which was without." Further, "That, if the light in the Sanctuary was to be always burning before Jehovah, the reason was, not that He needed such light, but that He honoured Israel with this as a symbolic command. In Messianic times God would, in fulfilment of the prophetic meaning of this rite, 'kindle for them a Great Light,' and the nations of the world would point to them, who had lit the light for Him Who lightened the whole world." Still further, "The Rabbis speak of the original light in which God had wrapped Himself as in a garment, and which could not shine by day, because it would have dimmed the light of the sun. From this light that of the sun, moon, and stars had been kindled. It was now reserved under the throne of God for the Messiah, in Whose days it would shine forth once more." And finally, the Midrash designates "the Messiah . . . as the Enlightener." Of him it says: "The light dwelleth with Him." (Edersheim 2:166.)

Thus, he, the Jewish Messiah, according to their own prophetic recitations and according to their Rabbinic teachings, was destined to be a light, not alone to the scattered remnants of Jewish Israel, but to the heathens, the Gentile nations, those always supposed by the devout among them to be outside the pale of saving grace. Their Messiah was to be the Light of the World.

Jesus is now about to proclaim himself as the Light of the World. He is choosing Tabernacles Times as the setting for such a proclamation for two very good reasons: (1) This is the feast, as we have seen, when sacrifices are offered for the nations of heathendom, the season when the chosen seed turn their thoughts to sending forth light and truth to those who sit in darkness; and (2) this is the festal season when each night the great candelabra are lighted in the temple to symbolize the sending forth of light to the inhabitants of the city and the world. Perhaps some circumstance arose to point the attention of the multitudes to these gigantic candelabra, fifty cubits in height, whereon were the lamps from which the light went forth. In any event Jesus took occasion, in this setting and at this feast, to announce:

I am the light of the world: he that followeth me shall not walk in darkness, but shall have the light of life.

The Light of the World! Jew and Gentile alike—all persons—must look to him. How well Jesus has applied the symbolisms of the feast to himself. 'I, Jesus, am the Source; light and truth shine forth from me. My word is light; it is truth. Follow me; I am the Exemplar. Believe my gospel and ye shall no longer walk in darkness; do as I do, and ye shall be as I am. Ye shall have the light which giveth life, the light leading to eternal life.'

The Pharisees Reject the Light
(John 8:13-20)

We now see something that makes us weep, weep for the spiritual blindness and depravity of a whole race of religionists. It is not as though the prophecies and Messianic concepts are foreign to them. They know, and have been taught for thousands of years, that one will come and announce himself as the Light of the World. They and their fathers have looked forward to this day for four millennia, a day when they that sit in darkness shall see a great light, a day when the Deliverer shall come to Israel to pierce the darkness of the night with the light of life, with the light of eternal life.

Here in the midst of the chosen race is a man like none other they have ever seen; here sitting in the treasury in the holy temple is one who says: 'I am the Light of the World; I am your promised Messiah; I am the Son of God. Come unto me and ye shall be saved.' He is the same man who is known by all the people as the one who opens blind eyes, unstops deaf ears, and commands the spirits of men to enter embalmed corpses so that dead men live again. He is the one who is known by all of them to cleanse lepers, cast out evil spirits, and to say to raging storms, 'Cease,' and it is so. He is the one who speaks—and this none of them can deny—as never man spake. His simple eloquence surpasses that of their greatest orators and their most profound preachers.

And yet they do not believe; they choose to reject him and his message. In direct response to his personal witness that he is the Light of the World, the Pharisees say: "Thou bearest record of thyself; thy record is not true." There are none so blind as they who will not see, none so deaf as those who will not hear. Why this utter disbelief? Why do they say the sun does not shine while they see it? The answer has been given before. It was at the First Passover. It is that men love darkness rather than light because their deeds are evil, and they come not to the light lest their evil deeds should be reproved. (See chapter 30, Book 1.)

But no man, least of all these pious Pharisees, says, 'I choose to walk in darkness because I am a sinner.' What, then, is the excuse they give for rejecting the Light? It is that his words do not comply with the requisites of their divine law of witnesses because he alone is attesting to their verity. This also is a matter that he has answered before, at the

Second Passover, when he acclaimed his divine Sonship in pointed and precise words and showed that the same witness had also been borne by John the Baptist, by his Father, by inspired witnesses as they were moved upon by the Holy Spirit, and by their whole body of scriptural writ. (See chapter 38, Book 2.) Now his response is:

Though I bear record of myself, yet my record is true: for I know whence I came, and whither I go; but ye cannot tell whence I come, and whither I go.

By claiming Jesus could not bear a true witness of his own divinity, the Pharisees were attempting to use a rule of judicial procedure that rejected uncorroborated personal testimony. In court procedures all things were established in the mouths of two or three witnesses. They were thus presuming to sit in judgment on him. In a moment he will name another, his Father, who is also his witness; but first he rejects their assertion that even his unsupported testimony is not true, and in doing so makes himself the judge rather than the one on trial.

He knows his origin, whence he came, and whither he will soon go; they do not. He can testify of these things. He knows; they are without knowledge and can give only negative testimony, as it were. Witnesses can testify only to what they know, not what they do not know. Jehovah tells his people, "Ye are my witnesses, saith the Lord, that I am God." (Isa. 43:12.) Thus, those saints who know of the existence of God by revelation from the Holy Ghost can testify "I know God lives," but someone else who does not know this cannot testify "There is no God." The fact that someone does not know something is not evidence that the thing is not true. In this case Jesus can testify as to who he is because he knows; the Pharisees cannot deny this because it is something they do not know. Their only valid testimony would be that they did not know one way or the other. And so Jesus continues:

Ye judge after the flesh; I judge no man. And yet if I

*judge, my judgment is true: for I am not alone, but I
and the Father that sent me.*

'Ye seek to judge me by the law, which requires added
witnesses. I do not involve myself in such contentions. When
I sit in judgment on any matter, my decisions are true and
righteous, for I do not judge by myself alone, but give the
decision of him who sent me, who is the Father.' This assertion determined the matter from the eternal standpoint; such
were the realities where the everlasting truths of salvation
were concerned. He was Christ, and Christ is God, and his
testimony alone sufficed on that point. But there was, in fact,
more; even if they chose to sit in judgment on him according
to their legal system, he nonetheless met their requirements.

*It is also written in your law, that the testimony of
two men is true. I am one that bear witness of myself,
and the Father that sent me beareth witness of me.*

This, as we have heretofore seen, is the divine law of witnesses. It operated in Jesus' case. Two "men" bore witness of
him; he was one man, the Father was the other. God himself
is a Holy Man.

Thereupon the Pharisees asked, not *who* is the Father—
Jesus had made that abundantly clear on this and numerous
occasions—but "Where is thy Father?" Perhaps in their
spiritually benighted state they assumed the Father should
come personally to bear witness of the Son, rather than
doing it, as his eternal law provides, by the power of the
Holy Ghost.

*Ye neither know me, nor my Father: if ye had known
me, ye should have known my Father also.*

This is the sum and substance of the whole matter. Because they did not believe in the Son, they were unable to
believe in the Father. How can anyone believe that the Son
is the offspring of the Father without believing that the
Father is the progenitor of the Son? To know one is to know
the other; and to disbelieve in one is to disbelieve in the
other. Having so spoken, having thus uttered words that had
the ring of blasphemy in Pharisaic ears, the expected reac-

tion should have been 'Let him be stoned as our law requires, for he maketh himself God.' But as John concludes, "No man laid hands on him; for his hour was not yet come."

'Believe in Me, or Die in Your Sins'
(John 8:21-30)

I go my way, and ye shall seek me, and shall die in your sins: whither I go, ye cannot come.

These words, spoken later, perhaps in one of the porches of the temple, are obviously the conclusion of some more extended teaching on Jesus' part. He is saying that the Son will go his own way back to the Father. He will not serve as the temporal Messiah whom they desire, though they will continue to seek for such a worldly ruler. But because they believe neither in him nor in his Father, they shall die in their sins. All men have sinned, and those only who believe, repent, are baptized, and receive the Holy Ghost become clean and qualify for a celestial inheritance. None others can go where he is.[3]

This doctrine is strong; the meaning is clear to Jewish ears; even these rebellious Jerusalemites know he is speaking of his atoning sacrifice and death, and of his heavenly abiding place with his Father. They know too that they have been plotting that very death. He must not, from their standpoint, be permitted to leave any implication that they, the Jews, will be guilty of his death. Alert to their own defense, they say—it is not a question to him but an assertion to the multitude—"Will he kill himself? because he saith, Whither I go, ye cannot come." 'See, he is going to commit suicide and go down to Sheol, where none of us Jews will go.'

Jesus knows their designs and intents. They shall not escape responsibility for their evil plans by such self-serving statements. He says:

Ye are from beneath; I am from above: ye are of this world; I am not of this world.

'Ye yourselves are from the nether realms; I am from

heaven. Ye are carnal, sensual, and devilish, and ye pursue a worldly course, a course that thirsts for my blood; I am righteous and live by a higher standard.'

I said therefore unto you, that ye shall die in your sins: for if ye believe not that I am he, ye shall die in your sins.

'I repeat; your deeds are evil; you are sinners; ye seek that which is evil; and ye shall die in your sins. I alone can save you; remission of sins comes by faith, repentance, and baptism. If you do not believe in me, ye shall die in your sins and be damned in eternity.'

Again the meaning is clear; again Jewish ears know he is hurling anathemas upon them for rejecting him; again they know he is damning them for their contempt toward him. What is their defense? Perhaps they can trap him into saying something that is clearly blasphemous and that will further their death-devising schemes. "Who art thou? " they ask. His reply:

Even the same that I said unto you from the beginning.

'Why try and trap me now? From the beginning of my ministry—throughout Judea and Galilee and among those who are aliens, always and everywhere—I have borne the same witness. My identity is of record. All who have heard me speak know what I have said about me and my Father.' And further:

I have many things to say and to judge of you: but he that sent me is true; and I speak to the world those things which I have heard of him.

Sadly, as John records, there were among them those who "understood not that he spake to them of the Father." In spite of all that he had said and now said, a veil of disbelief covered their hearts. Wicked and carnal men cannot comprehend the things of the Spirit; only those who hearken to the promptings of that light—the light of conscience, the Light of Christ, that light with which all men are endowed— only those are led to the truth.

When ye have lifted up the Son of man, then shall ye know that I am he, and that I do nothing of myself; but as my Father hath taught me, I speak these things.

And he that sent me is with me: the Father hath not left me alone; for I do always those things that please him.

'I shall be crucified. Ye shall, by Roman hands, lift me up upon the cross; ye shall, by a Roman spear, pierce my side; and finally, in a distant day, ye shall look on me whom ye have pierced, and know that I am he who came to bring salvation. And yet, even I can do nothing of myself. I serve at my Father's behest; he taught me all I know, and I speak his words. He sent me. I am his Son, and he is ever with me, for I keep his commandments.'

"As he spake these words," John says, "many believed on him." Or better, as we are about to see, many began to believe on him, for their faith was not yet perfect, and they had much yet to do to become his disciples indeed.

NOTES

1. Such was the proclamation of the Promised Messiah, spoken to the brother of Jared more than two millennia before his mortal birth.

2. Such were the words of the Risen Lord, spoken to the Nephites after he had tabernacled in the flesh.

3. "Remission of sins before death (and the consequent status of cleanliness and purity which assures the sin-free person of eventual salvation) comes to accountable men in one way and one way only. By conformity to the following eternal principles sins are remitted: (1) Men must believe in Christ as the very Son of God, the actual Redeemer and Savior through whose atoning sacrifice the whole plan of redemption and salvation is made operative; (2) Then being moved upon by a godly sorrow for sin they must forsake evil, turn to righteousness, and repent of their wrongdoings with all their hearts; (3) Thereafter they must be baptized in water for the remission of sins, under the hands of a legal administrator; and (4) Following this, also under the hands of a legal administrator, they must receive the gift of the Holy Ghost.

"Those who take these steps and who endure in righteousness thereafter are saved; all others are damned. Thus by rejecting their King-Messiah these Jews would inevitably and surely die in their sins and be precluded from going to that eternal kingdom where the Eternal King reigns forever. And what was true for them applies in principle to men of all ages." (*Commentary* 1:454-55.)

155

Chapter 72

ABRAHAM'S SEED

We be Abraham's children, the Jews said to Jove;
We shall follow our Father; inherit his trove.
But from Jesus our Lord came the stinging rebuke:
Ye are children of him whom ye list to obey;
Were ye Abraham's seed ye would walk in his path,
And escape the strong chains of the father of wrath.

We have Moses the seer, and the prophets of old;
All their words we shall treasure as silver and gold.
But from Jesus our Lord came the sobering voice:
If to Moses ye turn, then give heed to his word;
Only then can ye hope for rewards of great worth,
For he spake of my coming and labors on earth.

We have Peter and Paul; in their steps let us trod;
So religionists say, as they worship their God.
But speaks he who is Lord of the living and dead:
In the hands of those prophets, those teachers and
    seers,
Who abide in your day have I given the keys;
Unto them ye must turn, the Eternal to please.

"The Truth Shall Make You Free"
(*John 8:31-36*)

As the festal fellowship and sociality of the Feast of Tabernacles comes to a close, the temple courts present a disconcerting scene of confusion and contention. A motley multitude assembles in groups in the various porches to hear the words of prominent Rabbis. In the courts are lowing cattle and bleating sheep destined to die in the sacrificial rites. The autumn breezes carry the smell of dung and the stench of urine. Moneychangers ply their trade: the temple bazaars do a thriving business; and the sons of Annas gather extortionate sums into their rapacious pockets.

Large crowds gather around Jesus in one of the porches as he seats himself to continue the day-long doctrinal dialogues that have now been going on for four or five days. Some of the multitude are friendly, some unfriendly; some are meek and lowly in heart, others are conniving and mendacious. Sanhedrinists are present, those sanctimonious souls who delight to bear the religious burdens of the nation. There are pious priests and supercilious scribes. The Pharisees, who make broad their phylacteries and from whose garments hang the holy tassels in token of their covenant to be a people set apart, mingle among them. We see rude Galileans, haughty Judeans, worldly-wise Gentiles. There are pilgrims from afar, from Egypt and Greece and Rome, even, perhaps, from so distant a land as Spain, for the Jews in this day are everywhere. Herodians, ever alert to the interest of Rome, are infiltrated among them, and Roman soldiers are not far off, awaiting the call, if needed, to keep the peace. Mingling also with the group are the disciples, Peter and John and the others, hearing the words of the Master and participating in numerous gospel discussions.

At one time Jesus converses with one group, at another with a different one. Certain among the multitude have just heard him testify—with power beyond compare—of his coming atonement and that God is his Father. They believe his doctrine and their hearts are pricked by the power of his testimony, but they are not yet as those who have borne with him the heat of the day and who have worked miracles in his name. To these newly gained partial believers he says:

If ye continue in my word, then are ye my disciples indeed; And ye shall know the truth, and the truth shall make you free.

'You have begun to believe; you are exercising a particle of faith. My words, as a good seed, are beginning to sprout in your souls; and in this you have done well. But, if you are to be my true disciples—my intimate friends; those who are ever with me; those who sit with me in the kingdom of my Father—you must feast upon my words and keep my commandments. Then shall ye be my disciples. Then shall ye know the truth. Your minds shall be quick and active; ye shall receive revelation by the power of the Spirit; and the gifts of the Spirit shall be poured out upon you. Then ye shall know the truths of salvation; ye shall understand the gospel; ye shall know the things you must do to gain peace in this life and eternal life in the world to come. The truth will make you free—free from darkness, free from all the soul-shackling traditions that keep you from salvation.'

The truth shall make you free!—"Free from the damning power of false doctrine; free from the bondage of appetite and lust; free from the shackles of sin; free from every evil and corrupt influence and from every restraining and curtailing power; free to go on to the unlimited freedom enjoyed in its fulness only by exalted beings." (*Commentary* 1:456-57.)

With Jesus' statement—affirming that a knowledge of the truth as he revealed it would lead them to salvation—their faith died aborning. No, they would not continue in his word to gain the truth. Rather, "We be Abraham's seed," they said, "and were never in bondage to any man: how sayest thou, Ye shall be made free? "

'We are the chosen seed. God called Abraham, our father, and gave the truths of salvation to him and to his seed forever. None but the chosen seed have the truth; none but they shall be saved. All who are alien to Israel shall be damned. We are already free, free from all damning restraints of the heathens around us. We do not need you to make us free. You need not bring us another system of religion. We already have the Abrahamic covenant of salvation.'[1]

And all this has such a familiar spirit. These same Jews, when John the Baptist sought to introduce a new order of truth and salvation, said within themselves, "We have Abraham to our father." 'We do not need a new covenant. We are free from Gentile delusions; we shall be saved.' And such, sadly, is ever and always the cry of apostate peoples. Their wont is to rely on the promises made to prophets of old, rather than to accept the new revelation sent from heaven in their day. But to all this Jesus has a reply.

Verily, verily, I say unto you, Whosoever committeth sin is the servant of sin. And the servant abideth not in the house for ever: but the Son abideth ever. If the Son therefore shall make you free, ye shall be free indeed.

'True, you are Abraham's seed in the literal and temporal sense; you are descended from him; and his blood flows in your veins. As such you abide in his house here in this life and suppose you shall so abide forever.' "Temporally speaking, only members of the family abide permanently in the house; servants come and go in their menial ministrations; they cannot abide forever in the house unless freed from their station as bondsmen; they remain outside the inner circle unless adopted as members of the family, thus being made legal heirs of all its privileges."

'But you are not Abraham's seed in the spiritual and eternal sense, because you commit sin and are therefore the servants of sin. Said I not unto you, If ye believe not that I am the Messiah, ye shall die in your sins? ' "Only the family members, the freemen, the sons and daughters of God, shall abide forever in his kingdom; the servants, those bound by the chains of sin, shall minister in their assigned spheres; they cannot abide in the Father's house unless freed from sin through the cleansing power of the Son. To gain an inheritance in the spiritual kingdom, they must be spiritually begotten of the Father, adopted into his family as joint-heirs with the Son."

Thus: 'You may belong to the household of Abraham now in mortality, but it may not be so always. Only those who believe in me as the Son of God shall abide in the household of faithful Abraham in the eternal worlds. If ye forsake sin, and believe in the Son, he shall make you free from spiritual bondage, and only the free shall be Abraham's seed hereafter.' (*Commentary* 1:457.)

Who Are the Children of Abraham?
(John 8:37-50; JST, John 8:43, 47)

"Ye are the children of the prophets; and ye are of the house of Israel; and ye are of the covenant which the Father made with your fathers, saying unto Abraham: And in thy seed shall all the kindreds of the earth be blessed." So spoke the Risen Lord to the Nephite remnant of Israel; so might the Mortal Lord have spoken to those Jews who stood in his presence on this 18th day of October, A.D. 29, on the octave of the Feast of Tabernacles in that year; and so might he speak to that remnant of his ancient people who have been gathered into the true fold and kingdom in our day.

Children of the prophets! The literal seed of Abraham, the seed of his body, his posterity who are natural heirs of the blessings of their father! And those blessings are the blessings of celestial marriage, of an enduring family unit, of posterity both in the world and out of the world, as numerous as the sands upon the seashore or as the stars in the heavens. They are the blessings of eternal increase, of eternal life in the Everlasting Presence.

"The Father having raised me up unto you first, and sent me to bless you in turning away every one of you from his iniquities; and this because ye are the children of the covenant—And after that ye were blessed then fulfilleth the

Father the covenant which he made with Abraham, saying: In thy seed shall all the kindreds of the earth be blessed— unto the pouring out of the Holy Ghost through me upon the Gentiles." (3 Ne. 20:25-27.)

Children of the covenant! God covenanted with Abraham to save and exalt him, and his literal seed, and also all the Gentiles who would join his family by adoption—all on condition that those to be honored thus in eternity would accept the Messiah and keep his commandments. Even the Gentiles who were adopted into the family of Abraham would receive the Holy Ghost, the greatest gift that can be conferred upon men in mortality.

With reference to the dialogue digested in John 8:37-50, which we are here considering, I have written elsewhere: "For nearly 2,000 years all Israel had clung tenaciously to God's promise to Abraham: 'I will establish my covenant between me and thee and thy seed after thee in their generations for an everlasting covenant, to be a God unto thee, and to thy seed after thee.' Also: 'And in thy seed shall all the nations of the earth be blessed.' Now these unbelieving Jews, a remnant of the seed of faithful Abraham, glorying in their Abrahamic descent, contended with Jesus about their assumed preferential status as the 'seed' of that ancient patriarch.

"To understand this discussion between Jesus and his Jewish detractors, it must be remembered that men are born in various families, nations, and races as a direct result of their preexistent life. Many choice spirits from preexistence are sent in selected families. This enables them to undergo their mortal probations under circumstances where the gospel and its blessings will be more readily available to them.

"Abraham gained the promise from the Lord that his descendants, his 'literal seed, . . . the seed of the body,' would be natural heirs to all of 'the blessings of the Gospel.' His seed were to be 'lawful heirs, according to the flesh,' because of their 'lineage.' Accordingly, since Abraham's day, the Lord has sent a host of righteous spirits through that favored lineage.

"Further, Abraham also gained the divine assurance that all those who thereafter received the gospel, no matter what their literal lineage, should be 'accounted' his seed and should rise up and bless him as their father. By adoption such converts would 'become . . . the seed of Abraham.' Conversely, and in this spiritual sense, such of the literal seed of Abraham as rejected the gospel light would be cut off from the house of their fathers and be denied an eternal inheritance with Israel and Abraham. 'For they are not all Israel, which are of Israel,' as Paul explained it. 'Neither, because they are the seed of Abraham, are they all children: . . . That is, They which are the children of the flesh, these are not the children of God: but the children of the promise are counted for the seed.'

"Thus there are two distinct meanings of the expression, 'seed of Abraham': (1) There are his literal descendants who have sprung from his loins and who by virtue of their favored family status are natural heirs of the same blessings which Abraham himself enjoyed; and (2) There are those (including adopted members of the family) who become the 'seed of Abraham' in the full spiritual sense by conformity to the same gospel principles which Abraham obeyed. In this spiritual sense, the disobedient literal descendants of Abraham, being 'children of the flesh,' are not 'accounted' as Abraham's seed, but are cut off from the blessings of the gospel." (*Commentary* 1:458-60.)

Now we are ready for the conversation itself. Jesus said: "I know that ye are Abraham's seed; but ye seek to kill me, because my word hath no place in you. I speak that which I have seen with my Father: and ye do that which ye have seen with your father." 'Ye are Abraham's seed in this life, but you are not his children spiritually, because ye reject Him in whom Abraham believed and whose gospel he lived. Nay, more, ye even seek to kill me in whom Abraham believed. Ye seek to kill me because I speak that which I have received from my Father for your good. But in seeking to kill me, you do that which your father desires.' To this, without thought or reason, they chant back: "Abraham is our father." Jesus replies:

> *If ye were Abraham's children, ye would do the works of Abraham. But now ye seek to kill me, a man that hath told you the truth, which I have heard of God: this did not Abraham. Ye do the deeds of your father.*

The works of Abraham! The works of righteousness—for "Abraham believed God, and it was counted unto him for righteousness" (Rom. 4:3)—Abraham's works of righteousness were these: He had faith in the Lord Jehovah, whose gospel he believed and in whose paths he walked; he repented of his sins, was baptized, after the manner of his fathers, and received the gift of the Holy Ghost. Thereafter he endured in good works all his days—honoring the priesthood, living in the patriarchal order of matrimony, receiving visions and revelations and the gifts of the Spirit, and worshipping the Father in the name of the Son, as did Adam and all of the ancients. As to that celestial marriage practiced by Abraham and that eternal life which grows out of it, the revealed word to latter-day Israel is: "This promise is yours also, because ye are of Abraham, and the promise was made unto Abraham; and by this law is the continuation of the works of my Father, wherein he glorifieth himself. Go ye, therefore, and do the works of Abraham; enter ye into my law and ye shall be saved." (D&C 132:31-32.)

But these rebellious sons—sons physically but not spiritually—seek to slay the very Jehovah whom Abraham their father revered. And they do it because he tells them some of the same truths he revealed to Abraham, truths that he learned from his Father, Elohim. Such a course was counter to all that the ancient patriarch stood for, and these Jews, therefore, were doing the deeds not of righteous Abraham, but of an evil father. 'Ye are apostates who walk in the way of wickedness, being led by the devil whom ye have adopted as your father.'

"We be not born of fornication," they reply; "we have one Father, even God." 'The devil is not our father; we are not spiritually illegitimate. We are the children of Abraham and have the true religion, and hence God is our Father.'

If God were your Father, ye would love me: for I proceeded forth and came from God; neither came I of myself, but he sent me.

'If ye had the true religion, thus making God your Father, ye would accept me, for God sent me to lead men to him. How can you believe in the Father and reject the Son, who is in the express image of the Father and who came forth from him, and who speaks his words and does his works? '

Why do ye not understand my speech? even because ye cannot bear my word. Ye are of your father the devil, and the lusts of your father ye will do.

The wicked and ungodly cannot bear the word of God; it is a burden that crushes their souls and leaves them lifeless in the dust of despair. And further, "Just as surely as the obedient 'receive the adoption of sons,' becoming 'children of God,' so the disobedient are adopted into the Church or kingdom of the devil, thus becoming children of the devil." (*Commentary* 1:461.)[2] As to the satanic father of these satanic sons, Jesus now says:

He was a murderer from the beginning, and abode not in the truth, because there is no truth in him. When he speaketh a lie, he speaketh of his own: for he is a liar, and the father of it.

Satan is real; he is personal; he is an entity, a personage, a spirit being. He is as personal and real as any of the spirit offspring of the Father—for such he is: "Lucifer, a son of the morning"; "Perdition," over whom "the heavens wept" (D&C 76:26); the devil, who rebelled and defied God and all the hosts of Michael; the old dragon, whose tail drew a third of the stars of heaven, in the day when there was war in heaven. He was a murderer from the beginning in that he sought to destroy light and truth and whispers to every evil Cain to choose and slay a righteous Abel. As the enemy of truth he is the friend of falsehood. He was a liar in preexistence and is so now. Any truths spoken by him or his servants are interlaced with lies in an effort to make his own "gospel" more palatable to the minds of men. He is the one who "stirreth up the children of men"—as in the case of these Jews—"unto secret combinations of murder and all manner of secret works of darkness." (2 Ne. 9:9.)

And because I tell you the truth, ye believe me not. Which of you convinceth me of sin? And if I say the truth, why do ye not believe me? He that is of God receiveth God's words; ye therefore receive them not, because ye are not of God.

'I am without sin; my course of life is perfect. Since none of you can find any sin in me, it should be apparent that my life and teachings are in perfect harmony with the truth, and consequently what I tell you is true. Why then do ye not believe me? If ye had the truths of salvation so as to be the children of God, ye would accept the word of God which I now deliver unto you. But the very fact you do not accept my words shows you are not of God and do not have the true religion which is of God.'

Unable to answer him, and in a pitch of hatred and fury, the Jews ask—though it is more of a proclamation than a question—"Say we not well that thou art a Samaritan, and hast a devil? " How often they resort to the cry, 'Thou hast a devil,' to justify in their own minds their violent opposition. The demeaning slur that he is a Samaritan, however, is not an accusation that he came from Samaria or was one of that hated race. At this very feast they have attempted to belittle him as a Galilean, not a Samaritan. Edersheim tells us that the word meaning *Samaritan* "is almost as often used in the sense of heretic," and that it is "sometimes used as the equivalent of . . . the Prince of the demons." (Edersheim 2:174.) These evil men, steeped in iniquity and trained in priestcraft, are thus saying that he has a devil and is a heretic, or, worse, the very prince of demons himself. Our Lord's reply is simply to say:

I have not a devil; but I honour my Father, and ye do dishonour me. And I seek not mine own glory: there is one that seeketh and judgeth.

'I am not possessed of a devil. If I were, my teachings and works would not honor and glorify my Father as they do. But ye dishonor me because I am of God and ye are not. I seek not mine own glory, as do those who are of the devil; but there is one, even God, who seeketh it for me, and he will judge those who dishonor me.'

'Before Abraham Was I Jehovah'
(John 8:51-59)

This period of preaching is rising toward its glorious climax. Soon, in a perfectly orchestrated crescendo of divine music, the Sinless One will acclaim his divine Sonship in words we have never before heard him use; his witness will be as when a bush burned and was not consumed, or when smoke and fire and quaking spread themselves over Sinai as the Lord Jehovah wrote the law on tablets of stone with his own finger. This time, however, the Man Jesus will write the witness in the broken hearts of believing disciples, while the stony hearts of the sons of Satan will maintain their granitic hardness. As the tempo and tone of the great orchestration takes on new power, Jesus says:

Verily, verily, I say unto you, If a man keep my saying, he shall never see death.

Again he speaks of "my word," of "my saying," as well he might, for he is God; and the word comes from him even as it comes from his Father. "My word . . . is my law." (D&C 132:12.) Prophets speak of the word of the Lord; Jesus speaks of his own word and that of his Father. Those who keep his commandments shall never see death; they shall not die spiritually. It is the same doctrine he has taught before; it is a thoroughly Jewish way of speaking. According

166

to their own traditions, the Messiah would come bringing salvation, having life in himself, ransoming and redeeming his people both temporally and spiritually. That is to say: "They knew he would come bringing those truths by which men are born again, enjoy spiritual life and avoid spiritual death. . . . These Jews knew that those who believed and obeyed the words of the true Messiah would never see spiritual death." (*Commentary* 1:463.)

Their disbelief on this occasion did not stem from any misunderstanding of his spoken word. Rather, it was an affirmative denial of his Messiahship. "Now we know that thou hast a devil," they said. Such is the only explanation that can justify their course in their own eyes. "Abraham is dead, and the prophets; and thou sayest, If a man keep my saying, he shall never taste of death. Art thou greater than our father Abraham, which is dead? and the prophets are dead: whom makest thou thyself? "

It may be they were baiting him. Would he make a plain Messianic claim for which he could be stoned? Was he on the verge of such a blasphemous claim to divinity—as they would interpret it—that a mob, in a panic-borne burst of zeal for their law, would strike him with death-inflicting stones? In their hearts they sought his death by whatever means might arise. His answer ignored the repeated charade of false pretense that insinuated demoniac possession. He said instead:

> *If I honour myself, my honour is nothing: it is my Father that honoureth me; of whom ye say, that he is your God: Yet ye have not known him; but I know him: and if I should say, I know him not, I should be a liar like unto you: but I know him, and keep his saying.*

'If I make myself the Messiah, my claim to divinity is of no validity; it is God my Father who honors me with divine Sonship. My honor comes from him who ye say is your God, but whom in truth ye have not known. Nevertheless, I know him for I am his Son, and if I should say that I know him not and am therefore not the Messiah, I would be a liar

167

like unto you. But that I do know him and am the Messiah is shown by the fact that I keep his sayings perfectly, as only his Son could.' Then came the penultimate climax. After this there was but one blinding flash of eternal light, one thunderous roll of eternal truth, one supreme witness to bear. Its prelude came in these words:

Your father Abraham rejoiced to see my day: and he saw it, and was glad.

Abraham saw the day of Christ. Nearly two millennia before the Son of God made flesh his tabernacle, Abraham, the friend of God, the father of the faithful, saw in vision what would be in time's meridian. Abraham had the gospel. (Gal. 3:8.) Jehovah came personally to our great progenitor to tell him of the gospel, the priesthood, and eternal life. (Abr. 2:6-11.) To him the Almighty said: "The day cometh, that the Son of Man shall live." And he "looked forth and saw the days of the Son of Man, and was glad, and his soul found rest, and he believed in the Lord; and the Lord counted it unto him for righteousness." (JST, Gen. 15:11-12.)[3]

"Thou art not yet fifty years old," was the Jewish response, "and hast thou seen Abraham? " Either this question was a deliberate reversal and twisting of Jesus' statement—he had said Abraham saw his day, not that he had seen Abraham's day—or there is something left out of the account to which it is responsive. We may well suppose that the Jews did not want so much as to admit that Abraham saw the day of Jesus, lest it be concluded that this man was greater than their foremost patriarch. In any event, their assertion completed the foundation for the divine proclamation now to fall from Jesus' lips:

Verily, verily, I say unto you, Before Abraham was, I am.

Jesus-Jehovah has spoken, and so it is. "This is as blunt and pointed an affirmation of divinity as any person has or could make. 'Before Abraham was I Jehovah.' That is, 'I am God Almighty, the Great I AM. I am the self-existent,

Eternal One. I am the God of your fathers. My name is: I AM THAT I AM.'

"To Moses the Lord Jehovah had appeared, identified himself as the God of Abraham, Isaac, and Jacob, and said: 'I AM THAT I AM: . . . Thus shalt thou say unto the children of Israel, I AM hath sent me unto you. . . . This is my name for ever, and this is my memorial unto all generations.'

"Of a later manifestation, the King James Version has Deity say: 'I am the Lord: And I appeared unto Abraham, unto Isaac, and unto Jacob, by the name of God Almighty, but by my name JEHOVAH was I not known to them.' From latter-day revelation we know that one of our Lord's great pronouncements to Abraham was: 'I am the Lord thy God; . . . My name is Jehovah,' and accordingly we find the Inspired Version account reading: 'I appeared unto Abraham, unto Isaac, and unto Jacob. I am the Lord God Almighty; the Lord JEHOVAH. And was not my name known unto them?' " (*Commentary* 1:464.)

"Then took they up stones to cast at him," John says—for nothing could have been more blasphemous in their eyes than what they had just heard—"but Jesus hid himself, and went out of the temple, going through the midst of them, and so passed by."

He had preached his doctrine and borne his witness, and his crowning words were:

BEFORE ABRAHAM WAS I, JEHOVAH.

NOTES

1. It is unthinkable to me, as the weight of opinion assumes, that these Jews had any reference whatever to political freedom in their response to Jesus. They knew full well that their fathers had been slaves in Egypt for four hundred years; that ten of their tribes had been taken into Assyrian bondage and were lost to the knowledge of men; that their fathers had suffered a Babylonian exile, with only a remnant returning; and that even then a Roman yoke weighed heavily upon their bowed shoulders. In my mind the dialogue here involved is, in the mind of both Jesus and his opponents, one dealing with spiritual freedom, with the gospel freedom that leads to eternal life.

2. Some of the paraphrasing quotes involved in the dialogue here involved are also taken from this portion of my *Commentary*, vol. 1.

3. These words are not, of course, in the King James Version of the Bible. It is of con-

siderable interest and import, therefore, to note Edersheim's comment that "even Jewish tradition" asserted that "Abraham had, in vision, been shown not only this [that is, our Lord's day], but the coming world—and not only all events in the present 'age,' but also those in Messianic times." And further: "In the Targum Jerusalem on Gen. 15 also it seems implied that Abraham saw in vision all that would befall his children in the future, and also Gehenna and its torments." (Edersheim 2:176, including footnote 1.)

Chapter 73

JESUS SPEAKS OF SPIRITUAL THINGS

I will hear what God the Lord will speak:
for he will speak peace unto his people,
and to his saints: ...
Surely his salvation is nigh them that fear
him. (Ps. 85:8-9.)

The Seventies Report on Their Apostleship
(Luke 10:17-20; JST, Luke 10:19-20)

Shortly after the Feast of Tabernacles—at which all Israel worshipped for themselves; at which they offered sacrifices on behalf of the nations of heathendom; at which their rites symbolized the outpouring of the Holy Spirit upon the Gentiles—shortly after this great festal season, the seventies returned from their missions to report to that Lord whose witnesses they were. He had sent them—not as he soon would into all the world to declare his word to every creature, but to the cities and towns of Israel—to prepare the way for him, that receptive congregations might be assembled to hear the gospel, that attentive ears might be attuned to the Messianic voice.

All save one of the Twelve were Galileans. We suppose a like ratio was found among the Seventy. The Galilean chose his Galilean friends and kinsmen to echo his words of blessing and hope to Jew and Gentile alike. The Seventy were, like their brethren of the Twelve, rugged, forthright, and faithful souls who were scholastically untainted. The damning curse of scribal theology and the unbearable yoke of Rabbinic ritual weighed less heavily upon them than upon their Judean kinsmen. They had less of the doctrine of Hillel and fewer of the sayings of Shammai to forsake when they accepted the gospel than did the theologically contentious Judeans. Their present mission had commenced in the summer or autumn and now, three or four months later, they came together in a spirit of thanksgiving and rejoicing to report their labors. They had been successful. "Lord, even the devils are subject unto us through thy name," they said.

To cast out the spirit followers of Lucifer from their ill-gotten abodes, thus freeing suffering souls from physical maladies and spiritual suffering, could be accomplished only by the power of God. The Goliath of evil can only be slain by the David of righteousness. But Jesus had given them power—power to preach and heal and save. The gospel is power—the power of God by which salvation comes. The holy priesthood is power—the power and authority of God to act in all things for the salvation of men. The Holy Ghost comes with power—power to cleanse and perfect a human soul. Ministers without the power of the gospel, the power of the priesthood, the power of eternal truth, can never lead a soul to salvation. Satan is as naught only when he faces true ministers, and these seventies had subjected the evil one to their will through their Master's will. Rejoicing with them, Jesus said:

As lightning falleth from heaven, I beheld Satan also falling.

'When there was war in heaven, the rebel spirits were cast out. The same power that sent them as lightning from the realms of light to their benighted state on earth still controls them.' These seventies have ministered well, and they are now prepared for a greater ministry and a higher spiritual endowment.

> *Behold, I will give unto you power over serpents and scorpions, and over all the power of the enemy; and nothing shall by any means hurt you.*

How glorious is the Cause that makes every warrior a general, every soldier in the ranks a hero, every servant of the Lord the master of all things! What are the combined powers of earth and hell when arrayed against the servants of the Lord? "Nothing shall by any means hurt you." In the eternal sense there is nothing but glory and triumph for faithful ministers.

> *Notwithstanding in this rejoice not, that the spirits are subject unto you; but rather rejoice, because your names are written in heaven.*[1]

Christ Is the Father and the Son
(Matthew 11:25-30; JST, Matthew 11:27-29; Luke 10:21-24; JST, Luke 10:22-23)

Would that we knew all that the seventies said and could feel anew the fierce fervor and be warmed by the flaming faith that attended the testimonies they then bore. This must have been an occasion of spiritual refreshment comparable to that other day in Caesarea Philippi when the apostles themselves were bearing their testimonies. On this later occasion, as Matthew says, "there came a voice out of heaven," and as Luke says, in this hour "Jesus rejoiced in spirit." We cannot doubt that the words then spoken by the Father of us all placed a seal of divine approval upon the work and words of the seventies, which, naturally, would cause his Son, Jesus, to rejoice. Our Lord then said:

> *I thank thee, O Father, Lord of heaven and earth, that thou hast hid these things from them who think they are wise and prudent, and hast revealed them unto babes; even so, Father; for so it seemed good in thy sight.*

What things are hidden from the worldly wise but are revealed unto babes and sucklings, as it were? The truths just spoken by the Father; the testimonies just borne by the seventies; the revealed witness in the hearts of the faithful of the truth and divinity of the Lord's work; everything that pertains to God and godliness, to faith and faithfulness, to the Spirit and spirituality—all these things being of heavenly origin can only be understood by heavenly power. Among them are the great truths upon which Jesus now discourses. From Matthew's account we read:

All things are delivered unto me of my Father; and no man knoweth the Son, but the Father; neither knoweth any man the Father, save the Son, and they to whom the Son will reveal himself; they shall see the Father also.

As with almost all of Jesus' recorded words, our Gospel authors are selecting for preservation the portions that they feel most completely summarize the great truths then presented. In this case, Luke's account preserves these blessed words:

All things are delivered to me of my Father; and no man knoweth that the Son is the Father, and the Father is the Son, but him to whom the Son will reveal it.

It is evident that much more was said, but from these brief quotations from the transcripts of eternity, we receive a sunburst of truth seldom expressed in words so few. 'My Father, who is God, has placed all things in my hands because I am his Son and Heir, and I do ever those things which please him. And no man can know that I am the Son except by revelation from the Father; and no man can know my Father unless he comes unto me, for I am sent to bear record of the Father. And those who know by the power of the Holy Ghost that I am the Son of God, if they abide in me and keep my commandments, they shall see the Father also.

'And further, I, the Son, will reveal to the faithful that the Son is the Father, and the Father is the Son. We are one;

the Father is in me and I am in the Father. I am the manifestation of God in the flesh. God is in me revealing himself to the world, so much so that if you have seen me, you have seen the Father. The Father is as I am, for I am in his image and live and am as he is. I, the Son, am to you as the Father; and the Father, in whose image I am, is as the Son.'[2]

At this point, as Luke expresses it, "he turned him unto his disciples"—the seventies and others—"and said privately, Blessed are the eyes which see the things that ye see: For I tell you, that many prophets and kings have desired to see those things which ye see, and have not seen them; and to hear those things which ye hear, and have not heard them." And with this we concur completely, for we are among the number in question.

Thus, to his disciples he has spoken of the mysteries of the kingdom, telling them of his own divinity and how he is the incarnation of God so that it is as though he were the Father. In these disciples, already converted to the truth, he rejoices in spirit. But the message must not stop with them; what he has said to the seventies must go to all who will qualify to receive it. New disciples must be won; the kingdom is for all men. Downtrodden, burdened, suffering mankind; men staggering under the weight of their sins; children of a common Father, all with the potential of advancing and progressing and becoming like him—these may find rest in Christ. To them the cry goes forth:

Come unto me, all ye that labour and are heavy laden, and I will give you rest.

Those who then heard these words wore the yoke of Rabbinism. Around their necks and weighted upon their shoulders hung the yoke of the law, the yoke of the kingdom. This yoke—and it was so named by the Rabbis— was "one of laborious performances and of impossible self-righteousness. . . . Indeed, this voluntary making of the yoke as heavy as possible, the taking on themselves as many obligations as possible, was the ideal of Rabbinic piety."

175

(Edersheim 2:143-44.)[3] It is in this Rabbinic setting that we hear Jesus say:

Take my yoke upon you, and learn of me; for I am meek and lowly in heart: and ye shall find rest unto your souls. For my yoke is easy, and my burden is light.

'Rid yourselves of the yoke of Rabbinism; cease from all your self-righteous washings and ordinances and performances; forsake the insane Sabbath restrictions which say ye cannot even heal the sick or care for the suffering on that day. Remove the yoke placed upon you by the scribes and Pharisees; they are the degenerate defenders of the dead days of old. Come unto me; learn of me; believe that I am the Messiah by whom salvation comes. I am meek and lowly in heart, not proud and pompous and austere as are those whom you now serve. Wear my yoke—the yoke of the gospel; compared to your religious restrictions my yoke is easy and my burden is light. In me ye shall find rest. No longer will ye be wafted about by every word of Rabbinic doctrine; no longer will you have to judge between Hillel and Shammai, or this Rabbinic school or that. I will give you rest.'

Parable of the Good Samaritan
(Luke 10:25-37; JST, Luke 10:32-33, 36)

Jesus now encounters one of those intellectual religionists who thrive on contention and delight in dissension. Found in every sect and cult, particularly in Jewish Israel, their self-appointed mission is to ask questions for question's sake. Their interests are primarily academic and theoretical, and they deal with hypothetical rather than real situations. They are the lawyers whose interest are in the dicta rather than the decision; the medical students who ask how to treat nonexistent diseases; the religionists who solve problems that may never arise in the lives of people. If they can ask questions that—to the embarrassment of their opponents—cannot be answered, so much the better.

Jesus must have been teaching something about eternal life, that glorious state of exaltation reserved for the faithful for whom the family unit continues in the realms ahead. As he did so, "a certain lawyer stood up, and tempted him," or, better, stood up to *test* him, to see how he as a Rabbi would answer one of the points of debate in the Rabbinical schools. The question: "Master, what shall I do to inherit eternal life?"

Jesus parried the question. He declined to stoop to the level of the debating Rabbis; let them revel in polemics—he would not do so. "What is written in the law? how readest thou?" he asked. 'It is your problem, not mine. You have the law before you; answer your own question.'

And the answer that was forthcoming from the learned lawyer was perfect; it was the very answer Jesus himself gave on at least two other occasions. Combining the statement in Deuteronomy 6:5, which is part of the *Shema* itself, with that in Leviticus 19:18—these two passages being the heart and core of the Mosaic law—the lawyer answered: "Thou shalt love the Lord thy God with all thy heart, and with all thy soul, and with all thy strength, and with all thy mind; and thy neighbour as thyself." Moses, who spoke for Jehovah, had phrased perfectly the two commandments by conformity to which eternal life is won, and the lawyer had quoted correctly that which he had read in the law.

But the question had been asked not to gain information, but rather, in the hope that Jesus might not give the proper answer—an answer already known to his interrogator and preserved for all to read in the law—and therefore that he would be embarrassed at his own lack of Rabbinical understanding. Do we not, then, detect a touch of irony in our Lord's response: "Thou hast answered right: this do, and thou shalt live." 'You knew the answer all along; if you would do the things you already know, you shall gain eternal life.'

Hoping to salvage such reputation as he could in a confrontation that had gone against him; desiring to justify his own hatred rather than love for many of his fellowmen; and knowing, by instinct or from some previous statement of Jesus, that our Lord and the other Rabbis differed widely as to who fell in the category of a neighbor, the lawyer asked: "And who is my neighbour? "

Had Jesus, this time, asked, "What says the law on this point? " he would have called forth all the old expressions of approved hatred toward all those of other nations. He himself had summarized the Mosaic standard by saying, "Ye have heard that it hath been said, Thou shalt love thy neighbour, and hate thine enemy," but 'I give unto you a higher standard.' To the Jews their neighbors were the members of the congregation of Israel; the Gentiles and all who opposed the Jewish people not only failed to qualify as neighbors, but were, in fact, enemies. "Whatever modern Judaism may say to the contrary, there is a foundation of truth to the ancient heathen charge against the Jews of *odium generis humani* (hatred of mankind)." (Edersheim 2:237.) And so Jesus himself gave the answer, his answer, the gospel answer, to the query "Who is my neighbour," and the divine definition shines forth in that wondrous parable of the good Samaritan.

A certain man went down from Jerusalem to Jericho, and fell among thieves, which stripped him of his raiment, and wounded him, and departed, leaving him half dead.

A Jew, one of the elect, a member of the chosen people, traveling alone through the rocky gorges and rough terrain along the twenty-two-mile road from Jerusalem to Jericho, falls among Bedouin thieves. It is an evil area where men like Gadianton lurk. The thoroughfare itself was known as the Red Path or Bloody Way. On it our present victim is robbed, wounded, and left naked and half dead. The merciless thieves, perhaps frightened away by other itinerants, leave him to die while they hide nearby to await other victims.

And by chance, there came down a certain priest that way; and when he saw him, he passed by on the other side of the way.

By chance, or, rather, in the providences of the Almighty—for the seeming chances of life provide the testing experiences for men in this mortal probation—by chance a priest, a son of Aaron, one ordained to a holy calling, one whose divine appointment was to minister for the temporal well-being of his fellowmen, came, saw, recognized a Jewish brother, and chose to pass by. A priest, without compassion, left his brother, whom he could have saved, to die of wounds and thirst in a Bedouin desert.

And likewise a Levite, when he was at the place, came and looked upon him, and passed by on the other side of the way; for they desired in their hearts that it might not be known that they had seen him.

As with the priest, so with the Levite: both dishonored their priesthood; both brought disgrace upon their nation; both failed one of the great tests of mortality, choosing, rather, to say within themselves, "Am I my brother's keeper?" And they thought: "No man knows that I have seen this wounded and dying man, and who can condemn me?" And yet, there was a man who did know, and he is Judge of all.

But a certain Samaritan, as he journeyed, came where he was: and when he saw him, he had compassion on him, And went to him, and bound up his wounds, pouring in oil and wine, and set him on his own beast, and brought him to an inn, and took care of him.

A Samaritan, a hated Samaritan, a half-heathen and apostate worshipper of Jehovah, one through whose land the pilgrims from Galilee en route to Jerusalem would not even travel! A Samaritan, who could not be saved, and who some Rabbis said would not even be resurrected! A

Samaritan, who was an enemy and not a neighbor, chose to make this half-dead Jew his brother. Wine cleanses the wounds; oil salves the pain and removes the smart; bandages—perhaps torn from the benefactor's own clothing—protect the torn flesh; the ass of the one from the despised race carries the wounded Jew; and the owner of the beast walks. They go to the *khan* or hostelry by the road, where lodging is free but victuals for men and beasts can be had for a price. The Samaritan took care of the Jew, watched over him, and saved his life.

And on the morrow when he departed, he took out two pence, and gave them to the host, and said unto him, Take care of him; and whatsoever thou spendest more, when I come again, I will repay thee.

Two pence, or, better, two dinars, the sum a laborer earned in two days—this, and an assurance of more if need be, was left with the host. "Which now of these three, thinkest thou, was neighbour unto him that fell among the thieves?" Jesus asked. The lawyer, even now not daring to commend a hated Samaritan by national designation, responded, "He that shewed mercy on him." Jesus said, "Go, and do thou likewise."

A Familial Scene
(Luke 10:38-42)

He who had not where to lay his head—not so much as the foxes who have holes and the birds of the air who have nests—yet during the whole of his mortality among us partook of the culture and sociality of many Jewish abiding places. A sliver of knowledge here, a ray of light there, an incidental comment somewhere else, all let us catch fleeting glimpses of the life he lived and the sociality that was his among those with whom he shared the intimacies incident to the days of his flesh.

We attuned our voices to those of the seraphic hosts in the heavenly choir when he made flesh his tabernacle in a roadside caravanserai in Bethlehem of Judea. We saw him draw his first mortal breath amid the tethered beasts of burden because there was no room in the inns for a woman big with child and whose travail was upon her. We watched as loving hands cared for his needs in the homes of Jewish friends and relatives in Bethlehem and Egypt and Nazareth. It was pleasant to see him learn to crawl and walk and speak in the Jewish home of Jewish Joseph there in the hill country of Galilee. There it was that he learned to pray, where he memorized the *Shema* and reverenced the *Mezuzah* attached to the doorpost as a symbol of Jehovah's protecting care over the homes of Israel.

We have seen his wants cared for in many homes by many people; have feasted with him at many banquets; have slept with him under the stars and in the little booths into which all Israel moved at Tabernacle Times. In the home of Peter in Capernaum of Galilee we saw him hold a child in his arms as he taught who was greatest in the kingdom of heaven. And in the guest chamber of the home of John, in Jerusalem, at the time of the First Passover, we listened attentively as he conversed with Nicodemus, a ruler of the Jews, one who sat on the Great Sanhedrin.

But at no other time and in no other place have we seen such a sweet and tender scene as now opens before us in the home of Martha in Bethany. Blessed Bethany, hidden from Jerusalem by a spur of the Mount of Olives, yet only two miles away, was the retreat to which Jesus so often went to rid himself of the influence and contentions of those who knew not God and who, because of priestcrafts, chose to reject his Son.

It seems clear that the two sisters, Martha and Mary, and their brother Lazarus, all dwelt in the house owned by Martha, who therefore must have been the oldest of the three. It seems apparent that they were well-to-do and had the means and facilities to care for their blessed guest. Because of the reverent curtain of silence drawn by the inspired authors over the family relationship and social intercourse of

Jesus and his friends, we know only that the three who dwelt in Bethany were loved by Jesus. It is of interest to note that the name *Martha* was truly Jewish and meant "lady" or "mistress," that *Mary* was the Greek equivalent of the ancient Hebrew "Miriam," and that *Lazarus* was the Greek form of "Eleazer." The inference is that the three children had been so named by parents who rejoiced in the present and looked forward to the future, including the coming of the Messiah, and the new kingdom, rather than looking back to the old glory of the old kingdom.

That Jesus came to Bethany for the express purpose of being with the sisters we cannot doubt; his disciples apparently had found lodging in other homes. Nor can we doubt there was an open, congenial, and friendly respect and association between them and our Lord. There must have been considerable prior association so that the parties knew each other well and were not restrained in their association by feelings of awe.

On this occasion Mary, whom Jesus loved, sat at his feet to hear his words. No doubt she asked questions and was fed spiritually as few of her sex have ever been. We feel to rank her, in spiritual stature, along with the other Marys—the Blessed Virgin who gave birth to God's Son, and the Mary called Magdalene, whom we have seen as one of the traveling missionary companions of Jesus, and whom we shall yet see as the first mortal to behold the Resurrected Person. Shall we not also rank her with Eve and Sarah and the widow of Zarephath, and the faithful ones of old who ministered to the prophets in their days?

Would that we knew what conversations passed between them, what questions Mary asked, what answers Jesus gave. Did they discuss the atonement through which all men are raised in immortality, while those who believe and obey ascend unto eternal life? Was eternal life defined as that state of glory and peace reserved for those who live everlastingly in the family unit? Were the glories of the celestial realm unfolded to the view of this true believer who had prepared herself by baptism and otherwise to receive the mysteries of the kingdom? Perhaps it is not amiss to say— and we so express ourselves reverently—that in that day when all things are revealed we shall learn of even these sacred and now secret hours in the life of the Divine Person and those whom he chose as his intimates.

Also on this occasion Martha, whom also Jesus loved, "was cumbered about much serving"; as the official hostess, so to speak, it was incumbent upon her to attend to the physical needs of her guest. Perhaps she was envious of the attention given her younger sister and wished herself to be seated at the feet of the Master and to hear those things which then fell from his lips. We cannot suppose she was one whit less spiritual than Mary; indeed, it will be Martha, a short while hence, on the occasion of the raising of their brother Lazarus from death, who will bear a witness of the divine Sonship that would do credit to a Peter, or a Moses, or an Abraham. Nor can we rank her a hair's breadth behind Mary in personal righteousness and in the desire to hear the words of eternal life here and now and be an inheritor of immortal glory hereafter. It just happens that on this occasion the burdens of hospitality had fallen primarily upon the older sister. It is not unnatural to think that Martha may have asked Mary for help that up to that moment had not been forthcoming.

In any event Martha says: "Lord, dost thou not care that my sister hath left me to serve alone? bid her therefore that she help me." Such a statement spoken to Jesus under these circumstances carries a wealth of meaning. It is as though Jesus had some obligation to see that Martha had help. It is not the plea of a person who is so awed by the presence of the Lord Jesus that she fears to speak up on a relatively trivial matter. It is not a statement in which a hostess is careful to avoid any seeming annoyance in the presence of a guest because of a family problem. Geikie even says her "complaint to Jesus" was "not free from irreverence," and that it was as though she had said, " 'Lord, do you not care that my sister has left me to do all the work alone? If *you* speak to her, she will help me.' " (Geikie, p. 601.)

Thereupon Jesus, as was his invarying wont, turned the circumstances at hand into a teaching situation. "Martha, Martha," he said in words of endearing tenderness, "thou art careful and troubled about many things: But one thing is needful: and Mary hath chosen that good part, which shall not be taken away from her."

"From Martha's housewifely complaint and Jesus' mild reproof, we learn the principle that, though temporal food is essential to life, once a reasonable amount has been acquired, then spiritual matters should take precedence. Bread is essential to life, but man is not to live by bread alone. Food, clothing, and shelter are essential to mortal existence, but once these have been gained in reasonable degree, there is only 'one thing' needful—and that is to partake of the spiritual food spread on the gospel table." (*Commentary* 1:473.)

That there is no mention on this occasion of Lazarus, whom also Jesus loved, neither adds to nor detracts from the domestic scene. He may well have been present, as an observer rather than a participant. We shall shortly meet Martha, and then Mary, and then Lazarus, under the most unusual circumstances ever to confront humankind in all the four millennia since mortality began.

NOTES

1. "Records are kept in heaven as well as on earth, and the faithful saints who have gained the promise of eternal life have their names recorded in the Lamb's Book of Life." (*Commentary* 1:465.)

2. This whole glorious concept of how Christ is both the Father and the Son is dealt with at length in *The Promised Messiah*. See particularly chapter 20.

3. In this connection, the Midrash says of Isaiah: "He had been privileged to prophesy of so many blessings, 'because he had taken upon himself the yoke of the Kingdom of Heaven with joy.' " (Edersheim 2:143.)

Chapter 74

THE WONDROUS WORD POURS FORTH

Lo, I come: in the volume of the book
it is written of me, I delight to do thy will,
O my God: yea, thy law is within my heart.
I have preached righteousness. . . .
I have declared thy faithfulness and thy salvation:
I have not concealed thy lovingkindness
and thy truth from the great congregation.
(Ps. 40:7-10.)

Parable of the Friend at Midnight
(Luke 11:1-13; JST, Luke 11:4-5, 14)

The Galilean ministry has come to Judea; Jesus is now doing among the Judeans what he did in Galilee insofar as the people will receive it. The time period is from the Feast of Tabernacles (October 11-18, A.D. 29) through the Feast of Dedication (December 20-27, of the same year), and on into January of A.D. 30, a period of about three months.

His message is what it has always been—that he is the Messiah; that the gospel he brings from God, who is his Father, will save them; that he will work out the infinite and eternal atoning sacrifice and bring all men unto him on conditions of repentance. He speaks in plain words, by symbolic representations, and in parables. His deeds are now as they always have been: he heals the sick, speaks peace to sorrowing souls, and frees the penitent from the bondage of sin. The reaction to his words—it also is the same: a few believe, and the leaders and most of the Jews reject his sayings, claim he casts out devils by Beelzebub, and seek to slay him lest his new religion destroy their craft.

We have now seen his doings and heard his words at the Feast of Tabernacles; we have heard the report of the seventies and felt the impact of the deep and hidden things he then revealed to them. We heard the lawyer test his Rabbinic knowledge, and rejoiced in the spirit and meaning of the parable of the good Samaritan. Then for a few brief moments we sat with him in the home of the beloved sisters in Bethany.

Now we shall drink a few draughts of the living water that flow from the Eternal Fountain—and they are so few in comparison to the endless streams then sent forth to water men's arid hearts. We shall hear him repeat some things he has said before, climaxing it all with the grand pronouncement that he is the Good Shepherd and the stirring testimony: *"I am the Son of God."* Then we shall go with him to Perea, as he testifies there before returning to Jerusalem for the week of his passion.

But first we encounter the situation that brought forth the parable of the friend at midnight. Jesus himself "was praying in a certain place." Prayers may be offered in all places and at all times, but we are dealing here with a particular prayer of the Divine Son to the Divine Father. Clearly it was a prayer in marked contrast to those customarily offered by the Jews in general. "When he ceased, one of his disciples said unto him, Lord, teach us to pray, as John also taught his disciples."

Not all prayers are the same; some are thoughtless chants filled with ritualistic mockery; others are the repetitious and meaningless cries of the heathen. Some consist of memorized phrases learned in youth or of scriptures learned in days past; others—albeit they are few in number—are the heart-stirring pleas of the righteous, poured forth with all the energy and power and faith that their whole souls can possess. John had led his followers away from the ostentatious and mechanical recitations of Rabbinic delight; would Jesus now teach the true order of prayer as found in the new religion that he was restoring? He had done so in Galilee; it was part of the Sermon on the Mount. Now he will do so in Judea for other ears to hear. For that matter, we suppose that he gave over again, perhaps then, perhaps frequently, the whole Sermon on the Mount. Gospel truths are not forever restricted to those who happen to be present when a legal administrator first utters the eternal words. And so now, as a sample and a pattern—with no intent to specify the exact words to be repetitiously chanted, with a religious mien, as some suppose—Jesus said:

Our Father which art in heaven, Hallowed be thy name. Thy kingdom come. Thy will be done, as in heaven, so in earth. Give us day by day our daily bread. And forgive us our sins; for we also forgive every one who is indebted to us. And let us not be led unto temptation; but deliver us from evil; for thine is the kingdom and power. Amen.

These are not—probably advisedly so—the exact words used previously in Galilee, nor should they be. The Lord's Prayer for the Galileans need not be the Lord's Prayer for the Judeans or Pereans or anyone else. And the Lord's Prayer in Judea on one day may not be what it would be on any other. Prayers are to fit the needs of the moment; the models and patterns proffered by Jesus simply channel the thoughts and desires of mortal suppliants in the proper course. There is, however, a universal principle that Jesus then enunciated: "Your heavenly Father will not fail to give unto you whatsoever ye ask of him." Following this came the parable.

Which of you shall have a friend, and shall go unto him at midnight, and say unto him, Friend, lend me three loaves; For a friend of mind in his journey is come to me, and I have nothing to set before him?

This is a realistic setting. Eastern hospitality required that the host provide food and shelter. Having no bread in his own house, the host naturally turns, notwithstanding the hour, to his neighbor and friend.

And he from within shall answer and say, Trouble me not: the door is now shut, and my children are with me in bed; I cannot rise and give thee.

I say unto you, Though he will not rise and give him, because he is his friend, yet because of his importunity he will rise and give him as many as he needeth.

We need not seek for elaborate explanations nor varying applications. The meaning is clear. If a churlish, selfish man—annoyed and resentful because of a seemingly inopportune petition—will yet discommode himself and come to the aid of a friend, how much more will a gracious Father, who seeks to bless his children, grant petitions offered to him in faith. If there are special difficulties and great obstacles standing in the way, seemingly to prevent an answer to our prayers, yet our heavenly Friend will give heed to our petitions when they ascend to him in faith and righteousness.

And I say unto you, Ask, and it shall be given you; seek, and ye shall find; knock, and it shall be opened unto you. For every one that asketh receiveth; and he that seeketh findeth; and to him that knocketh it shall be opened.

To ask is one thing; to seek is a greater thing; and to knock at the very doors of heaven assures that those holy portals will be opened and that the desired blessings will be forthcoming. Those who take no thought save it be to ask are denied the blessing. "Let him ask of God, . . . But let him ask in faith" is the divine decree. (James 1:5-6; D&C 9:7-9.) Nothing is withheld from those who seek the Lord with all their heart. Those whose search falls short of the utmost bounds to which it should extend shall not find the desired treasure.

If a son shall ask bread of any of you that is a father, will he give him a stone? or if he ask a fish, will he for a fish give him a serpent? Or if he shall ask an egg, will he offer him a scorpion?

If ye then, being evil, know how to give good gifts unto your children, how much more shall your heavenly Father give good gifts, through the Holy Spirit, to them who ask him.

He Ministers in Judea as in Galilee
(Luke 11:14-54; JST, Luke 11:15, 18-19, 23, 25-27, 29, 32-33, 37; Luke 12:13-21; JST, Luke 12:23)

Jesus now continues to do in Judea what he did before in Galilee, and, predictably, is faced with the same reactions, to which he gives the same responses. He casts out a devil from one who is dumb, who then speaks, and the old familiar charge is hurled: "He casteth out devils through Beelzebub the chief of devils." His detractors also demand a sign from heaven, as those with a kindred evil spirit had done in the land to the north. There then follows the same discussion about a kingdom divided against itself; of Satan casting out Satan; of how their children can cast out devils; and of an evil generation of sign seekers who shall receive only the sign of the prophet Jonas. All this we have discussed in its Galilean setting in chapter 48 (Book 2).

Here also in Judea, Jesus is invited to eat in the home of a Pharisee, who marvels when our Lord refrains from the ritualistic washings imposed with such rigor upon the people. These burdensome washings we have considered at some length in their Galilean setting in chapter 59 (Book 2). Using the absurdities of these traditions of the elders as a basis, Jesus launches forth in a severe and merciless castigation of the Pharisees, scribes, and lawyers for their hypocrisy and evil deeds. He will repeat all this again on Tuesday, April 4, A.D. 30, the third day of the week of his atoning sacrifice, at which time we shall consider it in extenso.

It was also at this time that Jesus set forth the great and

wondrous concepts recorded in Luke 12. Those dealing with blasphemy and the unpardonable sin are considered in chapter 48 (Book 2); those pertaining to the preaching of the gospel boldly and in plainness, to the persecution and trials of the saints, and to the divisions among men that are created by the spread of the gospel are set forth in chapter 54 (Book 2). We shall hereafter come to grips with the portion of this chapter dealing with the second coming of the Son of Man, when Jesus delivers his great sermon on the Mount of Olivet on the third day of the week of the atoning sacrifice. We shall now, however, consider Luke's account of the parable of the rich fool.

Parable of the Rich Fool
(Luke 12:13-21; JST, Luke 12:23)

Jesus is speaking; words of wisdom are flowing forth from the Son of God; he who speaks as none other before or since is telling "an innumerable multitude of people," as Luke describes them, the very truths that will prepare the penitent for the riches of eternity. "Behold, he that hath eternal life is rich." (D&C 6:7.) He is speaking of spiritual things and telling the disciples that the Holy Ghost will guide them in the very hour in meting that measure of gospel truth which should go to every man.

At this point he is interrupted. There is one present whose thoughts are not on the riches of eternity that it is Jesus' good pleasure to give his disciples, but on the things of this world. The preached words are finding no lodgment in his soul; he is concerned about some petty baubles of mortal pelf that shall fade away with the setting sun. Who but a fool interrupts the Son of God—and shortly Jesus will so designate him. "Master," he says, "speak to my brother, that he divide the inheritance with me."

Perhaps he reasoned that the majesty and persuasiveness of this man, this Rabbi of such excelling wisdom, would force his brother to give him an equal share of their inherited wealth. Under Jewish law the eldest son always inherited a double portion. Clearly, this man sought to use Jesus for worldly gain, even as some in all ages seek to use the Church and the gospel to further their financial interests.

"Man, who made me a judge or a divider over you?" Jesus responds. He will neither intervene in nor override their earthly judicial system. No more did he when they brought before him the woman taken in adultery and demanded of him whether she should be put to death, nor when the tax collectors demanded of Peter why his Master, the Messiah, had not paid the temple assessment due for Messiah's house.[1] But Jesus will and does take occasion to teach the people the perils of selfishness and trusting in uncertain riches.

Take heed, and beware of covetousness: for a man's life consisteth not in the abundance of the things which he possesseth.

"How often, in one dramatic way after another, do we find Him who had not where to lay his head, teaching that worldly wealth is of little eternal worth; that men should lay up for themselves treasures, not on earth, but in heaven; that they should seek first the kingdom of God and let the things of this world take a position of secondary importance; that one thing above all others is needful—to love and serve God and the Son whom he hath sent!

"In this conversation with a covetous, worldly-minded man, and in the resultant parable of the rich fool which grew out of it, our Lord teaches that those whose hearts are set on the things of this world shall lose their souls. The parable itself condemns worldly-mindedness, reminds men that death and judgment are inevitable, and teaches that they should seek eternal riches rather than those things which moth and rust corrupt and which thieves break through and steal." (*Commentary* 1:474.) This, then, is the parable:

The ground of a certain rich man brought forth plen-

tifully: And he thought within himself, saying, What shall I do, because I have no room where to bestow my fruits?

There is no hint of ill-gotten gain here. A gracious Father has given the rich man the means of acquiring great wealth, and through his industry he has done so. But he supposes he has no place to bestow the fruits of his labors. What? Are there no hungry mouths to feed, no naked bodies to clothe, no derelict souls who long for a roof over their heads? Are not the poor always with us? Are there none to whom a crust of bread and a sip of wine would make the difference between life and death? And for what purpose does the Lord bestow the bounties of earth except to care for the just needs and wants of all his children? Truly the law of riches is summed up in these prophetic words: "Think of your brethren like unto yourselves, and be familiar with all and free with your substance, that they may be rich like unto you. But before ye seek for riches, seek ye for the kingdom of God. And after ye have obtained a hope in Christ ye shall obtain riches, if ye seek them; and ye will seek them for the intent to do good—to clothe the naked, and to feed the hungry, and to liberate the captive, and administer relief to the sick and the afflicted." (Jacob 2:17-19.) But back to the parable and the feelings of the rich man:

And he said, This will I do: I will pull down my barns, and build greater; and there will I bestow all my fruits and my goods. And I will say to my soul, Soul, thou hast much goods laid up for many years; take thine ease, eat, drink, and be merry.

'*My* barns, *my* fruits, *my* goods, and *my* soul—I, a rich man, revel in the delicacies and power which *my* riches bring. I will rejoice in worldliness and ease; I will make "provision for the flesh, to fulfil the lusts thereof." ' (Rom. 13:14.)

But God said unto him, Thou fool, this night thy soul shall be required of thee: then whose shall those things

192

be, which thou hast provided? So is he that layeth up treasure for himself, and is not rich toward God.

Truly, the prosperity of fools shall destroy them! O that all men might be rich toward God—"Rich in the currency negotiable in the courts above; rich in eternal things; rich in the knowledge of the truth, in the possession of intelligence, in obedience to gospel law, in the possession of the characteristics and attributes of Deity, in all of the things which will continue to be enjoyed in eternity." (*Commentary* 1:474.)

"And then our Lord expanded the thought. He told them that the life was more than food, and the body than raiment. Again He reminded them how God clothes, in more than Solomon's glory, the untoiling lilies, and feeds the careless ravens that neither sow nor reap. Food and raiment, and the multitude of possessions, were not life: *they* had better things to seek after and to look for; let them not be tossed on this troubled sea of faithless care; be theirs the life of fearless hope, of freest charity, the life of the girded loin and the burning lamp—as servants watching and waiting for the unknown moment of their lord's return." (Farrar, p. 362.)

Parable of the Barren Fig Tree
(Luke 13:1-9; JST, Luke 13:1, 6, 9)

Jesus has just spoken of the signs of the times and of the desolations and sorrows that are ahead. These matters, as before noted, will be considered later in connection with other parallel pronouncements relative to the perils and destructions that shall come upon the Jewish nation because of their rebellion and rejection of their Redeemer. They are mentioned here only to show the setting in which the parable of the barren fig tree was given.

As though to illustrate the punishments they supposed were sent of God upon sinners, some of those then present told Jesus "of the Galileans, whose blood Pilate had mingled with their sacrifices." Overlooking the temple grounds was the fortress of Antonia, from which Roman soldiers had ready access to the sacred grounds. Apparently they had been called upon to quell some nationalistic uprising or other disturbance, slaying the Galileans involved as they offered sacrifices on the great altar.

A not-uncommon Jewish belief was that special punishments were meted out for special sins. It may be that in telling Jesus of this bloody turmoil in the temple itself, these Jews were saying: "Yes, signs of the times and of the coming storm! These Galileans of yours, your own countrymen, involved in a kind of Psuedo-Messianic movement, a kind of 'signs of the times' rising, something like that towards which you want us to look—was not their death a condign punishment?" (Edersheim 2:222.)

To such a charge Jesus had no intention of acceding. "Suppose ye that these Galileans were sinners above all the Galileans, because they suffered such things?" he asked. "I tell you, Nay: but, except ye repent, ye shall all likewise perish." Then our Lord chose a like illustration of his own. "Or those eighteen, upon whom the tower of Siloam fell, and slew them," he asks, "think ye that they were sinners above all men that dwelt in Jerusalem?" His answer: "I tell you, Nay: but, except ye repent, ye shall all likewise perish."

Jesus' illustration was even more persuasive than that concerning the Galileans. Pilate had taken the sacred temple monies—the *Qorban*—and used them to build an aqueduct into Jerusalem. As a result there was a terrible uprising, vengefully quelled with Roman steel. Surely if a tower at the Siloam pool fell and killed eighteen persons engaged in this hated Gentile building project, this was just retribution. But Jesus says, 'Not so. Their sins were as the sins of all Jerusalem, and all of you will perish spiritually as they perished temporally, except ye believe in me, repent of your sins, and work the works of righteousness.'

"True it is, as a general principle, that God sends disasters, calamities, plagues, and suffering upon the rebellious, and that he preserves and protects those who love and serve him. Such indeed were the very promises given to

Israel—obedience would net them the preserving and protecting care of the Lord, disobedience would bring death, destruction, desolation, disaster, war, and a host of evils upon them.

"But to say that particular individuals slain in war, killed in accidents, smitten with disease, stricken with plagues, or shorn of their property by natural calamities, have been singled out from among their fellows as especially deserving of such supposed retribution is wholly unwarranted. It is not man's prerogative to conclude in individual cases of suffering or accident that such has befallen a person as a just retribution for an ungodly course." (*Commentary* 1:475.)

These principles Jesus now illustrates with the parable of the barren fig tree. With reference to the choice of the fig tree as his illustration, we should be aware of the following: "Fig-trees, as well as palm and olive trees, were regarded as so valuable, that to cut them down if they yielded even a small measure of fruit, was popularly deemed to deserve death at the Hand of God. . . . The fig-tree was regarded as the most fruitful of all trees." However, "as trees were regarded as by their roots undermining and deteriorating the land, a barren tree would be of threefold disadvantage: it would yield no fruit; it would fill valuable space, which a fruit-bearer might occupy; and it would needlessly deteriorate the land. Accordingly, while it was forbidden to destroy fruit-bearing trees, it would, on the grounds above stated, be duty to cut down a 'barren' or 'empty' tree." (Edersheim 2:246-47.) And so now to the parable itself:

A certain man had a fig tree planted in his vineyard; and he came and sought fruit thereon, and found none. Then said he unto the dresser of his vineyard, Behold, these three years I come seeking fruit on this fig tree, and find none: cut it down; why cumbereth it the ground?

And he answering said unto him, Lord, let it alone this year also, till I shall dig about it and dung it: And if it bear fruit, the tree is saved, and if not, after that

*thou shalt cut it down. And many other parables spake
he unto the people.*

"A certain husbandman (God) had a fig tree (the Jewish
remnant of Israel) planted in his vineyard (the world); and
he came (in the meridian of time) and sought fruit thereon
(faith, righteousness, good works, gifts of the Spirit), and
found none. Then said he unto the dresser of his vineyard,
(the Son of God), Behold, these three years (the period of
Jesus' ministry) I come seeking fruit on this fig tree, and find
none: cut it down (destroy the Jewish nation as an organized
kingdom); why cumbereth it the ground (why should it
prevent the conversion of the world by occupying the
ground and preempting the time of my servants)? And he
(the Son of God) answering said unto him (God, the husbandman), Lord, let it alone this year also till I shall dig
about it, and dung it (preach the gospel, raise the warning
voice, show forth signs and wonders, organize the Church,
and offer every opportunity for the conversion of the Jewish
nation). And if it bear fruit, the tree is saved (the Jewish nation shall be preserved as such and its members gain salvation), and if not, after that thou shalt cut it down (destroy the
Jews as a nation, make them a hiss and a byword, and scatter them among all nations)." (*Commentary* 1:477.)[2]

NOTES

1. "Christ had not only no legal authority for interfering, but the Jewish law of
inheritance was so clearly defined, and, we may add, so just, that if this person had any just
or good cause, there could have been no need for appealing to Jesus. Hence it must have
been 'covetousness,' in the strictest sense, which prompted it—perhaps, a wish to have, besides his own share as a younger brother, half of that additional portion which, by law,
came to the eldest son of the family." (Edersheim 2:243.)

2. "God called Israel as a nation, and planted it in the most favored spot: as a fig-tree
in the vineyard of His own Kingdom. 'And he came seeking,' as He had every right to do,
'fruit thereon, and found none.' It was the third year that He had vainly looked for fruit,
when He turned to His Vinedresser—the Messiah, to Whom the vineyard is committed as
its King—with this direction: 'Cut it down—why doth it also deteriorate the soil?' It is barren, though in the best position; as a fig-tree it ought to bear figs, and here the best; it fills
the place which a good tree might occupy; and besides, it deteriorates the soil. And its
three years' barrenness has established its utterly hopeless character. Then it is that the
Divine Vinedresser, in His infinite compassion, pleads, and with far deeper reality than
either Abraham or Moses could have entreated, for the fig-tree which Himself had planted

and tended, that it should be spared 'this year also,' 'until then that I shall dig about it, and dung it'—till He labour otherwise than before, even by His Own Presence and Words, nay, by laying to its roots His most precious Blood. 'And if then it bear fruit'—here the text abruptly breaks off, as implying that in such case it would, of course, be allowed to remain; 'but if not, *then* against the future (coming) *year* shalt thou cut it down.'" (Edersheim 2:247-48.)

Chapter 75

THE MAN
BORN BLIND

The Lord openeth the eyes
of the blind. (Ps. 146:8.)

The Miracle—One Born Blind Is Healed
(*John 9:1-12; JST, John 9:4*)

It is the joyous Sabbath—a day of rest, a day of peace, a
day of worship. It is also the burdensome Sabbath—a day on
which Rabbinism goes wild in enforcing petty, Satan-
inspired restrictions that defy all sense and reason, restrictions that serve no purpose except to stand as a witness of
the dire apostasy then prevailing among a once-chosen and a
once-enlightened people.

Jesus and his disciples pass by one of the gates of the
temple, as we suppose. It is a place where beggars ask alms,
perhaps the same sacred site where a man lame from his
mother's womb will one day entreat Peter and John for a
few pence and receive instead full strength in his feet and
ankles. But on this autumn day, a beggar is present who has
been blind from birth. He cannot ask alms, for it is the Sabbath, though it would be legal for kindly disposed persons to
make voluntary contributions to his welfare. The man and
his state are well known to the disciples and, as we shall see,
to great hosts of Jerusalemites. No doubt he is sitting in the
place where he commonly plied his unhappy trade.

"Master, who did sin, this man, or his parents, that he was born blind?" the disciples ask. This question, propounded by spiritually enlightened disciples—men who, like Peter, James, and John, had seen within the veil and heard the voice of God—presupposes two verities: (1) that the sins of the fathers may be visited upon the children in the form of physical impairment, and (2) that mortal souls are capable of committing sin before they ever breathe the breath of life. Both of these concepts are true.

As we have seen—with reference to the slaughter of the Galileans, whose blood Pilate mingled with their sacrifices, and with reference to the eighteen upon whom the tower of Siloam fell—the Jews believed that calamities and accidents came as punishment for sin. Jesus denounced this heresy; those so slain, though sinners, were not unlike all of their fellows; their misfortunes were not the result of any evil in their lives that was greater than that of their neighbors.

On the other hand, God sent calamities and plagues upon Israel, as a people and as a nation, because they forsook him and kept not his commandments. And there may be specific parental sins that impose penalties upon children; immoral parents may contract a venereal disease that causes blindness in unborn children. And personal sins may bring physical punishment to individuals, as when illness is caused by disobedience to the Lord's law of health.

The question asked is not one that can be answered by glib generalities. Birth deformities may or may not result from parental disobedience, but we have no reason to believe that children are so afflicted because of acts done in the premortal life. All children are born free from the taint of sin because of the great plan of redemption ordained for them by a gracious God. And yet, again on the other hand, children, though starting life in innocence, are born in one race or another, at one time or another, with one talent or another—all as a direct result of the life lived before mortal birth. The question asked by the disciples is, in fact, a good one that presupposes a knowledge of the plan of salvation.

They are asking about *this case,* to gain a better understanding of how the eternal laws operate in all cases.

Jesus answers: "Neither hath this man sinned, nor his parents: but that the works of God should be made manifest in him." 'This is a special case, set apart from all others. This man has never seen; no ray of light has ever entered his eyes; he has seen no sunrise or sunset, no birds of the air, no lilies of the field. He is born thus for a purpose—so that I may heal him and he may stand forever as a witness that I am the Son of God. Through him the works of God shall be manifest forever to all those to whom my gospel comes.'

I must work the works of him that sent me, while I
am with you; the time cometh when I shall have
finished my work, then I go unto the Father. As long as
I am in the world, I am the light of the world.

'Let there be no misunderstanding with reference to what I shall now do. My Father sent me to do this work, and do it I shall as long as I am with you. When I have finished my work—all my work, this act of healing, my preaching, and finally my atoning sacrifice—then I shall return to the Father. And know this: I am the light of the world. Whenever, from this time forth, you remember that I opened these blind eyes, physically, remember also that I came to bring light to eyes, spiritually.'

Now comes the miracle. Jesus himself has set the stage; he has told the people *what* he is going to do and *why.* It but remains for them to see *how* it is done, and in this instance the how is of surpassing import. Their Messiah stoops down; he spits on the ground, he makes clay with the spittle; and he anoints the eyes of the blind man with the saliva-filled lump of the dust of the earth. Sick persons are healed by faith through the laying on of hands, not by rubbing them with daubs of spittle-made mud. Why, then, does Jesus so act? There can be little doubt that he is deliberately violating the law of the Sabbath in two major respects: (1) he made clay, and (2) he applied a healing remedy to an impaired person, which of itself was forbidden, and in addition there was a

200

specific prohibition against the application of saliva to the eyes on the Sabbath. This strange restriction came into being because of a common belief that saliva was a remedy for diseases of the eye.

Thus Jesus is putting the people in the position of choosing between him as one sent of God to do the work of the Father, as one who can open blind eyes, and the traditions of the elders about Sabbath observance. They must make their choice at the peril of their salvation. Once again it will be a day in Israel when the trumpet sounds: "Choose ye this day whom ye will serve."

So far, be it noted, Jesus has said nothing to the man. He has made no effort to plant even the seeds of faith in the man's heart; the blind one does not even know who Jesus is, or that he is believed by some to be the Messiah. This miracle is being done at Jesus' initiative, by his own power, for his own purposes. He now says, "Go, wash in the pool of Siloam"—just that and nothing more. John here inserts the comment that Siloam means *sent*, thus signifying, as we suppose, that as the Father sent the Son, so the Son sent the man—all to the end that what was done might be for the glory of God. In any event, the man went, washed as directed, gained sight, and returned seeing. The miracle has been wrought.

The blind eyes that now see create a sensation everywhere; word of the event is on every tongue; neighbors, friends, kinsmen, those who merely knew him by sight—all marvel at what has happened. "Is not this he that sat and begged?" they ask. Some say, "This is he"; others, "He is like him." But he says, "I am he." "How then were thine eyes opened?" they demand. Having now learned Jesus' name, he responds: "A man that is called Jesus made clay, and anointed mine eyes, and said unto me, Go to the pool of Siloam, and wash: and I went and washed, and I received sight." Such a beautiful and straightforward account, glorious in its simplicity! "Where is he?" they ask, and he says, "I know not."

The Testing of the Miracle—Pharisaic Contention
(John 9:13-29; JST, John 9:13, 27)

It is the Sabbath. There are both believers and skeptics among those who know of the miracle. Some who are rigid formalists—zealous for the strict observance of the day—take him that was blind to the Pharisees in council and report: 'Jesus made clay and opened this man's eyes on the Sabbath.'

"The Rabbis had forbidden any man to smear even one of his eyes with spittle on the Sabbath, except in cases of mortal danger. Jesus had not only smeared *both* the man's eyes, but had actually mingled the saliva with clay! This, an act of mercy, was in the deepest and most inward accordance with the very causes for which the Sabbath had been ordained, and the very lessons of which it was meant to be a perpetual witness. But the spirit of narrow literalism and slavish minuteness and quantitative obedience—the spirit that hoped to be saved by the algebraical sum of good and bad actions—had long degraded the Sabbath from the true idea of its institution into a pernicious superstition. The Sabbath of Rabbinism, with all its petty servility, was in no respect the Sabbath of God's loving and holy law. It had degenerated into that which St. Paul calls it, a 'beggarly element.' And these Jews were so imbued with this utter littleness, that a unique miracle of mercy awoke in them less of astonishment and gratitude than the horror kindled by a neglect of their Sabbatical superstition." (Farrar, p. 439. Gal. 4:9.)

Those in the Pharisaic council inquired how the man had received sight. He told his story again. "He put clay upon mine eyes, and I washed, and do see." Clearly, this miracle was either of God or of Satan. Some among the Pharisees said of Jesus: "This man is not of God, because he keepeth not the sabbath day." Others replied: "How can a man that is a sinner do such miracles?" Faced with this division in their own ranks, the inquisitors asked further of the healed

202

man: "What sayest thou of him, that he hath opened thine eyes?" The answer came in majestic simplicity: "He is a prophet."[1]

There was yet one ray of Pharisaic hope that might explain all this away. Perhaps the man had not been blind at all. 'How could blind eyes be opened?' they argued. With this in mind they called the parents and questioned them. "Is this your son, who ye say was born blind? how then doth he now see?" they asked.

To us the obvious answer should have been: 'He is our son. He was born blind. The man Jesus anointed his eyes with clay made of his own spittle; our son, at his direction, washed in the pool of Siloam, and now his eyes are open.' All this the parents knew to be true; and next to the healed one himself, who should have rejoiced more in the miracle than his parents? But in the Jewish setting, and because they were faced with the social and religious pressures of Rabbinism, their answer was lacking in full integrity of expression and failed to manifest the same moral courage found in the words of their son. "We know that this is our son, and that he was born blind," they said, for this none could deny; "But by what means he now seeth, we know not; or who hath opened his eyes, we know not: he is of age; ask him: he shall speak for himself."

A great miracle has been wrought; a man who was blind from birth now sees; it should be a time to rejoice and thank God for his goodness and grace. But the issue is not that a blind man sees; he is but a pawn, an infinitesimal nothing, in a great warfare that is raging in the souls of rebellious Israel. The issue is that the miracle was wrought by Jesus, by a sinner who breaks the Sabbath, by one who casts out devils by Beelzebub, by one who opens blind eyes by Satan's power; yes, by one who is Satan Incarnate. Thus John, in explaining the parental response, says: "These words spake his parents, because they feared the Jews: for the Jews had agreed already, that if any man did confess that he was Christ, he should be put out of the synagogue. Therefore said his parents, He is of age; ask him."

Lucifer, our common enemy, using as his agents those on earth who heed the whisperings of his voice, is here exerting on these parents, and upon all who do or may believe that Jesus is the Christ, such pressure as we can scarcely envision. They are to be "put out of the synagogue." Had the Judaic-Mosaic worshippers, who chose to reject their Messiah, simply excommunicated all who did believe in him, we would have little fault to find with their decision. Certainly a religious society is entitled to drop from membership those who depart from its beliefs and standards.

Excommunication among them, however, came successively and by degrees, until it built up to a terrible climax of hate and vengeance. Certain temporary restrictions might be imposed to begin with; these might be increased in extent and intensity; finally, the penalties included curses and anathemas, unbearable social and economic pressures, and all of the fears and torments of an eternal hell. One of the incomplete excommunications, when thrust upon a prominent person, included these restrictions: "Henceforth he would sit on the ground, and bear himself like one in deep mourning. He would allow his beard and hair to grow wild and shaggy; he would not bathe, nor anoint himself; he would not be admitted into an assembly of ten men, neither to public prayer, nor to the Academy; though he might either teach, or be taught, by single individuals. Nay, as if he were a leper, people would keep at a distance of four cubits from him. If he died, stones were cast on his coffin, nor was he allowed the honor of the ordinary funeral, nor were they to mourn for him."

This was only the beginning of what might be. "Still more terrible was the final excommunication, or *Cherem* [by which is meant being put out of the synagogue], when a ban of indefinite duration was laid on a man. Henceforth he was like one dead. He was not allowed to study with others, no intercourse was to be held with him, he was not even to be shown the road. He might, indeed, buy the necessaries of life, but it was forbidden to eat or drink with such an one."

There were twenty-four grounds for imposing this final type of excommunication, including resisting "the authority of the Scribes, or any of their decrees," and leading others "either away from 'the commandments,' or to what was regarded as profanation of the Divine Name." (Edersheim 2:184.) Those who confessed that Jesus was the Messiah would, of course, be guilty of these violations.

To be put out of the synagogue was more than excommunication; it was persecution, which led Jesus to say to the disciples: "They shall put you out of the synagogues: yea, the time cometh, that whosoever killeth you will think that he doeth God service." (John 16:2.) The dreadful burden of such a penalty was more than these parents—already so poor that their son begged for a living—dared to assume.

An evil spirit of bitterness and contention now blazes forth anew. Having failed utterly in their assault upon the parents; being unable to deny or explain the miracle; feeling a sense of sheer and utter perplexity—the Pharisaic council again calls in the man that once was blind. They will try another approach. "Give God the praise: we know that this man is a sinner," they say. In effect they are asking the man to recant. 'We now admit you have been healed; your parents make that clear; but give God the credit. Confess that Jesus had nothing to do with it; he is a sinner—one who has desecrated the Sabbath by molding a ball of clay and by rubbing saliva on your eyes—and, therefore, he could not perform a miracle.' They were asking the man to side completely with them, to deny Christ and to glorify—even deify—traditionalism. They sought the condemnation of Christ and the apotheosis of Rabbinism.

But our once blind friend is fearless. He may not know all the intricacies and nuances of Rabbinic reasoning; he may not know whether it is a sin to rub a glob of mud together on your fingers on the Sabbath or not; but one thing he does know: whereas once he was blind, now he sees. His response is his testimony: "Whether he be a sinner or no, I know not: one thing I know, that, whereas I was blind, now I see."

Shamed and discomfited, the Pharisees make one more attack. Perhaps a renewed recitation of the details will reveal some undotted "I" or an uncrossed "T" that they can twist into proof the miracle was wrought by demoniac power. If their questions cease now, it is an admission of defeat at the hands of an unlearned beggar. "What did he to thee? how opened he thine eyes?" they demand. Their star witness is wearied with the repeated wanderings over the same course. He has told his story; it stands; there is nothing to add. "I have told you already, and ye did not believe," he says. Then in a master stroke, filled with inspired irony, the man asks: "Wherefore would ye hear it again? will ye also be his disciples?" 'Why are you asking me again? Is it because I have converted you? Do you now believe? Are you ready to become his disciples?'

Reviling and bitterness pour forth in the Pharisaic response: "Thou art his disciple," they say, "but we are Moses' disciples. We know that God spake unto Moses: as for this fellow, we know not from whence he is." And with these words they rejected their King, cast their lot with Lucifer, and sealed their own doom.

The Purpose of the Miracle: Jesus Acclaims His Divinity
(*John 9:30-41; JST, John 9:32*)

The Pharisaic witness has been given: 'This fellow, this Nazarene of Galilee, this friend of publicans and sinners, we do not know whether he is of God or not.'

Now comes the true witness, contained in words of irrefutable logic, spoken—we cannot doubt—by the power of the Spirit. The man says: "Why herein is a marvellous thing, that ye know not from whence he is, and yet he hath opened mine eyes. Now we know that God heareth not sinners: but if any man be a worshipper of God, and doeth his will, him he heareth. Since the world began was it not heard that any man opened the eyes of one that was born blind, except he be of God. If this man were not of God, he could do nothing."

To this there is no answer; it cannot be gainsaid; the words carry within themselves the evidence of their own verity. There is nothing left for the Pharisees to do but to revile and to persecute. "Thou wast altogether born in sins" is their screeching cry—as though that had any bearing on the issue one way or the other—"and dost thou teach us? " Truly out of the mouths of babes and sucklings fall gems of eternal truth; the weak and the simple confound the wise and the learned, and the purposes of the Lord prevail. He had taught them, and they knew it, and he knew it. As a consequence, "they cast him out," and he was subjected to the dire penalties of excommunication and persecution. And so ever is it with those who forsake the world and cleave unto Christ. The world loves its own and hates those who are Christ's.

But the Lord loveth and careth for those who are his own, and when he who came to minister to his fellowmen learned of the excommunication, he sought out the man to teach him the truths of his everlasting gospel. No doubt he told him many things about a loving Father, the fall of man, and the atonement yet to be wrought by God's own Son. We know he asked this question:

Dost thou believe on the Son of God?

There is nothing figurative, nothing hidden, nothing left for interpretation, about the query. It is as plain as language can be; it strikes, as an arrow, into the very heart and core of revealed religion. "Who is he, Lord, that I might believe on him? " Jesus answers:

Thou hast both seen him, and it is he that talketh with thee.

And the man said, "Lord, I believe." And he worshipped

Jesus. That is, he who was born blind, whose eyes Jesus opened, received now a greater gift than sight itself. His lifelong spiritual blindness ceased also; his spirit eyes were opened; he knew Jesus was the Son of God through whom salvation comes, and he was prepared to follow him, worship him, and keep his commandments. Because of his belief in the Son, he was ready to enter in at the gate of repentance and baptism and to plant his feet firmly on the path leading to eternal life.

Here is a man who was born blind so that he might one day be a sign and a witness of the One who should open his eyes. And such came to pass according to that divine providence which cares for all things so that even a sparrow's fall merits divine notice. Here also is a man who was spiritually blind, upon whose soul the rays of gospel light had never shone, until one came who opened his spiritual eyes so that he saw in Jesus the Son of God. Can there be any doubt as to which is the greater miracle—to see with the eyes of mortality the things of this benighted sphere which shall pass away, or to see with the eyes of the spirit the things of a better world that shall endure forever? And does not the fact that Jesus opened the eyes that were blind physically testify that he also has power to open men's spiritual eyes so they can see the things of the Spirit and walk in the strait and narrow path leading to eternal life? And so Jesus said:

> For judgment I am come into this world, that they which see not might see; and that they which see might be made blind.

'I am come into the world to sit in judgment upon all men, to divide them into two camps by their acceptance or rejection of my word. Those who are spiritually blind have their eyes opened through obedience to my gospel and shall see the things of the Spirit. Those who think they can see in the spiritual realm, but who do not accept me and my gospel shall remain in darkness and be made blind to the true spiritual realities.' (*Commentary* 1:482.)

Knowing full well the meaning and import of Jesus'

words, some of the Pharisees asked, "Are we blind also? " The reply: "If ye were blind, ye should have no sin: but now ye say, We see; therefore your sin remaineth." 'If you did not have the law of Moses and the words of the prophets; if you did not profess to worship the God of Israel in your synagogues and to sacrifice to him in your temple; if you were not the chosen people to whom the word of truth once came, you would not be condemned as severely as you are. But because you have the greater light, and rebel against it, you commit sin.'[2]

NOTES

1. Farrar's footnote relative to this proclamation, "He is a prophet," is instructive: "And the Jews themselves went so far as to say [and what he now quotes is from Maimonides] that 'if a prophet of undoubted credentials should command all persons to light fires on the Sabbath day, arm themselves for war, kill the inhabitants &c., it would behove all to rise up without delay and execute all that he should direct without scruple or hesitation.' " (Farrar, p. 439, footnote 2.)

2. " 'He who sins against the greater light shall receive the greater condemnation.' (D&C 82:3.) 'Where there is no law ... there is no condemnation.' (2 Ne. 9:25.) Modern sectarians, to whom the message of the restoration is presented, are in this same state of blindness and sin. They have the scriptures before them; they study the gospel doctrines contained in them; they are concerned about religion in general; and then they hear the latter-day elders, speaking as those having authority, present the message of salvation—and yet they choose to remain in the churches of the day rather than accept the fulness of revealed truth. If they were blind, knowing none of these things, they would be under no condemnation for rejecting the light; but when the truth is offered to them and they reject it, claiming to have the light already, they are under condemnation, for their sin remaineth." (*Commentary* 1:482.)

Chapter 76

THE GOOD SHEPHERD

The Lord is my Shepherd. (Ps. 23:1.)
The Lord God will come. . . .
He shall feed his flock like a shepherd:
he shall gather the lambs with his arm,
and carry them in his bosom,
and shall gently lead those that are with young.
(Isa. 40:10-11.)

Jesus Is the Good Shepherd
(John 10:1-15; JST, John 10:7-8, 12-14)

No figures of speech, no similitudes, no parables or allegories brought greater joy to Israelite hearts than those which led to the glorious pronouncement: *Jehovah is our Shepherd*.

Israel's very lives depended upon the safety and procreant powers of their sheep. Physically and spiritually their interests centered in their flocks and herds. From them came food for their tables, clothes for their bodies, sacrifices for their altars. In the lonely deserts, on the mountain slopes, in the valleys of the shadow of death, a strong bond of love and mutual reliance grew up between the sheep and their pastor. Those who cared for the flocks were not sheepherders but shepherds; sheep were not driven, but led; they hearkened to him whose voice they came to know. At night the flocks were commingled in one safe sheepfold where a single shepherd stood guard against the wolves and terrors of the night. In the morning each shepherd called his own sheep out and they followed him to green pastures and still waters.

Thus in their hymns of praise Israel sang: "Know ye that the Lord he is God: it is he that hath made us, and not we ourselves; we are his people, and the sheep of his pasture." (Ps. 100:3.) When Jehovah rebuked his recreant priests and teachers, his cry was: "Woe be to the shepherds of Israel that do feed themselves! should not the shepherds feed the flocks? . . . And ye my flock, the flock of my pasture, are men, and I am your God, saith the Lord God." (Ezek. 34:2, 31.) And when the people were called to repentance, the cry was: "O ye workers of iniquity; ye that are puffed up in the vain things of the world, ye that have professed to have known the ways of righteousness nevertheless have gone astray, as sheep having no shepherd, notwithstanding a shepherd hath called after you and is still calling after you, but ye will not hearken unto his voice! Behold, I say unto you, that the good shepherd doth call you; yea, and in his own name he doth call you, which is the name of Christ; and if ye will not hearken unto the voice of the good shepherd, to the name by which ye are called, behold, ye are not the sheep of the good shepherd. And now if ye are not the sheep of the good shepherd, of what fold are ye? Behold, I say unto you, that the devil is your shepherd, and ye are of his fold; and now, who can deny this?" (Alma 5:37-39.) And many of their Messianic prophecies spoke of the Shepherd of Israel, and of the day when the Son of David, sitting on the throne of David, should be King over them, when "they all shall have one shepherd." (Ezek. 37:24.)

It is in this setting, then, among a people who understand the similitudes and figures from days of old, that Jesus now bears testimony of himself as the Shepherd of Israel. In what has come down to us as an allegory—John calls it a parable, and such it may have been in the fuller versions extant in his day—the Lord Jesus now says:

Verily, verily, I say unto you, He that entereth not by the door into the sheepfold, but climbeth up some other way, the same is a thief and a robber.

He is addressing himself to the priests and scribes, to the Pharisees and Rabbis in particular—to those who have made themselves guides and lights and teachers to the people. These ministers, these pastors, these shepherds, like their fathers, were those of whom Ezekiel said: "Ye eat the fat, and ye clothe you with the wool, ye kill them that are fed: but ye feed not the flock. The diseased have ye not strengthened, neither have ye healed that which was sick, neither have ye bound up that which was broken, neither have ye brought again that which was driven away, neither have ye sought that which was lost; but with force and with cruelty have ye ruled them." (Ezek. 34:3-4.)

These false ministers ruled over such of Israel as was then known, over congregations assembled in Palestine and other lands, upon whom, as thieves and robbers, they imposed the burdens of a dead law and forbade the sheep to find pasture in Christ and to drink of the waters of life that he brought. Of them Elder James E. Talmage says that they "sought by avoiding the portal and climbing over the fence to reach the folded flock; but these were robbers, trying to get at the sheep as prey; their selfish and malignant purpose was to kill and carry off. . . . Never has been written or spoken a stronger arraignment of false pastors, unauthorized teachers, self-seeking hirelings who teach for pelf and divine for dollars, deceivers who pose as shepherds yet avoid the door and climb over 'some other way,' prophets in the devil's employ, who to achieve their master's purpose, hesitate not to robe themselves in the garments of assumed sanctity, and appear in sheep's clothing, while inwardly they are ravening wolves." (Talmage, pp. 417-18.)

But he that entereth in by the door is the shepherd of

the sheep. To him the porter openeth; and the sheep hear his voice: and he calleth his own sheep by name, and leadeth them out.

Jesus himself—a true Minister, the Shepherd of the Sheep—comes openly, boldly, visibly to the door. To him the one—his Father—who has preserved Israel in one place for this very day opens the sheepfold. The Son preaches his gospel; those who are his sheep, who came from pre-existence with the special talent to recognize the truth, heed his voice, and he leads them out of the Rabbinical past into the revelation of the present.

And when he putteth forth his own sheep, he goeth before them, and the sheep follow him: for they know his voice. And a stranger will they not follow, but will flee from him: for they know not the voice of strangers.

Christ goeth before his sheep; he is the pattern. They follow him and seek to do what he has done, because they know his voice—the voice of testimony, the voice of true doctrine, the voice of righteousness, the voice of the Lord. True disciples will not follow the false shepherds of the world. Should they do so, they will be eaten by the wolves of wickedness and lose their souls.

It is not strange that the spiritually untuned ears of the Rabbinists failed to receive into their souls the deep and awesome portent of Jesus' divine words. Accordingly, by way of doctrine and of testimony, he continues:

Verily, verily, I say unto you, I am the door of the sheepfold. All that ever came before me who testified not of me are thieves and robbers; but the sheep did not hear them.

'I am the door by which men must enter to be saved. All the ministers of the past, of the present, and of the future, who do not testify of me and teach my gospel—including you priests, scribes, Pharisees, and Rabbis—are thieves and robbers; you are teachers in the employ of Satan and are seeking to steal the souls of men. But the true sheep will not follow you.'

I am the door: by me if any man enter in, he shall be saved, and shall go in and out, and find pasture.

'Salvation comes by me; it is not in the law of Moses, neither in the dead churches of Christendom, neither in the non-Christian religions. Come unto me; I am the Savior. Those in my sheepfold shall go forth to the pastures of salvation and drink the waters of eternal life.'

The thief cometh not, but for to steal, and to kill, and to destroy: I am come that they might have life, and that they might have it more abundantly.

We are hearing Ezekiel all over again. False ministers feed and clothe themselves. Let the sheep be slain; let them lose their souls; it matters not what happens to the flock so long as the purposes of priestcraft are served. "Woe be to the shepherds of Israel." But Jesus came to bring life. His atoning sacrifice will cause all to live again in immortality, and those who believe and obey shall have an abundant life. They shall be added upon. All that the Father hath shall be theirs, for they shall inherit eternal life which is the kind of life that God lives.

I am the good shepherd: the good shepherd giveth his life for the sheep.

What more can he say? How better can it be said? 'I am Jehovah, your Shepherd; because of me ye shall not want. I shall cause you to lie down in green pastures and shall lead you beside the still waters. I shall restore your souls and lead you in the paths of righteousness for my name's sake. Though you walk through the valley of the shadow of death, ye need fear no evil: for I will be with you; my rod and my staff shall comfort you. I shall prepare a table for you in the presence of your enemies; I shall anoint your head with oil; your cup runneth over. Surely goodness and mercy shall follow you all the days of your life; and you shall dwell in the house of the Lord forever in the eternities that are ahead—all because I am the Good Shepherd; I am the Lord

Jehovah, and I shall give my life for the sheep in the infinite and eternal atonement which is ahead.'

And the shepherd is not as a hireling, whose own the sheep are not, who seeth the wolf coming, and leaveth the sheep, and fleeth; and the wolf catcheth the sheep and scattereth them. For I am the good shepherd, and know my sheep, and am known of mine. But he who is a hireling fleeth, because he is a hireling, and careth not for the sheep. As the Father knoweth me, even so know I the Father.

'Now I shall tell you the difference between me and false ministers and teachers, between me and the scribes and Pharisees. I am the Shepherd, not a hireling. Those who practice priestcrafts—who preach for hire and divine for money, who seek the praise of the world—whose own the sheep are not, they forsake the sheep when trouble comes. But I am the Good Shepherd, the Lord Jehovah. The sheep are mine; I will care for them, even though it costs me my life. This is ordained by my Father, who is God, and who knoweth me, even as I know him.'

The Good Shepherd Has Power over Death
(John 10:15-21)

Jesus, as the Good Shepherd, came into the world to lay down his life for the sheep. He will save the sheep though he be slain; or, better, he will save the sheep because he is slain.

And I lay down my life for the sheep.

Then, before enlarging upon this theme—almost in a parenthetical pronouncement—he extends the Good Shepherd concept out beyond the borders of Palestine, beyond Egypt and Greece and Rome, beyond the Old World, to the utmost bounds of the everlasting hills, as Father Jacob described the place of the inheritance of the seed of his son Joseph. Jesus speaks thus of his Nephite sheep:

And other sheep I have, which are not of this fold: them also I must bring, and they shall hear my voice; and there shall be one fold, and one shepherd.

All Israel, all the promised seed, all the chosen race—all shall enter one sheepfold. All Israel, all of the seed of Abraham, all of the children of the prophets—all shall have one Shepherd. The flock of the Lord's pasture are men, the men of Israel. They shall hear his voice and see his face; theirs is the privilege, first and ahead of all others, to hear his voice. The time of the Gentiles is yet future. And so when the Risen Lord ministers among Nephite-Israel, he will say: "Ye are they of whom I said: Other sheep I have which are not of this fold; them also I must bring, and they shall hear my voice; and there shall be one fold, and one shepherd. And they understood me not, for they supposed it had been the Gentiles; for they understood not that the Gentiles should be converted through their preaching. And they understood me not that I said they shall hear my voice; and they understood me not that the Gentiles should not at any time hear my voice—that I should not manifest myself unto them save it were by the Holy Ghost. But behold, ye have both heard my voice, and seen me; and ye are my sheep, and ye are numbered among those whom the Father hath given me." (3 Ne. 15:21-24.)

Then the Lord told his Nephite sheep that he had yet "other sheep," the lost tribes of Israel, whom he would visit. (3 Ne. 16:1-5.) And finally, all who believe his gospel, Jew and Gentile alike, shall be gathered into his fold, "for there is one God and one Shepherd over all the earth." (1 Ne. 13:41.) But having digressed from his central theme, or, at least, having illustrated the magnitude and extent of his sheepfold, Jesus returns to the matter of his laying down his life for the sheep.

> *Therefore doth my Father love me, because I lay down my life, that I might take it again. No man taketh it from me, but I lay it down of myself. I have power to lay it down, and I have power to take it again. This commandment have I received of my Father.*

Thus Jesus proclaims the doctrine of the divine Sonship. From God who is his Father he inherited the power of immortality, the power to live forever. An immortal Being cannot die. No man can take his life from him. From Mary, who is his mother, he inherited the power of mortality, the power to separate body and spirit, the power to die. All mortal beings die; all lay down their lives in death. Jesus only of all mankind—Jesus, the Son of the living God; Jesus, the Son of the mortal Virgin—this One Man of all men had power to live or to die; and having chosen to die, he had power to live again in glorious immortality, never again to see death. All this is according to the commandment of the Father.

What possible response can his hearers—then or now—make to this divine doctrine? The response—then as now—can be but one of two things: belief or disbelief. There is no middle ground, no gray area, no room for compromise. Either he is the Atoning One or he is not. If he is not, the natural Jewish excuse for rejecting him, as it then came from those then present, is: "He hath a devil, and is mad; why hear ye him?" Of course he is mad, insane, totally devoid of reason or sense, unless these claims to divinity are true. Yet others who chose to believe did so on the basis of his words and his works. His words flowed forth with such a divine fluency and conviction that no Spirit-enlightened person could reject them. His works were those which none but one approved of God could perform. "These are not the words of him that hath a devil. Can a devil open the eyes of the blind?" And so, if one approved of God—as his works testify—says, in words, 'God is my Father,' how can his testimony be other than true?

Jesus Says: "I Am the Son of God"
(*John 10:22-42*)

"How long dost thou make us to doubt? If thou be the Christ, tell us plainly." So said the Jews to Jesus as he walked in the temple in Solomon's Porch at the Feast of Dedication.[1] It is December 20-27, A.D. 29; in just over three months, he will be lifted up upon the cross because he is the

217

Christ. Can it be that he has not as yet told the people plainly that he is their Messiah?

The fact is, for three years, of which we know, this man from Nazareth in Galilee has testified that he is the Christ, thousands upon thousands of times, always so couching his words as to avoid claiming the kind of political Messiahship of which so many of the Jews dreamed. He has said: 'I am the Christ; I am the Messiah; I am the Lord Jehovah; I am the Good Shepherd; God is my Father; in me and in me alone are the Messianic prophecies fulfilled.' During this same period he has accepted, freely and graciously, a like testimony from his disciples: 'Thou art he of whom Moses and the prophets spoke; thou art the Messiah; thou art the Christ, the Son of the living God. We worship thee.' And yet he has not let himself be hailed or crowned as the King-Messiah who would raise an army, throw off the Roman yoke, and lead a disconsolate people to national triumph and worldly renown.

The words of inquiry now spoken to him must have partaken of some of the nationalistic feeling that he should acclaim himself as an earthly king. His answer—that of one whose kingdom is not of this world—brings the matter of Messiahship back into the place and perspective where he intends it to be.

I told you, and ye believed not: the works that I do in my Father's name, they bear witness of me.

'I have told you over and over again, and you have not believed me. I have wrought wondrous miracles in my Father's name, which I could not do without his approval—an approval that includes the words I speak. My words and my works bear witness that I am the Christ.'

But ye believe not, because ye are not of my sheep, as I said unto you. My sheep hear my voice, and I know them, and they follow me.

'I am the Good Shepherd, the Lord Jehovah, who is the Shepherd of those who truly are of Israel. Ye are not my sheep; ye are not truly Abraham's seed. Ye are of your father, the devil, as I said unto you. My sheep hear my voice; they developed the talent for spirituality, the talent to recognize the truth, while yet in preexistence. It is easy for them to believe in me; and I know them; and they follow me, believe my gospel, join my church, and keep my commandments.'

And I give unto them eternal life; and they shall never perish, neither shall any man pluck them out of my hand.

My Father, which gave them me, is greater than all; and no man is able to pluck them out of my Father's hand.

I AND MY FATHER ARE ONE.

They asked to be told plainly that he was the Christ. He is answering their petition again, not in the language calling for a temporal Deliverer who will wield a worldly sword, but in language quoted from the registers of eternity. He, the Christ, will give his disciples eternal life; salvation is in him; and none can steal his sheep. The flocks of this world perish from hunger and cold and thirst. The Lord's sheep will never perish. The Father who gave the sheep to the Son and Shepherd has all power, and he, the Son, acts in the power of the Father. They are one.

Again there are two alternatives and two only. Either what he says is true or it is blasphemy. Either he is the Son of God, one with his Father, or he deserves to die for the most awesomely irreverent of all crimes. These Jews, who had been told many times that Jesus was the Christ but perhaps never so plainly and forcibly as on this occasion, and who always and ever rejected the divine witness, now took up stones again to stone him.

"Many good works have I shewed you from my Father," he says, "for which of those works do ye stone me?" 'Am I to die at your hands because I opened the eyes of a man born blind, or cleansed a leper, or fed thousands of hungry souls with a few barley loaves and a savory made of fish, or is it because I raised a widow's son from death?' The question is unanswerable. It is as though men would slay God because he created the earth, gave them life and being, and sends seedtime and harvest. Their answer: "For a good work we stone thee not: but for blasphemy; and because that thou, being a man, makest thyself God." Clearly they understood the meaning of the words Jesus had spoken. Now he says:

> *Is it not written in your law, I said, Ye are gods? If he called them gods, unto whom the word of God came, and the scripture cannot be broken; Say ye of him, whom the Father hath sanctified, and sent into the world, Thou blasphemest; because I said, I am the Son of God?*

'Do you not understand the plan of salvation that was revealed to your fathers? Do you not know that all of the children of the Father have power to advance and progress and become like him? Have you never read that those who received your law in olden times had the promise that they could attain godhood and be gods themselves? Why accuse me of blasphemy for testifying that I was sanctified and sent into the world by the Father? Does it offend you to hear me say that I am the Son of God? Do you not know that every righteous person to whom the word of God comes, and who then obeys the fullness of that law, shall become like the Father and be a god himself?'[2]

> *If I do not the works of my Father, believe me not. But if I do, though ye believe not me, believe the works: that ye may know, and believe, that the Father is in me, and I in him.*

'Ye say ye do not believe in me; very well, then believe in the works which I do, for ye cannot deny they have come by divine power; and if ye accept the works, then ye shall believe in me also, for I could not do the works alone; they came by the power of the Father. Then ye shall know and believe that the Father is in me and I in him; we are one; we have the same powers, perfections, and attributes.'

Then again they sought to take him, "but he escaped out of their hand." We suppose he overawed them with his presence, and that while they devised in their hearts some way to put him to death, he passed through the throng, out of the temple, and out of Judea, into Perea, to the place beyond Jordan "where John at first baptized." There he abode for a season, and "many resorted unto him" to be taught. "John did no miracle," they said, "but all things that John spake of this man were true."

"And many believed on him there."

NOTES

1. At this point we face, as we have on several previous occasions, a problem of chronology that cannot be resolved on the basis of the Gospel accounts as we now have them. Almost every scholar who pays for himself the full price of analytical and in-depth research comes up with a different conclusion. Our friend Farrar, for instance, at this point in his writings says: "Almost every inquirer seems to differ to a greater or less degree as to the exact sequence and chronology of the events which follow. Without entering into minute and tedious disquisitions where absolute certainty is impossible, I will narrate this period of our Lord's life in the order which, after repeated study of the gospels, appears to me to be the most probable, and in the separate details of which I have found myself again and again confirmed by the conclusions of other independent inquirers." (Farrar, p. 444.)

Other equally competent analysts find themselves at odds with Farrar and are able to call upon yet others to sustain their views. Contention in the field is needless; and in view of the present state of things, we are not inclined to feel harshly toward any sincere student, regardless of the conclusions he reaches. The issues are such that reasonable men can differ without in any way demeaning or questioning the grand design of the Grand Life. Our own President J. Reuben Clark, Jr., and our own Elder James E. Talmage, for instance, are in complete disagreement as to when various things happened on this and other occasions. It is only important for us to know there are problems in the field of chronology and to confess that we, as well as others of greater insight and capacity, can err on the points involved. And yet this is of no great import, for the over-all witness will be the same, and someday the true eventualities will be unraveled and set forth for all to know.

Regardless of the chronology conclusions reached, it is logical, for our purposes, to consider Jesus' statements about the Good Shepherd who gives his life for the sheep as though they were part of the same sermon given at the Feast of Dedication. Such may, in fact, have been the case; there are so many similar threads that it seems as though Jesus is weaving one grand tapestry by all that is recorded in John 10.

2. "Though 'there is none other God but one' for men on this earth to worship, yet 'there be gods many, and lords many' throughout the infinite expanse of eternity. (1 Cor. 8:4-7.) That is, there are many exalted, perfected, glorified personages who reign as gods over their own dominions. John saw 144,000 of them standing with Christ upon Mount Zion, all 'having his Father's name written in their foreheads' (Rev. 14:1), which is to say that they were gods and were so identified by wearing crowns so stating. Indeed, to each person who overcomes and gains exaltation, Christ has promised: 'I will write upon him the name of my God,' and he shall 'sit with me in my throne, even as I also overcame, and am set down with my Father in his throne.' (Rev. 3:12, 21.)

"Joseph Smith said: 'Every man who reigns in celestial glory is a god to his dominions.' (Teachings, p. 374.) All exalted persons 'are gods, even the sons of God.' (D&C 76:58.) Through obedience to the whole gospel law, including celestial marriage, they attain the 'fulness of the glory of the Father' (D&C 93:6-28) and 'a continuation of the seeds forever and ever. Then shall they be gods, because they have no end; therefore shall they be from everlasting to everlasting, because they continue; then shall they be above all, because all things are subject unto them. Then shall they be gods, because they have all power, and the angels are subject unto them.' (D&C 132:19-20.)

"But to us there is but one God, who is Elohim, and one Lord, who is the Lord Jehovah; the Holy Ghost acts as their minister; and these three are one Godhead, or as it is more graphically expressed, one God. Thus we find the Psalmist, whom Jesus quoted, saying: 'God standeth in the congregation of the mighty; he judgeth among the gods. . . . I have said, Ye are gods; and all of you are children of the most High.' (Ps. 82:1, 6.)" (*Commentary* 1:491.)

SECTION IX

THE PEREAN MINISTRY

THE PEREAN MINISTRY

But as it is written,
Eye hath not seen, nor ear heard,
neither have entered into the heart of man,
the things which God hath prepared for them that
love him.
But God hath revealed them unto us by his Spirit:
for the Spirit searcheth all things,
yea, the deep things of God.
(1 Cor. 2:9-10.)

Jesus speaks; his words are wondrous; salvation is his theme.

Jesus ministers; his deeds are divine; blind men see and dead men live.

Jesus journeys; Jerusalem is his bourn; a cross awaits him there.

"Lord, are there few only that be saved?" he is asked. We hear his answer.

We learn that little children have eternal life; that men must be willing to lay their all on the altar—their possessions and families, even their very lives—to gain salvation.

We are told plainly: To gain eternal life, we must keep the commandments.

We stand before a sealed tomb and see the greatest

miracle of his mortal ministry: Lazarus after four days of decomposing death steps forth in vibrant life.

And we hear from his own lips the soul-filling testimony: "I AM THE RESURRECTION, AND THE LIFE: HE THAT BELIEVETH IN ME, THOUGH HE WERE DEAD, YET SHALL HE LIVE."

We see ten lepers healed; rejoice with blind Bartimeus as he sees again; and are grateful that the man with dropsy and the woman with an eighteen-year infirmity are now well and whole.

We hear sermons—his discourse on the kingdom of God; his discourse on marriage and divorce; his pronouncement that the law and the prophets testify of him.

What is this we hear? Peter asks what reward shall the Twelve receive. Jesus places them on twelve thrones, judging the twelve tribes of Israel. James and John seek a place on his right hand and on his left in the eternal worlds, and are rebuked for their presumption.

And there are parables, not a few: the prodigal son, that sweet story of infinite mercy and tenderness; Lazarus and Dives, which sets forth the divisions in the spirit world; the laborers in the vineyard, all of whom are paid alike; the parable of the pounds, of the lost sheep, of the great supper, and many others.

As we hear and see and feel of the miracle that he is, there comes also the satanic voice, heard in the Sanhedrin, as that spiritually dead quorum plots his death.

Truly, the one perfect ministry of the one perfect man is proceeding on its foreordained course—to a cross and to a crown!

Chapter 77

SACRIFICE AND SALVATION

How can ye be saved,
except ye inherit the kingdom of heaven? . . .
Ye cannot be saved in your sins. . . .
Those who believe on his name . . .
these are they that shall have eternal life,
and salvation cometh to none else.
(Alma 11:37-40.)

More Sabbath Healings
(Luke 13:10-17; 14:1-6; JST, Luke 13:11, 14, 17)

As the day approaches for the final great conflict that will bring death to God's Son and doom to a once-chosen people, it seems as though Jesus is deliberately widening the gulf between him and them. Their sad perversion of true Sabbath worship creates an arena in which the conflict can be waged. On that holy day he openly chooses to defy their traditions and to place them in a position where they must choose between him as a Divine Healer sent of God and the burdensome traditions of Rabbinism.

Luke tells us of two such healings that took place on different Sabbaths in different cities in Perea. In one of these, while Jesus taught on the Sabbath in a synagogue, he healed a woman who had suffered for eighteen long years with a sickly, serious malady; in the other, while eating in the home of a leading Pharisee, he chose to heal a man afflicted with dropsy. Both healings comforted the afflicted, enraged the rebellious, and bore irrefutable witness of the divine power of the one who made his acts of healing of more import than all the inane Sabbatarianism that seemed so important to the Jews.

Jesus is teaching in a synagogue in Perea on the Sabbath. And we say again—though the repetition may seem monotonous—he is teaching the gospel. He is teaching the plan of salvation, the tender mercies of a loving Father, the Messianic mission of Israel's Deliverer, the salvation that God's Son is offering to the chosen people. Such is his message; he has none other.

There is present a devout and deserving woman—one of the regular worshippers in this synagogue—who for eighteen years has been bound by Satan with a malady having deep spiritual roots. Hers is both a moody and melancholic state and one in which her sickly and crooked frame is bound and crippled. She is unable to straighten up and use her muscles. Jesus sees her, calls her to him, and says: "Woman, thou art loosed from thine infirmity." As is his not uncommon practice, he lays his hands upon her, and, as is always the case when he speaks, she is healed. Jesus thus acts on his own initiative, without supplication, because he desires to bless mankind. And she glorifies God. After eighteen years of sorrow and suffering, bowed in grief and crippled in body, she arises whole, clean, mentally and spiritually renewed and refreshed. Jesus speaks and so it is.

Jesus is now interrupted. The ruler of the synagogue—a pitiful, petty scrub of a man—arises in his Satan-spawned wrath and pours out his venom, not directly upon Jesus, not directly upon the woman, but upon the people who were silent witnesses of the power of God. "There are six days in which men ought to work," he says; "in them therefore come and be healed, and not on the sabbath day."

What a scene we have just beheld! One of God's

daughters has been healed, and one of Satan's ministers has risen in wrath to condemn the Healer and warn his congregation against the sin of permitting such a thing to happen to them on the Sabbath. The healed woman broke forth into utterances of gratitude to God. "But her strain of thanksgiving was interrupted by the narrow and ignorant indignation of the ruler of the synagogue. Here, under his very eyes, and without any reference to the 'little brief authority' which gave him a sense of dignity on each recurring Sabbath, a woman—a member of *his* congregation—had actually had the presumption to be healed! Armed with his favorite 'texts,' and in all the fussiness of official hypocrisy, he gets up and rebukes the perfectly innocent multitude, telling them it was a gross instance of Sabbath-breaking for them to be healed on that sacred day, when they might just as well be healed on any of the other six days of the week. . . .

"Now, as the poor woman does not seem to have spoken one word of entreaty to Jesus, or even to have called His attention to her case, the utterly senseless address of this man could only by any possibility mean either, 'You *sick* people must not come to the synagogue at all on the Sabbath under present circumstances, for fear you should be led into Sabbath-breaking by having a miraculous cure performed upon you;' or 'If any one wants to heal you on a Sabbath, you must decline.' And these remarks he has neither the courage to address to Jesus Himself, nor the candour to address to the poor healed woman, but preaches *at* them both by rebuking the multitude, who had no concern in the action at all, beyond the fact that they had been passive spectators of it! The whole range of the Gospels does not supply any other instance of an interference so illogical, or a stupidity so hopeless." (Farrar, pp. 466-67.)

Jesus' response contains a stinging rebuke and an irrefutable argument. "Thou hypocrite," he acclaims, "doth not each one of you on the sabbath loose his ox or his ass from the stall, and lead him away to watering?" Such was their practice. No penalty attached to the labor of leading an animal, which had been without water for a few hours, to the place of watering. Animals must be cared for; their well-being was important. "And ought not this woman, being a daughter of Abraham"—surely, as such, she was as important as an ox or an ass—"whom Satan hath bound, lo, these eighteen years, be loosed from this bond on the sabbath day?"

It is no wonder that "when he had said these things, all his adversaries were ashamed; and all his disciples rejoiced for all the glorious things which were done by him." In this setting Jesus continued to teach and gave over again the parables of the mustard seed and of the leaven.

On yet another Sabbath, in yet another Perean city, we find Jesus in the house of "one of the chief Pharisees," perhaps one who is a member of the Great Sanhedrin itself. A great company is present, including many who are prominent and influential; it is a festal-Sabbath meal. There are also unbidden guests present, as custom allows; these are welcome to enter and observe, as did the woman who washed Jesus' feet with her tears and anointed them with ointment in the home of another Pharisee, but these observers are not among the banqueters themselves. One of these unofficial guests has dropsy. He and his condition are visible to all; the chief Pharisee, planning to taunt or test Jesus, may even have arranged for the prominent display of the afflicted man. In any event, all present watch Jesus to see what he will do, and he does not hesitate to use the occasion for his own purposes.

To the lawyers and Pharisees, he asks, "Is it lawful to heal on the sabbath day?" For an answer there is silence only, no spoken word. "They *would* not say, 'Yes;' but, on the other hand, they dared not say, 'No!' Had it been unlawful, it was their positive function and duty to say so then and there, and without any subterfuge to deprive the poor sufferer, so far as in them lay, of the miraculous mercy which was prepared for him. If they dared not say so—either for fear of the people, or for fear of instant refutation, or because the spell of Christ's awful ascendency was upon them, or out of a mere splenetic pride, or—to imagine better motives—because in their inmost hearts, if any spot remained in them uncrusted by idle and irreligious prejudices, they felt that it *was* lawful, and more than lawful, RIGHT—then, by their own judgment, they left Jesus free to heal without the possibility of censure. Their silence, therefore, was, even on their own showing, and on their own principles, His entire justification. His mere simple question, and their inability to answer it, was an absolute decision of the controversy in His favour. He therefore took the man, healed him, and let him go." (Farrar, pp. 470-71.)

"Which of you shall have an ass or an ox fallen into a pit," Jesus then asks, "and will not straightway pull him out on the sabbath day?" He has cited their own custom and practice; to care for their beasts was lawful and right on the Sabbath. This being established—and even they knowing that a man is more important than a beast—there is nothing more to be said. And so they said nothing.

Before leaving the arena where this Sabbath-warfare is being waged—an arena in which we see Jesus contend for the real meaning and purpose of the Lord's holy day, while the Pharisees seek rather to follow the base traditions of their fathers—before leaving this field of contest, we should note these instructive words of Farrar, which show why a whole people will submit to such a system of inanity, of scribal scrupulosity, and of Pharisaic perversion. "Again and again was our Lord thus obliged to redeem this great primeval institution of God's love from these narrow, formal, pernicious restrictions of an otiose and unintelligent tradition," he says. "But it is evident that He attached as much importance to the noble and loving freedom of the day of rest as they did to the stupefying inaction to which they had reduced the normal character of its observance.

231

Their absorbing attachment to it, the frenzy which filled them when He set at naught their Sabbatarian uncharities, rose from many circumstances."

It is these circumstances and this religious climate that illustrate why people will follow false and strict systems of religion to their doom. "They were wedded to the religious system which had long prevailed among them," our analyst says, "because it is easy to be a slave to the letter, and difficult to enter into the spirit; easy to obey a number of outward rules, difficult to enter intelligently and self-sacrificingly into the will of God; easy to entangle the soul in a network of petty observances, difficult to yield the obedience of an enlightened heart; easy to be haughtily exclusive, difficult to be humbly spiritual; easy to be an ascetic or a formalist, difficult to be pure, and loving, and wise, and free; easy to be a Pharisee, difficult to be a disciple; very easy to embrace a self-satisfying and sanctimonious system of rabbinical observances, very difficult to love God with all the heart, and all the might, and all the soul, and all the strength. In laying His axe at the root of their proud and ignorant Sabbatarianism, He was laying His axe at the root of all that 'miserable micrology' which they had been accustomed to take for their religious life." (Farrar, p. 469.)

Parable of the Wedding Guests
(Luke 14:7-11; JST, Luke 14:7, 9-10)

After the Sabbath-healing of the dropsical man, and while yet at the festal table of the chief Pharisee, Jesus gave two parables—the parable of the wedding guests and the parable of the great supper. Many persons of great eminence were then present—noted scribes, renowned scholars, respected Rabbis, prominent Pharisees, rich merchants. All had assembled to partake of the rich delicacies heaped high on the banquet board. As the setting for the parable of the wedding guests, there must have been some struggles for seating precedence among the ego-inflated guests. Their protocol placed prominent people in preferred positions. This raised the question of comparative prominence and of ruling on the problems raised by their own self-esteem and self-exaltation. And so, Luke says, Jesus "put forth a parable unto them concerning those who were bidden to a wedding; for he knew how they chose out the chief rooms, and exalted themselves one above another."

When thou art bidden of any man to a wedding, sit not down in the highest room; lest a more honourable man than thou be bidden of him; And he who bade thee, with him who is more honorable, come, and say to thee; Give this man place; and thou begin with shame to take the lowest room.

To their shame, some of their chief concerns centered around rank and precedence, which, if it did nothing more, attested to the essential hollowness of their Rabbinical religion.

But when thou art bidden, go and sit down in the lowest room; that when he who bade thee, cometh, he may say unto thee, Friend, go up higher; then shalt thou have honor of God, in the presence of them who sit at meat with thee.

Those who bridle their Pharisaic self-esteem and control their inflated self-satisfaction prepare themselves to receive honor from God. What matter the petty preferences of this probation as compared to the eternal honors that are his to confer?

For whosoever exalteth himself shall be abased; and he that humbleth himself shall be exalted.

Parable of the Great Supper
(Luke 14:12-24; JST, Luke 14:12)

As a setting for this parable we have an assemblage of renowned persons. They are the friends of "one of the chief Pharisees." Also, Jesus has just given the parable of the wedding guests. Now, "concerning him who bade to the wedding," and speaking to a host whose assembled guests are the noble and great among men, he says: "When thou makest a dinner, or a supper, call not thy friends [an Oriental idiom meaning call not *only* thy friends], nor thy brethren, neither thy kinsmen, nor rich neighbors; lest they also bid thee again, and a recompense be made thee. But when thou makest a feast, call the poor, the maimed, the lame, and the blind"—the man healed of dropsy might well have been asked to stay and partake of the banquet delicacies—"And thou shalt be blessed; for they cannot recompense thee: for thou shalt be recompensed at the resurrection of the just."

Clearly these words were a reproof and a rebuke to a self-exalted host who esteemed highly those of his own ilk, but who looked with disdain and ill-will toward those in a lower caste. Perhaps to break the tension thus created, one of the self-esteeming, self-ennobling, self-exalting persons among the banqueters—one of those who in his own self-righteous frame of mind could, religiously, do no wrong—said: "Blessed is he that shall eat bread in the kingdom of God." In this reply there was more than meets the eye. Having in mind the Jewish tradition that the resurrection of the just and the setting up of the kingdom of God would be ushered in by a great festival of which all the members of the kingdom would partake, it was as though the speaker had acclaimed: 'Yea, Lord, we know that men will be rewarded for their good deeds in the resurrection of the just; and since we as members of the chosen people will be there at that time to partake of the feast of God, surely we shall be fully rewarded.'

In this setting, then, the Master Parabolist gave the parable of the great supper. "A certain man made a great supper, and bade many," he said. 'The Lord of all prepared for his people a great feast of fat kine, of wine on the lees well refined, of corn and cakes and honey. He offered to feed them with food celestial; theirs would be the privilege of eating at his table and never hungering more, of drinking at his board and never again wanting for water. He made ready a great gospel banquet that they might feast on the rich delicacies of eternity.'

He then "sent his servant at supper time to say to them that were bidden, Come; for all things are now ready." 'He sent his Servant, the Suffering Servant of whom Isaiah spoke; he sent his Son, sent him to the chosen people. Come, the Servant would say; Come, feast upon the words of Christ. The banquet table is set; there is meat and drink here for the soul. After fifteen hundred years of Mosaic preparation all things are now ready. The fulness of the everlasting gospel is now yours for the taking.'

"And they all with one consent began to make excuse." The whole nation sought to excuse themselves from attendance. The banquet was not to their liking; the food was seasoned with a new salt, the salt of humility and lowliness of heart. The fatted calf, now roasted before them, smelled not of the smoke of Mosaic fires, but was prepared more delicately for those of more refined sensitivities. This was no feast for them; they preferred rather to fatten themselves on the traditions of the elders and the teachings of the Rabbis.

"The first said unto him, I have bought a piece of ground, and I must needs go and see it: I pray thee have me excused." 'I am lawfully and properly engaged in tilling the soil of the past. My heart rejoices in the worldly possessions I have acquired. Why should I forsake all and believe in this new religion?' "And another said, I have bought five yoke of oxen, and I go to prove them: I pray thee have me excused." 'I am engaged in business enterprises of my own. If I spend the time required in this new religion, my business will suffer.' "And another said, I have married a wife, and therefore I cannot come." 'Mine are the pleasures of this present world; let me rejoice in my wife. Am I expected to give up the pleasant things of this world simply because a new religion promises me greater joys in the life to come?'

"So that servant came, and shewed his lord these things. Then the master of the house being angry said to his servant,

Go out quickly into the streets and lanes of the city, and bring in hither the poor, and the maimed, and the halt, and the blind." 'Turn from the scribes and Pharisees, from the rich and the noble in Israel; turn from those who are self-ennobling and self-exalting. Go to the publicans and sinners in your streets; go to the poor, to those who are considered to be spiritually maimed and halt and blind. Go to the common people, to the man born blind who in Pharisaic eyes knew not anything.' And it was done.

And then—because the gospel is for all men, because all are alike unto God, whether Jew or Gentile, bond or free, black or white—"Go out into the highways and hedges, and compel them to come in, that my house may be filled." 'Go outside the Holy City; go beyond the chosen people; go out upon the highways of the world; go to the heathen and the pagan. They have never heard of the gospel; they must be taught and commanded and compelled. Bring them in that my house may be filled.' "For I say unto you, That none of those men which were bidden shall taste of my supper."

"The application to all present was obvious. The worldly heart—whether absorbed in the management of property, or the acquisition of riches, or the mere sensualisms of domestic comfort—was incompatible with any desire for the true banquet of the kingdom of heaven. The Gentile and the Pariah, the harlot and the publican, the labourer of the roadside and the beggar of the streets, these might be [nay, would be] there in greater multitudes than the Scribe with his boasted learning, and the Pharisee with his broad phylactery." (Farrar, p. 474.) But the application to the whole nation and the manifestation of the eternal purposes of him who prepared the table and who issued the invitations are even more important. The gospel supper was spread, first, before the Jews as a nation and as a people. When the delicacies remained untouched—nay, when they were spurned and ignored and left to be carried as garbage to Gehenna—then the Gentiles and the ends of the earth were invited to come, to drink of the waters of life, to eat of the manna from heaven, to gain all of the blessings of the gospel.

Will Many or Few Be Saved?
(Luke 13:22-33; JST, Luke 13:23-25, 27-34)

Jesus, somewhere in Perea, is journeying toward Jerusalem. It is a missionary journey "through the cities and villages." Everywhere, as his custom is, he is telling people what they must do to be saved; his gospel, which he everlastingly preaches, is a gospel of salvation. He is asked: "Lord, are there few only that be saved?"

Few or many in comparison to what? Few as compared to the general masses of worldly men, or many when the billions of millennial men—almost all of whom will be saved—are thrown into the scales? The total number of saved souls is of academic interest only; it is of no especial concern in the real world of applied truth. A far better question is: What must we do to be saved? And so Jesus answers not the question that was asked, but the question that should have been asked.

Strive to enter in at the strait gate; for I say unto you, Many shall seek to enter in, and shall not be able; for the Lord shall not always strive with man.

Men must seek salvation. They must labor and strive and struggle. The gate is both strait and straight. Even among those who seek to enter, many shall fail. The Lord wants people to be saved and he will strive with them—personally while he dwells among them, and by his Spirit, the Light of Christ, at all times. But his Spirit will not always strive with men. When they harden their hearts and sear their consciences, his Spirit ceases to plead, to enlighten, to guide. Men are then left unto themselves, to pursue the inevitable and unfailing course which dooms them to outer darkness. Now we hear Jesus say:

Therefore, when once the Lord of the kingdom is

*risen up, and hath shut the door of the kingdom, then
ye shall stand without, and knock at the door, saying,
Lord, Lord, open unto us. But the Lord shall answer
and say unto you, I will not receive you, for ye know
not from whence ye are.*

There comes a time when the judgment is set, when the
books are opened, when the eternal decrees are issued.
There is a day when the door to the kingdom closes with
eternal finality. Thereafter no new citizens are admitted to
the Celestial Presence.

*Then shall ye begin to say, We have eaten and drunk
in thy presence, and thou hast taught in our streets. But
he shall say, I tell you, ye know not from whence ye
are; depart from me, all ye workers of iniquity.*

The Lord Jesus who then walked among them is the
Eternal King. He it is from whom the workers of iniquity
shall hear their dread doom: Depart from me. He invites
men to repent here and now; if they do not do so, theirs is an
everlasting sorrow hereafter.

*There shall be weeping and gnashing of teeth among
you, when ye shall see Abraham, and Isaac, and Jacob,
and all the prophets, in the kingdom of God, and you
are thrust out.*

This is literal. Those who reject the testimony of the legal
administrators who are sent to preach to them; those who
fail to heed the witness of the elders of Israel who come
preaching the gospel of peace; those who reject the living
oracles of God in their day—those shall see, as it were, these
very rejected ones with crowns on their heads, reigning in
immortal glory, in the presence of the Great King. And O
what weeping and howling there will be among those in
whose streets these very witnesses once walked!

*And verily I say unto you, They shall come from the
east, and the west; and from the north, and the south,
and shall sit down in the kingdom of God.*

All the ends of the earth shall hear the message of salvation—Jew and Gentile alike—and the righteous among

them shall come out of Babylon into Zion, there to prepare themselves for celestial rest.

And, behold, there are last which shall be first, and there are first which shall be last, and shall be saved therein.

" 'There are those Gentiles in all nations to whom the gospel is offered *last* who shall be saved ahead of you Jews to whom the word of God came *first,* and there are those among you who *first* had opportunity to hear the truth, who shall be *last* as to honor, preference, and salvation hereafter.' (1 Ne. 13:42.)" (*Commentary* 1:497.)

As Jesus thus spoke—of the Jews who would be cast out for rejecting Him who had taught in their streets, and of the Gentiles who would come from the ends of the earth to sit down with Abraham, Isaac, and Jacob, and all the prophets, in the kingdom of God—at this point, "certain of the Pharisees" came and said: "Get thee out, and depart hence: for Herod will kill thee."

That Jesus believed this Pharisaic report, and also that it was a matter of complete indifference to him whether Antipas sought his life or not, is evident from his reply: "Go ye and tell Herod," he said, "Behold, I cast out devils, and do cures to-day and to-morrow, and the third day I shall be perfected." For the present and for the immediate future he would continue his ministry; the day of his death, resurrection, and eternal perfection was a few months away. He would, in due course, be slain, not in Perea but in Jerusalem. "I must walk to-day and to-morrow, and the third day; for it cannot be that a prophet perish out of Jerusalem," he said. And Luke added, "This he spake, signifying of his death."

Sacrifice Prepares Disciples for Salvation
(Luke 14:25-35; JST, Luke 14:25-26, 28-31, 35-38)

After giving the parable of the wedding guests and the parable of the great supper—both in the house of one of the chief Pharisees—Jesus "departed thence, and there went great multitudes with him." To these he taught the law of

239

sacrifice required of all disciples. Better for these throngs if they turned back now unless they were ready to pay the full price of discipleship. Better for them to remain with such light as they had in the dead law of the dead past, unless they were prepared to lay their all, including their very lives, upon the altar of sacrifice.

If any man come to me, and hate not his father, and mother, and wife, and children, and brethren, and sisters, or husband, yea and his own life also; or in other words, is afraid to lay down his life for my sake, cannot be my disciple.

"A true disciple, if called upon to do so, forsakes all—riches, home, friends, family, even his own life—in the Master's Cause." (*Commentary* 1:503.) "And whoso is not willing to lay down his life for my sake is not my disciple." (D&C 103:28.) Are they even to hate their family members? "Not hate in the sense of intense aversion or abhorrence; such is contrary to the whole spirit and tenor of the gospel. Men are to love their enemies, to say nothing of their own flesh and blood. Rather, the sense and meaning of Jesus' present instruction is that true disciples have a duty toward God which takes precedence over any family or personal obligation." (*Commentary* 1:503.)

And whosoever doth not bear his cross, and come after me, cannot be my disciple. Wherefore, settle this in your hearts, that ye will do the things which I shall teach, and command you.

Only those who make up their minds to do so—come what may come—have power to keep the commandments in times of trial and tribulation. To dramatize his teaching "that converts should count the cost *before* joining the Church; that they should come into the kingdom only if they are prepared to make the sacrifices required; that they should go the whole way in the gospel cause, or stay out entirely; that they 'not . . . follow him, unless' they are 'able to continue' in his word, to 'do the things' which he teaches and commands" (*Commentary* 1:504)—Jesus now gives two parables, the parable of the rash builder and the parable of the rash king.

For which of you intending to build a tower, sitteth not down first, and counteth the cost, whether he have money to finish his work? Lest, unhappily, after he has laid the foundation and is not able to finish his work, all who behold, begin to mock him, Saying, This man began to build, and was not able to finish.

"And this he said," Luke tells us, "signifying there should not any man follow him, unless he was able to continue."

Or what king, going to make war against another king, sitteth not down first, and consulteth whether he be able with ten thousand to meet him that cometh against him with twenty thousand? Or else, while the other is yet a great way off, he sendeth an ambassage, and desireth conditions of peace.

Then, by way of conclusion to the whole matter, Jesus said:

So likewise, whosoever he be of you that forsaketh not all that he hath, he cannot be my disciple.

All that he hath! Possessions, family, life itself—all things—must be forsaken, if to retain them means losing the gospel and eternal life.[1]

These teachings that men must forsake all and follow Christ raise again the issue of Moses and his law. They crystallize in the Jewish mind the essential contrariety of their whole system of worship and the new doctrine proclaimed by this man who is neither a priest, nor a Levite, nor a scribe, nor a Pharisee, nor even, as they suppose, a follower of Moses, the man of God. It is time, as his antagonists reason, to ask again the question that will remind the people, as they also suppose, that there is no need for this Nazarene because they already have Moses and the plan of salvation set forth in the law that he gave. Accordingly, "certain of them came to him, saying, Good Master, we have Moses and the prophets, and whosoever shall live by them, shall he not have life?"

Salvation is available through Moses and his law! What need is there for you and your teachings? We have the sayings of all the seers, the prophecies of all the prophets, the ordinances and sacrifices ordained by Jehovah; what more do we need? Our fathers were saved because of Moses and the prophets; surely we also shall gain eternal life in the same way. Such was their reasoning. To it Jesus could make but one reply.

Ye know not Moses, neither the prophets; for if ye had known them, ye would have believed on me; for to this intent they were written. For I am sent that ye might have life.

It is the age-old answer to the age-old heresy. Apostate peoples always look back to their fathers; always suppose they are treading where the saints have trod; always reject new prophets who seem to them to teach a new doctrine that differs from their traditions. And the answer always is: The old prophets foretold the coming of the new ones, and if men believed the ancient scriptures they would accept the new revelations that come in their day. And, in the case of Jesus, not only did Moses and all the prophets foretell his ministry and mission, but also, in his case he, and he alone, had come to make eternal life available for all men because he was the Son of God.

"Therefore I will liken it unto salt which is good," he continues; "But if the salt has lost its savor, wherewith shall it be seasoned? It is neither fit for the land, nor yet for the dung hill; men cast it out. He who hath ears to hear, let him hear." Luke adds: "These things he said, signifying that which was written, verily must all be fulfilled."

Thus we have Jesus saying in effect:

"1. 'Ye do err, for ye neither know nor understand the teachings of Moses or the prophets. If ye understood their teachings, ye would believe in me, for all their teachings

242

were given to prepare men for my coming and the salvation which I would bring.'

"2. 'Further, even assuming that ye believe Moses and the prophets, yet ye must turn to me, for "salvation doth not come by the law alone," for it is only in and through my atoning sacrifice that life and salvation come.'

"3. 'And now that I have come, the law of Moses has lost such saving power as it had; it has become as salt that has lost its savor and it cannot be seasoned again; yea, the law is dead in me, and from henceforth it is not fit for anything except to be cast out. He who hath ears to hear, let him hear.' " (*Commentary* 1:506.)

NOTE

1. Nowhere do we find a better statement of this, the law of sacrifice, than that set forth by the Prophet Joseph Smith in these words: "For a man to lay down his all, his character and reputation, his honor, and applause, his good name among men, his houses, his lands, his brothers and sisters, his wife and children, and even his own life also—counting all things but filth and dross for the excellency of the knowledge of Jesus Christ—requires more than mere belief or supposition that he is doing the will of God; but actual knowledge, realizing that, when these sufferings are ended, he will enter into eternal rest, and be a partaker of the glory of God. . . .

"A religion that does not require the sacrifice of all things never has power sufficient to produce the faith necessary [to lead] unto life and salvation; for, from the first existence of man, the faith necessary unto the enjoyment of life and salvation never could be obtained without the sacrifice of all earthly things. It was through this sacrifice, and this only, that God has ordained that men should enjoy eternal life; and it is through the medium of the sacrifice of all earthly things that men do actually know that they are doing the things that are well pleasing in the sight of God. When a man has offered in sacrifice all that he has for the truth's sake, not even withholding his life, and believing before God that he has been called to make this sacrifice because he seeks to do his will, he does know, most assuredly, that God does and will accept his sacrifice and offering, and that he has not, or will not seek his face in vain. Under these circumstances, then, he can obtain the faith necessary for him to lay hold on eternal life.

"It is vain for persons to fancy to themselves that they are heirs with those, or can be heirs with them, who have offered their all in sacrifice, and by this means obtained faith in God and favor with him so as to obtain eternal life, unless they, in like manner, offer unto him the same sacrifice, and through that offering obtain the knowledge that they are accepted of him. . . .

"From the days of righteous Abel to the present time, the knowledge that men have that they are accepted in the sight of God is obtained by offering sacrifice. . . .

"Those, then, who make the sacrifice, will have the testimony that their course is pleasing in the sight of God; and those who have this testimony will have faith to lay hold on eternal life; and will be enabled, through faith, to endure unto the end, and receive the crown that is laid up for them that love the appearing of our Lord Jesus Christ. But those who do not make the sacrifice cannot enjoy this faith, because men are dependent upon this sacrifice in order to obtain this faith: therefore, they cannot lay hold upon eternal life, because the revelations of God do not guarantee unto them the authority so to do, and without this guarantee faith could not exist." (*Lectures on Faith,* pp. 58-60.)

Chapter 78

THE LOST SHEEP, COIN, AND SON

Ye feed not the flock.
The diseased have ye not strengthened,
neither have ye healed that which was sick,
neither have ye bound up that which was broken,
neither have ye brought again
that which was driven away,
neither have ye sought that which was lost.
(Ezek. 34:3-4.)

Parable of the Lost Sheep
(Matthew 18:11-14; JST, Matthew 18:11; Luke 15:1-7;
JST, Luke 15:1, 4)

We have no doubt that Jesus gave all of the parables many times. It strains the bands of sense and reason to suppose that each of his wise sayings was spoken only once. He came to preach the gospel and to save sinners, and the same message saves all men in all situations. If there were Galileans near Capernaum who were entitled to hear the Sermon on the Mount, surely there were Judeans near Jerusalem to whom the same words should be spoken. The Gospel authors repeatedly mention that Jesus was teaching and healing, but only occasionally do they record what he said or describe the cures he performed.

As to the parable of the lost sheep, we know he gave it twice, once in Galilee in response to claims of preeminence by those who wanted to be first in the kingdom of God, and later in Perea in response to murmurings that he ate with publicans and sinners. On that occasion in Capernaum he placed a little child in the midst of the disciples and taught them that they must become as little children in order to enter into the kingdom of heaven. "For the Son of Man is come to save that which was lost, and to call sinners to repentance; but these little ones have no need of repentance, and I will save them," he said. Then, with reference to those who are accountable for their sins, he asked:

> How think ye? if a man have an hundred sheep, and one of them be gone astray, doth he not leave the ninety and nine, and goeth into the mountains, and seeketh that which is gone astray?

He is speaking as the Good Shepherd; he is making himself the pattern. He has come to save the "little ones" who otherwise would be lost. "The emphasis is on keeping the sheep from getting lost, on showing how precious the sheep are, and on how reluctant the Shepherd is to lose even one." (*Commentary* 1:508.) And as he, the Chief Shepherd, does, so also should we do who are his servant-shepherds.

> And if so be that he find it, verily I say unto you he rejoiceth more of that sheep, than of the ninety and nine which went not astray.

> Even so it is not the will of your Father which is in heaven, that one of these little ones should perish.

In Perea the setting and tone are different. Jesus is consorting with publicans and sinners—eating at their tables, teaching in their homes, offering to such despised and lowly ones the same truths he made available to the noble and the great. Such is contrary to Rabbinical standards; these social outcasts are to be shunned, not received as equals. "And the Pharisees and scribes murmured, saying, This man receiveth sinners, and eateth with them."

To these complaining, self-esteeming ones, Jesus asked

which of them would not search for his one lost sheep and, finding it, place it on his shoulders with rejoicing.[1]

And when he cometh home, he calleth together his friends and neighbours, saying unto them, Rejoice with me; for I have found my sheep which was lost.

I say unto you, that likewise joy shall be in heaven over one sinner that repenteth, more than over ninety and nine just persons, which need no repentance.

"This time the Master Teacher places the emphasis on finding that which is lost; he shows the length the Shepherd will go to find the sheep and the rejoicing that takes place when the lost is found. This time, in applying the parable, the complaining religious leaders, who considered themselves as just men needing no repentance, become the shepherds who should have been doing what the Chief Shepherd was doing—seeking to find and save that which was lost." (*Commentary* 1:508.)

Jesus is speaking to Jews—to scribes and Pharisees in particular—and they and their friends and neighbors all rejoice when a lost sheep is found. Such was the practice. But what about the saving of a lost soul? Are there any like feelings when such occurs? We cannot, of course, answer as to the feelings of rejoicing that may have been in the hearts of individual Jews when Gentiles were converted, but we can quote the Rabbinic word that has come down to us. It is: "There is joy before God when those who provoke Him perish from the world." (Edersheim 2:256.) What a contrast this is to the gospel view of joy in heaven when a sinner repents!

It is not unlikely that Jesus, in the Perean rendition of this parable, was contrasting their rejoicing over their sheep with their almost total indifference toward human souls, even as he had recently contrasted their concern for thirsty cattle with the physical well-being of diseased and crippled humans.

Parable of the Lost Coin
(*Luke 15:8-10*)

As a second illustration of the joy in the heavenly kingdom that results from the reclaiming of a lost member of the earthly kingdom, Jesus gave the parable of the lost coin:

> *Either what woman having ten pieces of silver, if she lose one piece, doth not light a candle, and sweep the house, and seek diligently till she find it? And when she hath found it, she calleth her friends and her neighbours together, saying, Rejoice with me; for I have found the piece which I had lost.*[2]

> *Likewise, I say unto you, there is joy in the presence of the angels of God over one sinner that repenteth.*

The lost sheep strayed from the fold by choice, seeking green pastures and still waters out in the deserts of the world. But the lost coin, a silver drachma, was lost through the inattention of the officers of the kingdom. The Lord's servants neglected their responsibility to care for the needs of the saints, and one of the saintly coins slipped to the floor and rolled into the dust in a dark corner where, except for diligent search, it would remain lost until swept out with the refuse.

"The woman who by lack of care lost the precious piece may be taken to represent the theocracy of the time, and the Church as an institution in any dispensational period; then the pieces of silver, every one a genuine coin of the realm, bearing the image of the great King, are the souls committed to the care of the Church; and the lost piece symbolizes the souls that are neglected and, for a time at least, lost sight of, by the authorized ministers of the gospel of Christ." (Talmage, p. 456.)

The angels rejoice! And why not? Are they not our brethren, children of the same Eternal Father? Who should have greater interest in the spiritual well-being of mortals than their immortal kin beyond the veil who are themselves also seeking that eternal life which consists in the perfecting of the eternal family unit?

Parable of the Prodigal Son
(Luke 15:11-32)

As a gem in a crown of gold, so is the parable of the prodigal son among the parables. Even Jesus' words are not all of equal splendor, and the Son of God in this parable climbs the mountain height. In wonder and reverence we view his terse eloquence.

A certain man had two sons: And the younger of them said to his father, Father, give me the portion of goods that falleth to me. And he divided unto them his living.

And not many days after the younger son gathered all together, and took his journey into a far country, and there wasted his substance with riotous living.

Each son received his portion; each was entitled, according to the Jewish law of inheritance, to a specified share of his father's possessions, though neither could claim it while the father lived. The eldest son received a double portion; the younger gained one-third of the movable property, which apparently is all that was bequeathed at this time. "The demand of the younger son for a portion of the patrimony, even during his father's lifetime, is an instance of deliberate and unfilial desertion; the duties of family cooperation had grown distasteful to him, and the wholesome discipline of the home had become irksome. He was determined to break away from all home ties, forgetful of what home had done for him and the debt of gratitude and duty by which he was morally bound. He went into a far country, and, as he thought, beyond the reach of his father's directing influence. He had his season of riotous living, of unrestrained indulgence and evil pleasure, through it all wasting his strength of body and mind, and squandering his father's substance; for what he had received had been given as a concession and not as the granting of any legal or just demand." (Talmage, p. 458.)

And when he had spent all, there arose a mighty famine in that land; and he began to be in want. And he went and joined himself to a citizen of that country; and he sent him into his fields to feed swine. And he would fain have filled his belly with the husks that the swine did eat: and no man gave unto him.

Divine Providence uses the forces of nature to humble the children of men and to lead them to repentance. Deity speaks to earth's inhabitants by "the voice of thunderings, and the voice of lightnings, and the voice of tempests, and the voice of the waves of the sea heaving themselves beyond their bounds." (D&C 88:90.) Here his voice is heard in "a mighty famine," which forces the hunger-driven younger son into the most degrading of all occupations—herding swine. Jews who kept swine were cursed, and the husks that these particular swine ate were totally unfit for human consumption. "The Jews detested swine so much, that they would only speak of a pig euphemistically as *dabhar acheer,* 'another thing.' The husks are the long bean-like pods of the carob-tree, or Egyptian fig. . . . They are stringy, sweetish, coarse, and utterly unfit for human sustenance. . . . The tree was called the 'locust-tree,' from the mistaken notion that its pods are the 'locusts' on which St. John fed." (Farrar, p. 328, footnote 1.)

And when he came to himself, he said, How many hired servants of my father's have bread enough and to spare, and I perish with hunger! I will arise and go to my father, and will say unto him, Father, I have sinned against heaven, and before thee, And am no more worthy to be called thy son: make me as one of thy hired servants.

"Where, in the entire range of human literature, sacred or profane, can anything be found so terse, so luminous, so full of infinite tenderness—so faithful in the picture which it furnishes of the consequences of sin, yet so merciful in the hope which it affords to amendment and penitence—as this little story? How does it summarise the consolations of religion and the sufferings of life! All sin and punishment, all penitence and forgiveness, find their best delineation in these few brief words. The radical differences of temperament and impulse which separate different classes of men— the spurious independence of a restless free-will—the preference of the enjoyments of the present to all hopes of the future—the wandering far away from that pure and peaceful region which is indeed our home, in order to let loose every lower passion in the riotous indulgence which dissipates the rarest gifts of life—the brief continuance of those fierce spasms of forbidden pleasure—the consuming hunger, the scorching thirst, the helpless slavery, the unutterable and uncompassionated degradation that must inevitably ensue—where have these myriad-times-repeated experiences of sin and sorrow been ever painted—though here painted in a few touches only—by a hand more tender and more true than in the picture of that foolish boy demanding prematurely the share which he claims of his father's goods; journeying into a far country, wasting his substance with riotous living; suffering from want in the mighty famine; forced to submit to the foul infamy of feeding swine, and fain to fill his belly with the swine-husks which no man gave? And then the coming to himself, the memory of his father's meanest servants who had enough and to spare, the return homewards, the agonised confession, the humble, contrite, heart-broken entreaty, and that never-to-be-equalled climax which, like the sweet voice from heaven, has touched so many million hearts to penitence and tears." (Farrar, pp. 327-28.)

And he arose, and came to his father. But when he was yet a great way off, his father saw him, and had compassion, and ran, and fell on his neck, and kissed him. And the son said unto him, Father, I have sinned against heaven, and in thy sight, and am no more worthy to be called thy son.[3]

The father, who yet loved his wayward son, was waiting, hoping, praying for his return. He has a fatted calf in the stall for a planned feast; now he sees the erring one a great way off, hastens to him, and greets him with tender compassion. The son confesses his sins—without which forgiveness cannot come—and because he has been so graciously received as a son, he does not make the contemplated offer to serve in a menial capacity as a hired servant. The two of them return to the home.

But the father said to his servants, Bring forth the best robe, and put it on him; and put a ring on his hand, and shoes on his feet: And bring hither the fatted calf, and kill it; and let us eat, and be merry: For this my son was dead, and is alive again; he was lost, and is found. And they began to be merry.

Back came the prodigal, into the household, as a member of the family; back he came to a position of honor and dignity, where his wants and needs would be cared for by the servants; back came the repentant son—not to inherit all that his father had, for such was reserved for the faithful son who had served during the heat of the day, but back he came from reveling with harlots, eating husks, and wallowing in a pigsty to his place with the family in the ancestral home. From his back the servants took the ragged, tattered, and coarse garb of the swineherd and replaced it with a choice *stola,* the upper garment of the higher classes. On his finger went the ring of a ruler, and his bare and mire-encrusted feet were cleansed and shod with sandals. Thus crowned with the three symbols of wealth and position—the robe, the ring, and the shoes—he joined in eating the fatted calf and making merry with the family. A lost sheep had returned to the sheepcote.

Now his elder son was in the field: and as he came and drew nigh to the house, he heard musick and dancing. And he called one of the servants, and asked what

*these things meant. And he said unto him, Thy brother
is come; and thy father hath killed the fatted calf, because he hath received him safe and sound.*

*And he was angry, and would not go in: therefore
came his father out, and intreated him. And he answering said to his father, Lo, these many years do I serve
thee, neither transgressed I at any time thy commandment: and yet thou never gavest me a kid, that I might
make merry with my friends: But as soon as this thy
son was come, which hath devoured thy living with
harlots, thou hast killed for him the fatted calf.*

"Never certainly in human language was so much—such
a world of love and wisdom and tenderness—compressed
into such few immortal words. Every line, every touch of the
picture is full of beautiful eternal significance. The poor
boy's presumptuous claim for all that life could give him—
the leaving of the old home—the journey to a far country—
the brief spasm of 'enjoyment' there—the mighty famine in
that land—the premature exhaustion of all that could make
life noble and endurable—the abysmal degradation and
unutterable misery that followed—the coming to himself,
and recollection of all that he had left behind—the return in
heart-broken penitence and deep humility—the father's far-
off sight of him, and the gush of compassion and tenderness
over this poor returning prodigal—the ringing joy of the
whole household over him who had been loved and lost, and
had now come home—the unjust jealousy and mean complaint of the elder brother—and then that close of the parable in a strain of music—"

*And he said unto him, Son, thou art ever with me,
and all that I have is thine. It was meet that we should
make merry, and be glad: for this thy brother was dead,
and is alive again; and was lost, and is found.*

"All this is indeed a divine epitome of the wandering of
man and the love of God such as no literature has ever
equalled, such as no ear of man has ever heard elsewhere.
Put in the one scale all that Confucius, or Sakaya Mouni, or

Zoroaster, or Socrates ever wrote or said—and they wrote and said many beautiful and holy words—and put in the other the Parable of the Prodigal Son alone, with all that this single parable connotes and means, and can any candid spirit doubt which scale would outweigh the other in eternal preciousness—in divine adaptation to the wants of man?" (Farrar, p. 483.)

"All that I have is thine!" The elder and younger sons no longer stand on a plane of equality. Though received back to honor and dignity, the erstwhile wayward one does not receive all that his father hath; though he wears the *stola,* has a ring on his finger, and is shod with sandals, he does not reign on the throne, nor exercise control, rulership, and dominion in the place and stead of the father. Such an inheritance is reserved for the one whose service and devotion merit that inestimably great inheritance.[4]

NOTES

1. "The Midrash relates how, when Moses fed the sheep of Jethro in the wilderness, and a kid had gone astray, he went after it, and found it drinking at a spring. As he thought it might be weary, he laid it on his shoulder and brought it back, when God said that, because he had shown pity on the sheep of a man, He would give Him his own sheep, Israel, to feed." (Edersheim 2:257-58.)

2. From the Midrash we learn, as "a Rabbi notes, that, if a man had lost a *Sela* (drachm) or anything else of value in his house, he would light ever so many lights till he had found what provides for only one hour in this world. How much more, then, should he search, as for hidden treasures, for the words of the Law, on which depends the life of this and of the world to come!" (Edersheim 2:258.)

3. "As marking the absolute contrast between the teaching of Christ and of Rabbinism, . . . we have in one of the oldest Rabbinic works a Parable exactly the reverse of this, when the son of a friend is redeemed from bondage, not as a son, but to be a slave, that so obedience might be demanded of him. The inference drawn is, that the obedience of the redeemed is not that of filial love of the pardoned, but the enforcement of the claim of a master. How otherwise in the Parable and teaching of Christ!" (Edersheim 2:262.)

4. Speaking of those who magnify their callings in the Holy Priesthood and who are thereby true and faithful in all things, fulfilling all the terms and conditions of their priesthood covenant, the Lord promises: "All that my Father hath shall be given unto" them. (D&C 84:33-40.) All that the Father hath is eternal life or exaltation; it is to inherit, receive, and possess that which the Father now has and to be like him. Such was the promise to the elder son in this parable of parables.

Chapter 79

THE TWO PECULIAR PARABLES

Give ear, O my people, to my law:
incline your ears to the words of my mouth.
I will open my mouth in a parable:
I will utter dark sayings. (Ps. 78:1-2.)

Parable of the Unjust Steward
(Luke 16:1-13)

This parable and that of Lazarus and the rich man are difficult to understand, sow seeds of confusion and uncertainty among sectarian scripturalists, and in fact can only be understood by the saints as they are enlightened by the power of the Holy Spirit. In them Jesus opens his mouth to "utter dark sayings," as far as the scriptural exegetes of the world are concerned. But both of them, when received and understood for what they are, shed wondrous light on glorious gospel verities.

The parable of the unjust steward was spoken to the disciples, to members of the Church—to the publicans and sinners who now followed Jesus, to the extreme annoyance and displeasure of the Pharisees—and was intended not to countenance their prior evil deeds, but to show what they could learn from their previous life of sin.

There was a certain rich man, which had a steward;

and the same was accused unto him that he had wasted his goods. And he called him, and said unto him,

How is it that I hear this of thee? give an account of thy stewardship; for thou mayest be no longer steward.

As Eliezer of Damascus ruled over all that Abraham possessed, so was this steward the overseer of all his master's property. But unlike Eliezer, to whom Abraham entrusted the high duty of getting Rebekah as a wife for Isaac, our unnamed steward was untrue to his trust. He squandered his master's money and wasted his goods, perhaps in riotous living. Summoned before his employer, he made no defense, was discharged, and was given time to get his accounts in order for his successor.

Then the steward said within himself, What shall I do? for my lord taketh away from me the stewardship: I cannot dig; to beg I am ashamed. I am resolved what to do, that, when I am put out of the stewardship, they may receive me into their houses.

So he called every one of his lord's debtors unto him, and said unto the first, How much owest thou unto my lord? And he said, An hundred measures of oil. And he said unto him, Take thy bill, and sit down quickly, and write fifty. Then said he to another, And how much owest thou? And he said, An hundred measures of wheat. And he said unto him, Take thy bill, and write fourscore.

And the lord commended the unjust steward, because he had done wisely: for the children of this world are in their generation wiser than the children of light.

Here we see an unjust servant, an unrighteous steward— an evil Eliezer—violating every standard of honesty and integrity. His acts are within the letter of the law, for his power of attorney is still in force, and he can still buy and sell and contract at will. But he defrauds his employer and enriches the debtors, who he is confident will feel an obligation to favor him in future business arrangements. For such conduct we would anticipate, at the least, a severe rebuke, and, more likely, an attempt at legal prosecution. Instead we hear praise for his wise and prudent acts, with which conclusion Jesus concurs as he gives this moral: "For the children of this world are in their generation wiser than the children of light."

Having spiritual insight, the disciples to whom the dissertation has come could not have failed to see in this parable an endorsement, not of dishonesty and perfidy, but of worldly sagacity and wisdom in caring for one's own interests. To claim it, as some have done, as a parable that commends and sanctions cheating simply shows how far afield uninspired commentators can go. But now we hear how Jesus himself interpreted and applied the account.

And I say unto you, Make to yourself friends of the mammon of unrighteousness; that, when ye fail, they may receive you into everlasting habitations.

"Our Lord's purpose was to show the contrast between the care, thoughtfulness, and devotion of men engaged in the money-making affairs of earth, and the half-hearted ways of many who are professedly striving after spiritual riches. Worldly-minded men do not neglect provision for their future years, and often are sinfully eager to amass plenty; while the 'children of light,' or those who believe spiritual wealth to be above all earthly possessions, are less energetic, prudent, or wise. By 'mammon of unrighteousness' we may understand material wealth or worldly things. . . .

"If the wicked steward, when cast out from his master's house because of unworthiness, might hope to be received into the homes of those whom he had favored, how much more confidently may they who are genuinely devoted to the right hope to be received into the everlasting mansions of God!"

He that is faithful in that which is least is faithful also in much: and he that is unjust in the least is unjust also in much. If therefore ye have not been faithful in the unrighteous mammon, who will commit to your trust the true riches? And if ye have not been faithful in that which is another man's, who shall give you that which is your own?

No servant can serve two masters: for either he will hate the one, and love the other; or else he will hold to the one, and despise the other. Ye cannot serve God and mammon.

"Make such use of your wealth as shall insure you friends hereafter. Be diligent; for the day in which you can use earthly riches will soon pass. Take a lesson from even the dishonest and the evil; if they are so prudent as to provide for the only future they think of, how much more should you, who believe in an eternal future, provide therefor! If you have not learned wisdom and prudence in the use of 'unrighteous mammon,' how can you be trusted with the more enduring riches? If you have not learned how to use properly the wealth of another, which has been committed to you as a steward, how can you expect to be successful in the handling of great wealth should such be given you as your own? Emulate the unjust steward and the lovers of mammon, not in their dishonesty, cupidity, and miserly hoarding of the wealth that is at best but transitory, but in their zeal, forethought, and provision for the future. Moreover, let not wealth become your master; keep it to its place as a servant." (Talmage, pp. 463-64.)

The Law and the Prophets Testify of Christ
(Luke 16:14-18; JST, Luke 16:16-18, 20-23)

Never in all history was there a people unto whom God sent his word, by the mouths of his servants the prophets, who were left so completely without excuse for their disbelief as were these Jews. They had the law and the prophets; the scriptures lay open before them; the mind and will of the Lord was recorded for all to read. And the man of whom the ancient records taught stood among them, spake

257

as never man spake, performed miracles as none other had ever done, and lived and was as only God's Son could live and be. And yet their sins led them to reject him.

He has just taught his disciples, among whom are repentant publicans—and sinners—a group detested by the Pharisees—that to gain a heavenly reward they must use their earthly wealth in accordance with gospel standards. If men cannot be faithful in handling the unrighteous mammon—the things of this world—why should they think their heavenly Father will place in their hands the true riches of eternity?

Mingling with the disciples, and also hearing the parable of the unjust steward, were pious Pharisees who loved money and had their hearts set on the mammon of unrighteousness. They were covetous, grasping, avaricious. To cheat in business was a way of life with them.[1] And their reaction to Jesus' instruction on the proper use of wealth was to scoff and sneer and deride. In response Jesus said: "Ye are they which justify yourselves before men; for that which is highly esteemed among men is abomination in the sight of God."

These words, coming with a voice of authority, from one having authority, stand as a divine rejection of them and their way of life. Either they must be refuted or these Pharisees stand condemned before their race; and the sole means of overthrowing a divinely inspired prophetic utterance is to attack the prophet. If the word came from God, it is true; if the prophet can be rejected, his words fall with him. And so, "they said unto him, We have the law, and the prophets; but as for this man we will not receive him to be our ruler; for he maketh himself to be a judge over us."

How often they have taken this approach: 'What need have we for Jesus and his new doctrine? His gospel is a needless appendage to our system of religion; we already have the plan of salvation as given by Moses and all the prophets. As for this man Jesus, he and his doctrine are nothing to us.'

To such rebellious feelings, testimony mingled with doctrine is the only perfect answer. Thus Jesus says:

The law and the prophets testify of me; yea, and all the prophets who have written, even until John, have foretold of these days. Since that time, the kingdom of God is preached, and every man who seeketh truth presseth into it.

By definition and in its very nature, a prophet is one to whom the Holy Ghost reveals that Jesus Christ is the Son of God. The testimony of Jesus is the spirit of prophecy. Every prophet from Adam to John foretold the coming of him who then preached in their streets and ate at their tables. Had they not done so, they would not have been prophets. But now the new kingdom is being proclaimed, and every man who seeketh truth, who desires righteousness, who yearns for salvation—all such come and join the Church.

And why teach ye the law, and deny that which is written; and condemn him whom the Father hath sent to fulfill the law, that you might all be redeemed?

O fools! for you have said in your hearts, There is no God. And you pervert the right way; and the kingdom of heaven suffereth violence of you; and you persecute the meek; and in your violence you seek to destroy the kingdom; and ye take the children of the kingdom by force. Woe unto you, ye adulterers!

To all this—their condemning of the One who came to fulfill the law; the announcement that he had come to redeem them; the assertion that in their hearts they did not even believe in God; the charges of perverting the truth, of persecuting the Church, of using violence against the kingdom, of physically assaulting his disciples—to all this they gave no heed. Passing over their whole Satan-guided rejection of him, his laws, and his new kingdom—let these things be as they were—they came to the one thing that gave them supreme offense. He said they were adulterers. All else for which they were arraigned was openly known and could not be denied. Their immoral acts, however, were done in secret; and because Jesus lifted this veil and charged them openly with sex immorality, they reviled him. His response was to single out certain acts of adultery that were public knowledge, and that we shall consider later in connection with his teachings on marriage and divorce. He said:

> Whosoever putteth away his wife, and marrieth another, committeth adultery; and whosoever marrieth her who is put away from her husband, committeth adultery.

Such, then, were the words and feelings that called forth the parable of Lazarus and the rich man.

Parable of Lazarus and the Rich Man
(Luke 16:19-31; JST, Luke 16:23-24)

Jesus is facing his Pharisaic foes. Because of their love of money, their obdurate refusal to accept him, and their vicious persecution of his disciples, he is speaking sharp and stinging words. He calls them fools and adulterers. Then to climax his acrid and harsh sayings against these imperious self-exaltants who worship the mammon of unrighteousness, he says:

> Verily I say unto you, I will liken you unto the rich man. For there was a certain rich man, who was clothed in purple, and fine linen, and fared sumptuously every day.
>
> And there was a certain beggar named Lazarus, which was laid at his gate, full of sores, And desiring to be fed with the crumbs which fell from the rich man's table: moreover the dogs came and licked his sores.

Two more extreme opposites could scarcely have been chosen. A rich Pharisee, not so much as dignified by name, revels in wealth and luxury. His linen apparel and his upper garment, dyed a royal and costly violet-purple, are his constant dress. He banquets daily on all the delicacies money can buy. He is rich, powerful, and selfish, using his wealth to gratify his love of luxury. There is here none of that wise use of the mammon of unrighteousness which will prepare his soul for an everlasting inheritance.

On the other hand we see a poor, diseased beggar—one Lazarus by name, a name that means "God help him," and from which we derive the word *lazar*, meaning leper. He is laid at the gate of the opulent Pharisee, to beg, to plead, to cry out—along with the whining dogs—for crumbs that fall from the banquet board. Dressed in rags, burdened with disease, famished for want of food, he is seen by the lordly Pharisee, who worships before the great altar and makes broad his phylactery, but who has no dried crust of barley bread for his suffering fellow mortal. He is too immersed in the weighty things of wealth and in the intricacies of Mosaic performances to concern himself with a diseased and starving son of Abraham. And the dogs lick Lazarus's sores, which neither alleviates the pain nor softens the suffering; the uninvited canines merely aggravate the ache.

Such, then, is the temporal and physical state of Lazarus, who, however, from what follows, we know to have been a morally upright and righteous person. And such also is the earthly state of the rich man, whom we have come to call Dives, such being the Latin designation for his state of riches. But one's earthly state, be he Lazarus or Dives, is transitory; and so Jesus continues:

> And it came to pass, that the beggar died, and was carried by the angels into Abraham's bosom: the rich man also died, and was buried; And in hell he lift up his eyes, being in torments, and seeth Abraham afar off, and Lazarus in his bosom.[2]

Then death came—as come it must to all—first to Lazarus, hastened by hunger and assured by disease; then to Dives, who lived out his days of wealth and worship and high self-esteem. But how different were their deaths. For Dives there was earthly pomp and ceremony, an embalmed corpse, a costly funeral with paid mourners, a carved tomb in a choice cave where marble statuary was placed. Lazarus, his body uncared for, unwrapped, without ointment or spices or embalming service, was hauled on a wooden cart to a pauper's grave in a potter's field.

So much for their mortal remains. As to their immortal spirits things were quite different. One went to paradise, the other to hell. Lazarus was carried by the angels to Abraham's bosom, there to mingle with prophets and patriarchs; there to find rest and peace from all care and sorrow; there to enjoy the companionship of the righteous of all past ages until the day of resurrection. Dives descended to hell, to Hades, to Sheol, to the spirit prison, to outer darkness, to a place of weeping and wailing and gnashing of teeth, a place where sinners sorrow and howl because of the torments that have come upon them. Nor can we refrain from reciting that revelation in which the Lord says: "If any man shall take of the abundance which I have made, and impart not his portion, according to the law of my gospel, unto the poor and the needy, he shall, with the wicked, lift up his eyes in hell, being in torment." (D&C 104:18.) Then Dives speaks:

And he cried and said, Father Abraham, have mercy on me, and send Lazarus, that he may dip the tip of his finger in water, and cool my tongue; for I am tormented in this flame.

But Abraham said, Son, remember that thou in thy lifetime receivedst thy good things, and likewise Lazarus evil things: but now he is comforted, and thou art tormented.

And beside all this, between us and you there is a great gulf fixed: so that they which would pass from hence to you cannot; neither can they pass to us, that would come from thence.

How things have changed. The beggar on earth—whose body was pained with sores, whose belly cried out for food—now, well and whole, clothed in robes of righteousness, feasts on eternal bread in paradisiacal palaces. The rich man on earth—who rejoiced in the multitude of things that his soul possessed—now begs for a drop of water to cool the flame of tormented conscience that burns unchecked in his miserably small soul. Lazarus's mask of pain and poverty has been stripped away to reveal a healthy soul prepared to receive and manage the riches of eternity, while Dives's removed mask reveals the shriveled soul of a moral weakling who, now stripped of wealth and influence, suffers eternal pain in an eternal hell.[3]

And as they knew each other in mortality, so they remember their former acquaintanceship. But no longer are they accessible to each other so that one might minister to the needs of the other. Christ has not yet bridged the gulf between the prison and the palace, and there is as yet no communion between the righteous in paradise and the wicked in hell.

Then he said, I pray thee therefore, father, that thou wouldest send him to my father's house: For I have five brethren; that he may testify unto them, lest they also come into this place of torment.

Abraham saith unto him, They have Moses and the prophets; let them hear them. And he said, Nay, father Abraham: but if one went unto them from the dead, they will repent.

And he said unto him, If they hear not Moses and the prophets, neither will they be persuaded, though one rose from the dead.

To pass from this life to the next, to die, as we are wont to say, simply means that the eternal spirit—wherein the mind of man is found, and which is the believing, knowing, sentient, intelligent part of the human personality—steps out of the mortal body and continues to live in another sphere. Beliefs do not change; prejudices remain; faith or its absence is still the order of the day. Those who believe the truth in this life believe it in the next; those who reject God's eternal laws here reflect that same rebellion hereafter. There may and will be repentance and changes in process of time, but there is no immediate change. Dives's five brethren—were they the five sons of Annas, the high priest, as some have speculated?—knew Jesus had raised the dead, and they did not believe in him. Why would they be converted if a ghostly apparition—which could be rationalized away as a misty nothingness—should appear to them? Faith does not come in that way. Only those who accept Moses and the prophets would have the spiritual insight to recognize what was involved should one rise from the dead. There is indeed a certain eternal finality connected with death. It is this day of life that is given to men to prepare for eternity, and the day of death is one of rejoicing for all the Lazaruses of life and a day of sorrow for all the Diveses of death.

Parable of the Unprofitable Servant
(Luke 17:1-10; JST, Luke 17:5-6, 9-10)

Jesus now has somewhat to say to his disciples about those who bring offenses, saying that it were better for them if a millstone were hanged about their necks and they drowned in the sea than that they should offend one of his little ones. This is a repetition of similar expressions made earlier in Capernaum that we have considered in chapter 66. He also repeats some counsel about rebuking and forgiving our erring brethren—"And if he trespass against thee seven times in a day, and seven times in a day turn again to thee, saying, I repent; thou shalt forgive him"—all of which we also considered in the Capernaum setting in chapter 67. Now the apostles say unto him: "Increase our faith." Only a brief sentence of what must have been an extended exposition is preserved for us by Luke, and then Jesus gives the parable of the unprofitable servant. As to faith he says:

If you had faith as a grain of mustard seed, you might say unto this sycamore tree, Be thou plucked up by the roots, and be thou planted in the sea; and it should obey you.

We cannot doubt that Jesus on this and many occasions discoursed to the apostles, to all of his disciples, and to Jew

264

and Gentile alike, that faith was the first principle of the gospel and that it came by obedience to those laws upon which its receipt is predicated.

Faith, the moving cause of all action in intelligent beings; faith, the hope in that which is not seen which is true; faith, the assurance of things hoped for, the evidence of things not seen; faith, the mighty, moving power by which the worlds were made and by which all things are upheld and sustained in their ordained spheres; faith, the power by which miracles are wrought, by which God's work goes forth, by which the gospel is preached and souls are saved; faith, the very power of the Lord Almighty himself—faith is power.

Faith is borne of knowledge and matures through righteousness. To gain faith unto life and salvation, men must first adopt the concept that God actually exists; they must have a correct idea of his character, perfections, and attributes; and they must obtain an actual knowledge that the course of life they are pursuing is according to his omnipotent will. These and many like things we know about faith; would that we knew all that Jesus said to the apostles on this occasion, for who can know too much about faith and righteousness? But now for the parable:

> But which of you, having a servant plowing or feeding cattle, will say unto him by and by, when he is come from the field, Go and sit down to meat? And will not rather say unto him, Make ready wherewith I may sup, and gird thyself, and serve me, till I have eaten and drunken; and afterwards thou shalt eat and drink?

> Doth he thank that servant because he doeth the things which were commanded him? I say unto you, Nay. So likewise ye, when ye shall have done all those things which are commanded you, say, We are unprofitable servants. We have done that which was no more than our duty to do.

Jesus thus teaches that his saints grow in faith by obedience and service in the kingdom; also, "that Deity has a claim upon the services of his saints, and that even though they serve him with all their hearts, mights, mind, and strength, yet they are unprofitable servants." (*Commentary* 1:527.) As to faith growing in the hearts of men, first the seed sprouts; then, as it is cared for, the plant grows and the fruit ripens; and finally the faithful saints pluck and eat the fruit of eternal life. As to faithful service that yet leaves the servant as unprofitable, how can it be expressed better than King Benjamin did it: "If ye should serve him who has created you from the beginning, and is preserving you from day to day, by lending you breath, that ye may live and move and do according to your own will, and even supporting you from one moment to another—I say, if ye should serve him with all your whole souls yet ye would be unprofitable servants. And behold, all that he requires of you is to keep his commandments; and he has promised you that if ye would keep his commandments ye should prosper in the land; and he never doth vary from that which he hath said; therefore, if ye do keep his commandments he doth bless you and prosper you. And now, in the first place, he hath created you, and granted unto you your lives, for which ye are indebted unto him. And secondly, he doth require that ye should do as he hath commanded you; for which if ye do, he doth immediately bless you; and therefore he hath paid you. And ye are still indebted unto him, and are, and will be, forever and ever; therefore, of what have ye to boast?" (Mosiah 2:21-24.)

NOTES

1. In an instructive footnote dealing with Pharisaic covetousness, Farrar says: "The vice of avarice seems inherent in the Jewish race. To this day, says Dr. Thomson, speaking of the Jews in Palestine, 'Everybody trades, speculates, cheats. The shepherd-boy on the mountain talks of *piastres* from morning till night; so does the muleteer on the road, the farmer in the field, the artisan in the shop, the merchant in his magazine, the pacha in his palace, the kadi in the hall of judgment, the mullah in the mosque, the monk, the priest, the bishop—money, money, money! the desire of every heart, the theme of every tongue, the end of every aim. Everything is bought and sold—each prayer has its price, each sin its tariff.' Quarrels about the money, complaints of the greed and embezzlement of the Rabbis, wrong distribution of the *chaluka*, or alms, and the *kadima*, or honorary pay, form the main history of the Jews in modern Jerusalem. It is a profoundly melancholy tale, and no

one who knows the facts will deny it—least of all pious and worthy Jews." (Farrar, p. 475, footnote 1.)

2. "Now, concerning the state of the soul between death and the resurrection—Behold, it has been made known unto me by an angel, that the spirits of all men, as soon as they are departed from this mortal body, yea, the spirits of all men, whether they be good or evil, are taken home to that God who gave them life. And then shall it come to pass, that the spirits of those who are righteous are received into a state of happiness, which is called paradise, a state of rest, a state of peace, where they shall rest from all their troubles and from all care, and sorrow. And then shall it come to pass, that the spirits of the wicked, yea, who are evil—for behold, they have no part nor portion of the Spirit of the Lord; for behold, they chose evil works rather than good; therefore the spirit of the devil did enter into them, and take possession of their house—and these shall be cast out into outer darkness; there shall be weeping, and wailing, and gnashing of teeth, and this because of their own iniquity, being led captive by the will of the devil. Now this is the state of the souls of the wicked, yea, in darkness, and a state of awful, fearful looking for the fiery indignation of the wrath of God upon them; thus they remain in this state, as well as the righteous in paradise, until the time of their resurrection." (Alma 40:11-14.)

3. In this connection, these words of *Chrysostom* are worthy of preservation: "For as on the stage some enter, assuming the masks of kings and captains, physicians and orators, philosophers and soldiers, being in truth nothing of the kind; so also in the present life, wealth and poverty are only masks. As then, when thou sittest in the theatre, and beholdest one playing below who sustains the part of a king, thou dost not count him happy, nor esteemest him a king, nor desirest to be such as he; but knowing him to be one of the common people, a ropemaker or a blacksmith, or some such a one as this, thou dost not esteem him happy for his mask, and his robe's sake, nor judgest of his condition from these, but holdest him cheap for the meanness of his true condition: so also, here sitting in the world as in a theatre, and beholding men playing as on a stage, when thou seest many rich, count them not to be truly rich, but to be wearing the masks of rich. For as he, who in the stage plays the king or captain, is often a slave, or one who sells figs or grapes in the market, so also this rich man is often in reality poorest of all. For if thou strip him of his mask, and unfold his conscience, and scrutinize his inward parts, thou wilt there find a great penury of virtue; thou wilt find him to be indeed the most abject of men. And as in the theatre, when evening is come and the spectators are departed, and the players are gone forth thence, having laid aside their masks and their dresses, then they who before showed as kings and captains to all, appear now as they truly are; so now, when death approaches and the audience is dismissed, all, laying aside the masks of wealth and poverty, depart from hence, and, being judged only by their works, appear some indeed truly rich, but some poor; and some glorious, but others without honor."

Chapter 80

THE RAISING
OF LAZARUS

For behold, this is my work and my glory—
to bring to pass the immortality
and eternal life of man.
(Moses 1:39.)

The Message That Lazarus Is Sick
(*John 11:1-6; JST, John 11:1-2, 6, 16*)

Who shall say what was the greatest miracle performed
by the Man of Miracles during the years of his ministry?
Clearly the most wondrous event of the ages was to bring to
pass the immortality and eternal life of man. This he alone
could do because God was his Father; and this he did do—
commencing in Gethsemane when he sweat great drops of
blood from every pore; continuing on the cross when he
voluntarily gave up his life; and crowned in the
Arimathean's tomb when his spirit entered again that body
which never would see corruption.

What greater miracle did he perform than to come forth
from the tomb; than to rise in glorious immortality; than to
unite his body and spirit inseparably in the resurrected state?
What miracle compares with that of passing on to all men
the effects of his resurrection, so that all shall rise from death
to life; so that all shall put off this corruption and put on in-

corruption; so that all shall rise from mortality to immortality? And what greater joy and attainment is there—miraculous joy and attainment—than to be raised in immortality and unto eternal life in the everlasting kingdom of the Everlasting Father?

But as to the miracles that mortals can perform—and how he labored and lived and loved in the full bloom and beauty of that mortality which is the happy lot of all the worthy offspring of the Father—as to these miracles, which was the greatest? Was it to open blind eyes, cast out devils, or cleanse lepers? Was it to calm storms, walk on water, or feed thousands with a few barley loaves and a little savory of fish? Or was it to raise from death the daughter of Jairus in Capernaum or the widow's son near Nain, thus giving life to cold corpses and calling back spirits from the realms of the departed?

Perhaps the greatest miracle is none of these; perhaps it is the healing of sin-sick souls so that those who are spiritually blind and deaf and diseased become again pure and clean and heirs of salvation. Perhaps the greatest miracle of all is that which happens in the life of each person who is born again; who receives the sanctifying power of the Holy Spirit of God in his life; who has sin and evil burned out of his soul as though by fire; who lives again spiritually, and, perchance, if need be, is also healed physically.

With these words of introduction we now turn to the raising of Lazarus from death. We shall hear and see and feel what the Lord of Life—and blessed be his name—chose to do near Bethany of Judea a short while before he also chose to lay down his own life and take it up again at Jerusalem. We shall seek to tune our spirits to his as he performs what has become known as the miracle of miracles—this raising of Lazarus—the miracle that he singled out as the chief one to bear witness that he is the resurrection and the life; that by him immortality and eternal life come; and that he would in due course perform the infinitely and miraculously great atoning sacrifice. And as we weep with the mourners, including Jesus himself, and rejoice with the faithful when a decomposing body again becomes the tenement of an eternal spirit, perhaps we shall envision why this miracle stands preeminent over them all.

Now Lazarus lived in the town of Bethany some two miles east of Jerusalem, but hidden from the Holy City by a spur of the mount of Olives. There also dwelt in this Judean village of blessed memory the beloved sisters Mary and Martha, in whose family circle the Lord Jesus so often found surcease from toil and rest from his labors. They and their brother Lazarus were three of the most intimate friends Jesus had on earth. Of this intimacy we shall speak more particularly when we see Mary, just before the Fourth Passover, anoint Jesus' feet with very costly spikenard. At this time Mary "lived with her sister Martha, in whose house her brother Lazarus was sick." Whether Lazarus at this time was married and had a family of his own, we know not, only that in connection with this illness the industrious and compassionate Martha was caring for him in her home. If he was about the age of Jesus, the custom of the day would have required him long since to assume the normal familial responsibilities.

Jesus is in Perea at least a score of miles away, perhaps more, but his whereabouts are known to the two sisters in Bethany. We cannot escape the conclusion that they kept in touch with each other as friends and intimates normally do. From the two sisters came this message: "Lord, behold, he whom thou lovest is sick." Perhaps the messenger also said, 'It is urgent that you come immediately, for Lazarus lieth at the door of death. He cannot last much longer; only you can heal him.' The fact is, by that time Lazarus was dead and his body lay in a tomb, which thing Jesus must have known by the power of inspiration. It would take one day for the messenger to travel from Bethany to Perea and find Jesus. Our Lord then remained two days, teaching and ministering among the people, without apparent concern for his beloved friend; it took him another day to reach the Judean town, and when he finally arrived Lazarus had lain four days in the grave.

"This sickness is not unto death," Jesus said, "but for the glory of God, that the Son of God might be glorified thereby." No doubt the messenger returned bearing this somewhat enigmatic reply, which meant, as the subsequent events witness, 'Lazarus shall die—nay, has already passed from life to death—but he shall not remain long in the tomb. His passing was for the glory of God. At my command he shall return to mortality to stand as a witness to all generations that I am the Son of God and have power over life and death. He shall live again as a sign that he and all men shall rise in the resurrection because of me, for I am the resurrection and the life.'

Lazarus's sickness was "for the glory of God"! Shall we not set it forth plainly? Lazarus was foreordained to die; it was part of the eternal plan. His spirit must separate from its mortal tenement; it must remain in paradise until the tabernacle of clay began to decay, until corruption and decomposition were well under way. Then his destiny was to live again; to take up a physically renewed mortal body; to dwell again in mortality, from which temporal state he could escape only by dying again.

One wonders why this beloved friend of Jesus was not chosen as one of the Twelve. One answer is that he may have been at a later time, filling a vacancy caused by the martyrdom of one of the original special witnesses. Or Lazarus may have been one of the Seventy; or his may have been a special work that would heap upon him respect and renown in all ages, as is the case with many of the Lord's valiant servants today who serve neither in the Twelve nor among the Seventy.

When Jesus' work in Perea was finished; when sufficient time had elapsed for the purposes of the Father to be fulfilled in Lazarus's death; when he had "tarried two days, after he heard that Lazarus was sick"—then our Lord said: "Let us go into Judea again." Such a course was fraught with peril. His disciples remonstrated with him: "Master, the Jews of late sought to stone thee; and goest thou thither again?" Jesus, using figurative language, attempted to calm their fears:

Are there not twelve hours in the day? If any man walk in the day, he stumbleth not, because he seeth the light of the world. But if a man walk in the night, he stumbleth, because there is no light in him.

"During the twelve hours of His day of work He could walk in safety, for the light of His duty, which was the will of His Heavenly Father, would keep Him from danger." (Farrar, p. 506.) 'Though it be the eleventh hour of my life, yet there are twelve hours in the day, and during that designated period, I shall do the work appointed me without stumbling or faltering. This is the time given me to do my work. During the appointed day I shall walk in safety; my Father will preserve me. I cannot wait for the night when perchance the opposition will die down. He that shirks his responsibilities and puts off his labors until the night shall stumble in darkness and his work shall fail.'

Then, that they might more fully understand, he said: "Our friend Lazarus sleepeth; but I go, that I may awake him out of sleep." Though it was as common a figure among the Jews as it is among us to speak of those who have passed away as being asleep; though this was the obvious meaning of Jesus' statement, otherwise anyone could have awakened him and Jesus' presence would not have been needed; and though they knew he had raised the sleeping dead on at least two previous occasions—yet the disciples failed to grasp his meaning. "Lord, if he sleep, he shall do well," they said.

"Then said Jesus unto them plainly, Lazarus is dead. And I am glad for your sakes that I was not there, to the intent ye may believe; nevertheless let us go unto him." What Jesus will soon do will be a witness of his own divine Sonship that none, either in that day or this, can reject without losing his soul. It will be done in such a way that none can fail to envision the event or avoid discerning its meaning. None but a God can do what he is about to do.

Seeing, then, that he is determined to go, Thomas, who was willing to lay down his life in the gospel cause, but who had failed to understand Jesus' statement that he would be preserved during the appointed twelve hours of his mortal ministry, said to the group: "Let us also go, that we may die with him." As soon would be evident, however, Jesus' death must await the time of the coming Passover, and the martyrdom of Thomas and the others must not take place until after the apostolic witness of a resurrection has been borne to the nations of the world.

And so the holy party went to the Judean town of Bethany, there to become witnesses of the miracle of miracles, the raising of Lazarus after four days of death.

"Lazarus, Come Forth"
(John 11:17-46; JST, John 11:17, 29)

"And when Jesus came to Bethany, to Martha's house, Lazarus had already been in the grave four days." Such was part of the divine program. After four days, according to Jewish tradition, the spirit no longer remained near his erstwhile tenement, and the uninhabited corpse was considered as the dust of the earth. Decay and decomposition were in full swing; the finality of death was a reality; mourning and weeping would continue for thirty days, as the lives of the living adjusted to an existence without the presence of the dead one.

From all that is written about them, it is clear that the two sisters and their brother were part of a prominent family that was amply endowed with this world's goods. Lazarus, therefore, his body having been anointed with myrtle, aloes, and many spices, was laid in a cave or rock-hewn tomb, probably in a garden, as befitted his station in life. Even those of moderate means had their own private burial places, which were passed on to their heirs as was the case with all realty.

Many friends of the family had come out from Jerusalem to comfort the bereaved sisters. Though all the family members were disciples, whose belief in Christ was openly avowed, they had not as yet been put out of the synagogue and made subject to the penalties and persecutions of excommunication. Had Lazarus been esteemed as an apostate of Judaism, his death would have called for demonstrations, not of mourning but of rejoicing, from his Jewish neighbors and associates. But here we find hosts of people participating in the overly ostentatious weepings and howlings that substituted for genuine mourning in that day. We may assume, since the refining fires of the gospel had long burned in the hearts of Martha and Mary, that the pretentious and pompous wailings so common among them were somewhat modified.

Word of Jesus' coming was brought first to Martha, who immediately went forth to meet him, while Mary, apparently unaware of the Master's return, remained in the house mourning with her friends. And from Martha's lips, when she met Jesus, fell some of the sweetest words ever uttered, words of faith and surety that were Petrine in caliber:

Lord, if thou hadst been here, my brother had not died. But I know, that even now, whatsoever thou wilt ask of God, God will give it thee.

Martha, who served in the household; Martha, who was cumbered about with many things; Martha, whose younger sister had chosen the better part, as she sat at Jesus' feet, and who would yet again do so when she anointed them with oil; Martha of blessed memory, this day both spoke herself and heard from him such divine words as seldom have saluted the ears of mortal. Her words so far spoken can have but one meaning: 'I know thou wouldst have healed him hadst thou been here. But even now—as it was with the daughter of Jairus; as it was with the widow's son—I know thou canst call him forth from the death of the tomb to the life of

274

mortals. God will hear thee.' The full import of these words, spoken by the power of the Holy Ghost, may not, as we shall soon see, have dawned fully upon this faithful and sweet sister, but she was in tune with the Spirit, and her faith enabled her to speak them, and glorious is her name for so doing.

Jesus said to her, "Thy brother shall rise"—meaning, 'I shall call him back to mortal life.' To this Martha, relying on that faith and knowledge which long had been hers, replied: "I know that he shall rise again in the resurrection at the last day." Then Jesus, in all the awesome majesty of his eternal godhood, spoke to his beloved Martha, in the presence of his Father, of the holy angels, and of his mortal apostolic witnesses; then Jesus, speaking as the Great Jehovah, speaking as God's Almighty Son, gave this divine testimony of his own divine Sonship:

I am the resurrection, and the life: he that believeth in me, though he were dead, yet shall he live: and whosoever liveth and believeth in me shall never die. Believest thou this?

Thus saith the Lord. He has spoken and so it is. He is the resurrection; it comes by him; without him there would be no immortality; he is the personification of that power which molds the dust of the grave into an immortal man. He it was who asked: "Can these bones live?" And he it was who answered: "Thus saith the Lord God unto these bones; Behold, I will cause breath to enter into you, and ye shall live: And I will lay sinews upon you, and will bring up flesh upon you, and cover you with skin, and put breath in you, and ye shall live; and ye shall know that I am the Lord." (Ezek. 37:3, 5-6.)

He also is the life; eternal life comes by him. Without him there would be no salvation in the highest heaven, no exaltation, no continuation of the family unit in eternity, no fulness of joy in the realms ahead. He is the personification of that power which gives eternal life to all those who are born again, who are alive in Christ. Those who believe and obey, though they die the natural death, yet shall they gain eternal life in the resurrection. Yea, those who believe in Christ shall never die spiritually; they shall be alive to the things of the Spirit in this life, and they shall have eternal life in the world to come. Death, as men view it, is nothing to sorrow about where the faithful saints are concerned; what if they, as do all men, lose their lives here—they shall yet gain the far more glorious reward of eternal life hereafter.

To Jesus' question, "Believest thou this?" Martha—still guided by the power of the Spirit, still speaking with certainty from the depths of her soul, still uttering words that are Petrine in caliber, but now building on the foundation Jesus has just laid, that immortality and eternal life come by him—the blessed Martha, in this setting, replies:

Yea, Lord: I believe that thou art the Christ, the Son of God, which should come into the world.

In spiritual things there is no difference between men and women. Adam and Eve both teach their children by the power of the Spirit. Peter and Martha both bear witness that Jesus is the Christ, the Son of the Living God. Mary Magdalene, even ahead of the apostles, bows before the Risen Lord and hails him yet with the affectionate *Rabboni*. Martha has now borne her testimony, and that she might do so is one of the reasons all things relative to Lazarus's death and raising were arranged as they are now unfolding. Martha is on record; her testimony is recorded by the angels; and as Jesus said aforetime, with reference to such cases, her sins are forgiven. Now he must give Mary the same opportunity.

Martha came to Jesus while he was yet outside the town. Now she returned and spoke to Mary in secret. "The Master is come, and calleth for thee," she said. Mary arose quickly and, without even excusing herself from those who were comforting her in the house, hastened to Jesus, all of which indicates there were dangers in Jesus' coming and that his friends felt the need to take precautions. Those who were with Mary followed. "She goeth unto the grave to weep there," they said.

Coming to Jesus, Mary fell at his feet and said the same words Martha had first spoken: "Lord, if thou hadst been here, my brother had not died," indicating that this was something the beloved sisters probably had discussed between themselves. Perhaps also she added the same sure witness of Christ's eternal power that had fallen from the lips of her older sister; and the Lord Jesus may have said to her what he had already said to Martha about being the resurrection and the life, even receiving back from the younger sister the same inspired testimony of his own divinity. We have no reason to believe that Jesus would do other than treat his two friends with equal tenderness and solicitude, and that he would try the faith of each of them to the full in the same way.

When Jesus saw Mary weeping, "and the Jews also weeping which came with her, he groaned in the spirit, and was troubled, And said, Where have ye laid him? They said unto him, Lord, come and see." Perhaps there were other events, not recorded, that brought forth this display of divine emotion. It may be that John is telling us that Jesus was troubled in spirit because of the artificial wailings of the paid mourners, or the rebellion that he saw in the hearts of many who were present, or that his reaction was one of pure love and tenderness toward the two sisters and their now seemingly lost Lazarus.

Or perhaps it may be, as Farrar speculates, with reference to the sorrow of Mary and her friends, something along this line: "The sight of all that love and misery, the pitiable spectacle of human bereavement, the utter futility at such a moment of human consolation, the shrill commingling of a hired and simulated lamentation with all this genuine anguish, the unspoken reproach, 'Oh, why didst Thou not come at once and snatch the victim from the enemy, and spare Thy friend from the sting of death, and us from the more bitter sting of such a parting?'—all these influences touched the tender compassion of Jesus with deep emotion. A strong effort of self-repression was needed—an effort which shook His whole frame with a powerful shudder—before He could find words to speak, and then He could only ask, 'Where have ye laid him?' " (Farrar, pp. 507-8.)

We now see Jesus himself weeping, his eyes streaming with silent tears. Among the observing Jews are both friends and enemies. Those who are kindly disposed say: "Behold how he loved him!" Others whose hearts are hardened and who seek to discount his powers say: "Could not this man, which opened the eyes of the blind, have caused that even this man should not have died?" It was as though they said: 'True, this man opened the eyes of a blind man, whom he did not know, but he could not save his own friend from death. Perhaps after all his powers are of a limited, uncertain, and capricious nature.' And so again, confronted with such a malignant outpouring of unbelief, Jesus groaned in himself. Or perhaps, as Farrar says, "Jesus knew and heard their comments, and once more the whole scene—its genuine sorrows, its hired mourners, its uncalmed hatreds, all concentrated around the ghastly work of death—came so powerfully over His spirit, that, though He knew that He was going to wake the dead, once more His whole being was swept by a storm of emotion." (Farrar, p. 508.)

Jesus is now at the grave; it is a cave; a stone lies upon it, sealing the entrance. "Take ye away the stone," he says. He who can raise the dead can surely find a grave site, and yet he asked to be shown where Lazarus lay. He who can call forth a dead corpse can surely cause a stone to roll aside, and yet he called for human hands to move the obstacle that barred the way. Each step was taken with deliberation, to test and purify the faith of those who believed. And so Martha, who had before spoken of Jesus' power to raise the dead, now, fearful for the moment, struggling to believe that which almost no mortal could believe, said, "Lord, by this time he stinketh: for he hath been dead four days." And Jesus, strengthening, encouraging, desiring to see her faith increase, asks: "Said I not unto thee, that, if thou wouldest believe, thou shouldest see the glory of God?" Then Martha, strengthened and reassured, reminded of the assurances that had already come to her by the power of the Spirit, nodded the legal approval needed to unseal the tomb, and strong arms pushed aside the great stone that covered the place where Lazarus lay.

Before the great miracle, one thing yet remained. "And Jesus lifted up his eyes, and said, Father, I thank thee that thou hast heard me. And I knew that thou hearest me always: but because of the people which stand by I said it, that they may believe that thou hast sent me." This miracle is going to prove that Jesus is the Christ, the Messiah, the Promised One. None but the Son of God could do what he is about to do. He had prayed and struggled and prepared for this moment, and the Father, whose power he held, had granted his pleas.

Thus, at this moment—with the hearts of Martha and Mary perfectly united with that of their beloved Lord; with the body of Lazarus lying in the dust, eaten by worms, every vital organ in process of rotting away; with the spirit of this man of divine destiny, in paradise, awaiting the Promised Voice—at this moment the Lord of Life spoke: "LAZARUS, COME FORTH."

"Those words thrilled once more through that region of impenetrable darkness which separates us from the world to come; and scarcely were they spoken when, like a spectre, from the rocky tomb issued a figure, swathed indeed in its white and ghastly cerements—with the napkin round the head which had upheld the jaw that four days previously had dropped in death, bound hand and foot and face, but not livid, not horrible—the figure of a youth with the healthy blood of a restored life flowing through his veins; of a life restored—so tradition tells us—for thirty more long years to life, and light, and love." (Farrar, p. 510.)

"Loose him, and let him go," Jesus said. And there the inspired account ends. A reverent curtain of silence drops over the sayings and doings of Lazarus—from his youth to the day he fell asleep in the arms of death; during the four days his spirit visited with friends in paradise, as he awaited the call to come back to the turmoils of life; and from the time he again breathed the breath of life until he laid down again his mortal tabernacle, this time to await that glorious day of resurrection of which Martha spoke. Lazarus lived and Lazarus died and Lazarus rose again—that he might continue his mortal probation; that he might die again; that he might be, for his day and for all days, a living witness of the power of him who ministered in Bethany as the Son of God. We cannot doubt that he bore many fervent testimonies to many Jewish brethren relative to the life and death and life that was his.

We have now heard Jesus claim divine Sonship and accept the concurring witness of his beloved Martha. Then we have seen him prove the truth of his own testimony by creating a living Lazarus where only a dead one lay. What effect did this miracle have on the Jews? John says: "Then many of the Jews which came to Mary, and had seen the things which Jesus did, believed on him." And well they might, for which glory be to God. "But some of them went their ways to the Pharisees, and told them what things Jesus had done," and they as a result plotted his death.

Truly we are hearing an echo here in Bethany and in Jerusalem of a Perean Voice acclaiming: "If they hear not Moses and the prophets, neither will they be persuaded, though one rose from the dead." Or is it an echo? Perhaps what we hear are rolling claps of thunder, roaring and crashing from one end of heaven to the other, as part of the dooming storm that shall destroy all those who willfully close their eyes and ears to eternal truth.

The Sanhedrin Plots Jesus' Death
(John 11:47-54; JST, John 11:47)

There is no language to describe the religious idiocy and the Pharisaic fanaticism that swept through Jerusalem and Judea because Jesus raised Lazarus from death. Lazarus lives and therefore Jesus must die; indeed, it would be well if Lazarus's own testifying lips could be sealed in death also. Let us slay them both and be done with this menace that subverts our Mosaic religion and runs counter to the traditions of the elders.

Within an hour of the time Lazarus walked from his tomb in or near Bethany, Jewish zealots were in the temple in Jerusalem reporting to the Pharisees and rulers on all that they had seen and heard in that Judean town. The prayers of thanksgiving and the hymns of praise that were then ascending in the home of Martha found their counterpart in the curses and revilings being poured forth in the now desecrated house of Jewish worship. The great Sanhedrin convened immediately to hear the witnesses.

Their detailed investigation of the opening of the eyes of the man born blind and their complete discomfiture in the presence of an unlearned beggar who testified that Jesus was a mighty prophet were fresh in their minds. And now this—a man whose decaying body had rotted and spewed out stench for four days—was alive and well and vibrant. What kind of a man was it who opened blind eyes and reanimated cold corpses? This thing must be stopped even if it requires the death of a god. "If we let him thus alone," they reasoned, "all men will believe on him"—and what a sad thing that would be—"and the Romans shall come and take away both our place and nation." Their dilemma was both religious and political. 'If this man's gospel is true, the day of Moses and the law is past, and we shall lose our prominence and power as rulers in Israel. The people will rally round him as their Messiah and Deliverer, and Rome will then destroy us with the sword.'

281

As hatred and perplexity dominated the Sanhedrinists, the high priest, Joseph Caiaphas, a civil appointee of Rome who had gained his position by bribery, rose to address them. Apparently his intention was to advocate Jesus' death on the theory that it was better for this one man to die than that the whole nation should perish at the hands of Rome. His was to be a political speech of expediency. The problem before them was not a matter of right or wrong; they must forget whether Jesus was the Messiah or not. Regardless of anything, he must be destroyed lest their nation be brought to ruin.

But whatever Caiaphas's intention was, Deity ordained otherwise. And however evil and wicked he was, yet he held the office of high priest, and as such he had a commission to speak for God to the people, which he then, unwittingly, did. The words that came out were these: "Ye know nothing at all, Nor consider that it is expedient for us, that one man should die for the people, and that the whole nation perish not." John says: "This spake he not of himself: but being high priest that year, he prophesied that Jesus should die for that nation; And not for that nation only, but that also he should gather together in one the children of God that were scattered abroad."

Caiaphas's intent had been evil but his words had been prophetic; however, the Sanhedrin was no more inclined to believe prophetic words than they were to accept the divinity of one who raised the dead. Their decision was that Jesus must die for political reasons. "Then from that day forth they took counsel together for to put him to death."

Thereupon Jesus and his disciples slipped quietly away to a small village called Ephraim, whose locale is no longer known, and there they remained some weeks in seclusion, awaiting the appointed time for his return to Jerusalem and for the crowning events of the life of earth's only Divine Being. The time in Ephraim was spent preparing the disciples for the ministerial teachings and trials that lay ahead.

Chapter 81

MORE HEALINGS, PARABLES, AND SERMONS

To day if ye will hear his voice,
Harden not your heart, as in
the provocation,
and as in the day of temptation
in the wilderness:
When your fathers tempted me,
proved me, and saw my work.
(Ps. 95:7-9.)

Jesus Cleanses Ten Lepers
(Luke 17:11-19)

As Jesus, after a few weeks of seclusion in Ephraim, begins his last journey to Jerusalem, no doubt by a leisurely and circuitous route, he continues to warn and teach and heal. He continues to work wonders in Israel as he did among their fathers in generations past, and Jacob's seed, as always, seeks to tempt and prove and provoke him. His words and his works are as they have ever been; he preaches the gospel and takes upon himself the infirmities of his suffering kinsmen.

Just two years ago in Galilee we saw him heal a leper; we then marveled as he freed a faithful soul from leprosy—that dread and evil plague which makes of life a living death. (See chapter 36, Book 2.) No doubt since then there have been scores or hundreds of lepers cleansed, for what affliction would create in the heart of the Healing One such compassion as this stench-spreading sickness, which rotted away the organs of the body piecemeal? Our inspired authors, however, as we are aware, sift out selected samples of his healing power to teach such general principles and illustrate such special virtues as the needs of their respective narratives warrant.

Now, as Jesus passes through the midst of Samaria and Galilee, he enters an unnamed village where he meets, standing afar off, ten men who are lepers. Either this is a place where lepers are segregated to keep their putrefying plague from spreading, or, which accords with the sense and feeling of the whole episode, these ten, alerted to the coming of the Lord, had assembled that perchance his shadow, as it were, might touch them as he passed by. As is the requisite for those who seek healing blessings, they believed in him and had faith in his name and power. Their call to him, no doubt uttered with repetitious urgency, is a plea for healing from their deathlike doom: "Jesus, Master, have mercy on us."

"There was something in that living death of leprosy— recalling as it did the most frightful images of suffering and degradation—corrupting as it did the very fountains of the life-blood of man, distorting his countenance, rendering loathsome his touch, slowly encrusting and infecting him with a plague-spot of disease far more horrible than death itself—which always seems to have thrilled the Lord's heart with a keen and instantaneous compassion." (Farrar, p. 462.) Jesus calls out: "Go shew yourselves unto the priests." His meaning is clear: they must show themselves to the priests and be pronounced clean, free from leprosy, before they can again mingle with their fellowmen. True, it is a test of their faith to start their journey before they are healed, but so be it. He has spoken, and they are assured of that blessed physical relief that none but the leprous can desire so devoutly. There is none of the spirit of Naaman the Syrian in their souls. And so, as they journey, they are healed, we suppose, degree by degree, as health and vigor and strength return.

Ten lepers are now clean and whole; ten men whose fate was worse than death now glory in a new life of health and vigor; ten of the discards of society are now returned to the mainstream of life. It is with them as when Lazarus came forth from his tomb; where once there was death, now there is life. When a leper lives again, what does he do? Nine of the group—apparently all Jews—rushed home to embrace their loved ones; to weep with joy on the necks of their friends; to show themselves to the priests, lest any scrupulosity of the law be forgotten. One of the ten—and he a Samaritan—hastened back to Jesus, fell at his feet, gave thanks, "and with a loud voice glorified God." His loved ones and the priests could wait; first, let God be praised and his Healing Son be thanked.

"Were there not ten cleansed?" Jesus asked, "but where are the nine?" Surely there is sorrow in his voice as he continues: "There are not found that returned to give glory to God, save this stranger." And then, to the Samaritan he said: "Arise, go thy way: thy faith hath made thee whole"—which can only be interpreted to mean that this one Samaritan, singled out of the group, received added spiritual blessings that were withheld from the nine.

The sin of ingratitude, how common it is! As Jesus cleansed ten lepers physically, so he cleanses all his saints spiritually from the leprosy of sin. Are we more grateful for our blessings than were the healed lepers who hastened on their ways, heedless of the beneficent goodness of the One whose words had made them new creatures?

Well might we remember that he, who in his life healed men physically, is the one who, in his death, made it possible for all men to be healed spiritually. Well might we rejoice because he who cleansed the lepers, when he dwelt on earth, is the one who, through his atoning sacrifice, enables all men to cast off their leprous bodies of corruption, exchanging them for those glorious bodies which are refreshed and renewed in immortality.

And well ought we—lest the sin of ingratitude overtake us—praise his holy name forever.

The Discourse on the Kingdom of God
(Luke 17:20-37; JST, Luke 17:21)

This is a day of Pharisaic confrontation, one in which Jesus is repeatedly harassed, harried, and heckled by these pious preservers of the Mosaic status quo. After the healing of the ten lepers and while the holy party is still in Galilee, traveling with Jerusalem as their destination, these learned Rabbinists decide to put our Lord's Messianic claims to the test. He has testified everywhere that he is the Promised One, the Deliverer sent of God to Israel; he speaks everlastingly of the gospel of the kingdom of God. And yet he utterly refuses to wear a Messianic crown, rally the people round him, and lead the assault on their Romish-Gentile overlords that will free the chosen people from an alien yoke. Has not the time come to wring from him a declaration as to when the kingdom will be restored to Israel? If his answers are found wanting, perhaps his followers can be weaned away. Haughtily, imperiously, the Pharisees "demanded" to know "when the kingdom of God should come." 'Once and for all answer this question,' they say.

But they are not equal to him whose kingdom is not of this world, and who came not to lead a revolt against Rome, nor to place swords and shields in the hands of his followers, but to wage a revolution in the hearts of men. Their imperious demands are deftly swept aside as he restates the simple gospel verity that equates his earthly church with the kingdom of God on earth:

The kingdom of God cometh not with observation: Neither shall they say, Lo, here! or, Lo, there! For, behold, the kingdom of God has already come unto you.

'My kingdom is already here; there will be no martial displays of military might; no bands will play, no legions march. My soldiers will not capture the fortress of Antonia, nor overrun Machaerus, where John was slain. Heralds will not go forth crying, Assemble here, or, Go there, for my kingdom, which is not of this world, has already come. It is the Church which I have set up, which Church administers the gospel, which gospel is the power of God unto salvation. And these Twelve hold the keys; they shall direct the destiny of my kingdom.' Nothing more is recorded of this confrontation, leaving us to suppose the Pharisees had no more to say on the subject.

But the issue of the future glorious millennial reign having thus been raised, Jesus turned from the Pharisees to his disciples and delivered a great discourse relative to that kingdom which shall sweep away the decadent kingdoms of men and hold sway over all the earth. In substance and thought content he will repeat these same truths in the Olivet discourse, during the last week of his mortal life, and we will there consider them.

Parable of the Unjust Judge
(Luke 18:1-8; JST, Luke 18:8; D&C 101:81-92)

Having spoken *to the Pharisees* about the kingdom of God then set up among men, meaning the Church, and having spoken *to the disciples* about that great millennial kingdom which will be established when he comes again, Jesus now teaches, in a parable, how the preserving prayers *of the saints* will finally prevail in the day of his coming. He is not here speaking of the simplistic principle that earnest and repetitious importunings will eventually be heard and answered, though this may be true in some cases. It is not a matter of an importunate widow gaining redress from an unjust judge because of her insistent pleadings, and that therefore those who pray to Him who is just will have their petitions granted if they earnestly and everlastingly importune at the throne of grace. Prayers are answered when there is faith; faith is founded on truth and can only be exercised in harmony with the plan of heaven. Only those petitions which are just and right are granted. Rather, this parable, as we shall see, teaches that if the saints will continue to importune in faith for that which is right, and because their cause is just, though the answers to their prayers may be long delayed, yet, finally in the day of vengeance when he judges whose judgment is just, when he comes again to rule and reign, the faithful shall be rewarded.

"Men ought always to pray, and not to faint," Luke says in introducing the parable, meaning that the disciples, the saints of God, the children of Zion, the members of that kingdom which is the Church, ought to importune everlastingly for the success and triumph of their cause because their cause is just and right.

> *There was in a city a judge, which feared not God, neither regarded man.*

These introductory words have a ring of reality to his hearers, for such all too frequently was the case with those non-Jewish judges in Palestine. Appointed by Herod or the Romans, many of these magistrates were amenable to bribery; cared nothing for public opinion; were openly contemptuous of principles of equity and justice; flouted the divine law in their decisions; and issued decrees that were grossly unjust.

> *And there was a widow in that city; and she came unto him, saying, Avenge me of mine adversary. And he would not for a while: but afterward he said within himself, Though I fear not God, nor regard man; Yet because this widow troubleth me, I will avenge her, lest by her continual coming she weary me.*

The widow's plea is for the magistrate to make legal inquiry; to call in him who has wronged her; to set things right and let justice be done. The judge's sole concern is expediency: what is the political thing to do; how can he benefit most from the case; why not grant the petition and be free of the annoyance of repetitious importunings.

*And the Lord said, Hear what the unjust judge saith.
And shall not God avenge his own elect, which cry day
and night unto him, though he bear long with them?*

This parable is one of contrasts. If an evil magistrate, caring nothing for a poor widow, will finally adjudge her case, how much more shall the Judge of all the earth, who loves his saints, finally, in the day of vengeance at his coming, avenge his elect upon all their enemies.

*I tell you that he will come, and when he does come,
he will avenge his saints speedily. Nevertheless, when
the Son of Man cometh, shall he find faith on the
earth?*

In his own providences, and for their own development—that they may be tested to the full—it will seem to the Lord's praying saints as if the Just Judge delayeth his coming so that he will scarcely find any left who have faith.[1]

We must not overlook the fact that the Church itself, in Christ's absence, is a widow. And in the latter-day version of this parable, we find the Lord directing "the children of Zion" to importune for redress of grievances at the feet of the judge, the governor, and the president, each in turn; and if none of these heed their pleas,

*Then will the Lord arise and come forth out of his
hiding place, and in his fury vex the nation; And in his
hot displeasure, and in his fierce anger, in his time, will
cut off those wicked, unfaithful, and unjust stewards,
and appoint them their portion among hypocrites, and
unbelievers; Even in outer darkness, where there is
weeping, and wailing, and gnashing of teeth.*

*Pray ye, therefore, that their ears may be opened
unto your cries, that I may be merciful unto them, that
these things may not come upon them.*

Parable of the Pharisee and the Publican
(Luke 18:9-14)

In every major sect, party, and denomination there are both Pharisees and publicans. Among the Jews the Pharisees were the pious, proud, pompous self-appreciators who boasted of their charities and extolled their own good works. They esteemed themselves as far superior to the common, garden-variety of mankind, and they rejoiced in their separate, superior status. The publicans, on the other hand, were the tax collectors who made their living by extorting from the people more than they turned in to the Roman treasury. Almost without exception they were sinners whose hearts were so hardened that they could appropriate—with greed and avarice—the last sheep of the shepherd and the last mite of the widow. The nature of their employment, by an alien power, dulled their sensitivities and left them to ponder and plan how to exact by force a poor man's last farthing. In this parable Jesus speaks of the haughty pride of all Pharisees and of a welcome display of humility of a certain publican whose soul was wracked because of the sorrows of his avaricious life. It is addressed to "certain which trusted in themselves that they were righteous, and despised others."

Two men went up into the temple to pray; the one a Pharisee, and the other a publican. The Pharisee stood and prayed thus with himself, God, I thank thee, that I am not as other men are, extortioners, unjust, adulterers, or even as this publican. I fast twice in the week, I give tithes of all that I possess.

And the publican, standing afar off, would not lift up so much as his eyes unto heaven, but smote upon his breast, saying, God be merciful to me a sinner.

I tell you, this man went down to his house justified rather than the other: for every one that exalteth himself shall be abased; and he that humbleth himself shall be exalted.

"By the parable of the haughty, respectable, fasting, alms-giving, self-satisfied Pharisee—who, going to make his boast to God in the Temple, went home less justified than the poor Publican, who could only reiterate one single cry for God's mercy as he stood there beating his breast, and with downcast eyes—He taught them that God loves better a penitent humility than a merely external service, and that a broken heart and a contrite spirit were sacrifices which He would not despise." (Farrar, p. 482.)

It is clear that the prayer of the Pharisee portrayed the life he lived—a separatist life full of holier-than-thou conduct that was offensive to God and man. As for the publican, he had come to himself, as did the prodigal son, and we may safely assume he then was or soon would become a disciple of the One through whose blood mercy is dispensed to the penitent.

The Discourse on Marriage and Divorce
(Matthew 19:1-12; JST, Matthew 19:2, 11; Mark 10:1-12; JST, Mark 10:1-2; Luke 16:18; JST, Luke 16:23)

Still en route to Jerusalem, traveling from Galilee into Perea, Jesus and the holy party come to that Perean area where a few weeks ago he encountered violent Pharisaic opposition. On that occasion he called these Pharisees adulterers and lashed out at their loose marriage and divorce practices with the bold assertion: "Whosoever putteth away his wife, and marrieth another, committeth adultery: and whosoever marrieth her that is put away from her husband committeth adultery." (Luke 16:18.) We then reserved consideration of this pronouncement until the discourse on marriage and divorce he is now about to deliver.

Great multitudes now follow him; he teaches the gospel; many believe on him, and he heals them. Into this setting where there is peace and righteousness, and where the grace of God is being poured out in abundant measure upon penitent souls, there now comes an evil, divisive, hateful influence. Those Pharisees whom he had condemned as adulterers come to mingle with the multitudes. With the help of Satan, their master, these malignant and evil devils, clothed in human form, have built a trap from which, as they suppose, Jesus can find no escape. It may be that even their hellish cunning has never devised a question fraught with so many difficulties and so much emotion as that which they now use to tempt him. No matter what answer he gives, he will surely alienate, they reason, a large portion of the people; and if he takes the same view thundered forth by his forerunner, the Blessed Baptist, then they hope Herod Antipas will send forth his soldiers and carry off Jesus, as he did John, to the dungeons of Machaerus, there to await a convenient time for the headsman's ax to fall. Their question, which calls for a religious decision in a sensitive field, and which may pull down political wrath upon Him to whom it is asked, is couched thus: "Is it lawful for a man to put away his wife for every cause?"

Marriage and divorce, the one a blessing, the other a curse; how long a family unit endures; how to salvage all that may be saved in the case of divorce—these matters are of more concern in the society of men than are any others. It is the divine design that men create for themselves eternal family units patterned after the family of God the Eternal Father. In such a process there can be no divorce; if all men and all women lived in complete harmony with the law of the gospel, there would be no divorces. It is the purpose of the Almighty to create eternal family units; under his system, when it operates perfectly, families are never divided by divorce.

But just as God exalts and glorifies the family, so Satan seeks to weaken and destroy this most basic of all units of society. If Lucifer had his way, no men would ever marry; they would live like animals and breed like cattle; or, being married, they would live without sexual restraint and as if there were no moral law; or divorces would be so easy to obtain, and the dissolution of the family unit so common, that men would interchange wives freely; or divorces would be so hard to obtain that marriage partners would leave each other and live in open sin with others because no realistic system of divorce prevailed; or whatever circumstances or situations might be devised to increase immorality and demean the family as such.

Manifestly, the marriage discipline and the divorce requirements among various cultures and peoples depend upon that portion of the Lord's law which they are able to live. The Lord may allow divorces in one day among a certain people and deny them in another day among a more enlightened populace. Marriage and divorce may be regulated one way among the heathen, another in the Gentile nations, and yet another according to Mosaic discipline. Even in the church and kingdom of God on earth—where men have the gospel itself—the divinely approved laws of marriage and divorce may vary from time to time. Plural marriage is practiced under certain circumstances and at designated times; divorce is allowed—with consequent remarriage of divorced persons—when such laws are in the best interest of the people; and in the highest type gospel situation, there is no divorce and all families become eternal.

In the Jewish culture of Jesus' day there were many discordant and divisive voices crying out in defense of divergent divorce standards and advocating differing marriage disciplines. Plural marriage, handed down from their fathers, was still practiced, though it does not seem to have been the dominant order of matrimony. Their main difficulties, however, seem to have grown out of the meaning of this Mosaic statement: "When a man hath taken a wife, and married her, and it come to pass that she find no favour in his eyes, because he hath found some uncleanness in her: then let him write her a bill of divorcement, and give it in her hand, and send her out of his house. And when she is departed out of his house, she may go and be another man's wife." (Deut. 24:1-2.)

The Pharisaic question assumes the propriety of divorce; the issue, as they express it, is, may it be granted "for every cause"; and, in theory at least, this depends upon the meaning of the Mosaic phrase "some uncleanness," which may also be translated "some unseemly thing," or "some matter of shame," or, literally, "some matter of nakedness." On this point the School of Shammai interpreted the Mosaic standard so as to allow divorce only for unchastity, while the School of Hillel allowed almost any trivial act to sever a marriage. Among these the Mishnah recites such things as: seeing another woman who pleased him more; feeling any disgust toward the wife; spoiling her husband's dinner; breaking the law of tithing, or other Mosaic requirement; going in public with an uncovered head; spinning in the public streets; brawling or being troublesome, or quarrelsome, or of ill repute; being childless for ten years; and on and on and on. These differences between the two major schools led, it is said, to the Jewish proverb: "Hillel loosed what Shammai bound." In practice there were many divorces for minor reasons. But Jesus, in his reply, as his wont was, rose above the battleground of the Rabbinists and went back to first principles.

Have ye not read, that he which made them at the beginning made them male and female, And said, For this cause shall a man leave father and mother, and shall cleave to his wife: and they twain shall be one flesh?

Wherefore they are no more twain, but one flesh. What therefore God hath joined together, let not man put asunder.

This is the very heart and core of the whole matter. God made man, male and female created he them, so they could marry; so they could provide bodies for his spirit children; so they could create for themselves eternal family units. God brought the woman unto the man and gave her to him to be his wife. He did it in Eden, before the fall; all things were then immortal; death had not entered the world. The first marriage—performed by the Lord God himself—was a celestial marriage, an eternal marriage, a union of Adam and Eve that was destined to last forever. There was no death; there was to be no divorce; the man and his wife were to be one flesh forever. Such was the pattern. All men thereafter should be as their first parents. Men and women should marry as did Adam and Eve—in celestial marriage—and should cleave unto each other as the divine pattern required.

What God does is forever. And what he hath joined in eternal union, let not man put asunder. Divorce is no part of the eternal plan. That these caviling, querulous, quarrelsome Pharisees understood these words and knew exactly what Jesus was saying, there can be no doubt. When we consider the conversation with the Sadducees about marriage in heaven, we shall see that the concept of eternal marriage was part of Jewish theology. And so the Pharisees now ask, "Why did Moses then command to give a writing of divorcement, and to put her away?"

Needless to say, Moses never gave any such command. What he did was to permit the recalcitrant and rebellious rebels who went by the name of Israel, but who were unable to live the full law as the Lord gave it to them—for they had the Melchizedek Priesthood, the sealing power, and celestial marriage—to divorce each other in proper cases. Hence Jesus replies:

Moses because of the hardness of your hearts suffered you to put away your wives: but from the beginning it was not so.

And I say unto you, Whosoever shall put away his wife, except it be for fornication, and shall marry another, committeth adultery: and whoso marrieth her which is put away doth commit adultery.

Moses permitted divorce because Israel was unable to live the perfect law. His teachings were a schoolmaster to prepare men for the fulness of the gospel. That gospel is now among them, and under this perfect law, marriage once again is eternal. Once again it is performed by the Lord or by his word; and once again it has no end. Such marriages can only be put asunder as a result of unchastity. If the man and his wife sever their union for lesser reasons and marry others, all concerned commit adultery, for in the eyes of the Lord his eternal marriage compact has never been broken. All of its terms and conditions are in force and have full efficacy and divine standing.

Thus Jesus recited the full and perfect law to the

Pharisees. Its provisions were only binding upon those who received his gospel, but he had declared unto them that very gospel, and they must accept it—including its law of marriage and divorce—at the peril of their salvation. Later, in a house away from the multitudes, the disciples, themselves troubled at the severity and strictness of the doctrine, "asked him again of the same matter." Later they said: "If the case of the man be so with his wife, it is not good to marry."

Jesus repeated to the disciples the basic law of marriage and divorce, applying its principles to both men and women—for women can gain divorces as well as men—and then added:

All cannot receive this saying; it is not for them save to whom it is given. For there are some eunuchs, which were so born from their mother's womb: and there are some eunuchs, which were made eunuchs of men: and there be eunuchs, which have made themselves eunuchs for the kingdom of heaven's sake.

He that is able to receive it, let him receive it.

From these words it is clear that the high standards of marriage and divorce of which Jesus speaks were for those only to whom they were given by revelation. Needless to say they have not been given to us in our day in their eternal fulness, and marriages to divorced persons do not of themselves constitute adultery. That this high state of marriage discipline will prevail again during the millennium also goes without saying. It is difficult for us, however, to envision fully the illustration here used about eunuchs. The record must be incomplete, for these words cannot, as is sometimes assumed, have reference to a celibate ministry. Perhaps they simply mean that even as special provision must be made for those who for physical reasons cannot marry, so the Lord makes special provision in his marriage discipline, so that all things required will meet the needs and circumstances of people in whatever society and culture they live.

NOTE

1. "Yet ere the Son of man comes to redress the wrongs of His Church, so low will the hope of relief sink, through the length of the delay, that one will be fain to ask, 'Will He find any faith of a coming avenger left on the earth?' From this we learn, (1.) That the *primary* and *historical* reference of this parable is to the Church in its *widowed*, desolate, oppressed, defenceless condition during the present absence of her Lord in the heavens; (2.) That in these circumstances importunate, persevering prayer for deliverance is the Church's fitting exercise; (3.) That notwithstanding every encouragement to this, so long will the answer be delayed, while the need of relief continues the same, and all hope of deliverance will have nearly died out, and 'faith' of Christ's coming scarcely to be found." (Robert Jamieson, A. R. Fausset, and David Brown, *Commentary on the Whole Bible,* Grand Rapids, Mich.: Zondervan Publishing House, 2:118.)

Chapter 82

GAINING ETERNAL LIFE

If thou wilt do good,
yea, and hold out faithful to the end,
thou shalt be saved in the kingdom of God,
which is the greatest of all the gifts of God;
for there is no gift greater
than the gift of salvation.
(D&C 6:13.)
Salvation consists in the glory, authority,
majesty, power and dominion
which Jehovah possesses and in nothing else;
and no being can possess it
but himself or one like him.
(*Lectures on Faith,* p. 64.)
And, if you keep my commandments and endure
to the end you shall have eternal life,
which gift is the greatest
of all the gifts of God. (D&C 14:7.)

Little Children Shall Be Saved
(*Matthew 19:13-15; JST, Matthew 19:13-14; Mark 10:13-16; JST, Mark 10:12; Luke 18:15-17*)

A scene of surpassing sweetness now unfolds before our eyes. Little children, still retaining the sinless purity of the sacred seraphs who surround the throne of God, are brought to Jesus to be blessed. He enfolds them in his arms, lays his hands upon them, and speaks wondrous words about them. Then he commands all men to be as they are.

We are still with our Blessed Lord and his select group of disciples in a Perean house. He has just proclaimed the sacred and holy nature of the marital union. It is ordained of God for the benefit of man; the Lord God made man, male and female, that they might marry and provide bodies for his spirit children. "And they twain shall be one flesh, and all this that the earth might answer the end of its creation; And that it might be filled with the measure of man, according to his creation before the world was made," and "Whoso forbiddeth to marry is not ordained of God." (D&C 49:15-17.) As the Pauline word has it: "Marriage is honourable in all, and the bed undefiled." (Heb. 13:4.) Such is our Lord's doctrine. And so it is that we see Jesus take "part in a scene that has charmed the imagination of poet and painter in every age. For as though to destroy all false and unnatural notions of the exceptional glory of religious virginity, He, among whose earliest acts it had been to bless a marriage festival, made it one of His latest acts to fondle infants in His arms." We see "fathers and mothers and friends" bring "to Him the fruits of holy wedlock—young children and even babes—that He might touch them and pray over them." (Farrar, pp. 500-501.)

They are rebuked by the disciples, who say, "There is no need, for Jesus hath said, Such shall be saved." It is evident that the adult male followers of Jesus feel they should not be disturbed in the deep doctrinal discussions then in progress. To them women and children, in keeping with Jewish practice and tradition, should remain in the background. "But when Jesus saw and heard them, he was much displeased," and he rebuked his disciples. Then he uttered those words of wonder and beauty and glory that shall stand forever among the great doctrinal verities of pure Christianity:

Suffer little children to come unto me, and forbid them not; for of such is the kingdom of heaven.

For of such is the kingdom of heaven! Little children, blessed spirits, pure and holy children of the Father, scarce removed from the Celestial Presence—such, in their innocence and perfection, are heirs of full salvation. "And little children also have eternal life," Abinadi said (Mosiah 15:25); and Joseph Smith, in recording a vision of the celestial kingdom, tells us: "And I also beheld that all children who die before they arrive at the years of accountability are saved in the celestial kingdom of heaven" (D&C 137:10). Such being the law that Jesus had theretofore taught his meridian disciples, we can almost anticipate his next words:

Verily I say unto you, Whosoever shall not receive the kingdom of God as a little child shall in no wise enter therein.

Riches and Eternal Life
(Matthew 19:16-26; JST, Matthew 19:18, 26; Mark 10:17-27; JST, Mark 10:16, 22, 26; Luke 18:18-27; JST, Luke 18:27)

Jewish Rabbis in Jesus' day were often asked by their disciples what course they should pursue to gain an inheritance with Abraham, Isaac, and Jacob in the kingdom of God. Rabbinists discussed, freely and at length, what the chosen people must do to gain eternal life. It was a dominant theme of discussion in all the Rabbinical schools. And always the course leading to salvation was lighted by their varying views and interpretations of the Mosaic and prophetic writings. It is said, for instance, that "when the Angel of Death came to fetch the R. Chanina, he said, 'Go and fetch me the Book of the Law, and *see whether there is anything in it which I have not kept.*'" (Farrar, p. 502, footnote 2.) Jesus himself, but recently, encountered a lawyer who sought to test his Rabbinical knowledge, hoping to find a flaw or a fault, by asking: "Master, what shall I do to inherit eternal life?" And it was out of the resultant colloquy that the parable of the good Samaritan came.

We are now about to witness a scene that so impressed the Synoptists that all three preserved its essential details. With the same question weighing heavily upon him, a rich young ruler, probably the ruler of the local synagogue, came running to Jesus. He knelt, affirmatively doing obeisance. Evidently he was sincere, but his words were so phrased as to specify that Jesus was only a great and good Rabbi and not the Divine One, not the Messiah, not the one whose answer would be the *ipse dixit* that would settle the matter forever. His words, coupled with Jesus' reply, have always been somewhat troublesome and difficult to understand; but by placing them—and particularly Jesus' answer—in their Jewish setting, we get a radically different meaning than otherwise would be the case. The devout young man said: "Good Master, what good thing shall I do, that I may have eternal life?"

Now, in all Jewish literature there is no such thing as addressing a Rabbi as *good*. It is said that the whole Talmud contains no single instance of such an accolade. It simply was not done in that day. He might be called Rab, Rabbi, or Rabboni, as when Mary Magdalene knelt before the Risen Lord in the garden, but not Good Rabbi, or Good Master. We have seen his disciples and those made whole by his healing power kneel before him, worship his person, and call him the Messiah, the God of Israel, and the Son of God. This our rich young ruler does not do—he has some reservations about the claims of this Rabbi; and yet it is clear to him that here is one who is more than other Rabbis; and so he seeks a middle ground, one that will honor Jesus more than the mere title Rabbi, and yet one that will avoid ascribing to him divine Messianic status. He says, "Good Master." It is as though he said, 'I salute you as a great Rabbi, one whose wisdom is greater than these others, but I refrain from calling you the Messiah, as do your disciples.'

In reply, Jesus said: "Why callest thou me good? there is none good but one, that is, God." 'Do not address me by the title *good* unless you acknowledge me as God, for none but

301

God is good, none but he is sinless, none but he is perfect. I am indeed the Sinless One, and therefore I am good. As I have heretofore taught, no one convicts me of sin; and so unless you are ready to accede this, do not call me good.' By this answer, which carries a touch of irony, Jesus affirms by inference his divinity and makes it plain to the young ruler that his halfhearted attempt to laud the one who needs no honor from men does not suffice. "He would as little accept the title 'Good,' as He would accept the title, 'Messiah,' when given in a false sense. He would not be regarded as that mere 'good Rabbi,' to which, in these days, more than ever, men would reduce Him. So far, Jesus would show the youth that when he came to Him as to one who was more than man, his address, as well as his question, was a mistake. No mere man can lay any other foundation than that which is laid, and if the ruler committed the error of simply admiring Jesus as a Rabbi of preeminent sanctity, yet no Rabbi, however saintly, was accustomed to receive the title of 'good,' or prescribe any amulet for the preservation of a virtuous life." (Farrar, p. 502.) In this setting, then, Jesus turns to the issue at hand, and makes a pronouncement of wondrous import:

If thou wilt enter into life, keep the commandments.

This is the sum and substance of the whole matter. Salvation, eternal life, rewards in all their degrees and varieties—all come by obedience to the laws and ordinances of the gospel. Salvation must be won; it is not a free gift. "Let us hear the conclusion of the whole matter: Fear God, and keep his commandments: for this is the whole duty of man." (Eccl. 12:13.) But what of grace? Grace is the love, mercy, and condescension of God in making salvation available to men. "It is by grace that we are saved, after all we can do." (2 Ne. 25:23.) Eternal life is freely available; salvation is free in that all may drink of the waters of life; all may come and partake; but none gains so high a reward as eternal life until he is tried and tested and found worthy, as were the ancients.

This is the answer the rich young man should have expected to hear. Any reputable Rabbi would have said the same thing. The differences arose as to what the commandments were and what one must do to keep them. The law of marriage and divorce, but recently expounded by Jesus, is an illustration of the divergent views of recognized Rabbinical schools on some of the most important of all human conduct. And so in answer to Jesus' pronouncement calling upon men to keep the commandments, the young ruler of the local synagogue asks: "Which?" 'Do I follow the School of Shammai or the School of Hillel? Must I observe the Sabbath and fast twice a week as do the Pharisees? Must I eat the paschal lamb with my loins girded and my feet shod, as did our fathers? Everyone says, Keep the commandments; I need to know the particulars.' Jesus, as always, goes back to basics:

Thou shalt not kill. Thou shalt not commit adultery. Thou shalt not steal. Thou shalt not bear false witness. Honour thy father and thy mother: and, Thou shalt love thy neighbour as thyself.

To this recitation, the answer came: "All these things have I kept from my youth up: what lack I yet?" Clearly our young friend was a man of devotion, decency, and integrity. From his youth he had walked in the available light, as millions in modern Christendom do before they ever hear of the restoration of the fulness of the gospel. That he knew little of the real meaning of some of those commandments we are about to see when he declines to do more than give lip service to loving his neighbors. But at this point, "Jesus beholding him loved him," and said to him:

One thing thou lackest: go thy way, sell whatsoever thou hast, and give to the poor, and thou shalt have treasure in heaven: and come, take up the cross, and follow me.

Eternal life can come to those only who put first in their lives the things of God's kingdom; who love the riches of eternity more than a handful of mortal pelf; who are willing to forsake all and follow Christ. Where a man's treasure is, there will his heart be also. For this man, the needful thing was to overcome the love of money and the power of riches; for others of us, the testing process calls upon us to forsake some other prized possession or ardent desire; every man has his own Gethsemane.[1] Having heard Jesus' counsel, the young man was sad and went away grieving, for he was richly endowed with this world's goods. Jesus then said to the disciples:

> *How hardly shall they that have riches enter into the kingdom of God!*

Heretofore Jesus has said many things about laying up treasures in heaven. He has taught that a man's life consisteth not in the abundance of the things that his soul possesses; he has spoken of those who lay up treasures for themselves and are not rich toward God; he has repeatedly called upon men to forsake all and follow him, and many such like things; but now he makes it almost seem as though rich men cannot be saved. His disciples are astonished. This is a straiter gate and a narrower path than they had supposed was the case. Jesus, in words of tenderness, responds to their feelings by amplifying his words:

> *Children, how hard is it for them that trust in riches to enter into the kingdom of God! It is easier for a camel to go through the eye of a needle, than for a rich man to enter into the kingdom of God.*

Their astonishment increases. It is a common Jewish proverb that even in a man's dreams he will not see an elephant pass through the eye of a needle. It is a proverb that points to that which cannot be. As with an elephant, so with a camel; a bloated beast of gargantuan size cannot pass through an opening made only large enough for a silken thread. As Mark expresses it, "they were astonished out of measure," and asked among themselves, "Who then can be saved?" Jesus gives answer:

> *With men that trust in riches, it is impossible; but not impossible with men who trust in God and leave all for my sake, for with such all these things are possible.*

How better could it be said? Truly, never man spake as this man. And as to the rich young ruler whose questions and conduct brought forth these gems of eternal truth, no further mention is made. Our last view of him is one of a man who prefers the comforts and ease of great wealth to the riches of eternity; it is of a sincere and devout man who is nonetheless deceived by the deceitfulness of riches; it is of one who dares not pay out a *temporal-all* in the cause of truth and righteousness here, so as to purchase an *eternal-all* in the realms ahead. We cannot but hope that he—being one upon whom Jesus looked with affection—came to himself, returned and accepted our Lord as the Messiah, and made his means available to feed the hungry, clothe the naked, shelter the homeless, and further the eternal gospel cause.

Riches and Rewards in the Day of Regeneration
(Matthew 19:27-30; JST, Matthew 19:28; Mark 10:28-31; JST, Mark 10:30-31; Luke 18:28-30)

As the rich young ruler, clinging to his wealth as a miser grasps his pennies, departs in sorrow, choosing to revel in ease and comfort rather than to use his possessions to bless mankind; as Jesus ends his terse and piercing words about forsaking all to gain eternal life; and as the full significance of his sayings begins to dawn upon the disciples, showing them that those who trust in riches and will not forsake all to follow Christ and further his gospel cause cannot be saved—in this setting, in a boastful way, claiming an apostolic preference and preeminence, Peter says: "Behold, we have forsaken all, and followed thee; what shall we have therefore?" In answer Jesus speaks first to the Twelve:

Verily I say unto you, that ye who have followed me, shall, in the resurrection [in the regeneration, as the King James Version has it], *when the Son of Man shall come sitting on the throne of his glory, ye shall also sit upon twelve thrones, judging the twelve tribes of Israel.*

305

Not only shall the Twelve have eternal life, but these noble souls also shall continue to serve in their high and holy administrative roles in the eternal worlds. Neither Peter nor any of his fellow apostles could ever have dreamt of so high and exalted a station as is here named. Jacob begat Israel and sired them as a nation; Moses led the chosen people out of Egyptian bondage and gave them their law; Elijah and Isaiah and the prophets guided them in the hours of their despair; Jesus, the Son of God, had come to redeem them—but now it is revealed that the Twelve shall, at Christ's behest, sit in judgment on Abraham's seed. Thus saith the Lord: "It hath gone forth in a firm decree, by the will of the Father, that mine apostles, the Twelve which were with me in my ministry at Jerusalem, shall stand at my right hand at the day of my coming in a pillar of fire, being clothed with robes of righteousness, with crowns upon their heads, in glory even as I am, to judge the whole house of Israel, even as many as have loved me and kept my commandments, and none else." (D&C 29:12.)[2]

All this was to be in the day of regeneration, the day when the earth would be refreshed and renewed and receive again its paradisiacal glory. This is the day that Peter, James, and John had seen in vision in the holy mount when Christ and they were transfigured, and when the Father bore witness that Jesus was his Son. But the blessings of the gospel are not for the Twelve only. Jesus continues:

Verily I say unto you, There is no man that hath left house, or brethren, or sisters, or father, or mother, or wife, or children, or lands, for my sake, and the gospel's, But he shall receive an hundredfold now in this time, houses, and brethren, and sisters, and mothers, and children, and lands, with persecutions; and in the world to come eternal life.

Of what does sacrifice consist? In the eternal perspective it is giving up a handful of clay—held and owned but tremulously and for a moment on this lowly earth—in exchange for a universe in the eternal ages that are to be. And yet, from our mortal view, it may mean giving up that which is of great worth unto us for the moment. Do we forsake family and friends and possessions and receive persecutions instead? If so, the gospel cause provides us with kinfolk who become closer than blood relatives; we are welcome to use the lands of others; and the possessions of all the saints become ours as we need them—all of which is only the beginning. There are rewards—with persecutions—in this life; and, finally, there is eternal life in the world ahead, which eternal life is all that the Father hath.[3]

Having set forth these wondrous truths, Jesus turned to Peter, who, with some pride of self-accomplishment, had posed the question. "But there are many who make themselves first," Jesus said, "that shall be last, and the last first." To this Mark adds: "This he said, rebuking Peter." And this, we might also add, formed an introduction to the parable of the laborers in the vineyard, which was immediately forthcoming.

Parable of the Laborers in the Vineyard
(Matthew 20:1-16)

Peter's statement, "we have forsaken all, and followed thee," said after the rich young ruler made his great refusal, declining as he did to follow Christ, was followed by the question: "What shall we have therefore?" Jesus' answer— glorious beyond belief—we have heard, together with his rebuke of Peter relative to some who made themselves first and who would, in fact, be last. Such is the setting for the present parable. "To impress upon them still more fully and deeply that the kingdom of heaven is not a matter of mercenary calculation or exact equivalent—that there could be no bargaining with the Heavenly Householder—that before the eye of God's clearer and more penetrating judgment Gentiles might be admitted before Jews, and Publicans before Pharisees, and young converts before aged Apostles—He told them the memorable Parable of the Labourers in the Vineyard. That parable, amid its other

307

lessons, involved the truth that, while all who serve God should not be defrauded of their just and full and rich reward, there could be in heaven no murmuring, no envyings, no jealous comparison of respective merits, no base strugglings for precedency, no miserable disputings as to who had performed the maximum of service, or who had received the minimum of grace." (Farrar, p. 504.)

For the kingdom of heaven is like unto a man that is an householder, which went out early in the morning to hire labourers into his vineyard. And when he had agreed with the labourers for a penny a day, he sent them into his vineyard.

The kingdom of heaven on earth is the Church of Jesus Christ, which prepares men for an inheritance in the kingdom of heaven hereafter, which is the celestial kingdom. The householder is God; the hired laborers are his servants; the vineyard is his kingdom; it is also the house of Israel and all the inhabitants of the earth to whom his servants are sent. It was the practice of the day to employ daily laborers in the marketplace. The agreed compensation, a penny or denarius, was the normal wage for a single day's service. The great importance of the work is shown by the fact that the householder himself employed the laborers, not trusting it to a steward.

And he went out about the third hour, and saw others standing idle in the marketplace. And said unto them; Go ye also into the vineyard, and whatsoever is right I will give you. And they went their way. Again he went out about the sixth and ninth hour, and did likewise.

The work day lasted from sunup to sunset. The others were employed for a just but unspecified wage; the Lord's servants do not always know what rewards he has in store for them, nor, in reality, could they conceive of them if they were named and identified.

And about the eleventh hour he went out, and found others standing idle, and saith unto them, Why stand ye here all the day idle? They say unto him, Because no man hath hired us. He saith unto them, Go ye also into the vineyard; and whatsoever is right, that shall ye receive.

Laborers called throughout the day are assumed to have been available at any time, but were called only as indicated. Deity calls his own servants according to his own will and on his own schedule. A new and grander vision of those called into the Master's service at the eleventh hour is seen in the revelation, received June 8, 1978, offering the full blessings of the gospel, including the priesthood and the blessings of the temple, to those of every race and color. All such, called at the eleventh hour, have the same obligation of priesthood service that the divine Householder has given to any of his servants, and they shall be rewarded on an equal basis.

So when even was come, the lord of the vineyard saith unto his steward, Call the labourers, and give them their hire, beginning from the last unto the first. And when they came that were hired about the eleventh hour, they received every man a penny. But when the first came, they supposed that they should have received more; and they likewise received every man a penny.

And when they had received it, they murmured against the goodman of the house, Saying, These last have wrought but one hour, and thou hast made them equal unto us, which have borne the burden and heat of the day.

But he answered one of them, and said, Friend, I do thee no wrong: didst not thou agree with me for a penny? Take that thine is, and go thy way: I will give unto this last, even as unto thee. Is it not lawful for me to do what I will with mine own? Is thine eye evil, because I am good?

In its initial application, the parable applied to Peter and the apostles; they bore the burdens of the kingdom during the heat of the day and came off marvelously well. But there were others—Gentiles, heathen, the seed of Cain—all of whom in due course would be called to service in the vineyard of the world. What if some of them, laboring but for an hour, should receive equal or even greater rewards than the first laborers—all of which brings us back to the introductory statement, made to Peter, which Jesus now restates by way of summary.

So the last shall be first, and the first last: for many be called, but few chosen.

These concluding words—"many be called, but few chosen"—stand forth as the warning-climax of the parable, not alone to Peter and the other first laborers, but to all who are called to service in the vineyard of the Lord. Many are called into the earthly kingdom, but few shall gain full salvation in the heavenly kingdom; many are called to serve missions, but few shall reap the reward that might have been theirs; many are called to the holy priesthood—covenanting thereby to love and serve God and their fellowmen with all their hearts, might, mind, and strength—but few shall be chosen for eternal life in the kingdom of Him whose we are. As he who gave the parable anciently has said to us in our day: "There are many who have been ordained among you, whom I have called but few of them are chosen. They who are not chosen have sinned a very grievous sin, in that they are walking in darkness at noon-day. . . . If you keep not my commandments, the love of the Father shall not continue with you, therefore you shall walk in darkness." (D&C 95:5-6, 12; 121:34-40.)

Many are called but few are chosen. It is an awesome warning.

NOTES

1. "Keep my commandments, and seek to bring forth and establish the cause of Zion: Seek not for riches but for wisdom, and behold, the mysteries of God shall be unfolded unto you, and then shall you be made rich. Behold, he that hath eternal life is rich." (D&C 6:6-7.)

2. For a brief summary of how men are judged by a great hierarchy of judges—with Judge Jesus at the head—see *Commentary* 1:558-59.

3. Because the Prophet Joseph Smith laid his all on the altar, the Lord by revelation said of him: "I will bless him and multiply him and give unto him an hundred-fold in this world, of fathers and mothers, brothers and sisters, houses and lands, wives and children, and crowns of eternal lives in the eternal worlds." (D&C 132:55.)

Chapter 83

JOURNEYING TOWARD THE CROSS

Suffer it to be so now:
for thus it becometh us to fulfil
all righteousness. (Matt. 3:15.)

The Coming Baptism of Blood
(Matthew 20:17-28; JST, Matthew 20:23; Mark 10:32-45;
JST, Mark 10:40, 42; Luke 18:31-34; JST, Luke 18:34)

Two scenes now come into view that dramatize the agony and the glory that lie ahead for Him who came to ransom fallen man from the bottomless abyss. They are (1) the announcing anew of his coming death and resurrection, and (2) the strivings of two of the Twelve for precedence and dominion in the kingdom of heaven.

We are traveling with Jesus, en route to "the great city, which spiritually is called Sodom and Egypt," where also he will be "crucified." (Rev. 11:8.) He must needs go to Jerusalem; he left Ephraim with that fixed design. He has ministered and taught, somewhat leisurely along the way, but now the time of the Fourth Passover draws nigh. It must needs be that he arrive on schedule, enter the Holy City amid shouts of Hosanna, perform his final ministry there, and then submit to the Roman scourge and the crucifier's nails.

311

Jesus' feet have trod the dusty lanes of Palestine for some thirty-three years; he has been in and out of the gates of Jerusalem hundreds of times; but there has never been such a journey as this one. In the past his steps have taken him to scenes of joy and healing and friendly intercourse with beloved associates; now they are traversing a steady descent into the valley of the shadow of death. And there is a solemnity, an awe—yes, a reverence—about the journey itself. Mark tell us Jesus went before the Twelve, and that they were amazed and afraid as they followed him. As he went forth on "the journey which was to end at Jerusalem," Farrar—whose way with words is wondrous—tells us, "A prophetic solemnity and elevation of soul struggling with the natural anguish of the flesh, which shrank from that great sacrifice, pervaded His whole being, and gave a new and strange grandeur to every gesture and every look. It was the Transfiguration of Self-sacrifice; and, like that previous Transfiguration of Glory, it filled those who beheld it with an amazement and terror which they could not explain. There are few pictures in the gospels more pathetic than this of Jesus going forth to His death, and walking alone along the path into the deep valley, while behind Him, in awful reverence, and mingled anticipations of dread and hope—their eyes fixed on Him, as with bowed head He preceded them in all the majesty of sorrow—the disciples followed, and dared not disturb His meditations." (Farrar, pp. 516-17.) But as they journeyed, Jesus said:

Behold, we go up to Jerusalem, and all things that are written by the prophets concerning the Son of man shall be accomplished.

He was following a foreordained course; he came to preach and heal and die; his death lay just ahead. Of him all the prophets had testified, and every jot and tittle spoken by them must be fulfilled.

Behold, we go up to Jerusalem; and the Son of man shall be betrayed unto the chief priests and unto the scribes, and they shall condemn him to death, And shall

312

deliver him to the Gentiles to mock, and to scourge, and to crucify him: and the third day he shall rise again.

This is now the third time, of which we know, when this same Jesus has spoken in plainness of his betrayal, trial, scourging, death, and resurrection. It was said just before he and the Three went up the Mount of Transfiguration and, thereafter, when the apostolic party—including the women who were with them—returned to Galilee. But this is the first time the word *crucify* is recorded. Of what he has now said, Luke editorializes: "And they understood none of these things; and this saying was hid from them; neither remembered they the things which were spoken." As the apostles were to be observers, witnesses, and to some extent participants in the atoning events that lay ahead, and as those events were to be tests for them as well as for the Lord Jesus, their full meaning was kept from them and they were not permitted to remember them again until after the testing period was past.

Now the scene changes, though the holy party is still traveling their fateful course toward Jerusalem. Life with Jesus was like a refiner's fire. Day after day and conversation after conversation, his incisive words burned dross and imperfections out of the souls of his apostles and out of all others who could bear the heat of the fiery furnace. Now Salome—the wife of Zebedee, the sister of the Blessed Virgin, the mother of James and John, the aunt of the Lord Jesus—with her two sons, the sons of thunder, who one day sought to call down fire from heaven upon certain persons in Samaria who rejected Jesus—these three, a mother and her two sons, came to Jesus in secret. They fell before him in reverential worship; theirs was the sure knowledge, born of the Spirit, that the Man of Nazareth was the Holy Messiah who should reign on the throne of David forever.

Knowing they desired something of him, Jesus asked: "What wilt thou?" Salome answered: "Grant that these my two sons may sit, the one on thy right hand, the other on the left, in thy kingdom." James and John uttered the same peti-

313

tion. "Master, we would that thou shouldest do for us what-soever we shall desire," they said. And when he responded, "What would ye that I should do for you," they repeated the plea of their mother: "Grant unto us that we may sit, one on thy right hand, and the other on thy left hand, in thy glory."

The echo of Jesus' voice, rebuking Peter when the Chief Apostle sought to make himself first in the kingdom of God, has scarcely stopped ringing in their ears. The message of the parable of the laborers in the vineyard—that all servants worthy of exaltation would be rewarded alike—is still part of their ponderings. And yet, filled with holy zeal and bound-less ambition—as true saints should be, within proper limits—these intimates of the Lord asked for that which exceeded the bounds of propriety. "Jesus bore gently with their selfishness and error. They had asked in their blindness for that position which, but a few days afterwards, they were to see occupied in shame and anguish by the two crucified robbers. Their imaginations were haunted by twelve thrones; His thoughts were of three crosses. They dreamt of earthly crowns; He told them of a cup of bitterness and a baptism of blood." (Farrar, pp. 517-18.) "Ye know not what ye ask," he said. "Are ye able to drink of the cup that I shall drink of, and to be baptized with the baptism that I am baptized with?" Their answer, "We are able."

Then said Jesus: "Ye shall drink indeed of my cup, and be baptized with the baptism that I am baptized with: but to sit on my right hand, and on my left, is not mine to give, but it shall be given to them for whom it is prepared of my Father."[1] As Jesus was baptized by John in Jordan to fulfill all righteousness, so for the same reason would all of the Twelve be baptized in blood, as it were, when the severity of the scourge, and the cruelties of the cross, and the sharpness of the spear fell upon them. James would be slain at Herod's order and John would be banished to Patmos. The baptism of blood was indeed at their door.

When the rest of the Twelve heard what Zebedee's family sought, they were "much displeased with James and

John," and Jesus, calling them all together, used the occasion to teach them how true greatness in God's kingdom is gained:

> *Ye know that they who are appointed to rule over the Gentiles exercise lordship over them; and their great ones exercise authority upon them. But so shall it not be among you: but whosoever will be great among you, shall be your minister: And whosoever of you will be the chiefest, shall be servant of all.*
>
> *For even the Son of man came not to be ministered unto, but to minister, and to give his life a ransom for many.*

If Jesus came to be the servant of all; if he came to minister to the eternal well-being of all men; if he came to pay the ransom, by the shedding of his own blood, for the captive souls of men—then how ought his greater stewards and lesser servants labor in his vineyard?

The Healing of Zaccheus and of Bartimeus
(Luke 18:35-43; 19:1-10; JST, Luke 18:43; 19:7-8; Mark 10:46-52; Matthew 20:29-34)

In Jericho of ancient fame there dwelt two men, Zaccheus and Bartimeus, whose lives are about to be changed forever by the touch of the Master's hand. Zaccheus, the Jew, is a hated and despised publican; nay, more, he is "the chief among the publicans," of whom there is a large colony in this prosperous city. He is a rich man and a sinner who lives a life of extortion and fraud. How evil it is for a tax collector to take more than the law allows and to keep it for himself! Zaccheus has a sin-sick soul. Bartimeus, the Jew, is poor and blind and makes his living by begging on the streets. He is a social nonentity for whom none care, and whose life is tolerated only because blindness and begging go together in this culture, a culture that leaves its invalids to suffer alone and to gain such crumbs and crusts as chance to fall their way.

Jericho, a verdant tropical city filled with flowers and

315

palm trees, located on a watered plain, is called the paradise of God. It is truly the Eden of Palestine, the most fruitful area of the whole land, and to it masses of people flock as desert denizens to a flowery oasis. Through its streets pass many of the Perean and Galilean pilgrims en route to keep the Passover in Jerusalem. Among them this time are Jesus, the Twelve, and others of the disciples, including women, one of whom, Salome, has but recently interceded with him for her sons.

Jesus' fame is such that the whole city turns out to see him. This is he who sent one born blind to wash in the pool of Siloam and he came seeing. This is he who said to Lazarus of Bethany, whose decomposing body had lain in the tomb for four days, "Come forth," and it was so. This is he whom the scribes hate and the Sanhedrin seek that they may put him to death. Is he the Messiah, as we have heard, or does he do all these miracles by the power of Satan? Will he do any of his marvelous works in our streets? Is he the Messiah or the antichrist? Perhaps we will be able to tell as we see what happens to Zaccheus and to Bartimeus.

Jesus, now in Jericho, is surrounded by throngs of people; there are multitudes on every side. Zaccheus, who is small of stature, cannot so much as glimpse the Messianic face; he runs ahead and climbs a sycamore tree. Jesus stops under the tree, looks up, and says, "Zaccheus, make haste, and come down; for to day I must abide at thy house."

"And he made haste, and came down, and received him joyfully." He who ever stands at the door and knocks; he who is ever ready to come in and sup with all who will open unto him; he who seeks to be an unseen guest in every home at every meal—he this day chose a rich and hated publican to be his host. Why? No reasons are given, nor need they be. We cannot doubt that Zaccheus by study and prayer and pondering had made himself ready to receive the Guest of guests, and that Jesus came—as a Laborer worthy of his hire—to impart to a repenting publican that spiritual health which he alone can give. "And when the disciples saw it, they all murmured, saying, That he was gone to be a guest with a man who is a sinner."

Once there was no room for him in the inns; now he chooses to spend the night with a sinner who is hated by all, and that not without cause. Often he has slept with his disciples under the Palestinian stars to be rid of the conniving and evil influences of the day; now he elects to associate with a sinner of ill repute. In this self-selected abode there is time to relax and eat, to rest and to teach. Much is said by Jesus about the gospel and repentance and salvation and the glories of the eternal world. At a point of climax, Zaccheus's heart is pricked. He stands and says: "Behold, Lord, the half of my goods I give to the poor; and if I have taken any thing from any man by unjust means, I restore him fourfold."

Jesus has gained a convert. This man will be baptized and become a disciple. Jesus says: "This day is salvation come to this house, forsomuch as he also is a son of Abraham." And to all of this, then comes the grand climax:

For the Son of man is come to seek and to save that which was lost.

Such is the story of Zaccheus, as far as it has been preserved for us. His soul is healed and he is a new man. Jesus has wrought one of his greatest miracles. As to Bartimeus, the beggar, the blessing prepared for him is reserved until the next morning as Jesus and his party leave Jericho, and it becomes in effect a divine seal on the preaching and spiritual healing of which we have already spoken.

Luke tells us that as Jesus and his party approached Jericho, they met "a certain blind man" who sat begging by the way. Hearing the multitude, he asked what it meant, and was told, "Jesus of Nazareth passeth by." Immediately the sightless one cried out, "Jesus, thou son of David, have mercy on me." He was rebuked by those who accompanied Jesus and was told to hold his peace, which he did not do, but continued to cry out, "Thou son of David, have mercy on me." Jesus stopped, commanded the blind one to be brought, and asked, "What wilt thou that I shall do unto thee?" He said, "Lord, that I may receive my sight." Jesus said, "Receive thy sight: thy faith hath saved thee." Immediately his sight came, and he followed Jesus and glorified God. "And all the disciples when they saw this, gave praise unto God." Then, as Luke has it, "Jesus entered and passed through Jericho."

Mark tells us that this healing took place when Jesus "went out of Jericho with his disciples," and adds to Luke's account that the beggar was named Bartimeus, the son of Timeus; that when the beggar was called to come to Jesus, he was told, "Be of good comfort, rise; he calleth thee"; and that the beggar cast away his garment as he came. Matthew agrees with Mark as to when the blind eyes were opened, but says there were two beggars, not one, and that Jesus "touched their eyes." There is no question, of course, that if we had the full recitations, as originally written, there would be no contradictions. We are left, therefore, to draw our own conclusions as to the details here involved. We know Jesus normally taught the gospel first and then stretched forth his hands to work miracles so that the healing acts would place a seal of divinity upon his teachings. We suppose that is what he did in this instance also. In any event, as pertaining to Bartimeus, his repeated designation of Jesus as the Son of David, who had power to open blind eyes, shows that he had prior faith and qualified as one entitled to receive the divine blessing that came to him.

Parable of the Pounds
(Luke 19:11-28; JST, Luke 19:11, 14, 17, 23-25)

Jesus has set his face like flint to go to Jerusalem, where the cruel cross of crucifixion awaits his outstretched arms and nailed hands. He has many things yet to say in the few remaining days of his flesh, but, with it all, Jehovah must die so that together with his dead body many that sleep in the dust shall come forth. He as a nobleman sent of God must now travel to a far country, there, in the presence of his Father, to be crowned with glory and power everlasting.

318

Before he departs he will leave his earthly affairs in the hands of his servants to whom, in due course, he will return and call for an accounting of their stewardships.

This, however, is not what all Israel suppose. They are yet seeking a temporal deliverer upon whose head a kingly crown may be placed; they have yet to learn that the way to the crown is by the cross. Even some of the disciples—not, we suppose, those of the Twelve or of the Seventy—yet feel that this man should be crowned, not crucified, when he arrives in the Holy City.

And so now we find Jesus and his party, and a great host of Passover pilgrims, plodding onward from Jericho to Jerusalem. Mingled among them are many who could be drawn into the scribal stream of hostility and evil where the enemies of God will raise a sword against his Son. As a warning to them, and so that his disciples may understand more perfectly his purposes, and because they are "nigh to Jerusalem," "and because the Jews taught that the kingdom of God should immediately appear"—the scene being thus set—Jesus delivers the parable of the pounds.

A certain nobleman went into a far country to receive for himself a kingdom, and to return. And he called his ten servants, and delivered them ten pounds, and said unto them, Occupy till I come. But his citizens hated him, and sent a messenger after him, saying, We will not have this man to reign over us.

This is a story that friends and foes alike will ponder in their hearts. Hearing it, they will recall the numerous "noblemen" who left Palestine and went to far-off Rome to receive suzerainty from Caesar, that they might return and reign with blood and horror over the citizens of their assigned kingdoms. They will remember in particular that some thirty years before, Archelaus went to Augustus in Rome to gain confirmation of the provisions of the will of his father, Herod the Great, so that the Idumean's offspring could reign in his appointed kingdom. They will recall how the Jews sent to Augustus a deputation of fifty to recount the cruelties and oppose the claims of Herod's son; how "Philippus defended the property of Archelaus during his absence from the encroachments of the Proconsul Sabinus"; and how Archelaus, upon his return, avenged this Jewish act of rebellion with the blood of his enemies. (Farrar, p. 524, footnote 1; Edersheim 2:466.) They will also realize that Jesus is speaking of himself as the nobleman who goes to a far country; that his servants have a period of labor before his return; and that the Messianic kingdom for which they yearn will not be established until a future day.

And it came to pass, that when he was returned, having received the kingdom, then he commanded these servants to be called unto him, to whom he had given the money, that he might know how much every man had gained by trading.

Then came the first, saying, Lord, thy pound hath gained ten pounds. And he said unto him, Well done, thou good servant; because thou hast been faithful in a very little, have thou authority over ten cities. And the second came, saying, Lord, thy pound hath gained five pounds. And he said likewise to him, Be thou also over five cities.

And another came, saying, Lord, behold, here is thy pound, which I have kept laid up in a napkin: For I feared thee, because thou art an austere man: thou takest up that thou layedst not down, and reapest that thou didst not sow.

And he saith unto him, Out of thine own mouth will I judge thee, thou wicked servant. Thou knewest that I was an austere man, taking up that I laid not down, and reaping that I did not sow: Wherefore then gavest not thou my money into the bank, that at my coming I might have received mine own with usury?

And he said unto them who stood by, Take from him the pound, and give it to him who hath ten pounds.

Each servant has a like endowment and a like responsibility. It is with the elders and seventies as it is with the apostles. Each receives the Holy Priesthood; each is called to minister for the salvation of men; each takes upon himself the covenant and rejoices in the oath of the priesthood; and each has power to work out his own salvation and gain eternal reward if true and faithful in all things. As it turns out, the respective labors of each determine his kingdom and dominion in the day of his Lord's return. The power to work in the kingdom here becomes the power to rule in the kingdom hereafter. As to the slothful servant, who did no labor here, he enjoys no dominion hereafter. His pound is given to the one who can make the best use of it—it shall go "to him that hath ten pounds." Such is the surprise of his hearers at this decision that they interrupt Jesus to say, "Lord, he hath ten pounds." Our Lord's response is:

For I say unto you, That unto every one who occupieth, shall be given; and from him who occupieth not, even that he hath received shall be taken away from him.

Service is essential to salvation! Labor in the vineyard or be damned. Those who receive the Holy Priesthood must magnify their callings; they must use the priesthood to teach the gospel, to perform ordinances, and to work miracles, as Jesus did; otherwise they have no reward.

But those mine enemies, which would not that I should reign over them, bring hither, and slay them before me.

Jesus' enemies—worldly people; those who do not heed the voice of his servants; those who reject him and his gospel; those who will not have him to rule over them—they shall be slain at his coming. "And the day cometh that they who will not hear the voice of the Lord, neither the voice of his servants, neither give heed to the words of the prophets and apostles, shall be cut off from among the people." (D&C 1:14.) It shall be "when the Lord Jesus shall be revealed from heaven with his mighty angels, In flaming fire taking vengeance on them that know not God, and that obey not the gospel of our Lord Jesus Christ: Who shall be punished with everlasting destruction from the presence of the Lord, and from the glory of his power." (2 Thes. 1:7-9.)

Such is the eternal intent; such is the long-term meaning of the parable. But for that generation of Jews there was to be an immediate application of the curse pronounced upon those who would not have him to rule over them; who proclaimed, "We have no king but Caesar"; who said, "Write not, The King of the Jews; but that he said, I am King of the Jews"; who after he ascended into heaven continued to exhibit violent hostility against the infant Church—upon that generation of Jews the curse was to fall with unslaked fury. True, "The parable was one of many-sided application; it indicated His near departure from the world; the hatred which should reject Him; the duty of faithfulness in the use of all that He entrusted to them; the uncertainty of His return; the certainty that, when He did return, there would be a solemn account; the condemnation of the slothful; the splendid reward of all who should serve Him well; the utter destruction of those who endeavoured to reject His power." (Farrar, p. 525.)

"But as regards His 'enemies,' that would not have Him reign over them—manifestly, Jerusalem and the people of Israel—who, even after he had gone to receive the Kingdom, continued the personal hostility of their 'We will not that this One shall reign over us'—the ashes of the Temple, the ruins of the City, the blood of the fathers, and the homeless wanderings of their children, with the Cain-curse branded on their brow and visible to all men, attest, that the King has many ministers to execute that judgment which obstinate rebellion must surely bring, if His authority is to be vindicated, and His Rule to secure submission." (Edersheim 2:467.)

"And when he"—the Nobleman who will reign as King in a future day—"had thus spoken," Luke tells us, "he went before, ascending up to Jerusalem," allowing his hearers to ponder and marvel at the gracious words they had heard.

NOTE

1. As I have written elsewhere with reference to the statement that a position on his right hand or on his left was not his to give: "Certainly it is Christ's to give, for he has all power (Matt. 28:18) and all judgment is committed to the Son. (John 5:22.) Rather: 'It is not mine to give as a matter of favoritism; it can be given only in accordance with justice. To sit on my right hand or on my left is not mine to give, except to them for whom it is prepared according to the Father's will, and the Father and I are one.' " (*Commentary* 1:566.)

SECTION X

FROM THE ANOINTING
TO THE ROYAL REIGN

FROM THE ANOINTING TO THE ROYAL REIGN

THIS IS JESUS
THE KING OF THE JEWS.
(Matt. 27:37.)
Blessed be the King that cometh
in the name of the Lord:
peace in heaven,
and glory in the highest.
(Luke 19:38.)

As Samuel poured oil on the head of Saul and anointed him to be captain over the Lord's inheritance, and all Israel then marched at their king's word;

As he also poured oil on David and anointed him in the midst of his brethren, so that the Spirit of the Lord came upon him from that day forward;

And as Zadok took an horn of oil and anointed Solomon, and all the people said, "God save king Solomon"—

So Mary of Bethany, in the home of Simon the leper, as guided by the Spirit, poured costly spikenard from her alabaster box upon the head of Jesus, and also anointed his feet, so that, the next day, the ten thousands of Israel might acclaim him King and shout Hosanna to his name.

We see Jesus thus anointed and acclaimed, heading a triumphal procession into the Holy City. So commences the first day of the week of the atoning sacrifice.

On the second day he curses the barren fig tree and cleanses the temple a second time.

On the third day he discourses on faith; confounds the Jews on the question of authority, and delivers the three

327

parables to the Jews—the parable of the two sons, the parable of the wicked husbandmen, and the parable of the marriage of the king's son.

That same day the Jews provoke, tempt, and reject him; they seek to ensnare him on the question of tribute and are confounded; he proclaims the law of eternal marriage; and then he gives his great pronouncement about the first and great commandment.

Then he propounds the question: "What think ye of Christ?"

After all this comes the great denunciation. Such woes—eight in number—as seldom come from divine lips are heaped, with a vengeance, upon the rebellious scribes and Pharisees.

Thereupon he laments over doomed Jerusalem, speaks of the widow's mite, offers salvation to the Gentiles, and testifies boldly that he is the Son of Man. Thus endeth his public ministry.

During the closing hours of that day, he gives the incomparable Olivet Discourse.

In it his voice is raised, first, against Jerusalem and the Holy House soon to be left desolate.

He speaks of the persecutions and martyrdom that await his disciples.

He tells of the universal apostasy that will precede the Second Coming; then of the glorious era of Restoration; of the desolations of the latter days; and of the coming in of the Gentile fulness.

His disciples learn that the abomination of desolation shall again sweep Jerusalem; that signs and wonders shall fill the heavens and the earth; and that he shall come as a thief in the night.

Those who shall abide the day are identified, and all men are commanded to watch, pray, take heed, and be ready.

He then speaks the parable of the ten virgins and the parable of the talents, and, finally, gives the great decree that he and the Twelve shall sit on thrones in judgment upon the world.

And in that day all his saints who have served their fellow men shall learn that their good deeds were in fact done unto him, and they shall have eternal life.

Chapter 84

"HOSANNA TO THE SON OF DAVID"

Rejoice greatly, O daughter of Zion;
shout, O daughter of Jerusalem:
behold, thy King cometh unto thee:
he is just, and having salvation;
lowly, and riding upon an ass,
and upon a colt the foal of an ass. . . .
He shall speak peace unto the heathen:
and his dominion shall be from sea even to sea,
and from the river even to the ends of the earth.
(Zech. 9:9-10.)

Mary Anoints Jesus at Simon's Supper
*(John 11:55-57; 12:1-11; JST, John 11:56; 12:7; Matthew 26:6-13;
JST, Matthew 26:5-10; Mark 14:3-9; JST, Mark 14:4-8)*

As the time of the Fourth Passover draws near, fanatical
tides of religious anarchy sweep through Jerusalem—
through the Holy City, the City of David, through the religious capital of the world. Never in the whole history of the
world have religious feelings and fanaticism built themselves
up to such a crises as now impends—not when the Lord confounded the tongues at Babel; not when he slew the firstborn
in every Egyptian home; not when an evil and militant spirit
swept the Crusades across Europe; not at any time.

331

There is a veritable maelstrom of divergent opinion about Him who is everywhere proclaiming his own divine Sonship and then working miracles to attest the divinity of his word. For three and a half years Jesus has taught and preached and worked miracles in every city and village throughout the land. Apostles and seventies, and disciples without number, both male and female, have echoed his words and testified of his goodness and grace to them. His gospel message has been proclaimed from the mountaintops; nothing has been done in a corner. Just as all Israel knew that Moses led them through the Red Sea and that six days of each week Jehovah rained manna from heaven upon them, so these Jews all know that there is one among them who claims to be the Son of God. It is as though each day the press, radio, and television carry new banner headlines and relay extensive broadcasts telling his doings of that day. There are press releases quoting his words; accounts of eyewitnesses who saw his miracles; the testimonies of those who were healed; the views of his enemies that he works by the power of Beelzebub and is even Satan incarnate; and the analytical columns setting forth the marvels of his ministry, or the evils of forsaking Moses to follow him, as each author expounds the views he espouses. Every Sabbath in the synagogues his doings and sayings are discussed by friends and foes. Every marketplace is ablaze with gossip and rumor about him. On every street corner men congregate to exchange opinions and gain new views. The raising of Lazarus is discussed in every home; the name of Jesus is on every tongue.

Passover pilgrims from the country areas are arriving in Jerusalem ahead of the feast itself so they can "purify themselves" in the temple. Their conversations are about the one thing uppermost in all minds. "What think ye of Jesus?" they ask one another. His disciples, whose views are fixed, move among them and bear testimony of the knowledge of salvation that has come into their hearts. Many rustic Galileans speak of him in reverent tones. "Will he not come to the feast?" they ask, and none seem to know. Influenced by their Rabbis and swayed by their scribes, most of the sophisticated Judeans have gained an undying hatred of this man of Galilee—out of which country, as they pretend to believe, cometh no prophet. And the chief priests and the Pharisees have given a commandment that if anyone knows where Jesus is, "he should shew it, that they might take him."[1]

Before placing his person in the midst of this war of words and tumult of opinions; before showing himself to the people, that all things shall be fulfilled which have been spoken of him in the law and in the prophets; before carrying his cross for the week of his passion, Jesus chose to spend a quiet Sabbath, his last on earth, in his beloved Bethany. There in the home of Simon the leper, enjoying sociality with Mary and Martha and Lazarus and those of his intimate circle, he will receive the holy anointing preparatory to his kingly burial; there he will take into his lungs the last peaceful breaths of Judean air before the tumultuous hours and days of his passion. It is Friday, Nisan 8, A.U.C. 780— March 31, A.D. 30, according to our calendar—and Jesus and his select friends are just arriving from Jericho. As we learned in the passing and raising of Lazarus there was communication between our Lord and his associates in Bethany, and it would not surprise us if the beloved sisters and others came out to meet and greet him and his party as they neared the place where they designed to spend the approaching Sabbath.

But before recounting the circumstances surrounding the sacred ordinance, which will transpire in this Judean village of blessed memory, on the Sabbath which will dawn, as it were, with the setting sun, we must note the intimate and felicitous friendships that prevailed between Jesus and the beloved sisters and their brother Lazarus. We have reason to believe this relationship was like none other enjoyed by him who came to do all things well and gain all the experiences of mortality. All scripturalists and authors of insight and renown are aware of the unique and unusual familial scenes portrayed by the Gospel authors with reference to the various happenings in this secluded and peaceful village. Let us note, for instance, how Farrar speaks of Jesus' friends in Bethany.

"We seem to trace in the Synoptists a special reticence about the family at Bethany," he says. "The house in which they take a prominent position is called 'the house of Simon the leper'; Mary is called simply 'a woman' by St. Matthew and St. Mark; and St. Luke contents himself with calling Bethany 'a certain village,' although he was perfectly aware of the name. There are, therefore, good grounds for the conjecture that when the earliest form of the Gospel of St. Matthew appeared, and when the memorials were collected which were used by the other two Synoptists, there may have been special reasons for not recording a miracle [the raising of Lazarus] which would have brought into dangerous prominence a man who was still living, but of whom the Jews had distinctly sought to get rid as a witness of Christ's wonder-working power. Even if this danger had ceased, it would have been painful to the quiet family of Bethany to have been made the focus of an intense and irreverent curiosity, and to be questioned about those hidden things none have ever revealed. Something, then, seems to have 'sealed the lips' of those Evangelists—an obstacle which had been long removed when St. John's Gospel first saw the light." (Farrar, p. 511.)[2]

As to our Lord's last Sabbath on earth, we assume he preached in the local synagogue or counseled in quiet seclusion with the Twelve and other intimates. When the hour came for the festive Sabbath meal, they held it in his honor. John says, "they made him a supper," as though it were a community expression of goodwill toward their Guest of renown. Matthew and Mark placed the banquet "in the house of Simon the leper." Martha served—indeed, she seems to have been in charge of the serving and arrangements; Lazarus sat at the table with Jesus; the Twelve and others of the disciples partook of the feast; and—as the custom was—others milled about as observers.

Bethany that evening was the focal point of Jewish interest. Many people, learning that Jesus was there, came from Jerusalem to see him and to see Lazarus, "whom he had raised from the dead." Among them were those whose souls were penitent and who sought that righteousness which this Galilean brought; and among them also were those whose hearts were hardened and who were devising ways to slay both Lazarus and Jesus. Lazarus alive was a living witness of the power of Him whose new doctrine meant the death of the Mosaic system, and of all the religious formalities so dear to the hearts of those whose means of livelihood it was. And so, "the chief priests"—the very rulers of the nation—"consulted that they might put Lazarus also to death," John tells us, "Because that by reason of him many of the Jews went away, and believed on Jesus." Scarcely is there a lower depth than this to which malice and hatred and depravity can sink.

Emotions ran high this memorable evening in Bethany, not only among those who came to view and wonder, or to plot and connive, as their desires might be, but also among those in whose house the feast was held. And in the souls of none did the fires of love, and devotion, and worship, burn more brightly than in the soul of the beloved Mary. She who loved to sit at Jesus' feet and hear his words; she whose soul drank in truth as the parched desert absorbs the heavensent rain; she who had seen her brother Lazarus come forth from the tomb after four days of decomposing death—this beloved one now sought some means of expressing her love and worship of the Master before he went to his death. She took from her treasures an alabaster box containing "a pound of ointment of spikenard, very costly," and poured it on his head, and anointed his feet, and wiped them with her hair, "and the house was filled with the odour of the ointment." Truly the sweet smell of incense, symbolical of the prayers of the heart, ascended up on high this night.

"To understand this solemn scene one must both know and feel the religious significance of Mary's act. Here sat the Lord of Heaven, in the house of his friends, as the hour of his greatest trials approached, with those who loved him knowing he was soon to face betrayal and crucifixion. What act of love, of devotion, of adoration, of worship, could a mere mortal perform for him who is eternal? Could a loved one do more than David had said the Good Shepherd himself would do in conferring honor and blessing upon another, that is: 'Thou anointest my head with oil'?" (*Commentary* 1:700.)[3]

"But there was one present to whom on every ground the act was odious and repulsive. There is no vice at once so absorbing, so unreasonable, and so degrading as the vice of avarice, and avarice was the besetting sin in the dark soul of the traitor Judas. The failure to struggle with his own temptations; the disappointment of every expectation which had first drawn him to Jesus; the intolerable rebuke conveyed to his whole being by the daily communion with a sinless purity; the darker shadow which he could not but feel that his guilt flung athwart his footsteps because of the burning sunlight in which for many months he now had walked; the sense too that the eye of his Master, possibly even the eyes of some of his fellow-apostles, had read or were beginning to read the hidden secrets of his heart;—all these things had gradually deepened from an incipient alienation into an insatiable repugnancy and hate. And the sight of Mary's lavish sacrifice, the consciousness that it was now too late to save that large sum for the bag—the mere possession of which, apart from the sums which he could pilfer out of it, gratified his greed for gold—filled him with disgust and madness. He had a devil. He felt as if he had been personally cheated; as if the money were by right *his,* and he had been, in a senseless manner, defrauded of it. 'To what purpose is this waste?' he indignantly said; and, alas! how often have his words been echoed, for wherever there is an act of splendid self-forgetfulness there is always a Judas to sneer and murmur at it. 'This ointment might have been sold for three hundred pence and given to the poor!' *Three hundred pence*—ten pounds or more! There was perfect frenzy in the thought of such utter perdition of good money; why, for barely a third of such a sum, this son of perdition was ready to sell his Lord. Mary thought it not good enough to anele Christ's sacred feet: Judas thought a third part of it sufficient reward for selling His very life." (Farrar, 527- 28.)

Mary loved much and was rewarded infinitely. Her act of adoring worship—born, we cannot doubt, from the promptings of the Spirit—gained for her a name and a fame that shall endure everlastingly. How sweet the words we now hear Jesus speak:

Why trouble ye the woman? For she hath wrought a good work upon me.

Ye have the poor with you always, and whensoever ye will, ye may do them good; but me ye have not always.

Let her alone; for she hath preserved this ointment until now, that she might anoint me in token of my burial.

She has done what she could, and this which she has done unto me, shall be had in remembrance in generations to come, wheresoever my gospel shall be preached; for verily she has come beforehand to anoint my body to the burying.

And in this thing that she hath done, she shall be blessed; for verily I say unto you, Wheresoever this gospel shall be preached in the whole world, this thing that this woman hath done, shall also be told for a memorial of her.

He that hath ears to hear, let him hear!

Jesus Enters Jerusalem as King Messiah
(*Matthew 21:1-11; JST, Matthew 21:2, 4-5, 9; Mark 11:1-11; JST, Mark 11:10-13; Luke 19:29-44; John 12:12-19; JST, John 12:14*)

"Rejoice greatly, O daughter of Zion; shout, O daughter of Jerusalem"; let all who dwell in David's City cry

Hosanna. Come, all ye Judeans and Galileans and Pereans and Samaritans; come, ye Gentiles whose lives are touched by Israel and her divine destiny; come, ye three million souls who are celebrating the Passover in your capital city—for this day ye shall see the seeric words of Zechariah fulfilled.

"Behold," O Jerusalem, the Holy City, for "thy King cometh unto thee." He cometh from Bethany on the east, where but yesterday he sat at meat with Lazarus, whom he raised from death; where in the house of Simon the leper, his beloved Mary anointed his royal head and poured costly spikenard on his kingly feet—all in token of his burial, which is to be later this week.

Hail him as your King; heed his words, for "he is just, and having salvation." Accept him as the Just One, your Deliverer—from death, hell, the devil, and endless torment. Know that all who believe in him shall be saved; he is your Savior; salvation comes by him; he is the resurrection and the life, as he said.

How shall he come? As the prophetic word foretells, ye shall see him "lowly, and riding upon an ass," the symbol of Jewish royalty. He shall be "upon a colt the foal of an ass." Messianic shouts shall rend the air; his disciples shall wave palm branches of peace; and the Roman soldiers in Antonia will smile and say, "What manner of King is this," not knowing that his kingdom is not of this world.

Come, join in the celebration, for this is he of whom it is written: "He shall speak peace unto the heathen: and his dominion shall be from sea even to sea, and from the river even to the ends of the earth." And those who accept him now will reign with him then in that great millennial day.

It is Sunday, April 2, A.D. 30, and Jesus with his disciples—that all things shall be fulfilled which are written of him—departs from Bethany, going toward Jerusalem. Multitudes from the Judean village follow along. When he arrives at the mount of Olives, near Bethphage, a suburb of Jerusalem, he says, as we suppose, to Peter and John: "Go your way into the village over against you: and as soon as ye be entered into it, ye shall find a colt tied, whereon never man sat; loose him, and bring him. And if any man say unto you, Why do ye this? say ye that the Lord hath need of him; and straightway he will send him hither."

They went. All things happened as Jesus' seeric foresight had specified, and they "brought the colt, and put on it their clothes; and Jesus took the colt and sat thereon; and they followed him." Then many, "a very great multitude"—those who came out from Jerusalem to meet the Messianic party, and those who followed from Bethany—spread their garments, and the branches they cut from the trees, to make a path before him. His disciples—both Judeans and Galileans coming out from the City of the Great King, and those from Bethany who were with him "when he called Lazarus out of his grave, and raised him from the dead"—they all "took branches of palm trees" and waved them as they gave the Hosanna Shout. It was a spontaneous, Spirit-guided acclamation of holy praise and divine testimony, patterned after the acclamations of adulation and glory given to Jehovah at the Feast of Tabernacles. Their King—meek and lowly in heart, riding in their midst on a lowly ass—heard thousands of voices cry out in perfect praise:

Hosanna: Blessed is the King of Israel that cometh in the name of the Lord.

Blessed be the King that cometh in the name of the Lord: peace in heaven, and glory in the highest.

Hosanna to the son of David: Blessed is he that cometh in the name of the Lord; Hosanna in the highest.

Hosanna! Blessed is he that cometh in the name of the Lord; That bringeth the kingdom of our father David; Blessed is he that cometh in the name of the Lord; Hosanna in the highest.

Such blasphemy as this could not go unchallenged. This mob of unlearned followers of this discredited Galilean were ascribing to *him* the very cries of praise reserved for Jehovah alone. Here were men crying Hosanna—meaning *save now,* or *save we pray,* or *save we beseech thee*—to *him,* as though *he* were God and could save them. Here the very words of the Hallel—"Save now, I beseech thee, O Lord: O Lord, I beseech thee, send now prosperity. Blessed be he that cometh in the name of the Lord"—were being sung in praise to One whose works were from beneath. To the Pharisees among them this was as gall and wormwood; it was blasphemy. "Master, rebuke thy disciples," they said. But Jesus, knowing the full significance of what was then in process, replied: "I tell you that, if these should hold their peace, the stones would immediately cry out." These cries were destined to be made. He was the King of Israel and was to be acclaimed as such by believing people before Pilate wrote over his cross: "THIS IS JESUS THE KING OF THE JEWS."

Drawing near to Jerusalem, and beholding the city, Jesus wept. "He had dropped *silent* tears at the grave of Lazarus; here He wept aloud. All the shame of His mockery, all the anguish of His torture, was powerless, five days afterwards, to extort from Him a single groan, or to wet His eyelids with one trickling tear; but here, all the pity that was within Him overmastered His human spirit, and He not only wept, but broke into a passion of lamentation, in which the choked voice seemed to struggle for its utterance. A strange Messianic triumph! a strange interruption of the festal cries! The Deliverer weeps over the city which it is now too late to save; the King prophesies the total ruin of the nation which He came to rule!" (Farrar, pp. 534-35.) His lamenting words:

> *If thou hadst known, even thou, at least in this thy day, the things which belong unto thy peace! but now they are hid from thine eyes.*

'O that thou hadst known me and believed my gospel and gained that peace which I came to bring. O that thou hadst exchanged thy heart of flint for a heart of flesh and had hearkened unto the Son of Man who has taught in thy streets. But now all these things are hidden from thine eyes.'

340

For the days shall come upon thee, that thine enemies shall cast a trench about thee, and compass thee round, and keep thee in on every side, And shall lay thee even with the ground, and thy children within thee; and they shall not leave in thee one stone upon another; because thou knewest not the time of thy visitation.

"Sternly, literally, terribly, within fifty years was that prophecy fulfilled. Four years before the war began, while as yet the city was in the greatest peace and prosperity, a melancholy maniac traversed its streets with the repeated cry, 'A voice from the east, a voice from the west, a voice from the four winds, a voice against Jerusalem and the holy house, a voice against the bridegrooms and the brides, and a voice against this whole people.' No scourgings or tortures could wring from him any other words except, 'Woe! Woe! to Jerusalem; woe to the city; woe to the people; woe to the holy house!' until seven years afterwards, during the siege, he was killed by a stone from a catapult. His voice was but the renewed echo of the voice of prophecy.

"Titus had not originally wished to encompass the city, but he was forced, by the despair and obstinacy of the Jews, to surround it, first with a palisaded mound, and then, when this *vallum* and *agger* were destroyed, with a wall of masonry. He did not wish to sacrifice the Temple—nay, he made every possible effort to save it—but he was forced to leave it in ashes. He did not intend to be cruel to the inhabitants, but the deadly fanaticism of their opposition so extinguished all desire to spare them, that he undertook the task of well-nigh exterminating the race—of crucifying them by hundreds, of exposing them in the amphitheatre by thousands, of selling them into slavery by myriads. Josephus tells us that, even immediately after the siege of Titus, no one, in the desert waste around him, would have recognised the beauty of Judea; and that if any Jew had come upon the city of a sudden, however well he had known it before, he would have asked 'what place it was?' And he who, in modern

Jerusalem, would look for relics of the ten-times-captured city of the days of Christ, must look for them twenty feet beneath the soil, and will scarcely find them. In one spot alone remain a few massive substructions, as though to show how vast is the ruin they represent; and here, on every Friday, assemble a few poverty-stricken Jews, to stand each in the shroud in which he will be buried and wail over the shattered glories of their fallen and desecrated home." (Farrar, pp. 535-37.)

Then Jesus, continuing with the triumphal procession, entered Jerusalem, and, Matthew tells us, "all the city was moved, saying, Who is this?" It was never intended that the events of this day be hidden from view; for nearly six hundred years all Israel had awaited the fulfillment of Zechariah's prophecy, and now the divine Hosannas rent the air. The answer to their question came from the multitude who hailed him as the Son of David. "This is Jesus of Nazareth, the prophet of Galilee," they said.

Continuing into the courts of the temple, where two hundred and ten thousand can assemble at one time, Jesus "looked round about upon all things, and blessed the disciples." What a sweet and tender touch this is! The Son of David, whose Father is God, and who has this day been hailed by believing souls as the Blessed One who was to come, has in his heart a feeling of gratitude. However deserving he knows himself to be—of all the glory and honor and worship that this day has been heaped upon him—yet he now blesses his disciples for the spirit of adoration they have manifest. He blesses them for fulfilling the Messianic word, for crying out: "Blessed is he who cometh in the name of the Lord."

Meanwhile the Pharisees—oppressed, hateful, vengeful—unable to stay the surging tide of divine acclaim that is this day hailing Jesus as Israel's King, say among themselves: "Perceive ye how ye prevail nothing? behold, the world is gone after him." And Jesus, when "the eventide

342

was come," the work of this day being accomplished, "went out unto Bethany with the twelve."

NOTES

1. Something akin to this state of affairs in Palestine was also going on among the Israelite Nephites in the New World at this same time. The people were looking with great earnestness for the sign of the Messiah's death, as such had been given by Samuel the Lamanite. "And there began to be great doubtings and disputations among the people, notwithstanding so many signs had been given." (3 Ne. 8:1-4.)

2. Later, in discussing the supper in the home of Simon the leper, Farrar says: "We are again driven to the conclusion that there must have been some good reason, a reason which we can but uncertainly conjecture, for their marked reticence on this subject; and we find another trace of this reticence in their calling Mary 'a certain woman,' in their omission of all allusion to Martha and Lazarus, and in their telling us that this memorable banquet was served in the house of 'Simon the leper.' " (Farrar, p. 526.)

3. "To anoint the head of a guest with ordinary oil was to do him honor; to anoint his feet also was to show unusual and signal regard; but the anointing of head and feet with spikenard, and in such abundance, was an act of reverential homage rarely rendered even to kings. Mary's act was an expression of adoration; it was the fragrant outwelling of a heart overflowing with worship and affection." (Talmage, p. 512.)

Chapter 85

JESUS—ONE HAVING AUTHORITY

And no man taketh this honour unto himself,
but he that is called of God,
as was Aaron. So also Christ glorified
not himself to be made an high priest;
but he that said unto him,
Thou art my Son, to day have I begotten thee.
As he saith also in another place,
Thou art a priest for ever
after the order of Melchisedec. . . .
Called of God an high priest
after the order of Melchisedec.
(Heb. 5:4-6, 10.)

He Curseth a Barren Fig Tree
*(Mark 11:12-14, 20-26; JST, Mark 11:14-16, 24-26;
Matthew 21:18-22; JST, Matthew 21:17, 20)*

Here is a man who says he is the Son of God; who preaches a gospel that he says is the plan of salvation; who works miracles as a witness that his words are true and that God is his Father. Whence comes his authority, and in what power does he act?

Our Gospel authors do not preserve for us his sermons on priesthood and priestly offices; they do not speak of his

344

ordinations, or even have a great deal to say of the divine commissions conferred upon him by his Father. He is simply described as going forward doing what could not be done without authority. Our inspired writers do not tell how he received the same priesthood and power that was before held by Melchizedek, or how he was called by his Father to rule and reign in that priestly power forever. And yet, implicit in every word that he spoke and every deed that he did is the issue of divine authority. Never man spake as this man; he spake as one having authority and not as the scribes. Never man wrought as this man did; his works required power—the power of God. And priesthood is the power and authority of God delegated to man on earth to act in all things for the salvation of men. It is also the power and authority by which worlds come rolling into existence, by which mountains are moved and seas divided, and by which fig trees are cursed. And if ever there was a people who knew their prophets must have authority from on high, it was Jewish Israel. We are about to see Jesus curse a fig tree and cleanse again his Father's house, and then the chief priests will confront him on the very issue of authority itself. But first the matter of the fig tree.

Bethany of blessed memory—the beautiful and beloved village—has once again been the bivouac of the Bridegroom and of the twelve special friends who ever attend him. It is now early Monday. How the holy party spent the night we do not know—perhaps in communion with each other; perhaps in sacred and solitary prayer; perhaps resting in the home of Simon the leper. Now they are en route to the city and the temple. Jesus is hungry. Afar off he sees a solitary fig tree having leaves. Such trees are planted by the way, and their fruit is common property of all. It is not the season for newly ripened figs, but it is common to find autumn figs still clinging to the trees; and since the new crop develops before the leaves, there should have been a sweet and edible though unripened crop of spring figs.

"But when He came up to it, He was disappointed. The

345

sap was circulating; the leaves made a fair show; but of fruit there was none. Fit emblem of a hypocrite, whose external semblance is a delusion and sham—fit emblem of the nation in whom the ostentatious profession of religion brought forth no 'fruit of good living'—the tree was barren. And it was *hopelessly* barren; for had it been fruitful the previous year, there would still have been some of the *kermouses* hidden under those broad leaves; and had it been fruitful *this* year, the *bakkooroth* would have set into green and delicious fragrance before the leaves appeared; but on this fruitless tree there was neither any promise for the future, nor any gleanings from the past.

"And therefore, since it was but deceptive and useless, a barren cumberer of the ground, He made it the eternal warning against a life of hypocrisy continued until it is too late, and, in the hearing of His disciples, uttered upon it the solemn fiat, 'Never fruit grow upon thee more!' Even at the word, such infructuous life as it possessed was arrested, and it began to wither away." (Farrar, pp. 546-47.)

Matthew tells us that Jesus having so spoken, "Presently the fig tree withered away. And when the disciples saw it, they marvelled, saying, How soon is the fig tree withered away!" Mark says that the next morning as the little group passed by on the same route, "they saw the fig tree dried up from the roots." That this miracle is unique is apparent to all; it seems at first glance, from the standpoint of the fig tree, to be a miracle that curses instead of blesses. But miracles are for the benefit and blessing of men, not for trees and shrubs. All things are and were created for man, to whom dominion over them has been given. Man is the prince of creation. If created things do not serve him and his purposes, should they not be replaced with others that will? That it is also a manifestation of the power of faith resident in him who creates and destroys as seemeth good to him is also apparent. And who are we to question divine wisdom when destructions come?

To cavilers whose aim is to find fault, this miracle becomes an excuse to upbraid and question the justice of the One who does all things well. To all such it is perhaps sufficient answer to say: "When the hail beats down the tendrils of the vineyard—when the lightning scathes the olive, or 'splits the unwedgeable and gnarled oak'—do any but the utterly ignorant and brutal begin at once to blaspheme against God? Is it a crime under *any* circumstances to destroy a *useless* tree? If not, is it *more* a crime to do so by miracle? Why, then, is the Savior of the world—to whom Lebanon would be too little for a burnt-offering—to be blamed by petulant critics because He hastened the withering of one barren tree, and founded, on the destruction of its uselessness, three eternal lessons—a symbol of the destruction of impenitence, a warning of the peril of hypocrisy, an illustration of the power of faith?" (Farrar, p. 548.)

Did Jesus ever miss an opportunity to teach the principles of the gospel? It almost seems that everything he or his asssociates either saw or heard or did became a text for preaching a new and an everlasting doctrine. When Peter said to him on Tuesday, "Master, behold, the fig tree which thou cursedst is withered away," Jesus answered:

Have faith in God. For verily I say unto you, That whosoever shall say unto this mountain, Be thou removed, and be thou cast into the sea; and shall not doubt in his heart, but shall believe that those things which he saith shall come to pass; he shall have whatsoever he saith fulfilled.

Therefore I say unto you, Whatsoever things ye desire, when ye pray, believe that ye receive, and ye shall have whatsoever ye ask.

This is familiar doctrine, but by tying it now to a miracle of such a dramatic nature, who among his hearers will ever forget it? And if trees wither, will not mountains move? Clearly, faith is a power over both animate and inanimate objects. And all are governed for the benefit and blessing of Adam's seed. "But, since in this one instance the power had been put forth to destroy, He added a very important warning. They were not to suppose that this emblematic act gave them any licence to wield the sacred forces which faith and prayer would bestow on them, for purposes of anger or vengeance; nay, *no* power was possible to the heart that knew not how to forgive, and the *unforgiving* heart could never be forgiven. The sword, and the famine, and the pestilence were to be no instruments for *them* to wield, nor were they even to dream of evoking against their enemies the fire of heaven or the 'icy wind of death.' The secret of successful prayer was faith; the road to faith in God lay through pardon of transgression; pardon was possible to them alone who were ready to pardon others." (Farrar, p. 555.)

> *And when ye stand praying, forgive, if ye have ought against any: that your Father also which is in heaven may forgive you your trespasses. But if ye do not forgive, neither will your Father which is in heaven forgive your trespasses.*

Jesus Cleanseth the Temple the Second Time
(Matthew 21:12-17; JST, Matthew 21:13-14; Mark 11:15-19;
Luke 19:45-48; 21:37)

When we went with Jesus into the temple three years ago, at the time of the First Passover, and saw him drive out, with force and violence, the moneychangers and the wicked men who made merchandise of his Father's house, we took occasion to describe the desecrating filth and the evilness of spirit that there prevailed. (See chapter 29, Book 1.) We need not describe anew the physical filth, nor the spiritual degeneracy that then overspread those sacred courts. Suffice it to say that the cleansing of the past was but for a moment. Once again the changers of coins ply their dishonest course; the keepers of doves and the sellers of sheep still haggle over prices and shortchange the Passover pilgrims; the lowing of cattle and the bleating of sheep still add to the confusion and bespeak the spirit of religious anarchy that rages through the city; and the piles of dung and the stench of urine still foul the air. The House of the Lord at Passover time is still as filthy as a pig sty, and many who commune with each other in its courts are still breathing the spirit of hate and vengeance and murder.

Once again, in a spirit of righteous indignation, Jesus drives them out, we suppose with a scourge of cords, as in the first instance; once again he overturns the money tables, frees the doves, and refuses entrance to those who seek to carry vessels through the holy courts, as though they were streets of commerce. But this time he does not say "Make not my Father's house an house of merchandise," but, rather, "My house shall be called the house of prayer; but ye have made it a den of thieves." Three years have passed. Everywhere he has now testified that he and his Father are one; that he speaks the word of his Father; that whatsoever is the Father's is his also; and so now, it is Jesus' house. Let him be charged with blasphemy, if they will. It is his house. It is the house of the Lord Jehovah. He is Jehovah. And it must meet such standards of cleanliness as he can impose for these final hours and days of his teachings therein.

As peace and serenity fell over the sacred courts, Jesus resumed his teachings. The Gospel Voice was heard again; disciples crowded around him to drink deeply from the Everlasting Fountain; faith welled up in the hearts of men; "And the blind and the lame came to him in the temple; and he healed them." The same spirit of worship and adoration that fell mightily upon the multitudes the day before, in the triumphal entry into the city, came again. Shouts of hosanna rent the air; from the children of the kingdom came the cries, "Hosanna to the son of David," and believing souls knew in their hearts that this prophet of Galilee was the Promised Messiah.

But "when the chief priests and scribes saw the wonderful things that he did" and heard the shouts of hosanna and the pleas for salvation that came from the disciples, "they were sore displeased." "Hearest thou what these say?" they demanded. And Jesus said: "Yea; have ye never read the scriptures which saith, Out of the mouth of babes and sucklings, O Lord, thou hast perfected praise?" Then they sought how they might destroy him, and he returned to Bethany for the night.

Jesus Confoundeth the Jews on the Question of Authority
(Matthew 21:23-27; Mark 11:27-33; JST, Mark 11:34; Luke 20:1-8)

On Saturday, April 1, the holy Sabbath, the Lord Jesus—having but recently accomplished his glorious Perean ministry, with all its miracles and wonders—was honored by the people of Bethany with a banquet in the house of Simon the leper. There, while Lazarus whom he raised from the dead looked on, Mary anointed Jesus' head and feet; anointed him—shall we not say it?—as King in Israel; anointed him for his burial, for their King was to die and rise again, that glory and triumph might come to them all, if they would receive it. Though these deeds were done in comparative privacy, in an obscure village, this was a crowning day in the life of Him who would, first, be lifted up upon an earthly cross, and then, have placed on his head an eternal crown.

On Sunday, April 2, Jesus rode on an ass, in triumph, into Jerusalem, amid cries of Hosanna and bold acclamations that he was the Blessed One who came to establish the kingdom of his Father. That evening he returned to Bethany.

On Monday, April 3, he returned; cursed the barren fig tree en route; cleansed the temple a second time; and taught and healed, with great power, in the newly cleansed courts. Again he returned to Bethany for the night.

These were days of glory and honor and triumph. He was being received by believing souls, and they were pledging a Spirit-borne allegiance to him who came to fulfill the old

350

and establish the new. Those in Bethany rejoiced in his presence; many from Jerusalem and multitudes of Passover pilgrims who were there for the feast hailed him as King and Lord; and the common people found pleasure in the cleansing of the temple and the overturning of the money-gouging bazaars of the sons of Annas.

But days of glory and honor and triumph are also days of enmity and opposition and hatred. Mingling with the friendly folk in Bethany were those—taking their cues from the chief priests—who sought the death of Lazarus, that he might no longer stand as a witness of the power of Him who is the resurrection and the life. Infiltrating the hosannic chorus were Pharisaic voices that demanded, "Master, rebuke thy disciples," and that lamented among themselves, "Perceive ye how ye prevail nothing? behold, the world is gone after him."

And so, on Monday night, some of these voices—made up of the chief priests and the scribes and the elders—consulted together as to how they might halt the tide of popular acclaim now attending the ministry of this Galilean rebel, this disturber of the Mosaic order, this Rabbi from Nazareth who would destroy their craft. What arraignment can they bring against him? They have heretofore charged him with casting out devils by Beelzebub; they have demanded Messianic signs from heaven; they have raised questions of marriage and divorce and of doctrines without number; they have sought in every way for more than three years to silence his voice and void his message—all to no avail. Nay, more, all his replies and every rejoinder he has made have left them silent, embarrassed, beaten. What issue can they now raise? With that cunning which has guided them in the past, they devise a new trap. Perhaps they can show he is not an approved Rabbi and has no right even to speak, let alone work miracles. If only the people can be brought to see that he has no Rabbinical authority to utter a word of doctrine or lift a finger to perform a ministerial act, perhaps they will no longer give him glory and honor and cry out: "Lord, save us, we pray; O bring us salvation, we beseech thee; for, blessed is he that cometh in the name of the Lord; hosanna to the Son of David."

Thus, on Tuesday, April 4, Jesus comes again from Bethany; he discourses en route on faith, as the disciples view the smitten fig tree; he enters the temple, where—as always!—he "preached the gospel." The word of everlasting salvation is again going forth; he must be stopped; soon he will be causing the blind to see and the lame to leap, as he has done before. Now is the time for the chief priests and the scribes and the elders to make their confrontation. It is to be a formal and planned challenge. Thus, as Jesus taught the gospel to a receptive congregation, his enemies made their assault. "A formidable deputation approached them, imposing alike in its numbers and its stateliness. The chief priests—heads of the twenty-four courses—the learned scribes, the leading rabbis, representatives of all the constituent classes of the Sanhedrin were there, to overawe Him—whom they despised as the poor contemptible Prophet of Nazareth—with all that was venerable in age, eminent in wisdom, or imposing in authority in the great Council of the nation. The people whom He was engaged in teaching made reverent way for them, lest they should pollute those floating robes and ample fringes with a touch; and when they had arranged themselves around Jesus, they sternly asked Him, 'By what kind of authority doest thou these things, and who gave thee this authority?' They demanded of Him His warrant for thus publicly assuming the functions of Rabbi and Prophet, for riding into Jerusalem amid the hosannas of attendant crowds, for purging the Temple of the traffickers, at whose presence they connived." (Farrar, pp. 548-49.)

To envision the cunning import of these scribal demands—"By what authority doest thou these things? and who gave thee this authority?"—we must know the Jewish setting in which they were made. In Jesus' day, approved Rabbinical ministries must meet two standards:

1. *All formal teaching must be both authoritative and authorized.*

"There was no principle more firmly established by universal consent than that *authoritative* teaching required previous authorization," Edersheim tells us. "Indeed, this logically followed from the principle of Rabbinism. All teaching must be authoritative, since it was traditional—approved by authority, and handed down from teacher to disciple. The highest honour of a scholar was, that he was like a well-plastered cistern, from which not a drop had leaked of what had been poured into it. The ultimate appeal in cases of discussion was always to some great authority, whether an individual Teacher or a Decree by the Sanhedrin. In this manner had the great Hillel first vindicated his claim to be the Teacher of his time and to decide the disputes then pending. And, to decide differently from authority, was either the mark of ignorant assumption or the outcome of daring rebellion, in either case to be visited with 'the ban' [excommunication]."

2. *Authorization for Rabbinical teaching came by ordination.*

"No one would have thought of interfering with a mere Haggadist—a popular expositor, preacher, or teller of legends. But authoritatively to teach, required warrant. In fact there was regular ordination (*Semikhah*) to the office of Rabbi, Elder, and Judge, for the three functions were combined in one. . . . Although we have not any description of the earliest mode of ordination, the very name—*Semikhah*—implies the imposition of hands. Again, in the oldest record, reaching up, no doubt, to the time of Christ, the presence of at least three ordained persons was required for the ordination. . . . In the course of time certain formalities were added. The person to be ordained had to deliver a Discourse; hymns and poems were recited; the title 'Rabbi' was formally bestowed on the candidate, and authority given him to teach and to act as Judge [to bind and loose, to declare guilty or free]."

Thus, "at the time of our Lord, no one would have ventured authoritatively to teach without proper Rabbinic authorisation. The question, therefore, with which the Jewish authorities met Christ, while teaching, was one which had a very real meaning, and appealed to the habits and feelings of the people who listened to Jesus. Otherwise, also, it was cunningly framed. For, it did not merely challenge Him for teaching, but also asked for His authority in what He *did;* referring not only to His work generally, but, perhaps especially to what had happened on the previous day. They were not there to oppose Him; but, when a man did as He had done in the Temple, it was their duty to verify his credentials. Finally, the alternative question reported by St. Mark: 'or'—if thou has not proper Rabbinic commission—'who gave Thee this authority to do these things?' seems clearly to point to their contention, that the power which Jesus wielded was delegated to Him by none other than Beelzebub." (Edersheim 2:381-83.)

Then Jesus answered their question. He did not, as some have supposed, avoid the necessity of answering by asking a question of his own; rather, his question was so framed as to constitute a complete, though partially unspoken, answer. "I also will ask you one thing, which if ye tell me," Jesus said, "I in like wise will tell you by what authority I do these things." This, then, was his question: "The baptism of John, whence was it? from heaven, or of men?"

'The baptism of John—meaning, his whole work and ministry, the doctrines he taught, the testimonies he bore, the ordinances he performed—were they of God?' As to John—than whom there was not a greater prophet—we are reminded that "all the people that heard him, and the publicans, justified God, being baptized with the baptism of John. But the Pharisees and lawyers rejected the counsel of God against themselves, being not baptized of him." (Luke 7:29-30.) His baptism—the sign of his ministry; the witness that all that he taught was true—if they believed in John they must believe in Christ, for John's whole ministry was one of preparation for the One who came after. Here then was their answer. Jesus is saying *'John has already answered your questions. My authority comes from higher than Rabbinic sources; it comes from my Father, as John testified when he said: "Behold the Lamb of God!" If ye believed John, ye would believe in me, for he testified of me.'*

But they had not believed in John. How then could they respond? "If we shall say, From heaven," they reasoned, "he will say, Why then believed ye him not?" Their rebellion of the past bore witness of their sins of the present. "But and if we say, Of men," they continued, "all the people will stone us: for they be persuaded that John was a prophet." How then could they answer? "We cannot tell," they said.

"There is an admirable Hebrew proverb which says, 'Teach thy tongue to say, "I do not know." ' But to say, 'We do not know,' in this instance, was a thing utterly alien to their habits, disgraceful to their discernment, a deathblow to their pretensions. It was ignorance in a sphere wherein ignorance was for them inexcusable. They, the appointed explainers of the Law—they, the accepted teachers of the people—they, the acknowledged monopolisers of Scriptural learning and oral tradition—and yet to be compelled, against their real convictions, to say, and that before the multitude, that they *could not tell* whether a man of immense and sacred influence—a man who acknowledged the Scriptures which they explained, and carried into practice the customs which they reverenced—was a divinely inspired messenger or a deluding imposter! Were the lines of demarcation, then, between the inspired Prophet and the wicked seducer so dubious and indistinct? It was indeed a fearful humiliation, and one which they never either forgot or forgave. And yet how just was the retribution which they had thus brought on their own heads! The curses which they had intended for another had recoiled upon themselves; the pompous question which was to be an engine wherewith another should be crushed, had sprung with sudden rebound, to their own confusion and shame." (Farrar, p. 550.)

"Neither tell I you by what authority I do these things," Jesus said. 'Why try to involve me in your petty Rabbinical squabbles? What is this dead Rabbinical school or that? Of what concern is it whether some blind guide had ordained me to speak authoritatively or not? You have your answer; John gave it to you at Bethabara, and my Father confirmed it by his own voice out of heaven when he said at my baptism: "This is my Beloved Son, in whom I am well pleased. Hear ye him." '

Chapter 86

THREE PARABLES
TO THE JEWS

Utter a parable
unto the rebellious house.
(Ezek. 24:3.)

Parable of the Two Sons
(Matthew 21:23, 25, 28-32; JST, Matthew 21:31-34)

All Israel, as it were—through their legally designated
agents, the chief priests and the scribes and the elders, as
these arrayed themselves for combat in the courts of Jehovah's House—all Israel confronted Israel's Incarnate God
with the demand, made relative to all that he did and all that
he said, "By what authority doest thou these things? and
who gave thee this authority?"

The Incarnate One, by the way of reply, asked of them:
"The baptism of John, whence was it? from heaven, or of
men?" To this, as they knew in their hearts, there was only
one reply: 'John was sent of God; he bore testimony that
you are the Lamb of God, the Son of the Eternal Father; his
baptism was to prepare men to receive you; and therefore
you have divine authority that came to you from God who is
your Father. We heard John say of you, "The Father loveth
the Son, and hath given all things into his hand. He that
believeth on the Son hath everlasting life: and he that be-

lieveth not the Son shall not see life; but the wrath of God abideth on him." (John 3:35-36.) We have answered our own question. Yours is the authority of God, and he gave it to you.' To their shame they could not and did not respond in this way because they were among those who "rejected the counsel of God against themselves, being not baptized of him." (Luke 7:30.)

Their silence being an answer that all present understood, Jesus, nonetheless, means now to tell them vocally the answer to his question as to whether John's baptism was of God, and hence, also to tell them the source of his own authority and to do it by a parable.

But what think ye? A certain man had two sons; and he came to the first, and said, Son, go work to day in my vineyard. He answered and said, I will not: but afterward he repented, and went. And he came to the second, and said likewise. And he answered and said, I go, sir: and he went not. Whether of them twain did the will of his father?

It is a plain and simple story. So far there can be no misunderstanding, and there is only one answer to his question. They are compelled to say, "The first." And thereupon Jesus applies his teaching:

Verily I say unto you, That the publicans and harlots shall go into the kingdom of God before you. For John came unto you in the way of righteousness, and bore record of me, and ye believed him not; but the publicans and the harlots believed him; and ye, afterward, when ye had seen me, repented not, that ye might believe him.

For he that believed not John concerning me, cannot believe me, except he first repent. And except ye repent, the preaching of John shall condemn you in the day of judgment.

The Father of us all, the Great God, whose arm is not shortened that he cannot save, and who desires to save all his children, calls both of his sons to labor in his vineyard. The first son is wicked, rebellious, ungodly, unclean, having no interest in spiritual things. He refuses the call. Religion is not for him. He is, symbolically, as the harlots and the publicans. And what is more evil than the immoral degeneracy of a prostitute or the avaricious greed of an extortionate and dishonest tax collector? The second son—wearing a veneer of spirituality; fasting two days in each week; making broad his phylacteries and lengthening the fringes on his garments; praying on the street corners to be seen of men; keeping the traditions of the fathers with a scrupulosity beyond sense and reason; separating himself from the lesser breed of men—the second son, symbolically, is the chief priests and the scribes and the elders. He is the Pharisees and the Rabbinists, the leaders of Jewry. They are the ones who, professing to be about their Father's business, have let his vineyard degenerate into a fruitless wilderness. Tares grow where wheat was sown; vines shed their fruit untimely; fig trees are barren; olives rot on the ground; and swine forage in the fields.

John comes; he bears witness of Christ; his message is one of righteousness and salvation; the publicans and harlots repent; they join the people who are preparing themselves to receive the Coming One. The lawyers and the leaders believe not, no, not even after Christ himself ministers among them. Nor, having rejected John, can they believe in Christ, unless they repent. Jesus and John are one; they testify of each other; to believe in John is to believe in Jesus; each bears witness of the authority of the other, and the words of each shall condemn the rebellious and unbelieving in the day of judgment. Such is the message of the parable of the two sons.

Parable of the Wicked Husbandmen
(Matthew 21:33-46; JST, Matthew 21:34-35, 42-43, 48-56;
Mark 12:1-12; JST, Mark 12:12; Luke 20:9-19;
JST, Luke 20:10)

We are in the midst of a mighty confrontation. A religious war is in progress, reminiscent of—or better, a continuation of—the war in heaven when Michael led the armies of the just in their verbal conflict with Lucifer and his evil ones. We are in the temple, which but yesterday was cleansed again. Jesus is here to teach. His disciples rejoice in each spoken word; arrayed against them are the chief priests, scribes, Pharisees, and elders. It is a formal setting; the lawyers and leaders of the people have set themselves forth in their official capacity to defend and uphold the established order and to overthrow and destroy this new order being set up by this upstart Galilean who violates the traditions of their fathers. Our Lord's antagonists have just been defeated and humiliated on the issue of authority, and their souls have been cut to the quick by the parable of the two sons. Many hearers are assembled, some friendly and receptive, others vengeful and rebellious. Jesus says: "Unto you that believe not, I speak in parables; that your unrighteousness may be rewarded unto you." The spirit of rebellion that fills their souls denies them the right to hear the word of truth in plainness; it is their fate, as a rebellious house, to be told of their rebellion in story form. Both now and hereafter they will ponder these parables, see their application to themselves, and always wonder whether they have learned their full significance.

Hear another parable: There was a certain householder, which planted a vineyard, and hedged it round about, and digged a wine press in it, and built a tower, and let it out to husbandmen, and went into a far country:

And when the time of the fruit drew near, he sent his servants to the husbandmen, that they might receive the fruits of it. And the husbandmen took his servants, and beat one, and killed another, and stoned another. Again, he sent other servants more than the first: and they did unto them likewise.

All this was familiar business procedure. Householders commonly leased their lands or placed them in the custody of husbandmen who had full control over their management. Owners then traveled or attended to other business, and the fruits in due season were divided between them and the lessees or husbandmen.

Here the Eternal Householder—one Jehovah by name— had planted his people on earth, beginning with Adam, the first husbandman, and had then returned to a distant heaven, leaving the first man of all men to till and farm the garden. Or, more specifically, the Great Jehovah had planted his people Israel in their promised land; had entered into a covenant with them amid the smoke and fire and thunder of Sinai; had given direction in the Mosaic law for the care and keeping of his vineyard; had traveled back to his eternal abode; and had sent his servants the prophets from time to time to serve in the vineyard and receive an accounting with reference to the fruits thereof.

That Israel's prophets were tortured, mocked, scourged, imprisoned, stoned, sawn asunder, and slain was axiomatic. All who heard Jesus speak of the ill treatment received by the Householder's servants would remember how their own scriptures said of their fathers: "All the chief of the priests, and the people, transgressed very much . . . And the Lord God of their fathers sent to them by his messengers, rising up betimes, and sending; because he had compassion on his people, and on his dwelling place: But they mocked the messengers of God, and despised his words, and misused his prophets, until the wrath of the Lord arose against his people, till there was no remedy." (2 Chr. 36:14-16.) All who heard Jesus' words would know that even in their day "another servant," as both Mark and Luke call him—one John by name—had come and been rejected by the chief priests, arrested by Antipas, imprisoned in Machaerus, and slain to appease Salome.

And further: Jesus' words would seem but a distant echo of Isaiah's parabolic utterance: "Now will I sing to my well beloved a song of my beloved touching his vineyard. My well beloved hath a vineyard in a very fruitful hill: And he fenced it, and gathered out the stones thereof, and planted it

361

with the choicest vine, and built a tower in the midst of it, and also made a winepress therein: and he looked that it should bring forth grapes, and it brought forth wild grapes. And now, O inhabitants of Jerusalem, and men of Judah, judge, I pray you, betwixt me and my vineyard. What could have been done more to my vineyard, that I have not done in it? wherefore, when I looked that it should bring forth grapes, brought it forth wild grapes?" (Isa. 5:1-4.) In this setting, with a full understanding on the part of all concerned, Jesus continues the parable:

> But last of all he sent unto them his son, saying, They will reverence my son. But when the husbandmen saw the son, they said among themselves, This is the heir; come, let us kill him, and let us seize on his inheritance. And they caught him, and cast him out of the vineyard, and slew him.
>
> When the lord therefore of the vineyard cometh, what will he do unto those husbandmen?

"I will send my beloved son" are the words of the householder as Luke records them. 'This Is My Beloved Son' is the eternal testimony of the Father himself. "I am the Son of God" is the witness Jesus has everywhere been bearing of himself. And now be it noted, according to the words of the parable, the husbandmen—the chief priests, scribes, Pharisees, elders, Rabbinists, lawyers, and rulers of the people—the husbandmen appointed in that day to labor in the vineyard and raise fruit for the Lord knew who the Heir was and chose willfully to cast him out and slay him lest he disturb them in their petty Mosaic ministrations. And so now, for the third time in a row—the other two were in connection with the matter of authority and in the parable of the two sons—they are forced by their own lips to judge themselves. In answer to Jesus' question, they say: "He will destroy those miserable, wicked men, and will let out the vineyard unto other husbandmen, who shall render him the fruits in their season."

Such is the parable proper, together with the self-condemnation it heaped upon the wicked husbandmen against whom the forces of righteousness were then arrayed. And we cannot doubt that those so responding to Jesus knew they were echoing Isaiah's words: "And now go to," he says with reference to the song of the well-beloved and the vineyard, "I will tell you what I will do to my vineyard," because it brought forth wild grapes. "I will take away the hedge thereof, and it shall be eaten up; and break down the wall thereof, and it shall be trodden down: and I will lay it waste: it shall not be pruned, nor digged; but there shall come up briers and thorns: I will also command the clouds that they rain no rain upon it. For the vineyard of the Lord of hosts is the house of Israel, and the men of Judah his pleasant plant: and he looked for judgment, but behold oppression; for righteousness, but behold a cry." (Isa. 5:5-7.) But lest there be any question, Jesus then drew his own conclusions and said unto them:

Did ye never read in the scriptures, The stone which the builders rejected, the same is become the head of the corner: this is the Lord's doing, and it is marvellous in our eyes?

Therefore say I unto you, The kingdom of God shall be taken from you, and given to a nation bringing forth the fruits thereof.

And whosoever shall fall on this stone shall be broken: but on whomsoever it shall fall, it will grind him to powder.

In thus applying to himself the Messianic words of the Psalmist (Ps. 118:22-26),[1] Jesus is saying he is the one whom the wicked husbandmen will cast out and slay. When the chief priests, scribes, Pharisees, and others heard this parable, "they perceived that he spake of them, And they said among themselves, Shall this man think that he alone can spoil this great kingdom? And they were angry with him. But when they sought to lay hands on him, they feared the multitude, because they learned that the multitude took him for a prophet." Later, we suppose in answer to their questions, Jesus said to his disciples:

Marvel ye at the words of the parable which I spake unto them? Verily, I say unto you, I am the stone, and those wicked ones reject me.

I am the head of the corner. These Jews shall fall upon me, and shall be broken. And the kingdom of God shall be taken from them, and shall be given to a nation bringing forth the fruits thereof; (meaning the Gentiles.)

Wherefore, on whomsoever this stone shall fall, it shall grind him to powder. And when the Lord therefore of the vineyard cometh, he will destroy those miserable, wicked men, and will let again his vineyard unto other husbandmen, even in the last days, who shall render him the fruits in their season.

Following this, as Matthew so aptly concludes: "And then understood they the parable which he spake unto them, that the Gentiles should be destroyed also, when the Lord should descend out of heaven to reign in his vineyard, which is the earth and the inhabitants thereof."

Parable of the Marriage of the King's Son
(Matthew 22:1-14; JST, Matthew 22:3-4, 7, 14)

Jewish theology, Jewish tradition, and Jewish hope all united to fix in the minds of the Jews one great Messianic expectancy: the kingdom of their Messianic Deliverer would be ushered in by a great feast, a marriage feast, a feast to celebrate the marriage, symbolically, of the Promised Messiah and his covenant people. That this Messianic hope—though misunderstood, misinterpreted, and misapplied by the Rabbinic expounders of their law and tradition—is a true one, we shall see in the ensuing parable, as Jesus continues and, for the moment, climaxes his confrontation with the enemies of all righteousness who are arrayed before him in the temple court.

True it is, as we shall see, that there shall be a "supper of the Lord" to usher in his millennial reign, a great feast to which "all nations shall be invited"—a banquet held in honor of the Bridegroom, the Son of the Great King, whose bride is the Church. It will not be a closed and restricted feast attended only by the Jews, as the Rabbinists suppose, and it will not take place in full until the King's Son comes a second time to rule and reign on earth a thousand years. All this will now appear as the Master Parabolist gives the parable of the marriage of the king's son.

The kingdom of heaven is like unto a certain king, which made a marriage for his son, And when the marriage was ready, he sent forth his servants to call them that were bidden to the wedding; and they would not come.

Again he sent forth other servants, saying, Tell them that are bidden, Behold, I have prepared my oxen, and my fatlings have been killed, and my dinner is ready, and all things are prepared; therefore come unto the marriage.

The Church of Jesus Christ—which is the kingdom of God on earth; which organization administers the gospel of the kingdom; which gospel is the bread of life, upon which men may feast and never hunger more—this church, with all its saving power, is like unto a king who makes a marriage for his son. So begins the parable. Deity is the King; Jesus (Jehovah) is the Son; and those first invited to "the marriage of the Lamb"—those invited to come unto Christ and feast upon the good word of God—are the chosen and favored hosts of ancient Israel, to whom the saving truths were offered in days of old. The servants who heaped the banquet tables high with heavenly manna were Moses and Isaiah and all the prophets; they were all the messengers of old who testified of the Son of God and pled with Abraham's seed to feast upon the word of Christ and partake of that eternal bread which he alone can give. "Thy Maker is thine husband," Isaiah proclaimed to Israel, "the Lord of hosts is his name." (Isa. 54:5.)

Oriental custom called for two invitations to marriage feasts—the first, an invitation of preparation, the second, to announce that the seven- or fourteen-day feasting period, as the case may be, had arrived. With the advent of the Son, the second invitation went forth; the Old Testament proclamations prepared the way for the renewed proclamation of the same message in New Testament times. And so, "other servants" again bid the covenant people to come and eat. Again the dinner is ready. Again the Bridegroom will be the Husband of all who believe. Again the invitation goes forth to Israel: "The Lord hath called thee as a woman forsaken and grieved in spirit, and a wife of youth." (Isa. 54:6.) "Come unto the marriage" is the call.

But they made light of it, and went their ways, one to his farm, another to his merchandise: And the remnant took his servants, and entreated them spitefully, and slew them.

But when the king heard that his servants were dead, he was wroth; and he sent forth his armies, and destroyed those murderers, and burned up their city.

Jewish Israel is composed of murderous rebels. They have a form of godliness that cloaks their avaricious interest in farms and merchandise and the things of this world. They slay the apostles and prophets who invite them to the gospel table, and they defy and rebel against Him who sent them. He in turn, using Roman steel and the vengeance of fire, in A.D. 70 destroys the murderers and burns Jerusalem. The words of the parable are the voice of prophecy.

Then saith he to his servants, The wedding is ready, but they which were bidden were not worthy. Go ye therefore into the highways, and as many as ye shall find, bid to the marriage.

So those servants went out into the highways, and gathered together all as many as they found, both bad and good: and the wedding was furnished with guests.

Thus Israel's day of preferential treatment ends; having rejected their King and his Son, they are no longer worthy to receive the blessings of Abraham. Now the gospel goes to all men, Jew and Gentile alike. From Jerusalem to the highways of the world; from the seed of Abraham to all the seed of Adam; from the favored few to the whole body of mankind—thus is the new order prefigured in the parable.

And so it is today, as "those servants" appointed in this age perform their labors. Their voices cry out: "Prepare ye the way of the Lord, prepare ye the supper of the Lamb, make ready for the Bridegroom." (D&C 65:3.) They go forth "that a feast of fat things might be prepared for the poor; yea, a feast of fat things, of wine on the lees well refined, that the earth may know that the mouths of the prophets shall not fail; Yea, a supper of the house of the Lord, well prepared, unto which all nations shall be invited. First, the rich and the learned, the wise and the noble; And after that cometh the day of my power," saith the Lord. "Then shall the poor, the lame, and the blind, and the deaf, come in unto the marriage of the Lamb, and partake of the supper of the Lord, prepared for the great day to come." (D&C 58:8-11.)

And when the king came in to see the guests, he saw there a man which had not on a wedding garment: And he saith unto him, Friend, how camest thou in hither not having a wedding garment? And he was speechless.

Then said the king to the servants, Bind him hand and foot, and take him away, and cast him into outer darkness; there shall be weeping and gnashing of teeth.

For many are called, but few chosen; wherefore all do not have on the wedding garment.

Those gathered in are both bad and good; the gospel net catches fish of all kinds. Only those who make themselves worthy are saved. All who come into the Church must forsake the world, repent of their sins, and keep the commandments; otherwise they will be cast out with the wicked and rebellious and suffer the sorrows of the damned.

Salvation is a personal matter; it comes to individuals, not congregations. Church membership alone does not save; obedience after baptism is required. Each person called to the marriage feast will be examined separately, and of the many called to partake of the bounties of the gospel, few only will wear the robes of righteousness which must clothe every citizen in the celestial heaven. True it is that the Lord "hath bid his guests," as Zephaniah said, but "all such as are clothed with strange apparel" shall be cast out. (Zeph. 1:7-8.)

"Let us be glad and rejoice, and give honour to him: for the marriage of the Lamb is come, and his wife hath made herself ready. And to her was granted that she should be arrayed in fine linen, clean and white: for the fine linen is the righteousness of saints. And he saith unto me, Write, Blessed are they which are called unto the marriage supper of the Lamb." (Rev. 19:7-9.)

NOTE

1. These words are, of course, part of the *Hallel*, which all Jewry chanted in their ceremonies.

Chapter 87

THE JEWS PROVOKE, TEMPT, AND REJECT JESUS

He shall be . . . for a gin
and for a snare to the inhabitants
of Jerusalem. And many among them shall stumble,
and fall, and be broken,
and be snared, and be taken.
(Isa. 8:14-15.)
Him whom man despiseth, . . .
him whom the nation abhorreth, . . .
a servant of rulers (Isa. 49:7),
He is despised and rejected of men (Isa. 53:3).
For they that dwell at Jerusalem,
and their rulers, because they knew him not,
nor yet the voices of the prophets
which are read every sabbath day,
they have fulfilled them in condemning him.
(Acts 13:27.)

Render unto God and Caesar Their Own
(Matthew 22:15-22; Mark 12:13-17; Luke 20:20-26; JST, Luke 20:21)

If ever a plot was conceived in hell, born in hate, and
acted out with satanic cunning, it was the jointly concocted

369

stratagem of the Pharisees and Herodians on the matter of paying tribute to Caesar. When these two parties—the Pharisees whose extreme and intemperate devotion to Jehovah rejected the mere thought of Roman rule, and the Herodians whose fawning sycophancy toward Roman rule made them the open enemies of the Pharisees—when these political foes came forward to ask Jesus to rule in favor of one or the other of them (supposing that a pro-Pharisaic answer would cause his arrest by Roman authority, and a pro-Herodian answer his rejection by the people); when the hierarchical scrupulosity of the Pharisees and the political expediency of the Herodians united their voices, surely their questions must have been framed in the council rooms of Satan himself.

The Pharisees, Rabbinists, priests, elders, and leaders of the people, "foiled in their endeavor to involve Him with the ecclesiastical"—that is, having devised the questions, "By what authority doest thou these things? and who gave thee this authority?" in their attempt to show he had no Rabbinical right either to teach or perform miracles; having been humiliated by his answer and by their inability to account for John's testimony of his divine Sonship; and having been condemned, rebuked, and left bruised and bleeding, as it were, by the cutting words of the three parables that he directed against them—thus, "foiled in their endeavor to involve Him with the ecclesiastical, they next attempted the much more dangerous device of bringing Him in collision with the civil authorities," as Edersheim expresses it.

"Remembering the ever watchful jealousy of Rome, the reckless tyranny of Pilate, and the low artifices of Herod, who was at that time in Jerusalem, we instinctively feel, how even the slightest compromise on the part of Jesus in regard to the authority of Caesar would have been absolutely fatal. If it could have been proved, on undeniable testimony, that Jesus had declared Himself on the side of, or even encouraged, the so-called 'Nationalist' party, He would have quickly perished, like Judas of Galilee. The Jewish leaders would thus have readily accomplished their object, and its unpopularity have recoiled only on the hated Roman power. How great the danger was which threatened Jesus, may be gathered from this, that, despite His clear answer, the charge that He perverted the nation, forbidding to give tribute to Caesar, was actually among those brought against Him before Pilate." (Edersheim 2:383-84; Luke 23:2.)

Our dealings with the Pharisees, in many places and at numerous times, have left us wary of these religious extremists—these fanatics who fast twice in a week; who make broad their phylacteries and lengthen the sacred fringes on their garments; who pray on the streets to be seen of men; and who turn simple living into a morbid hell by their Sabbath restrictions, ceremonial washings, and baseless traditions. But who are the Herodians, and how do they fit into the social milieu of Jewry? They "occur but seldom in the Gospel narrative. Their very designation—a Latinised adjective applied to the Greek-speaking courtiers of an Edomite prince who, by Roman intervention, had become a Judean king—showed at once their hybrid origin. Their existence had mainly a *political* significance, and they stood outside the current of religious life, except so far as their Hellenising tendencies and worldly interests led them to show an ostentatious disregard for the Mosaic law.

"They were, in fact, nothing better than provincial courtiers; men who basked in the sunshine of a petty tyranny which, for their own personal ends, they were anxious to uphold. To strengthen the family of Herod by keeping it on good terms with Roman imperialism, and to effect this good understanding by repressing every national aspiration—this was their highest aim. And in order to do this they Grecised their Semitic names, adopted ethnic habits, frequented amphitheatres, familiarly accepted the symbols of heathen supremacy, even went so far as to obliterate, by such artificial means as they could, the distinctive and covenant symbol of Hebrew nationality.

"That the Pharisees should tolerate even the most tempo-

371

rary partnership with such men as these, whose very existence was a violent outrage on their most cherished prejudices, enables us to gauge more accurately the extreme virulence of hatred with which Jesus had inspired them. And that hatred was destined to become deadlier still. It was already at red-heat; the words and deeds of this day were to raise it to its whitest intensity of wrath." (Farrar, pp. 555-56.)

And so we find the Pharisees and Herodians counseling together, in secret, as to "how they might entangle him in his talk." Their plot: Certain disciples of the Pharisees—some of their young scholars who had not as yet openly confronted Jesus and who would be unknown to him—would join with the Herodians in asking him to decide the great political issue which divided them. These men—Luke calls them "spies"—"should feign themselves just men." They would raise the issue of paying tribute to Rome. If he sided with the Herodians and endorsed the Roman taxing power, he would antagonize the people, perhaps be rejected by them. If, by so much as an intimation, he questioned Romish rule and Romish taxes, their intent was to "deliver him unto the power and authority of the governor."

"If one, whom they take to be the Messiah, should openly adhere to a heathen tyranny, and sanction its most galling burdens, such a decision will at once explode and evaporate any regard which the people may feel for Him. If, on the other hand, as is all but certain, 'He should adopt the views of His countryman Judas the Gaulonite, and answer, '*No, it is not lawful*,' then, in that case too, we are equally rid of Him; for then He is in open rebellion against the Roman power, and these new Herodian friends of ours can at once hand Him over to the jurisdiction of the Procurator. Pontius Pilate will deal very roughly with His pretentions, and will, if need be, without the slightest hesitation, mingle His blood, as he has done the blood of other Galileans, with the blood of the sacrifices." (Farrar, p. 558.)

Their approach was respectful, deferential, courteous. Who but one so wise as he could guide their course in this matter upon which they were so widely divided? But their respect was feigned, their deference a sham, and their courtesy a thin veneer hiding an implacable hatred. "Master, we know that thou art true, and teachest the way of God in truth, neither carest thou for any man," came the sycophantic praise designed to catch him off guard, "for thou regardest not the person of men." 'Thou alone art true; thou alone speakest what God wants said; thou only can rise above the petty politics of the day; at long last thy divine wisdom will chart our course.' The problem: "Is it lawful to give tribute to Caesar, or not? Shall we give, or shall we not give?"

Matthew says that Jesus "perceived their wickedness"; Luke comments that "he perceived their craftiness"; and Mark says he knew "their hypocrisy." The time has long since passed when even these evil conspirators should presume to deceive him who has repeatedly said: 'I am the Son of God; all things are given me of my Father.' His reply was curt and pointed: "Why tempt ye me, ye hypocrites? Shew me the tribute money." They produced a penny, a Roman denarius, bearing the image of Tiberius Caesar, emperor of Rome. "Whose is this image and superscription?" Jesus asked. The answer: "Caesar's." His reply—nay, his decision, his decree—answered for then and for now the question of Church versus state:

Render therefore unto Caesar the things which are Caesar's; and unto God the things that are God's.

For their day and for ours, King-Messiah's kingdom is not of this world; it is a spiritual kingdom, an ecclesiastical kingdom, a church and congregation into which true believers may come to find peace in this world and gain a hope of eternal life in the world that is to be. For their day and for ours, men render unto Caesar that which is his own and in the process subject themselves to the powers that be. Having been so instructed, the conspirators marveled at his doctrine, "and left him, and went their way."

If there is a further lesson to be learned from this

confrontation, perhaps it is aptly summarized in these words of Elder James E. Talmage: "Every human soul is stamped with the image and superscription of God, however blurred and indistinct the line may have become through the corrosion or attrition of sin; and as unto Caesar should be rendered the coins upon which his effigy appeared, so unto God should be given the souls that bear His image. Render unto the world the stamped pieces that are made legally current by the insignia of worldly powers, and give unto God and His service, yourselves—the divine mintage of His eternal realm." (Talmage, pp. 546-47.)

Jesus Teaches the Law of Eternal Marriage
(Matthew 22:23-33; Mark 12:18-27; JST, Mark 12:23, 28, 32;
Luke 20:27-40; JST, Luke 20:35)

This very day—Tuesday, April 4, A.D. 30, the third day of the week of the atoning sacrifice—in the temple courts, Jesus has overcome the evil assaults and triumphed over the satanic plots of the Sanhedrinists, the chief priests, the scribes, the elders, the rulers and leaders of the people, the Rabbinists and teachers, the Pharisees and their disciples, and the hated Herodians. Now the Sadducees join the chorus of reviling rebels whose goal it is to goad, provoke, and belittle the Son of God, all with the hope that he will be rejected by the common people and condemned to death by the Roman Procurator.

Their devilish devisings take the form of a scoffing, sneering, deriding attack on the doctrine of the resurrection. Theirs is to be the weapon of ridicule. They already know the answer to the question they will ask; it is one commonly debated in the Rabbinical schools and for which the Pharisees and people generally have an accepted and prevailing view. They come with "an old stale piece of casuistry, conceived in the same spirit of self-complacent ignorance as are many of the objections urged by modern Sadducees against the resurrection of the body, but still sufficiently puzzling to furnish them with an argument in favour of their

374

disbeliefs, and with a 'difficulty' to throw in the way of their opponents." (Farrar, p. 561.) In this case their opponents are both Jesus, by whom the resurrection comes, and the Pharisees, who, with all their faults, do believe that the bodies of dead men will rise from their graves and live in glorious immortality.

Thus, from their malignant hearts of disbelief—for the Sadducees say "there is no resurrection"—and from spiteful Sadducean lips, in tones of scorn and derision, these agnostic worshippers, if such they may be called, began their colloquy with Jesus by saying: "Master, Moses said, If a man die, having no children, his brother shall marry his wife, and raise up seed unto his brother."

Such, as far as it went, was a true summary of the levirate law.[1] Moses had indeed given such a commandment to Israel when they were subject to all of the terms and conditions of the new and everlasting covenant of marriage—including plurality of wives. Moses had indeed included such a requirement in the revealed marriage discipline of his day, so that worthy men who died without seed might yet have them in eternity where they would live forever in the family unit. Moses had made such a provision for faithful holders of the Melchizedek Priesthood whose chief aim and goal in life was to create for themselves eternal family units patterned after the family of God their Heavenly Father. The Sadducean use of the Mosaic principle as a basis for their caviling query indicates that some remnant of levirate marriage—we assume a twisted and perverted one—still prevailed in Jewry.

Having given lip service to Moses' levirate declaration, the Sadducees now mention a certain woman who, seeking seed, married seven brothers in turn, each of whom predeceased her. "In the resurrection whose wife shall she be of the seven?" they ask, "for they all had her." It is difficult to understand why they would ask such a foolish question, even in ridicule, for every informed person already knew the answer. The matter had been fully analyzed and debated in the Rabbinical schools. "The Pharisees," for instance, as Farrar points out, "had already settled the question in a very obvious way, and quite to their own satisfaction, by saying that she should in the resurrection be the wife of the first husband." (Farrar, p. 561.) From our vantage point, we say she would be the wife of the one to whom she was married for time and for all eternity. Any other marriage, being only until death parted the covenanting parties, would end when the mortal life of one or the other of them ceased.

But underlying this seemingly innocent query is the unspoken ridicule of the doctrine of the resurrection. 'How foolish to believe in a literal resurrection in which the family unity continues—as the Pharisees believed and the Rabbis teach!—when everyone knows a sevenfold widow cannot have seven husbands at one time.' Such an approach, in its historical setting, seems to us to present a petty and a poor argument. But we suppose it was the best one the Sadducees—who, whatever else they may have been, were neither scripturalists nor theologians—could devise at the moment.

Jesus answered, as a tolerant teacher might, without the biting sarcasm and stinging invective that at this late date so often attended answers given to the scribes and Pharisees. "Ye do err," he said, "not knowing the scriptures, nor the power of God."

Not knowing the scriptures! How little they knew of the intent and meaning of that which was written. Had they "not read, that he which made them at the beginning"—*the beginning,* note it well; it is the time before death entered the world—"made them male and female"? Did they not know that the Eternal Creator who married Adam and Eve in an eternal union, there then being no death in the world, had said, "For this cause"—that they might live together forever—"shall a man leave father and mother, and shall cleave to his wife: and they twain shall be one flesh?" Had it escaped them that such married partners "are no more twain, but one flesh," and "what therefore God hath joined together"—again mark it well, what *God,* not *man*—"let not man put asunder"? (Matt. 19:4-6.) Was the scripture entirely new to them that "whatsoever God doeth, it shall be for ever"? (Eccl. 3:14.) Were they unaware of the scriptural teachings that only those who believe the gospel; only those who hold the Holy Priesthood; only those who believe in Christ and keep his commandments—that these alone are the ones to whom Moses' levirate law applies? There neither is nor can be a continuation of the family unit in eternity for any others. Celestial marriage and the resultant eternal relation as husband and wife have no application whatever to ungodly people who live after the manner of the world.

Not knowing . . . the power of God! As with all carnal men, they were incapable of knowing how he who created man from primal element could also call his dead body back from dust to life. The power of God—the power that creates, the power that snuffs out mortal breath, the power that gives life again to the dead elements of a hopeless corpse! If God creates, can he not also resurrect? And if he causes men to live again in glorious immortality, can he not solve such a petty little problem as whose wife she shall be of the seven? How narrow, inglorious, and grudging are the views of those who know neither the scriptures nor the power of God!

Three accounts follow as to what Jesus then said. Matthew gives his teaching thus:

> *For in the resurrection THEY neither marry, nor are given in marriage, but are as the angels of God in heaven.*

Mark gives the same teaching in substantially equivalent words:

> *For when THEY shall rise from the dead, THEY neither marry, nor are given in marriage; but are as the angels which are in heaven.*

In view of the common sectarian heresy, based on substantially the same scriptural ignorance as that which enveloped the Sadducees, that there is no marrying nor giving in marriage in the world of resurrected glory, we cannot stress too strongly the imperative need to identify who are *they* to whom Jesus here refers. It is, accordingly, to Luke that we turn for the most extended, complete, and enlightening account of the inspired words of him who, as Jehovah—before death had entered the world—sealed the first man, Adam, and the first woman, Eve, in an eternal marriage union:

THE CHILDREN OF THIS WORLD marry, and are given in marriage: But they which shall be accounted worthy to obtain that world, and the resurrection from the dead, neither marry, nor are given in marriage: Neither can they die any more: for THEY are equal unto the angels; and are the children of God, being the children of the resurrection.

Now, these words were spoken to Jesus' detractors who did not believe in a resurrection; they were spoken about a question on marriage that had been asked as a ploy only, and not because information was being sought about how marriage and the family unit operated in the realms ahead; and they were spoken to people who knew perfectly well that the Pharisees and the Rabbis and the people believed not only in a resurrection, but in the kind of a resurrection in which the same sociality—including marriage and the family unit—that exists among mortals would continue among immortals. It is true that some believed, as a certain "Rabbi Raf is reported to have often said, 'In the world to come they shall neither eat, nor drink, nor beget children, nor trade. There is neither envy nor strife, but the just shall sit with crowns on their heads, and shall enjoy the splendor of the Divine Majesty.' " This, however, was a minority view—shall we not say, as far as they were concerned, a heretical view. "The majority inclined to a materialistic view of the resurrection. The pre-Christian book of Enoch [from which Jude quotes in the New Testament] says that the righteous after the resurrection shall live so long that they shall beget thousands. The received doctrine is laid down by Rabbi

Saadia, who says, 'As the son of the widow of Sarepton, and the son of the Shunamite, ate and drank, and doubtless married wives, so shall it be in the resurrection'; and by Maimonides, who says, 'Men after the resurrection will use meat and drink, and will beget children, because since the Wise Architect makes nothing in vain, it follows of necessity that the members of the body are not useless, but fulfil their functions.' The point raised by the Sadducees was often debated by the Jewish doctors, who decided that 'a woman who married two husbands in this world is restored to the first in the next.' "[2]

Who then are *they* to whom Jesus refers when he says *they* neither marry nor are given in marriage in the resurrection? They are the children of this world; they are worldly and carnal and rebellious people; they are those who live after the manner of the world. They are the wicked and ungodly who "know not God, and that obey not the gospel of our Lord Jesus Christ: Who shall be punished with everlasting destruction from the presence of the Lord, and from the glory of his power; When he shall come to be glorified in his saints." (2 Thes. 1:8-10.) They are the Sadducees and their ilk who do not even believe in a resurrection, to say nothing of the eternal joy of eternal familyhood.

Of such persons the Lord says: "If a man marry him a wife in the world, and he marry her not by me nor by my word, and he covenant with her so long as he is in the world and she with him, their covenant and marriage are not of force when they are dead, and when they are out of the world; therefore, they are not bound by any law when they are out of the world. Therefore, when they are out of the world they neither marry nor are given in marriage; but are appointed angels in heaven, which angels are ministering servants, to minister for those who are worthy of a far more, and an exceeding, and an eternal weight of glory. For these angels did not abide my law; therefore, they cannot be enlarged, but remain separately and singly, without exaltation, in their saved condition, to all eternity; and from henceforth are not gods, but are angels of God forever and ever." (D&C 132:15-17.)

And as touching the dead, that they rise: have ye not read in the book of Moses, how in the bush God spake unto him, saying, I am the God of Abraham, and the God of Isaac, and the God of Jacob? He is not therefore the God of the dead, but the God of the living; for he raiseth them up out of their graves. Ye therefore do greatly err.

Addressing Sadducees—who believed neither the prophets, nor in preexistence, nor in angels, nor in spirits, nor in life after death, nor in a resurrection, nor in kingdoms of eternal glory where family felicities are perfected—addressing these Jewish agnostics, Jesus did not call up the words recorded by Isaiah that say to Israel: "Thy dead men shall live, together with my dead body shall they arise. . . . and the earth shall cast out the dead." (Isa. 26:19.) He did not hark back to the words of Daniel, which say that "many of them that sleep in the dust of the earth shall awake, some to everlasting life, and some to shame and everlasting contempt." (Dan. 12:2.) Nor did he remind them of Ezekiel's vision of the valley of dry bones—the bones of all Israel—which came forth with sinews and flesh and skin to live again; nor of the promise of the God of Israel to his people: "I will open your graves, . . . and bring you into the land of Israel." (Ezek. 37:1-14.) Nor did he call attention to anything that the prophets of old had spoken relative to that life and immortality which is brought to pass through the atonement of God's Son.

Rather, our Lord, turning to the Pentateuch, brought forth an irrefutable proof of the resurrection that is nobler and grander even than prophetic words or seeric visions. He equated the resurrection with the very existence of God and man. The Eternal One is not the God of the dead but of the living! How unworthy, how impotent, how lowly and base is God if all things are created for naught; if his mortal children vanish away and their bodies become "grey hand-fuls of crumbling dust." Unless Abraham, Isaac, and Jacob live; unless their spirits dwell with the just, as they await their resurrection; unless they shall rise again to become like Him whose children they are; unless there is victory over the grave—the purposes of creation vanish away, God is dethroned, and his plans and purposes fail.

But he is not the God of the dead. Indeed, there are no dead. All live unto him. To what, if there is no resurrection, had the trust of Abraham, Isaac, and Jacob come? "To death, and nothingness, and an everlasting silence, and 'a land of darkness, as darkness itself,' after a life so full of trials that the last of these patriarchs had described it as a pilgrimage of few and evil years! But God meant more than this. He meant—and so the Son of God interpreted it—that He who helps them who trust in Him here, will be their help and stay for ever and for ever, nor shall the future world become for them 'a land where all things are forgotten.'" (Farrar, pp. 562-63.)

It is no wonder that "when the multitude heard this [all that he had said both about marriage and about the resur-rection], they were astonished at his doctrine," and that "certain of the scribes answering said, Master, thou hast well said."

"The First and Great Commandment"
(Matthew 22:34-40; Mark 12:28-34)

Those who believed in a literal resurrection and in the continuation of the family unit in eternity found themselves with ambivalent feelings when Jesus routed the Sadducees. They gloried in his answer, but remained repulsed by his person. They took satisfaction in seeing the false Sadducean doctrines exposed, and yet this Galilean must be shown up as a false prophet and a fraud in some other way. Some of the scribes had the good grace to say, "Master, thou hast well said," as they saw the total discomfiture of the high and mighty Sadducees. But one of their number—one who was also designated as a lawyer, one who was an expert on their law, and who was held out as an expounder of the law and a teacher of the people—one held in high esteem among them, resorted to an observing group of Pharisees to consult as to what assault could be made on Him who always came off triumphant in the forays against him. Though these agnostic Sadducees, these nonscholars, these nontheologians, who made little pretense of scriptural knowledge, were no match for the Master, yet the learned scribes and Pharisees—they would yet devise a problem to which any answer he gave would cause division and opposition against him.

After consulting with the Pharisees, one of the scribes presented this problem: "Master, which is the greatest commandment in the law?" To us this may seem to be a perfectly normal and reasonable inquiry; in its Jewish setting, however, we soon see why Matthew says it was asked as a means of "tempting him." It was, in fact, a matter around which considerable contention centered. "The Rabbinical schools, in their meddling, carnal, superficial spirit of word-weaving and letter-worship, had spun large accumulations of worthless subtlety all over the Mosaic code. Among other things they had wasted their idleness in fantastic attempts to count, and classify, and weigh, and measure all the separate commandments of the ceremonial and moral law. They had come to the sapient conclusion that there were 248 affirmative precepts, being as many as the members in the human body, and 365 negative precepts, being as many as the arteries and veins, or the days of the year: the total being 613, which was also the number of letters in the Decalogue.

"They arrived at the same result from the fact that the Jews were commanded to wear fringes (*tsitsith*) on the corners of their *tallith,* bound with thread of blue; and as each fringe had eight threads and five knots, and the letters of the word *tsitsith* make 600, the total number of commandments was, as before, 613. Now surely, out of such a large number of precepts and prohibitions, *all* could not be of quite the same value; and some were 'light' (*kal*), and some were 'heavy' (*kobhed*). But which? and what was the greatest commandment of all? According to some Rabbis, the most important of all is that about the *tephillin* and the *tsitsith,* the fringes and phylacteries; and 'he who diligently observes it is regarded in the same light as if he had kept the whole Law.'

"Some thought the omission of ablutions as bad as homicide; some that the precepts of the Mishna were all 'heavy'; those of the Law were some heavy and some light. Others considered the *third* to be the greatest commandment. None of them had realised the great principle, that the wilful violation of one commandment is the transgression of all (James 2:10) because the object of the entire Law is the spirit of *obedience to God.* On the question proposed by the lawyer the Shammaites and Hillelites were in disaccord and, as usual, both schools were wrong: the Shammaites, in thinking that mere trivial external observances were valuable, apart from the spirit in which they were performed, and the principle which they exemplified; the Hillelites, in thinking that *any* positive command could in itself be unimportant, and in not seeing that great principles are essential to the due performance of even the slightest duties." (Farrar, pp. 565-66.)

Faced with these variant, petty, and uninspired views, these interpretations of the law that came from blind guides whose spiritual perceptions were almost nil, Jesus followed his usual course. He simply swept aside the minutia and haggling of the schools and turned their attention back to the foundation upon which the whole law rested. He may even have pointed to the *tephillin* (phylactery) worn by the inquiring scribe as he answered, for in it was the *Shema,* which all the faithful recited twice daily and which was itself a recitation of the first and great commandment.

The first of all the commandments is, Hear, O Israel;
The Lord our God is one Lord: And thou shalt love the
Lord thy God with all thy heart, and with all thy soul,
and with all thy mind, and with all thy strength: this is
the first commandment.

*And the second is like, namely this, Thou shalt love
thy neighbour as thyself. There is none other commandment greater than these.*

This answer, thus given, was not new. It contained none
of the "contentions, and strivings about the law" that Paul
acclaimed as "unprofitable and vain." (Titus 3:9.) And there
were among the Rabbis those with the sense and discernment to single it out for themselves. We have, in fact, heretofore heard a lawyer tempt Jesus with the question,
"Master, what shall I do to inherit eternal life?" and he
himself be asked in turn, "What is written in the law? how
readest thou?" This learned Jew gave the same answer here
repeated by Jesus, and then, "willing to justify himself,"
asked, "Who is my neighbour?" which brought forth from
our Lord the wondrous parable of the good Samaritan.
Jesus, however, to the two commandments, recorded as they
are in the law,[3] expanded their meaning by saying:

*On these two commandments hang all the law and
the prophets.*

To his everlasting credit, the scribal lawyer responded:
"Well, Master, thou hast said the truth: for there is one God;
and there is none other but he: And to love him with all the
heart, and with all the understanding, and with all the soul,
and with all the strength, and to love his neighbour as
himself, is more than all whole burnt offerings and
sacrifices."

Jesus then said, "Thou art not far from the kingdom of
God." We can only hope that the light of truth grew brighter
in the lawyer's heart until its full blaze and glory guided him
into the earthly kingdom where alone is found the course
leading to eternal life.

With this colloquy, the day of Rabbinic-Pharisaic-scribal
questioning ceased. "And no man after that durst ask him
any question." He had answered all things well, and aside
from some things that he would yet say and do on his own
motion, he had delivered his Father's message in full.

"What Think Ye of Christ?"
(Matthew 22:41-46; Mark 12:35-37; JST, Mark 12:40, 44; Luke 20:41-44)

Salvation is in Christ! He is the Son of the living God. No man cometh unto the Father but by him. He is the Savior of the world and the Redeemer of men. He came into the world to do the will of the Father. His Father sent him to ransom all men from the grave and to raise those who believe and obey unto eternal life in the eternal kingdom. To gain salvation, men must come unto him, believe his gospel, and live his laws. This is the doctrine he has taught and the witness he has borne from that day in the temple when he, but twelve years of age, asked Mary if she knew not that he must be about his Father's business, to this, his last day in the temple, when all but the climactic events of his ministry are passed. But as one of these crowning events he must once again let all who will hear know that he is God's Son.

He has defeated his enemies—God's enemies!—at every turn and on every hand. That is evident to all; but none must be left to assume, nor must there be the slightest intimation, that his triumphs have come simply because he is a great prophet, or a wise philosopher, or a learned Rabbi. He must be identified for what he is—the Son of the Highest. Thus, to the Pharisees assembled there in great numbers and dressed in regal splendor, while yet in the court of his Father's house, he says:

What think ye of Christ? whose son is he?

Their answer—he could have expected none other—crystallized the whole Jewish concept of a Temporal Deliverer who would once again wield the sword of David, wear the crown of that great king, and sit on a throne from which laws would go forth to the Gentile aliens whose yoke they now wore. Their answer presupposed that the downtrodden of Israel would, under their Messiah, tread on the necks of their enemies as they rejoiced in their new Messianic kingdom. They said: "The son of David." They said: 'A mighty king, a great deliverer, a supreme ruler.' In reply Jesus said:

> *How then doth David in spirit call him Lord, saying,*
> *The Lord said unto my Lord, Sit thou on my right*
> *hand, till I make thine enemies thy footstool? If David*
> *then call him Lord, how is he his son?*

Psalm 110, given to David by the power of the Holy Ghost—that glorious Messianic psalm in which the Eternal Father swore with an oath that his Son would be a priest forever after the order of Melchizedek—such is the scriptural source to which Jesus refers as a means of raising the issue of his own divinity. As interpreted by the Son of God— and here we may discard all the vagaries of men on the passage involved; we may ignore the higher critics who say David never wrote the psalm; we may throw aside the "learned" assumptions that someone other than Elohim was testifying of his Son—David's Messianic utterance speaks of one Lord saying to another—of one God saying to another, of Elohim saying to Jehovah, of the Eternal Father saying to his Beloved Son—sit thou on my right hand. Lo, that God who then spoke unto men by his Son; that Son whom he "hath appointed heir of all things"; that Son who is "the brightness of his glory, and the express image of his [Father's] person"; the very Son who now, having ascended into heaven, sits "on the right hand of the Majesty on high"—this Son and this Father, they are the Gods mentioned in the Messianic prophecy. (Heb. 1:1-3.) These are the ones of whom the inspired utterance speaks.

Jesus' logic was unassailable. "How say the scribes that Christ is the Son of David?" he asked. If "David . . . himself calleth him Lord," he continued, "whence is he then his son?" How could he be David's Son—as he was—if David also called him Lord? "How then could the Messiah be David's son? Could Abraham have called Isaac or Jacob or Joseph, or any of his own descendants near or remote, his *lord?* If not, how came David to do so? There could be but one answer—because that Son would be divine, not human—David's son by human birth, but David's Lord by divine subsistence. But they could not find this simple explanation, nor, indeed, any other; they could not find it, because Jesus was their Messiah, and they had rejected Him. They chose to ignore the fact that He was, in the flesh, the son of David; and when, as their Messiah, He had called Himself the Son of God, they had raised their hands in pious horror, and had taken up stones to stone Him." (Farrar, p. 567.)

Jesus' testimony of himself, implicit in the divine logic that he used, left the Pharisees without hope or answer, but brought rejoicing to those whose minds had not been poisoned by the theological seminaries of the day. Thus it is written: "And no man after that durst ask him, saying, Who art thou?" And also: "The common people heard him gladly; but the high priest and the elders were offended at him." So be it.

NOTES

1. Levirate marriage is so named from the Latin word *levir,* "a brother-in-law." Some of its original provisions are set forth in Deuteronomy 25:5-10.

2. J. R. Dummelow, *The One Volume Bible Commentary,* p. 698. In this connection it is worthy of note that Jesus, after his resurrection, ate fish and an honeycomb in the presence of his disciples. (Luke 24:41-43.) Peter says the disciples "did eat and drink with him after he rose from the dead." (Acts 10:41.)

3. Leviticus 19:18 speaks of loving one's neighbor as himself, and Deuteronomy 6:4-5 contains the great commandment to love the Lord above all. The passages contained in the four compartments of the *tephillin* were Exodus 13:1-10, 11-16; Deuteronomy 6:4-9 and 11:13-21. As set forth in the latter-day revelation, the two greatest of the commandments are given in these more perfected words: "Thou shalt love the Lord thy God with all thy heart, with all thy might, mind, and strength; and in the name of Jesus Christ thou shalt serve him. Thou shalt love thy neighbor as thyself." (D&C 59:5-6.)

Chapter 88

THE GREAT DENUNCIATION

Prophesy against the shepherds of Israel,
prophesy, and say unto them,
Thus saith the Lord God unto the
shepherds;
Woe be to the shepherds of Israel
that do feed themselves! should not the
shepherds feed the flocks? . . .
Behold, I am against the shepherds;
and I will require my flock at their hand,
and cause them to cease
from feeding the flock.
(Ezek. 34:2, 10.)
O the wise, and the learned, and the rich,
that are puffed up in the pride of their
hearts,
and all those who preach false doctrines,
and all those who commit whoredoms,
and pervert the right way of the Lord,
wo, wo, wo be unto them,
saith the Lord God Almighty,
for they shall be thrust down to hell!
(2 Ne. 28:15.)

Jesus Speaks with the Voice of Vengeance
(*Matthew 23:1-12; JST, Matthew 23:2, 4-7, 9; Luke 11:43*)

"Vengeance is mine; I will repay, saith the Lord" (Rom. 12:19), the Lord who is both Jehovah and Jesus. "Is God unrighteous who taketh vengeance?" Paul asks. He answers: "God forbid: for then [that is, if otherwise] how shall God judge the world?" (Rom. 3:5-6.) And be it remembered that the Father judgeth no man, but hath committed all judgment unto the Son. And so, as we now hear the meek and lowly One—who came to teach, and bless, and heal—raise his voice in cutting invective, we must be mindful that he is also a God of vengeance, and that the power to bless is also the power to curse. He who came, according to the Messianic word, "to preach good tidings unto the meek" and "to bind up the broken-hearted" came also "to proclaim the acceptable year of the Lord, and the day of vengeance of our God." (Isa. 61:1-2.) He it is whose destiny was to "bring forth judgment unto truth." He is the one concerning whom Isaiah promised: "He shall not fail nor be discouraged, till he have set judgment in the earth: and the isles shall wait for his law." (Isa. 42:1-7.)

When the Holy Messiah comes again—suddenly, as the promise is—to his temple, which is the earth, those whom he finds in its courts will fall into two categories. For some he calls it "the day of vengeance which was in my heart," and he says he will trample them in his fury and tread upon them in his anger. For others he names it "the year of my redeemed," those who "shall mention the loving kindness of their Lord, and all that he has bestowed upon them according to his goodness, and according to his loving kindness, forever and ever." (D&C 133:50-52.)

Even so now, here in his earthly temple, where tens of thousands of Passover pilgrims mill about, surrounded by faithful disciples who rejoice in his goodness and loving kindness, and in the midst of scribes and Pharisees, who hate his person and whose every faculty is bent on shedding his blood—here in a scene prefiguring the day of his later coming, he sits in judgment on his fellowmen. It is a present day in which he is revealing what shall be in the future day of judgment and burning. For his disciples it is a day of added doctrinal enlightenment and the consequent courage to hold fast to that iron rod which is the word of God. For the scribes and Pharisees it is a day of vengeance in which they shall hear about the fires of hell that await them.

In what has already taken place the priests and Rabbis and Pharisees and leaders of the people have been identified as blind leaders of the blind. "And they"—how sad it is to say—"loved their blindness," because, as we are so well aware, their deeds were evil. Further: "They would not acknowledge their ignorance," so fully demonstrated in all that has just transpired. And "they did not repent them of their faults; the bitter venom of their hatred to Him was not driven forth by His forbearance; the dense midnight of their perversity was not dispelled by His wisdom. Their purpose to destroy Him was fixed, obstinate, irreversible. If one plot failed, they were but driven with more stubborn sullenness into another. And, therefore, since Love had played her part in vain, 'vengeance leaped upon the stage;' since the Light of the World shone for them with no illumination, the lightning flash should at last warn them of their danger. There could now be no hope of their becoming reconciled to Him; they were but being stereotyped in unrepentant malice against Him. Turning, therefore, to His disciples, but in the audience of all the people, He rolled over their guilty heads, with crash on crash of moral anger, the thunder of His utter condemnation." (Farrar, p. 569.)

The scribes and the Pharisees sit in Moses' seat: All, therefore, whatsoever they bid you observe, they will make you observe and do; for they are ministers of the law, and they make themselves your judges. But do not ye after their works; for they say, and do not. For they bind heavy burdens and grievous to be borne, and lay them on men's shoulders; but they themselves will not move them with one of their fingers.

Moses' seat, the seat of judgment and power! For the few brief remaining hours until, at this very Passover, the Paschal Lamb is slain, the scribes and Pharisees continue as legal administrators of the Mosaic order. They are still the ministers of the law; none others on earth can offer up sacrifices on the great altar so as to make atonement for the sins of repentant souls. Theirs is still the obligation to teach, not their traditions, but the true principles set forth by Moses and the prophets. But O how men must be warned against their false teachings, their evil examples, their works of wickedness!

No man, before the judgment bar, will be excused for believing false doctrines or doing evil acts on the excuse that he followed a minister, who he supposed taught true principles and gave good counsel, but who in fact declared false doctrine and wrought evil works. No matter that, in showy piety, we bear grievous burdens in the name of religion (as all the Jews did), or win great theological conflicts (as the Rabbis and scribes were wont to do), or display a superabundance of supposed good works (as some modern religionists suppose they do); no matter what else we may do in a false hope of gaining salvation—all that will matter in the day of judgment will be whether we have kept, truly and faithfully, the commandments of God. Let false ministers be damned, if such is the judgment they deserve; the members of their congregations must nonetheless work out their salvation by conforming to true principles of religion.

And all their works they do to be seen of men. They make broad their phylacteries, and enlarge the borders of their garments, and love the uppermost rooms at feasts, and the chief seats in the synagogues, and greetings in the markets, and to be called of men, Rabbi, Rabbi (which is master.)

True ministers labor with an eye single to the glory of God. Their interests and concerns are in the welfare of the sheep and the salvation of the souls of men. False ministers supplant priesthood service with the self-exaltation of priestcraft. Their interests and concerns are in their own self-ennoblement, not in the welfare of the sheep. They have not strengthened the diseased, nor healed the sick, nor bound up the broken, nor brought again that which was driven away, nor sought that which was lost, as true shepherds must, "but with force and with cruelty" have they "ruled them." (Ezek. 34:4.)

Indeed, "priestcrafts are that men preach and set themselves up for a light unto the world, that they may get gain and praise of the world; but they seek not the welfare of Zion." (2 Ne. 26:29.) Scarlet robes and jeweled gowns, golden crowns and costly scepters, girdles of fine-twined linen, gold and silver and silks, and all manner of precious clothing—these become the desires of those who seek to serve God through personal exaltation. Did all the Jews wear their phylacteries—those leather straps placed on the foreheads and left arms, near the heart, and containing parchments reciting the *Shema* and other scriptures—when praying? Those of the scribes and Pharisees must be broader and bear witness of a showy display of supposed piety. Is it the practice of all to wear garments whereon dangle sacred blue tassels in remembrance of covenants made with Jehovah? Those plying their trade of priestcraft must have gaudy and distinguishable adornments, lest any fail to see the sign of their religious devotion. Are people seated by rank and greeted in public with laudatory titles? How the ministers of men must vie for preferential status in all situations! What a difference there is between true and false religion—even in outward symbols! Without true doctrines to ponder and teach, false ministers turn to the trappings of ritualistic formalism to satisfy man's innate leanings toward things in the spiritual realm. Of all this the disciples must beware.

> *But be not ye called Rabbi; for one is your master,*
> *which is Christ; and all ye are brethren.*
> *And call no one your creator upon the earth, or your*

392

heavenly Father; for one is your creator and heavenly Father, even he who is in heaven.

Neither be ye called masters; for one is your master, even he whom your heavenly Father sent, which is Christ; for he hath sent him among you that ye might have life.

But he that is greatest among you shall be your servant. And whosoever shall exalt himself shall be abased of him; and he that shall humble himself shall be exalted of him.

This counsel to the disciples seems of obvious and self-evident value to us. In its Jewish setting, however, it took on an even deeper import and meaning, a meaning that grew out of the unbelievable—sometimes even blasphemous— honor sought by and bestowed upon Rabbis. For instance: The heathen Governor of Caesarea was said to have seen Rabbis in vision with the faces of angels. The Governor of Antioch was supposed to have "seen their faces and by them conquered," which is not far different from the Catholic legend about Constantine the Great. Rabbis ranked higher than kings, their curses (though unjustified) always, as they supposed, came to pass, and one of them chose to "be buried in white garments, to show that he was worthy of appearing before his Maker." (Edersheim 2:409.) But perhaps the greatest illustration of pretentious self-assertion is seen in this Talmudic account: "They represent heaven itself as a Rabbinic school, of which God is the Head Rabbi. On one occasion God differs from all the angels on a question as to a leper being clean or unclean. They refer the decision to R. Ben Nachman, who is accordingly slain by Azrael, and brought to the heavenly Academy. He decides with God, who is much pleased." (Farrar, footnote 4, p. 569.) In the light of such monstrous and blasphemous absurdities, it is no wonder that Jesus commanded the disciples to designate no one on earth as their heavenly Father, which in effect is what this Rabbinic account does. No doubt there were numerous other local legends on this and related points that have not been preserved to our day.

The Eight Woes against the Scribes and Pharisees
(Matthew 23:13-33; JST, Matthew 23:11-13, 17, 21, 28-29;
Mark 12:38-40; Luke 11:37-42, 44-48; 20:45-47; JST, Luke 11:42-43)

Jesus now bursts forth with eight denunciations of woe upon the scribes and Pharisees.[1] He arraigns them "with a veritable torrent of righteous indignation, through which flashed the lightning of scorching invective, accompanied by thunder peals of divine anathema." (Talmage, p. 554.) For three and a half years he has offered them blessings—the Sermon on the Mount itself contains eight beatitudes, eight eternal blessings for all who will believe and obey—all of which blessings they have repeatedly rejected. The sun has now set on the day for blessings, and the darkness of night with its woeful cursings is upon them. Both blessings and curses grow out of a way of life; the righteous are blessed, the wicked are cursed. Upon them comes a deep and inconsolable grief and misery. So it is now with the scribes and Pharisees; divine wrath, holy wrath, the wrath of a Divine Being is now poured out upon them, almost without measure. We shall consider each woe in turn.

1. *The Woe for Rejecting Christ and Salvation:*
But woe unto you, scribes and Pharisees, hypocrites! for ye shut up the kingdom of heaven against men: for ye neither go in yourselves, neither suffer ye them that are entering to go in.

"Woe unto them, for the ignorant erudition which closed the gates of heaven, and the injurious jealousy which would suffer no others to enter in!"[2]

What false minister is ever content to damn himself alone, to lose his own soul only, to go without companions on his head-strong course to hell? It is inherent in the ministerial role to get others to believe and live as the preacher proclaims. Christ—whom the scribes and Pharisees rejected—is the door to salvation. Not only did they thus lose their own souls, but with all their power they sought to deny the gospel blessings to others.

2. *The Woe against Avarice and Hypocrisy:*

Woe unto you, scribes and Pharisees! for ye are hypocrites! Ye devour widows' houses, and for a pretence make long prayers; therefore ye shall receive the greater punishment.

"Woe unto them for their oppressive hypocrisy and greedy cant!"

Thou shalt not covet; the love of money is the root of all evil; how hardly can a rich man enter into the kingdom of heaven; where a man's treasure is, there will his heart be also—these and a host of scriptural truisms, taught by Jesus, accepted instinctively by the spiritually inclined, and known to the scribes and Pharisees—all these bore testimony against them. Avarice, greed, covetousness, the amassing of great wealth by questionable means—all such was a way of life among the leaders in Israel. Under cover of religious duty, they extorted enormous sums from the ever-present widows and orphans, salving their consciences with pretentious prayers. To gain salvation, they must not only repent of their rapacious and grasping ways, but they must also affirmatively make their riches available to the poor and the needy—sell all that they have and go and follow Christ, as he himself said to the rich young ruler. How truly and well it is written: "Wo unto you rich men, that will not give your substance to the poor, for your riches will canker your souls; and this shall be your lamentation in the day of visitation, and of judgment, and of indignation: The harvest is past, the summer is ended, and my soul is not saved!" (D&C 56:16.) Add to this the deliberate and designed vice of hypocrisy, and we have a scribal-Pharisaic person whose heart is fixed on the things of this world and who will inherit accordingly in the world to come.

3. *The Woe for Converting Souls to a False Church:*

Woe unto you, scribes and Pharisees, hypocrites! For

ye compass sea and land to make one proselyte; and when he is made, ye make him two-fold more the child of hell than he was before, like unto yourselves.

"Woe for the proselytising fanaticism which did but produce a more perilous corruption!"

O the wickedness of converting a soul, a human soul, a child of God to a false system of religion, be it Judaism or Pharisaism or one of the sects of Christendom! If a mortal child of the Eternal God is seeking truth and willing to forsake an undesirable past, how dire and calamitous it is to lead him into greater darkness! There may be times when truth seekers improve their lot by going from a sect that is more abominable to one that is less evil, but when the True Light is present, there can be only one acceptable course—turn to Him. It is said of Jewish proselytizing of that day: "Out of a bad heathen they made a worse Jew." As with the other woes, this one befell them because they rejected Him who came to bring them light and truth and salvation.

4. *The Woe against Moral Blindness Shown in the Breaking of Oaths:*

Woe unto you, blind guides, who say, Whosoever shall swear by the temple, it is nothing; but whosoever shall swear by the gold of the temple, he committeth sin, and is a debtor. Ye fools and blind: for whether is greater, the gold, or the temple that sanctifieth the gold?

And, Whosoever shall swear by the altar, it is nothing; but whosoever sweareth by the gift that is upon it, he is guilty. Ye fools and blind: for whether is greater, the gift, or the altar that sanctifieth the gift? Verily I say unto you, Whoso, therefore, sweareth by it, sweareth by the altar, and by all things thereon.

"Woe for the blind hair-splitting folly which so confused the sanctity of oaths as to tempt their followers into gross profanity!"

In few things did the moral depravity of Pharisaism rear

its ugly head with such studied wickedness as in their profane perversion of the divine law relative to oaths. From the beginning, down through the patriarchal dispensations, and through the whole Mosaic era, Jehovah had allowed his people the privilege of swearing with an oath—of making a divine affirmation, of asserting an assured verity in a sacred way—so as to guarantee the immutable verity of the spoken word. An oath made God a partner in the matter to which solemn attestation was being made. It could not, therefore, fail; for God does not fail, and the Cause of Righteousness is as prevailing and eternal as Deity himself.

But these Jews—in their apostate debauchery—had so perverted the true order of vows and oaths that they had become a sword of evil instead of a shield of good. Technical, trifling rules by which oaths could be annulled and avoided came forth from the Great Sanhedrin. An indulgence here, some special privilege there, as the Rabbinists taught, enabled men to ignore their solemn vows made in Jehovah's name. Causistry of the most complicated kind guided the Pharisees in their avoidance of their moral and sworn obligations. Thus: "If a man swore by the temple, the House of Jehovah, he could obtain an indulgence for breaking his oath; but if he vowed by the gold and treasure of the Holy House, he was bound by the unbreakable bonds of priestly dictum. Though one should swear by the altar of God, his oath could be annulled; but if he vowed by the corban gift or by the gold upon the altar, his obligation was imperative. To what depths of unreason and hopeless depravity had men fallen, how sinfully foolish and how wilfully blind were they, who saw not that the Temple was greater than its gold, and the altar than the gift that lay upon it! In the Sermon on the Mount the Lord had said 'Swear not at all'; but upon such as would not live according to that higher law, upon those who persisted in the use of oaths and vows, the lesser and evidently just requirement of strict fidelity to the terms of self-assumed obligations was to be enforced, without unrighteous quibble or inequitable discrimination." (Talmage, p. 556.)

5. *The Woe against Supplanting Eternal Principles with Religious Trifles:*

> *Woe unto you, scribes and Pharisees, hypocrites! for ye pay tithe of mint and anise and cummin, and have omitted the weightier matters of the law, judgment, mercy, and faith: these ought ye to have done, and not to leave the other undone. Ye blind guides, who strain at a gnat, and swallow a camel; who make yourselves appear unto men that ye would not commit the least sin, and yet ye yourselves, transgress the whole law.*

"Woe for the petty paltry sham scrupulosity which paid tithes of potherbs, and thought nothing of justice, mercy, and faith—which strained out animalculae from the goblet, and swallowed camels into the heart!"

One of the marks of personal or universal apostasy is to center on religious trifles to the exclusion of eternal principles. Abstain from the use of tea, coffee, and tobacco, but indulge in lustful acts or forsake standards of business integrity; refrain from picking an olive or shucking an ear of maize on the Sabbath, but ignore the command to worship the Father in spirit and in truth on his holy day; pay tithing on the leaves and stalks of herbs grown in pots on the windowsill, but give no heed to judgment, mercy, and faith—such are the marks of apostate fanaticism. By such a course it is easy to have a form of godliness and a zeal for religion without doing the basic things that require the whole heart and the whole soul. Those so doing filter their drinking water through a linen cloth to avoid swallowing an unclean insect while, figuratively, gulping down a camel.

6. *The Woe against Hiding Wickedness Under a Religious Cloak:*

> *Woe unto you, scribes and Pharisees, hypocrites! for ye make clean the outside of the cup and of the platter, but within they are full of extortion and excess. Thou blind Pharisee, cleanse first that which is within the cup and platter, that the outside of them may be clean also.*

"Woe for the external cleanliness of cup and platter contrasted with the gluttony and drunkenness to which they ministered!"

Again the woe pronounced by Jesus has application to the apostate scribes and Pharisees of all ages and among all peoples. Under a religious cloak, with unbounded zeal, they perform some ritualistic minutae, as though such solved all the problems of life and attuned them forever to the Infinite One. Cups and platters must be polished to perfection; they must be ceremonially clean; what does it matter that the contents are purchased with the gold of extortion, or that the meat will pander to gluttony, or that the wine will assure drunkenness. It is the form, not the substance, with which Rabbinism is concerned.

Earlier in Perea, while dining in the home of a Pharisee, Jesus abstained from the ritualistic washings that played such a vital role in their lives. On that occasion he denounced the same hypocritical pettiness with even greater exacerbation.

Now do ye Pharisees make clean the outside of the cup and the platter; but your inward part is full of ravening and wickedness. Ye fools, did not he that made that which is without make that which is within also?

But if ye would rather give alms of such things as ye have; and observe to do all things which I have commanded you, then would your inward parts be clean also.

7. *The Woe against a False Outward Appearance of Righteousness:*

Woe unto you, scribes and Pharisees, hypocrites! for ye are like unto whited sepulchres, which indeed appear beautiful outward, but are within full of dead men's bones, and of all uncleanness. Even so ye also outwardly appear righteous unto men, but within ye are full of hypocrisy and iniquity.

"Woe to the tombs that simulated the sanctity of temples—to the glistening outward plaster of hypocrisy which did but render more ghastly by contrast the reeking pollutions of the sepulchre within!"

"It was an awful figure, that of likening them to whitewashed tombs, full of dead bones and rotting flesh. As the dogmas of the rabbis made even the slightest contact with a corpse or its cerements, or with the bier upon which it was borne, or the grave in which it has been lain, a cause of personal defilement, which only ceremonial washing and the offering of sacrifices could remove, care was taken to make tombs conspicuously white, so that no person need be defiled through ignorance or proximity to such unclean places; and, moreover, the periodical whitening of sepulchres was regarded as a memorial act of honor to the dead. But even as no amount of care or degree of diligence in keeping bright the outside of a tomb could stay the putrescence going on within, so no externals of pretended righteousness could mitigate the revolving corruption of a heart reeking with iniquity." (Talmage, p. 558.)

On that previous occasion in Perea, while sitting at meat in a Pharisaic home, Jesus had likened the scribes and Pharisees to "graves which appear not, and the men that walk over them are not aware of them." This woe he has now perfected and expanded. Clearly, his gift of plain and incisive speech is without parallel in all history.

8. *The Woe against Rejecting Living Prophets:*
Woe unto you, scribes and Pharisees, hypocrites! because ye build tombs of the prophets, and garnish the sepulchres of the righteous, And say, If we had been in the day of our fathers, we would not have been partakers with them in the blood of the prophets.

Wherefore, we are witnesses unto yourselves of your own wickedness, and ye are the children of them who killed the prophets; And will fill up the measure then of your fathers; for ye, yourselves, kill the prophets like unto your fathers.

"Woe for the mock repentance which condemned their

fathers for the murder of the prophets, and yet reflected the murderous spirit of those fathers—nay, filled up and exceeded the measure of their guilt by a yet deadlier and more dreadful sacrifice!"

Of all the woes, this is the chief and crowning one. To reject living prophets, under the pretext of honoring the seers of old, is to deny all the prophets and forfeit any hope of eternal reward. We have long since learned that to believe in Abraham, or Moses, or any of the prophets, or John the Baptist, meant to believe in Christ, for they all testified of him. All the prophets of all the ages bear the same testimony; all preach the same saving truths; all bear witness of the same Atoning One. Salvation is in Christ, and the prophets are his messengers who announce his saving truths to the mortals of their day.

And to reject the prophets of any age is to reject those of all ages, for they all teach the same truths; they all bear the same witness; they all possess the same spirit. The spirit of murderous rebellion that thirsts for the blood of Christ is the same spirit that caused Jeremiah to be cast into a dungeon, Isaiah to be sawn asunder, and prophets without number to seal their testimonies with their own blood. The great test for all men is whether they will believe and obey the living oracles sent to them, not what they suppose they think about the prophets of old.

If these scribes and Pharisees, these priests and Rabbis, these Jewish elders and Israelite guides—if they and all the people would but believe in Christ, no woes would befall them. When any people believe the word which Deity sends to them—let it come from earth's Chief Prophet or the Lord's lowest elder—then past cursings slink away like a jackal before a lion, to be replaced by the blessed glories of the gospel. But always the religious pretext for rejecting living prophets, the conscience-salving excuse for turning away from living oracles, is a supposed belief in dead prophets and is an assumed reverence for buried seers. By professing to believe the prophetic word of old—which brought salvation to them of old—the door of salvation seems open and the need for new revelation to be done away. Come, then, let us slay the living prophets lest they muddy the prophetic message of the past.

On that previous occasion in Perea, our Lord's similarly phrased invective, against others equally evil, came forth in these words:

Woe unto you also, ye lawyers! for ye lade men with burdens grievous to be borne, and ye yourselves touch not the burdens with one of your fingers.

Woe unto you! for ye build the sepulchres of the prophets, and your fathers killed them. Truly ye bear witness that ye allow the deeds of your fathers: for they indeed killed them, and ye build their sepulchres.

Truly, the woe for rejecting living prophets is the woe of woes—the woe that thrusts men into the eternal woes of an eternal hell with its eternal damnation where their worm dieth not and the fire is not quenched!

Fill ye up then the measure of your fathers. Ye serpents, ye generation of vipers, how can ye escape the damnation of hell?

Jewish Accountability for the Sins of Their Ancestors
(Matthew 23:34-36; JST, Matthew 23:33-35; Luke 11:49-54; JST, Luke 11:53-54)

What other woes Jesus may have thundered forth on this ominous day—"with crash on crash of moral anger"—we do not know. Matthew records only the eight we have considered, and we cannot believe that he has preserved for us all that was said with reference to any of them. Inspired authors often write only in headlines and follow the practice of digesting and abridging much that falls from prophetic lips. We do know that on that prior Perean occasion when Jesus rebuked others whose hearts were black and whose deeds were evil, he had some cutting things to say about those who had not cared properly for the scriptural records entrusted to them.

Woe unto you, lawyers! For ye have taken away the key of knowledge, the fulness of the scriptures; ye enter not in yourselves into the kingdom; and those who were entering in, ye hindered.

"The holy scriptures"—the mind and will and word and voice of the Lord—how can their worth be weighed? Who can tell what wonders have been wrought because the pure word of the Perfect God lay open before men? And who can envision what evils have befallen the sons of men when the pure word has been tainted and twisted and made to say that which is not true?

"The holy scriptures," Paul said to Timothy, which "from a child thou hast known . . . are able to make thee wise unto salvation through faith which is in Christ Jesus." (2 Tim. 3:15.) Did not Jesus say, "They are they which testify of me"? (John 5:39.) Sad though it be, few are the men who hear the audible voice, thundering from Sinai, revealing in prophetic ears the mind and will of Jehovah; few are they who hear the still small voice, whispering in prophetic ears, revealing the principles and ordinances of the gospel; but millions comprise the hosts of earth's inhabitants who have before them the recorded words of holy men who wrote as they were prompted from on high. And all those who read these words—words preserved in the holy scriptures—and who do so by the power of the Holy Ghost can testify that they have heard the Lord's voice and know his words. (D&C 18:33-36.) And so, Paul continues, "All scripture is given by inspiration of God"—or, better, every scripture inspired of God—"is profitable for doctrine, for reproof, for correction, for instruction in righteousness: That the man of God may be perfect, throughly furnished unto all good works." (2 Tim. 3:16-17.)

And yet these evil leaders of an erring people had taken away the fulness of the scriptures. The word no longer lay open before the chosen seed. We have no reason to believe they had the writings of Abraham, the complete Book of Enoch, the portions of Genesis revealed anew through Joseph Smith, or the words of Zenos or Zenock or Neum or, perhaps, hosts of prophets whose very names are buried with their lost writings.

But let us return to the woes pronounced this day in the temple. In spite of all the evils of the scribes and Pharisees, Jesus yet offered his saving truths to the people. Though these blind spiritual guides comprised a generation of serpents and vipers whose assured destination was hell, the Blessed One said:

Behold, I send unto you prophets, and wise men, and scribes: and some of them ye shall kill and crucify; and some of them shall ye scourge in your synagogues, and persecute them from city to city: That upon you may come all the righteous blood shed upon the earth, from the blood of righteous Abel unto the blood of Zacharias son of Barachias, whom ye slew between the temple and the altar. Verily I say unto you, All these things shall come upon this generation.

Ye bear testimony against your fathers, when ye, yourselves, are partakers of the same wickedness. Behold your fathers did it through ignorance, but ye do not; wherefore, their sins shall be upon your heads.

This is strong doctrine. In it is a great principle of eternal truth that none but the true saints can comprehend; from it we learn, with an impact scarcely found elsewhere, how all generations of men tie together and how all of us are truly our brother's keeper.

Jesus sends apostles and prophets among the Jews of his day. He is Jehovah; he calls the prophets and wise men; the true scribes bear a true witness of him by the power of his Spirit. Even he himself ministers among them, testifying with words such as no other man ever spake, and in deeds such as no other man ever did, that he is truly God's Son. All this they reject, and they are damned; no man can reject the light of heaven and be saved—of course they are damned; they are a generation of vipers who cannot escape the damnation of hell. They shall die in their sins. Thus saith Jesus.

But this is not all. They are accountable for the sins of their fathers who through ignorance rejected the message of salvation. Such is the worst of woes, the crowning curse—to be accountable, not alone for their own sins, but for the sins of those who might have been saved had these spiritual leaders done their duty. From the day of Abel the son of Adam, whom Cain slew, to the day of Zacharias the father of John, who "was slain by Herod's order, between the porch and the altar"(*Teachings,* p. 261)—between these two days, which covered the whole span of earth history, many good men lived and died without a knowledge of the gospel. All these could have been freed from their spirit prison by the men of Jesus' day, if those to whom Jesus then preached had believed his words.

Joseph Smith, in the course of a sermon on salvation for the dead, and after quoting the denunciation of these scribes and Pharisees by Jesus, said: "Hence as they possessed greater privileges than any other generation, not only pertaining to themselves, but to their dead, their sin was greater, as they not only neglected their own salvation but that of their progenitors, and hence their blood [that of the progenitors] was required at their hands." (*Teachings,* pp. 222-23.)

"Am I my brother's keeper?" Cain responded when the Lord asked him about Abel (Gen. 4:9), whom he had slain, who was indeed slain for the love of God and the testimony of Jesus, as also was Zacharias. "My brother's keeper!" Truly it is so. All men, Jesus included, are brothers, children of the same Father. And as Christ laid down his life to save all men, his ministers are called to do all things necessary, even unto death, to save such portion of their brethren as they can.

NOTES

1. "The Talmud itself, with unwonted keenness and severity of sarcasm, has pictured to us the seven classes of Pharisees, out of which *six* are characterized by a mixture of haughtiness and imposture. There is the 'Shechemite' Pharisee, who obeys the law from self-interest (Gen. 34:19); the *Tumbling* Pharisee, who is so humble that he is always

stumbling because he will not lift his feet from the ground; the *Bleeding* Pharisee, who is always hurting himself against walls, because he is so modest as to be unable to walk about with his eyes open lest he should see a woman; the *Mortar* Pharisee, who covers his eyes as with a mortar, for the same reason; the *Tell-me-another-duty-and-I-will-do-it* Pharisee—several of whom occur in our Lord's ministry; and the *Timid* Pharisee, who is actuated by motives of fear alone. The seventh class only is the class of *Pharisees from love*, who obey God because they love Him from the heart." (Farrar, pp. 571-72.)

2. This statement, as well as each of the first-sentence quotations set forth in the discussion of the eight woes, is taken from Farrar, p. 570.

Chapter 89

JESUS' FINAL TEACHING IN THE TEMPLE

He that believeth on me,
believeth . . . on him that sent me.
I am come a light into the world.
I came . . . to save the world.
I have not spoken of myself.
. . . even as the Father said unto me, so I speak.
(John 12:44-50.)

He Laments over Doomed Jerusalem
(Matthew 23:37-39; JST, Matthew 23:36-41; Luke 13:34-35;
JST, Luke 13:34-36)

As the great denunciation of the evil guides of a blinded people ended, the rupture between Jesus and the Jews was complete. Virtue and vice can only be reconciled when vice becomes virtue, and those whom Jesus has just arraigned before Jehovah's bar have neither the desire nor the will to repent. Their hearts of stone will retain their flinty hardness until they are melted in the fires of Gehenna.

As the woes ceased, our Lord's lamentation began. As the rolling thunders of his moral indignation no longer echoed within the walls of Jehovah's House, Jesus was heavy of heart. These blind guides, these scribes and Pharisees whom he has just called serpents and vipers and for whom he has decreed the damnation of hell, have also led thousands of their fellow Israelites in the paths of destruction. The people are following the false teachings and supporting the dark deeds of their rulers even though the Light of Life in all its brilliance now shines in their streets, and in their synagogues, and is even, at this very moment, teaching in the temple courts. Can we imagine the sorrow that filled the Divine Being as he "began to weep over Jerusalem," saying:

O Jerusalem! Jerusalem! Ye who will kill the prophets, and will stone them who are sent unto you; how often would I have gathered your children together, even as a hen gathers her chickens under her wings, and ye would not. Behold, your house is left unto you desolate![1]

But yesterday when he cleansed the temple for the second time, he called it "my house," for such it was, and such it had been through the ages. Their fathers had built it at his behest. His ordinances were performed therein. Now, however, he is withdrawing his divine approval from that splendid and magnificent structure, which is no longer needed in his dealings with men on earth. The House of the Lord, constructed to meet Mosaic needs, is no longer needed in the eternal scheme of things. Jesus is establishing new ordinances—sacramental emblems instead of sacrificial offerings, among others—and the need for the old temple is over. He is now giving it back to men; it is no longer "my house," but "your house."

Nor was the temple to be the only desolate house. Jesus is also turning Jerusalem itself back into the hands of men. From the days of Melchizedek who was king in Salem, and with reference to Israel, from the days of David, who took Jerusalem from the Jebusites, it had been the Lord's own city, the Zion of God, the religious capital of the world. Soon it would be left to evil men and the new Zion would be the congregations of the pure in heart as they assembled to worship the Father in the name of Jesus in all the nations of the earth. It was as though "my city" was now to be "your city."

And so it became as we shall see in our consideration of the Olivet Discourse. (Chapter 90.) And all this came upon them because they rejected him whose temple it was, and him whose city it was. And so Jesus continued:

For I say unto you, that ye shall not see me henceforth, and know that I am he of whom it is written by the prophets, until ye shall say, Blessed is he who cometh in the name of the Lord, in the clouds of heaven, and all the holy angels with him.

Matthew says: "Then understood his disciples that he should come again on the earth, after that he was glorified and crowned on the right hand of God." And Luke, recording what was said in Perea, when our Lord said he must go up to Jerusalem, for—and what biting irony this is—"it cannot be that a prophet perish out of Jerusalem," Luke tells us that Jesus then said:

And verily I say unto you, Ye shall not know me, until ye have received from the hand of the Lord a just recompense for all your sins; until the time come when ye shall say, Blessed is he who cometh in the name of the Lord.

Jesus is withdrawing his face from the Jews until they pay the penalty for their sins and until they learn that he is their Messiah, the one of whom all the prophets have written! And in the providences of the Lord that is a not far distant day.

The Widow's Mite
(Mark 12:41-44; JST, Mark 12:50; Luke 21:1-4)

We pass now from the thunderous woes that consigned the scribes and Pharisees to hell, and from the tears of sorrow that wet the divine cheeks as Jesus withdrew his approval from the temple and the city, and turn rather to a sweet and hallowed scene. Jesus has left the porches and the wrangling, and the contentious mobs of men who are there debating his words and defaming his person. He seats himself "over against the treasury," apparently upon the steps that gave him a view of the Court of the Women. Under the colonnades that surround this court are thirteen trumpet-shaped boxes into which various religious and charitable contributions may be placed. Each of the trumpets bears an inscription that identifies the object of the contributions placed therein.

Jesus' heart is brimful with sorrow as he reflects on the sins of the people and their rejection of him. His tears of a few moments before have dried on his cheeks. The hour of the daily sacrifice is past, and those now in the court are engaged in private devotions, private sacrifices, and the paying of their various offerings. He watches as rich and affluent people, desiring to be seen of men and with that ostentation so common among them, drop great treasures of silver and gold into the receptacles. Among the worshippers is a poor widow, identified by her garb of mourning. She comes quietly, meekly, hoping perhaps that others will not see the smallness of her offering; she drops two mites—the smallest legal amount that can be given—into one of the chests.

Two mites! Together they are less than a farthing. Her total contribution is about half a cent in American money. But it is all she has. She has lived the law of sacrifice to the full. Jesus calls his disciples and says:

> *Verily I say unto you, That this poor widow hath cast more in, than all they which have cast into the treasury: For all the rich did cast in of their abundance; but she, notwithstanding her want, did cast in all that she had; yea, even all her living.*

No word was spoken to the sorrowing widow who in her penury had sacrificed her all, nor did she then so much as know that the Judge of all had weighed her gift in the eternal scales and found it of more worth than the wealth of kings. It is pleasant to suppose, however, that she now knows that her deed, done in secret and with no thought of reward, was not far removed from that of Mary of Bethany, who poured the anointing oil on the feet of the Master. Both acts have been memorialized forever among those whose hearts are centered upon sacred things.

Nor should we miss the message—that on the records kept by the angels of God in heaven, the meager gifts of faithful people far outweigh the ostentatiously bestowed largess of the rich who bestow their bounties to be seen of men; and that those who expend the Lord's money to build up his kingdom and further his interests should do so as though it all came from the mites of sorrowing widows.

Jesus Offers Salvation to the Gentiles
(John 12:20-33)

We are now nearing the end and the climax of Jesus' public ministry. He is yet in the temple on this the third day of the week of his passion. What is about to transpire, and which has been preserved for us by the Beloved John only, is Jesus' crowning demonstration that his saving truths are for all men, Jew and Gentile alike. After his resurrection he will tell his apostolic witnesses to go into all the world and preach the gospel to every creature, Jew and Gentile alike. Now he will foreshadow that glorious change of direction—a change from his previous command that they should go only to the lost sheep of the house of Israel—by himself proclaiming the message of salvation to certain Greeks. True they were proselytes of Judaism, but they were not Abraham's seed, and the blood of the ancient patriarch did not flow in their veins; they were not part of the chosen people in the true and full sense of the word.

These Greeks had come up to Jerusalem to the Passover "to worship at the feast." They were Jews by adoption and had submitted to circumcision so as to be allowed fellowship in the regular worship. As devout men they were now feeling the exhilaration of the first three days of Passover worship and more particularly the impact of Jesus on the festive celebration.

They may well have been caught up in the outpouring of

the Spirit that accompanied the triumphal entry into Jerusalem, amid shouts of Hosanna to the Son of David, on the first day; in any event they would have been fully apprised of that prophetically wondrous day. They must have been present when Jesus cleansed the temple on the second day, and manifestly on this third day they had heard and seen and felt such glorious things as have seldom fallen to the lot of men on earth to experience.

No doubt they were present when our Lord discomfited the chief priests and rulers on the question of authority, and then heard the parables of the two sons, the wicked husbandman, and the king's son. Jesus' discussion with the Pharisees on the tribute money and his pronouncements to the Sadducees about eternal marriage were still ringing in their ears. They had heard the discussion with the lawyer relative to the first and great commandment; had heard him ask the Pharisees, "What think ye of Christ? whose son is he?"; and had heard him heap woes upon the scribes and Pharisees, and seen him weep over doomed Jerusalem.

They were devout men in whose hearts a spirit of faith now welled up. Unlike those Jews who had in their veins the blood of Abraham naturally, these Greeks had not been led far astray by the blind guides of the day. They had come to the Passover as "Proselytes of Righteousness," as the Jews called their converts, but after hearing, and seeing, and feeling the message of Jesus, they had become in their hearts disciples of "the Lord our Righteousness," as Jesus was Messianically called.

But with it all they were timid, hesitant to approach Jesus directly. Perhaps they were overawed by his personal majesty; perhaps their cultural background called for a personal introduction; perhaps they felt that as Jewish non-Jews they might not receive the welcome reserved for Israel proper. The separation of the Jew from the Gentile was well fixed in every mind in that day. In any event they came to Philip and said, "Sir, we would see Jesus." Aware of the reasons for their timidity, and accepting them as proper,

Philip himself hesitated to approach Jesus with the Greek entourage. Instead he went to Andrew; then these two apostles, obviously after consultation together, took the matter to Jesus.

It is evident that these Gentile converts were then taught by our Lord, but only a few fragmentary portions of what was said have been preserved for us by John. We suppose the Greeks acclaimed him as Lord and testified of his Messiahship, perhaps in words that meant he was soon to rule and reign on an earthly throne, as some Jews had affirmed in the past. Our Lord's first recorded words to them were:

> *The hour is come, that the Son of man should be glorified. Verily, verily, I say unto you, Except a corn of wheat fall into the ground and die, it abideth alone: but if it die, it bringeth forth much fruit.*

"The simile is an apt one, and at once impressively simple and beautiful. A farmer who neglects or refuses to cast his wheat into the earth, because he wants to keep it, can have no increase; but if he sow the wheat in good rich soil, each living grain may multiply itself many fold, though of necessity the seed must be sacrificed in the process." (Talmage, pp. 518-19.) To this Jesus then added:

> *He that loveth his life shall lose it; and he that hateth his life in this world shall keep it unto eternal life.*

"The Master's meaning is clear; he that loves his life so well that he will not imperil it, or, if need be, give it up, in the service of God, shall forfeit his opportunity to win the bounteous increase of eternal life; while he who esteems the call of God as so greatly superior to life that his love of life is as hatred in comparison, shall find the life he freely yields or is willing to yield, though for the time being it disappear like the grain buried in the soil; and he shall rejoice in the bounty of eternal development. If such be true of every man's existence, how transcendently so was it of the life of Him who came to die that men may live? Therefore was it necessary that He die, as He had said He was about to do;

but His death, far from being life lost, was to be life glorified." (Talmage, p. 519.)

We suppose also that they said something about their Grecian ancestry and pleaded for the blessings of the gospel for those not of the chosen race. In any event Jesus said:

If any man serve me, let him follow me; and where I am, there shall also my servant be: if any man serve me, him will my Father honour.

Jesus' death was to be for *all men,* Jew and Gentile alike. *Any man*—let him be of whatever nation or kindred or tongue or people, black or white, bond or free, male or female, Jew or Gentile—*any man* may come unto Christ and be saved. There is no aristocracy except the aristocracy of personal righteousness, no nobility except the nobility of worthiness, no salvation except the salvation that comes by obedience to the laws and ordinances of the gospel. All are to be saved on the same terms and conditions, and the salvation involved is exaltation: it is to be where he is; it is to be like him: it is to sit down on his throne, even as he sits on the throne of his Father.

As thoughts of his coming suffering and death pressed in upon Jesus; as the awesome reality and nearness of it all hung heavily upon him; as he seemed to feel in advance some of the agonizing pains of Gethsemane and the cross, he exclaimed:

Now is my soul troubled; and what shall I say? Father, save me from this hour: but for this cause came I unto this hour. Father, glorify thy name.

Thus a God speaks to a God. Overwhelming as the coming agony might be, crushing as the weight of his burden might be, yet this was the very purpose for which he had come to earth; yet he would glorify the Father's name by drinking the dregs of the bitter cup. "Then came there a voice from heaven," the voice of the Father, saying:

I have both glorified it, and will glorify it again.

Twice has the Gentile world, prefiguring that which is to be, come to the Mortal Messiah to testify and worship—once at his birth in Bethlehem and now at his death in Jerusalem. Wise men from the East bowed before his cradle, and Gentiles from Greece now kneel before his cross. And thrice has the Father spoken from heaven to testify and strengthen his Son—once at Bethabara when the Holy Ghost descended bodily in calm serenity like a dove; then on Mount Hermon when Jesus was transfigured before the Three; and now in the temple as the message is given that the gospel is for all men. And on none of these occasions was it clear to the wicked and ungodly what wondrous realities were then being portrayed. This time, perhaps at all times, it was an audible voice that all present heard. This time, as also on the previous occasions, some besides Jesus understood the spoken words; others now said, "It thundered"; and yet others, "An angel spake to him." Then Jesus said:

This voice came not because of me, but for your sakes. Now is the judgment of this world: now shall the prince of this world be cast out. And I, if I be lifted up from the earth, will draw all men unto me.[2]

There is glory and triumph in these words. Jesus is comforted by his Father's voice; the people, having heard the sound from heaven, have a witness from on high of his divine Sonship, and Jesus, speaking of things to come as though they were already accomplished, announces that Satan, "the prince of this world," is doomed. Righteousness will eventually triumph. As to our Lord's being "lifted up," John says: "This he said, signifying what death he should die." After Gethsemane he would suffer the agony of the cross.

"Who Is This Son of Man?"
(John 12:34-50)

Jesus is to be lifted up and slain for all men, not for the Jews only. This message he has given to the Gentile Greeks. We cannot doubt that they understood his words and rejoiced in his goodness. But the captious, caviling critics among his own people chose to ignore this concept of a universal religion, brought by the Savior of all men, and to take issue with him instead on the matter of whether he could be the Savior of any people, let alone all men of all races.

"We have heard out of the law that Christ abideth for ever," the people then said, having reference to their Messianic traditions and the teachings of the Rabbis that Messiah's reign would be followed by the resurrection. How, then, could the Messiah be lifted up and slain as Jesus now said? "How sayest thou, The Son of man must be lifted up? who is this Son of man?" they asked. How can the Son of Man be the Messiah if he is to lose his life?[3]

Jesus will answer their question, with power and authority, in words of doctrine and of testimony. It is the very question he has been answering for nearly three and a half years from one end of Palestine to the other—to the Jews of Judea, the Galileans of Galilee, the Samaritans of Samaria, and the Pereans of Perea, and to the Gentiles in Phoenicia and the mixed races around Decapolis. There has not been, there is not now, and there never shall be any doubt in the minds of spiritually enlightened persons as to who this Son of Man is.

The Father is a Holy Man. "In the language of Adam, Man of Holiness is his name, and the name of his Only Begotten is the Son of Man, even Jesus Christ, a righteous Judge." (Moses 6:57.) Jesus will now make such a proclamation. He will not quibble about their interpretation of their law. What he has heretofore said about their false traditions, their legends and fantasies, their wicked wresting of holy writ—all such is well known to them. Rather he will deliver his last public sermon, and he will make it a fitting testimony of himself and his Father. He begins with these words:

Yet a little while is the light with you. Walk while ye have the light, lest darkness come upon you: for he that walketh in darkness knoweth not whither he goeth. While ye have the light, believe in the light, that ye may be the children of light.

He who is the Light of the World, whose spirit enlight-eneth every man born into the world, who invites all men to believe in him and come unto the Father by him—the Blessed Christ again issues his new and everlasting plea. 'Come, believe in me. I am the Light; believe in the Light. Become my sons and daughters, the children of Light. If ye do not this, darkness will come upon you, and those who walk in darkness trudge an undeviating course to everlasting doom.'

At this point, before the full sermon is preached, John makes some parenthetical comments about the disbelief of the Jews and includes this statement: "These things spake Jesus, and departed, and did hide himself from them." This statement clearly should have been made at the end, not in the middle of the sermon.

As is always the case when the gospel is preached, some believe, many disbelieve, and even among believers there are those who will not make an open confession. Of the Jews generally John says: "Though he had done so many miracles before them, yet they believed not on him."

Let there be no misunderstanding on this point: Some few accepted Jesus as the Messiah, but the generality of the people rejected him with a vengeance. This rejection was not the isolated act of their leaders or of a few rabble rousers. It had the sustaining support of the generality of the people and was the outgrowth of their whole religious system. As evidence that such would be the case, John quotes Isaiah's Messianic word: "Lord, who hath believed our report? and to whom hath the arm of the Lord been revealed?" Further, John says, "they could not believe," because as Isaiah prophesied: "He hath blinded their eyes, and hardened their heart; that they should not see with their eyes, nor under-stand with their heart, and be converted, and I should heal them."

A further sad note, interjected into John's account at this point, says: "Nevertheless among the chief rulers also many believed on him; but because of the Pharisees they did not

417

confess him, lest they should be put out of the synagogue:
For they loved the praise of men more than the praise of
God." Truly it was an onerous burden—religiously, socially,
economically—to be cast out of the synagogue by the judges
of men, but how much greater is it to be cast out eternally
from the society of the saved by the Eternal Judge.

Now we return to the sermon about the Son of Man. In it
Jesus probably said many things that are not preserved for
us. This we do know, however, that the rest of his recorded
words were proclaimed in a loud voice, and we cannot do
other than believe they were the climax of his sayings in this
his last public sermon.

*He that believeth on me, believeth not on me, but on
him that sent me. And he that seeth me seeth him that
sent me.*

"*Who is this Son of Man?*" He is the Son of Man of Holiness. There is a Father and a Son. Those who believe in the
Son must of necessity believe in the Father. It is not possible
to believe a man is a son without believing he has a father,
nor to believe a man is a father unless he has offspring. God
the Eternal Father is a father because he has children. The
Son of God is God because God is his Father. And in this
case, to see one is to see the other, as it were, because they
are in the express image of each other.

*I am come a light into the world, that whosoever
believeth on me should not abide in darkness.*

"*Who is this Son of Man?*" He is the Light of the World,
the perfect pattern for all men, the great Exemplar, the only
one who can say, without any limitation whatever: "What
manner of men ought ye to be? Verily I say unto you, even
as I am." (3 Ne. 27:27.) Those who believe in him leave the
darkness of the world and come into the marvelous light of
Christ.

*And if any man hear my words, and believe not, I
judge him not: for I came not to judge the world, but to
save the world.*

He that rejecteth me, and receiveth not my words,

hath one that judgeth him: the word that I have spoken, the same shall judge him in the last day.

"*Who is this Son of Man?*" He is a preacher of righteousness whose words have saving power. He came to save the world through the gospel. If men do not believe his words, they reject him; and if they reject him, his words will condemn them in the day of judgment when he standeth to judge the world.

For I have not spoken of myself; but the Father which sent me, he gave me a commandment, what I should say, and what I should speak.

"*Who is this Son of Man?*" He is the Son of God, his servant, his agent, his ambassador, his representative. The Father sent him into the world, and he speaks the word of the Father.

And I know that his commandment is life everlasting: whatsoever I speak therefore, even as the Father said unto me, so I speak.

"*Who is this Son of Man?*" He is the Son of God who speaks the word of the Father, and the Father's commandments lead men to eternal life, which is the greatest of all the gifts of God.

Thus Jesus ended his public teaching: ended it with a testimony of his own divine Sonship; ended it with a call to all men to believe in him and live his laws; ended it with the promise that all the obedient shall have eternal life in his Father's kingdom.

With this he left the temple forever.

NOTES

1. Be it noted that these are the words of the Lord Jesus; he is the One who shall gather his children. Implicit in the context is another affirmation of his divine Sonship. A similar lament has come from his lips in modern times: "O, ye nations of the earth," his solemn voice intones, "how often would I have gathered you together as a hen gathereth her chickens under her wings, but ye would not!" (D&C 43:24.)

2. To the Nephites, Jesus gave utterance to this same thought in these words: "My Father sent me that I might be lifted up upon the cross; and after that I had been lifted up upon the cross, that I might draw all men unto me, that as I have been lifted up by men even so should men be lifted up by the Father, to stand before me, to be judged of their works, whether they be good or whether they be evil—And for this cause have I been lifted

up; therefore, according to the power of the Father I will draw all men unto me, that they may be judged according to their works." (3 Ne. 27:14-15.)

3. "Of course the scriptures said Christ and his kingdom should abide forever (Isa. 9:7; Ezek. 37:25; and Dan. 7:14, among many others); and so shall it be commencing in the millennial day when 'the kingdoms of this world are become the kingdoms of our Lord, and of his Christ: and he shall reign for ever and ever.' (Rev. 11:15.)

"But the scriptures also said that King-Messiah 'was wounded for our transgressions, . . . bruised for our iniquities,' 'brought as a lamb to the slaughter,' and *'cut off out of the land of the living.'* They said, *'he made his grave with the wicked, and with the rich in his death'* (Isa. 53); that he, 'the Lord Jehovah' would 'swallow up death in victory,' and bring to pass the resurrection of all men. Indeed, it was the great Jehovah himself who had said to their fathers: 'Thy dead men shall live, *together with my dead body shall they arise.'* (Isa. 25:8; 26:4, 19.)

"There was no occasion for Jesus' captious critics either to have or to feign ignorance of the true mortal ministry of their Messiah." (*Commentary* 1:631.)

Chapter 90

THE OLIVET DISCOURSE: JERUSALEM AND THE TEMPLE

The end is come upon my people of Israel. . . .
And the songs of the temple
shall be howlings in that day,
saith the Lord God:
there shall be many dead bodies
in every place; they shall
cast them forth with silence.
(Amos 8:2-3.)
Messiah [shall] be cut off, . . .
and the people of the prince that shall come
shall destroy the city and the sanctuary;
and . . . he shall cause the sacrifice
and the oblation to cease,
and for the overspreading of abominations
he shall make it desolate,
even until the consummation,
and that determined shall be poured upon the
desolate. (Dan. 9:26-27.)

"*Your House Is Left unto You Desolate*"
(*Matthew 24:1-2; JST, Matthew 24:1-2; Mark 13:1-2; JST, Mark 13:1-6; Luke 21:5-6*)

To mortal eyes it seemed as though all the wealth and glory and grandeur of the world was centered in the Temple of Jehovah, which crowned the Holy City. We know of no other buildings either before or since that have shown forth such splendid architectural perfection and such surpassing beauty. And yet he who had blessed it with his presence now cursed it with his mouth: "Your house is left unto you desolate," he said as tears of sorrow streamed down his cheeks.

And now Jesus was leaving the temple forever. Henceforth the House of God could be a den of thieves; no matter, it had served its purpose, and its end had come. It was a sad moment; tears might well flow again on every cheek. Was all this glory and beauty to be as Sodom and Gomorrah? How could such grandeur turn to dust? Luke tells us that then "some spake of the temple, how it was adorned with goodly stones and gifts." But Jesus said:

> *As for these things which ye behold, the days will come, in the which there shall not be left one stone upon another, that shall not be thrown down.*

We can understand how the feelings of the disciples were engulfed in despair as the divine decree was uttered. "The feelings of the Apostles still clung with the loving pride of their nationality to that sacred and memorable spot. They stopped to cast upon it one last lingering gaze, and one of them was eager to call His attention to its goodly stones and priceless offerings—those nine gates overlaid with gold and silver, and the one of solid Corinthian brass yet more precious; those graceful and towering porches; those polished and bevelled blocks forty cubits long and ten cubits high, testifying to the toil and munificence of so many generations; those double cloisters and stately pillars; that lavish adornment of sculpture and arabesque; those alternate blocks of red and white marble, recalling the crest and hollow of the sea-waves; those vast clusters of golden grapes, each cluster as large as a man, which twined their splendid luxuriance over the golden doors.

"They would have Him gaze with them on the rising terraces of courts—the Court of the Gentiles with its monolithic columns and rich mosaic; above this the flight of fourteen steps which led to the Court of the Women; then the flight of fifteen steps which led up to the Court of the Priests; then, once more, the twelve steps which led to the final platform crowned by the actual Holy, and Holy of Holies, which the Rabbis fondly compared for its shape to a couchant lion, and which, with its marble whiteness and golden roofs, looked like a glorious mountain whose snowy summit was gilded by the sun.

"It is as though they thought that the loveliness and magnificence of this scene would intercede with Him, touching His heart with mute appeal. But the heart of Jesus was sad. To Him the sole beauty of a Temple was the sincerity of its worshippers, and no gold or marble, no brilliant vermilion, or curiously-carven cedar-wood, no delicate sculpturing or votive gems, could change for Him a den of robbers into a House of Prayer. The builders were still busily at work, as they had been for nearly fifty years, but their work, unblessed of God, was destined—like the earthquake-shaken forum of guilty Pompeii—to be destroyed before it was finished." (Farrar, pp. 577-78.)

Thus we find the disciples, as "Jesus went out, and departed from the temple," coming to him and saying: "Master, show us concerning the buildings of the temple; as thou hast said; They shall be thrown down, and left unto you desolate." His answer:

Behold ye these stones of the temple, and all this great work, and buildings of the temple? Verily I say unto you, they shall be thrown down and left unto the Jews desolate.

See ye not all these things, and do ye not understand them? Verily I say unto you, There shall not be left here upon this temple, one stone upon another, that shall not be thrown down.

Literal fulfillment of this dire prophecy came in 70 A.D. when Titus and his legions turned Jerusalem into a ghastly ruin and wrenched each temple stone from its place and foundation as the heathen forces searched out every carat of gold and every gem of worth, and the temple treasures were carried to Rome. What had once adorned the House of God found its way to the synagogue of Satan.

And Jesus, having so spoken, "left them and went upon the mount of Olives."

The Dispensation of Persecution and Martyrdom
(Matthew 24:3-5, 9-13; JST, Matthew 24:3-4, 8, 11;
Mark 13:3-6, 9, 11-13; JST, Mark 13:7-13;
Luke 21:7-8, 12-19; JST, Luke 21:7-8, 11-14, 16; D&C 45:15-21)

Upon that holy mount, east of Jerusalem—from which the Risen Lord shall soon ascend unto his Father, and where at the day of his glorious return he shall again place his feet—there Jesus and the Twelve rested quietly after an arduous day in the wicked city below them. Alone there, apart from the maddening throngs of Passover pilgrims and separated from the cursed leaders of a damned people, Jesus was prepared to teach and the Twelve to receive the mysteries of the kingdom. Thoughts of the doomed temple and of the Lord's return to receive the glad acclaim, "Blessed is he who cometh in the name of the Lord, in the clouds of heaven, and all the holy angels with him," are uppermost in the minds of the spiritual giants there seated. They propose to the Lord two questions:

1. "Tell us, when shall these things be which thou hast said concerning the destruction of the temple, and the Jews?"

2. "And what is the sign of thy coming, and of the end of the world? (or the destruction of the wicked, which is the end of the world.)"

Portions of our Lord's reply are found in Matthew, in

Mark, and in Luke, and a revealed account of other parts was given to the Prophet Joseph Smith. Each account lays emphasis upon one part or another of his reply. As nearly as we can piece his sermon together, the doctrine came forth as we shall now recite in this and the next three chapters.

As ye have asked of me concerning the signs of my coming, in the day when I shall come in my glory in the clouds of heaven, to fulfil the promises that I have made unto your fathers, For as ye have looked upon the long absence of your spirits from your bodies to be a bondage, I will show unto you how the day of redemption shall come, and also the restoration of the scattered Israel.

As is his wont, he will answer their questions by a recital of basic principles, and he will tell them additional things that even they had not been led to ask.

And now ye behold this temple which is in Jerusalem, which ye call the house of God, and your enemies say that this house shall never fall.

But, verily I say unto you, that desolation shall come upon this generation as a thief in the night, and this people shall be destroyed and scattered among all nations. And this temple which ye now see shall be thrown down that there shall not be left one stone upon another.

And it shall come to pass, that this generation of Jews shall not pass away until every desolation which I have told you concerning them shall come to pass.

Such is his introduction, given in general terms and reaffirming what had just fallen from his lips relative to the magnificent buildings comprising the holy temple, which the scribes and leaders boasted should never fall. And yet this very generation of proud and haughty ones shall see and feel and sorrow as desolations come upon them as a thief in the night. As pertaining to these desolations about to be poured out upon their generation, Jesus said:

The time draweth near, and therefore take heed that

ye be not deceived; for many shall come in my name,
saying, I am Christ; go ye not therefore after them.

False prophets always arise to oppose those who are truly
sent of God. False Christs will always be proclaimed when
the truth from heaven is being set forth by true ministers.
False religions will forever arise to fight the Lord's saints.
And because error cannot long stand against truth, evil men
will turn to persecution and begin to wield those satanic
forces of hatred and evil which have ever been hurled at the
faithful.

But take heed to yourselves: for they shall deliver
you up to councils; and in the synagogues ye shall be
beaten: and ye shall be brought before rulers and kings
for my sake, for a testimony against them.

'All the civil and religious power of the world will combine against you. The councils (the Sanhedrins, both local
and general) with their civil power; the synagogues, which
exercise the power of the church; kings and rulers, who
wield the sword and command armies—all these shall combine to fight against God.' Nor is it any different today.
Many governments in many lands, influenced by the religions of men and of devils, proscribe the preaching of true
religion and provide legal penalities for those sent to bear
witness of the truth.

But when they shall lead you, and deliver you up,
take no thought beforehand what ye shall speak,
neither do ye premeditate: but whatsoever shall be
given you in that hour, that speak ye: for it is not ye
that speak, but the Holy Ghost.

Though they are persecuted; though prison walls house
their bodies; though priests deride and rulers mock; though
all the forces of earth and hell combine to close the mouths
of the living witnesses of the Lord Jesus Christ, yet their
voices must and shall be heard; yet the words will be his, for
the Holy Ghost will speak by their mouths.

Now the brother shall betray the brother to death,
and the father the son; and children shall rise up

against their parents, and shall cause them to be put to death.

Then shall they deliver you up to be afflicted, and shall kill you, and ye shall be hated of all nations for my name's sake.

And then shall many be offended, and shall betray one another; and many false prophets shall arise, and shall deceive many;

And because iniquity shall abound, the love of many shall wax cold; but he that shall endure unto the end, the same shall be saved.

With two millennia to separate us from the early Christians, the agony of their sufferings, the burden of their pains, and the horrors of the persecutions heaped upon them seem to fade away. But if ever there was a dispensation of martyrdom it was in the day of Jesus and Peter and Paul. In that day to join the Church was to prepare to die. Lest we forget, let us note a few lines from the history of the past; let us view a small part of the persecutions of the saints in time's meridian.

Rome went up in flames, it is supposed by the hand of a mad tyrant, Nero. He immediately "endeavoured to fix the odious crime of having destroyed the capital of the world upon the most innocent and faithful of his subjects—upon the only subjects who offered heartfelt prayers on his behalf—the Roman Christians. They were the defenceless victims of this horrible charge; for though they were the most harmless, they were also the most hated and the most slandered of living men. . . .

"Nero sought popularity and partly averted the deep rage which was rankling in many hearts against himself, by torturing men and women, on whose agonies he thought that the populace would gaze not only with a stolid indifference, but even with fierce satisfaction. . . .

"It is clear that a shedding of blood—in fact, some form or other of human sacrifice—was imperatively demanded by popular feeling as an expiation of the ruinous crime which

had plunged so many thousands into the depths of misery.
. . . Blood cried for blood, before the sullen suspicion against
Nero could be averted, or the indignation of Heaven ap-
peased. . . .

"No man is more systematically heartless than a corrupted debauchee. Like people, like prince. In the then condition of Rome, Nero well knew that a nation 'cruel, by their
sports to blood inured,' would be most likely to forget their
miseries, and condone their suspicions, by mixing games and
gaiety with spectacles of refined and atrocious cruelty, of
which, for eighteen centuries, the most passing record has
sufficed to make men's blood run cold. . . .

"Tacitus tells us that '. . . *a huge multitude* were convicted, not so much on the charge of incendiarism as for
their hatred to mankind.'" Then he adds: "'And various
forms of mockery were added to enhance their dying
agonies. Covered with the skins of wild beasts, they were
doomed to die by the mangling of dogs, or by being nailed
to crosses; or to be set on fire and burnt after twilight by way
of nightly illumination. Nero offered his own gardens for
this show, and gave a chariot race, mingling with the mob in
the dress of a charioteer, or actually driving about among
them."

The gardens of Nero "were thronged with gay crowds,
among whom the Emperor moved in his frivolous degradation—and on every side were men dying slowly on their
crosses of shame. Along the paths of those gardens on the
autumn nights were ghastly torches, blackening the ground
beneath them with streams of sulphurous pitch, and each of
those living torches was a martyr in his shirt of fire. And in
the amphitheatre hard by, in sight of twenty thousand
spectators, famished dogs were tearing to pieces some of the
best and purest of men and women, hideously disguised in
the skins of bears or wolves. Thus did Nero baptize in the
blood of martyrs the city which was to be for ages the capital
of the world!"[1]

A compassionate providence impels us to draw the curtain over a further recitation of such scenes. It suffices for us to know that the saints in that day—in the dispensation of death, in the era of martyrdom—became followers of the lowly Nazarene, only to have their blood mingled with the blood of all the martyrs of the past, that together that great river of blood might cry unto the Lord of Hosts till he, in his own good time, chose to avenge it.

Jerusalem and the Abomination of Desolation
(*Matthew 24:15-22; JST, Matthew 24:12-21; Mark 13:14-20; JST, Mark 13:14-23; Luke 17:31-33; 21:20-24; JST, Luke 17:31; 21:20*)

Whatever may be said of the sufferings and sorrows and death of the Lord's saints in the age of martyrdom, it was but a type and a shadow of the vengeance and slaughter destined to be poured out upon the Jews of that generation. The synagogues in which apostles were scourged would soon be drenched in the blood of those who wielded the lash. The currents of hatred that swept many of Jesus' disciples to untimely deaths would soon become a great tidal wave of anger and animosity against the Jewish people that would destroy their city, overrun their nation, and scatter their people. Those who with Roman hands crucified their King at Jerusalem would soon themselves be hanging by the thousands upon Roman crosses in that same benighted area. The sensitivities of refined persons will overflow with revulsion as we now hear the dire predictions of Jesus against his own people and then see the beginning of their fulfillment in the very day of those then living.

When ye therefore shall see the abomination of desolation, spoken of by Daniel the prophet concerning the destruction of Jerusalem, then ye shall stand in the holy place.

At this point in Jesus' discourse, Matthew and Luke insert the statement, "Whoso readeth let him understand." We know that Daniel foretold that desolation, born of abomination and wickedness, would sweep Jerusalem as with a flood in the day that the Messiah was cut off from among the living. (Dan. 9:27; 11:31; 12:11.) According to Luke's account, Jesus said: "And when ye shall see Jerusalem compassed with armies, then know that the desolation thereof is nigh." The sorrows and evils of this dread day we shall relate shortly. The counsel that the saints should then "stand in the holy place" means that they should assemble together where they could receive prophetic guidance that would preserve them from the desolations of the day. The place of their assembly became holy because of the righteousness of the holy ones who comprised the Lord's congregation.[2] As Matthew recorded:

Then let them who are in Judea, flee into the mountains. Let him who is on the housetop, flee, and not return to take anything out of his house: Neither let him who is in the field, return back to take his clothes.

Luke's account speaks similarly: "Then let them who are in Judea flee to the mountains; and let them who are in the midst of it, depart out; and let not them who are in the countries, return to enter into the city." "Remember Lot's wife."

And woe unto them that are with child, and unto them that give suck in those days! Therefore, pray ye the Lord, that your flight be not in the winter, neither on the Sabbath day.

In all this, speedy flight is enjoined. 'Flee to the mountains. Let him who is on the housetop take the outside staircase, or go over the roofs of the houses. Let him who is in the field go in his work clothes. Abandon your property. Those who are in country areas must not return into the city. The time for escape will be short. Look not back to Sodom and the wealth and luxury you are leaving. Stay not in the burning house, in the hope of salvaging your treasures, lest the flame destroy you. Pray that your flight will not be impeded by the cold of winter or the shut gates and travel restrictions of the Sabbath. Flee, flee to the mountains.' (And when the day came, the true saints, guided as true saints always are by the spirit of revelation, fled to Pella in Perea and were spared.)

For then, in those days, shall be great tribulation on the Jews, and upon the inhabitants of Jerusalem; such as was not before sent upon Israel, of God, since the beginning of their kingdom, (for it is written their enemies shall scatter them,) until this time; no, nor ever shall be sent again upon Israel.

All things which have befallen them, are only the beginning of the sorrows which shall come upon them; and except those days should be shortened, there should none of their flesh be saved. But for the elect's sake, according to the covenant, those days shall be shortened.

Behold, these things I have spoken unto you concerning the Jews.

To this we must add those words of Jesus which Luke preserved: "For these be the days of vengeance, that all things which are written may be fulfilled. . . . For there shall be great distress in the land, and wrath upon this people. . . . And they shall fall by the edge of the sword, and shall be led away captive into all nations."

Before viewing the desolation that came upon them—lest we think the historical account be overdrawn—we must remind ourselves of the prophetic word that foresaw the awful horrors of that day. Jesus has just said: "For it is written their enemies shall scatter them," and "These be the days of vengeance, that all things which are written may be fulfilled." Though many prophets spoke of these days, none did so with such force and power as Moses, the man of God in whom they trusted. He it was who placed before their forebears the blessings of obedience and the cursings of disobedience.

Israel, the favored and chosen of Jehovah, in the very day of their birth as a nation, heard from the mouth of Moses such an array of curses as no other people has ever faced. In more than fifty consecutive verses of Holy Writ, Jehovah proclaimed the calamities, desolations, diseases, plagues, and evils that would befall his people if they forsook him and his law.

431

And now fourteen hundred years later that remnant of the chosen seed which resided in old Canaan had waged open war against Jehovah as he walked in their streets, taught in their synagogues, and worked wonders in the holy house that bore his name and that they viewed as the glory of the whole earth. And so the ax was laid at the root of the rotted tree; Jerusalem was about to suffer all that the prophets had foretold.

The specific word and the exact portion of the ancient curses about to be fulfilled were these: Thou shalt "serve thine enemies which the Lord shall send against thee, in hunger, and in thirst, and in nakedness, and in want of all things: and he shall put a yoke of iron upon thy neck, until he have destroyed thee.

"The Lord shall bring a nation against thee from far, from the end of the earth, as swift as the eagle flieth; a nation whose tongue thou shalt not understand; A nation of fierce countenance, which shall not regard the person of the old, nor shew favour to the young. . . .

"And he shall besiege thee in all thy gates, until thy high and fenced walls come down, wherein thou trustedst, throughout all thy land. . . .

"*And thou shalt eat the fruit of thine own body, the flesh of thy sons and of thy daughters,* which the Lord thy God hath given thee, in the siege, and in the straitness, wherewith thine enemies shall distress thee. . . .

"The tender and delicate woman among you, which would not adventure to set the sole of her foot upon the ground for delicateness and tenderness, her eye shall be evil toward the husband of her bosom, and toward her son, and toward her daughter, And toward her young one that cometh out from between her feet, and toward her children which she shall bear: for *she shall eat them for want of all things* secretly in the siege and straitness, wherewith thine enemy shall distress thee in thy gates. . . .

"And the Lord shall scatter thee among all people, from the one end of the earth even unto the other; . . . And among these nations shalt thou find no ease, neither shall the sole of thy foot have rest: but the Lord shall give thee there a trembling heart, and failing eyes, and sorrow of mind: And thy life shall hang in doubt before thee; and thou shalt fear day and night, and shalt have none assurance of life: In the morning thou shalt say, Would God it were even! and at even thou shalt say, Would God it were morning!" (Deut. 28:15-68.)

Thus saith Jehovah; such is the prophetic word, and his word shall not return unto him void. Summarizing the details given by Josephus of the siege of Jerusalem, our friend Farrar, with his usual literary craftsmanship, says: "Never was a narrative more full of horrors, frenzies, unspeakable degradations, and overwhelming miseries than is the history of the siege of Jerusalem. Never was any prophecy more closely, more terribly, more overwhelmingly fulfilled than this of Christ.

"The men going about in the disguise of women with swords concealed under their gay robes; the rival outrages and infamies of John and Simon; the priests struck by darts from the upper court of the Temple, and falling slain by their own sacrifices; 'the blood of all sorts of dead carcases—priests, strangers, profane—standing in lakes in the holy courts'; the corpses themselves lying in piles and mounds on the very altar slopes; the fires feeding luxuriously on cedar-work overlaid with gold; friend and foe trampled to death on the gleaming mosaics in promiscuous carnage; priests, swollen with hunger, leaping madly into the devouring flames, till at last those flames had done their work, and what had been the Temple of Jerusalem, the beautiful and holy House of God, was a heap of ghastly ruin, where the burning embers were half-slaked in pools of gore.

"And did not all the righteous blood shed upon the earth since the days of Abel come upon that generation? Did not many of that generation survive to witness and feel the unutterable horrors which Josephus tells?—to see their fellows crucified in jest, 'some one way, and some another,' till

433

'room was wanting for the crosses, and crosses for the carcases?'—to experience the 'deep silence' and the kind of deadly night which seized upon the city in the intervals of rage?—to see 600,000 dead bodies carried out of the gates?—to see friends fighting madly for grass and nettles, and the refuse of the drains?—to see the bloody zealots 'gaping for want, and stumbling and staggering along like mad dogs?'—to hear the horrid tale of the miserable mother who, in the pangs of famine, had devoured her own child?—to be sold for slaves in such multitudes that at last none would buy them?—to see the streets running with blood, and the 'fire of burning houses quenched in the blood of their defenders?'—to have their young sons sold in hundreds, or exposed in the amphitheatres to the sword of the gladiator or the fury of the lion, until at last, 'since the people were now slain, the Holy House burnt down, and the city in flames, there was nothing farther left for the enemy to do?'

"In that awful siege it is believed that there perished 1,100,000 men, besides the 97,000 who were carried captive, and most of whom perished subsequently in the arena or the mine; and it was an awful thing to feel, as some of the survivors and eyewitnesses—and they not Christians—*did* feel, that 'the city had deserved its overthrow by producing a generation of men who were the causes of its misfortunes;' and that 'neither did any other city ever suffer such miseries, nor *did any age ever breed a generation more fruitful in wickedness than this was, since the beginning of the world.'* " (Farrar, pp. 573-74.)[3]

Thus saith the Lord: "Vengeance is mine; I will repay." (Rom. 12:19.)

NOTES

1. F. W. Farrar, *The Early Days of Christianity* (London, 1882), 1:58-69.

2. Similarly the saints of latter days are to stand in holy places and be not moved when the scourges and desolations preceding the Second Coming sweep over the earth. (D&C 45:31-32.)

3. As an introduction to the quoted passage, Farrar says: "Speaking of the murder of

the younger Hanan, and other eminent nobles and hierarchs, Josephus says, 'I cannot but think that *it was because God had doomed this city to destruction as a polluted city, and was resolved to purge His sanctuary by fire,* that He cut off these their great defenders and well-wishers; while those that a little before had worn the sacred garments and presided over the public worship, and had been esteemed venerable by those that dwelt in the whole habitable earth, were cast out naked, and seen to be the food of dogs and wild beasts.' " (Farrar, *The Life of Christ,* pp. 572-73.)

Chapter 91

THE OLIVET DISCOURSE: THE LAST DAYS

He shall send Jesus Christ,
which before was preached unto you:
Whom the heaven must receive
until the times of restitution of all things,
which God hath spoken by the mouth
of all his holy prophets
since the world began.
(Acts 3:20-21.)

Universal Apostasy Before the Second Coming
(Matthew 24:23-27; JST, Matthew 24:22-24, 27; Mark 13:21-23;
JST, Mark 13:24-26, 28-29; Luke 17:22-25;
JST, Luke 17:22-24)

How sad and dire it is to hear the babble of discordant voices saying, "Lo, here is Christ, and lo, there," each voice supposing that his philosophy of religion is the one that will save men in the everlasting realms ahead!

How far from the truth it is for men to suppose that what Jesus taught would remain in its pure and perfect form, with all its saving power, so that men in the latter days would, through it, have the same blessings as their forebears!

Has no one read the promises made of old that the Lord Jesus cannot return "except there come a falling away first"

(2 Thes. 2:1-12); that before that day, "darkness shall cover the earth, and gross darkness the people" (Isa. 60:2; D&C 112:23-24); that the whole earth "is defiled under the inhabitants thereof; because they have transgressed the laws, changed the ordinance, broken the everlasting covenant" (Isa. 24:5)?

Does anyone really suppose that the sects of modern Christendom—with their silks and robes and rituals; with their notions of a salvation without works and by grace alone; with neither signs, nor miracles, nor apostles, nor prophets, nor revelation—does anyone really believe such a Christianity is the same as that of Jesus and Peter and Paul?

Truly, before the Lord returns, the divine decree is: Lucifer shall have his day; Satan shall reign in the hearts of men; the man of sin—who is the master of sin and the father of lies—shall hold dominion over all the earth. The Lord, according to the promises, will make the earth empty; his saving truths shall be taken away, and universal apostasy shall prevail.

Thus, Jesus—having spoken to the disciples of what shall be in their generation; having told of the destruction of Jerusalem and the scattering of the Jews; having warned those then living of what impends in their day—Jesus now raises his warning voice to us relative to what is to be in the latter days.

And again, after the tribulation of those days which shall come upon Jerusalem, if any man shall say unto you, Lo! here is Christ, or there; believe him not; For in those days, there shall also arise false Christs, and false prophets, and shall show great signs and wonders; insomuch that, if possible, they shall deceive the very elect, who are the elect according to the covenant.

In the day preceding our Lord's return, false religions will cover the earth. Each will be, as it were, a false Christ, inviting men to this or that system of salvation; each will have its own ministers and evangelists who, as false prophets, will propound its doctrines and extol its wonders.[1]

So great and wondrous will be these false systems that men will think, How could a church be false that builds such cathedrals as these? How could a church be false that crowns kings and emperors; that sends forth armies into battle; that commands the services of artists and sculptors; that has, as it seems, all the gold and power of earth? With such "signs" and "wonders" as these, will not all but the very elect be deceived?

> *Behold, I speak these things unto you, for the elect's sake. Behold, I have told you before. Wherefore if they shall say unto you, Behold, he is in the desert; go not forth: behold, he is in the secret chambers; believe it not.*

> *For as the light of the morning cometh out of the east, and shineth even unto the west, and covereth the whole earth; so shall also the coming of the Son of Man be.*

Let the elect know of the great apostasy of latter days; let them shun false teachers who would reveal Christ, as they suppose, in a life of asceticism in the deserts, or in the seclusion of secret monastic chambers; let them know that when the restored truths of everlasting life come again among men, they shall be as the rising sun which gradually sheds its wholesome rays over all the earth. Let them know that the Son of Man will not come to reign personally on earth until this light, in millennial brilliance, shall have cast out all the darkness of long ages of apostasy.

An Era of Restoration Before the Second Coming
(Matthew 24:14, 28; JST, Matthew 24:28, 32; Mark 13:10; JST, Mark 13:30-31, 36)

As set forth in our scriptural text that heads this chapter, Christ cannot come again—he must be retained in heaven—until the great era of restoration, "until the times of restitution" in which the Lord will restore all things which he hath spoken "by the mouth of all his holy prophets since the world began." Jesus now names two of these things—things that must be given again before his Second Advent. They are: the fulness of the everlasting gospel and the gathering together again of the house of Israel.

And now I show unto you a parable. Behold, wheresoever the carcass is, there will the eagles be gathered together; so likewise shall mine elect be gathered from the four quarters of the earth. . . .

And again, this gospel of the kingdom shall be preached in all the world, for a witness unto all nations, and then shall the end come, or the destruction of the wicked.

Nothing so touched the hearts of Jewish-Israel as the many prophetic assurances that the dispersed and scattered remnants of that once favored nation would someday come together to worship the Lord their God as in former days. Nothing instilled in them a greater hope of ultimate glory and triumph than the divine word that some day the kingdom would be restored to Israel and that the Gentiles would then bow beneath their rod. It is this very hope in the hearts of the Twelve that will cause them a little more than forty days hence, on this very Mount, to ask the then-risen Lord, ere he ascends to his Father, when it is that such a restoration shall take place. They will then be reminded of its deferral to a later day. But here Jesus tells them that the gathering of Israel will commence before he comes again. It is one of the signs of the times.

And in this connection the very gospel he has given them, the same saving truths, the same plan of salvation that they have received, will, in that future day, come forth to be preached in all the world for a witness unto all nations. Until this has been done the Lord Jesus will not return.

How aptly do these words of the Lord Jesus lay a foundation for those yet to be written by the Beloved John, who will tell of the angelic ministrant flying through the midst of heaven to restore, in a day subsequent to New Testament times, the fulness of the everlasting gospel. (Rev. 14:6-7.)[2]

Sad it is that there will be universal apostasy for a long

period before the great and dreadful day of the Lord. But, praise be to him, there shall also be a day of restoration when the ancient blessed truths shall come again, and when Israel shall be gathered to the ancient standard, a standard that shall again be set up on earth.

Desolations Precede the Second Coming
(Matthew 24:6-8; JST, Matthew 24:25, 29-31; Mark 13:7-8; JST, Mark 13:27, 32-35; Luke 21:9-11; JST, Luke 21:9)

In the latter-day age of restoration, when once again the glorious wonders of the gospel are available to men, and when Israel is gathering again round the ancient standard, the powers of evil will be unleashed as never before in all history. Satan will then fight the truth and stir up the hearts of men to do evil and work wickedness to an extent and with an intensity never before known.

And ye also shall hear of wars, and rumors of wars; see that ye be not troubled; for all I have told you must come to pass. But the end is not yet.

And they shall hear of wars, and rumors of wars. Behold I speak unto you for mine elect's sake. For nation shall rise against nation, and kingdom against kingdom; there shall be famine and pestilences, and earthquakes in divers places.

And again, because iniquity shall abound, the love of men shall wax cold; but he that shall not be overcome, the same shall be saved.

There will be wars and rumors of wars in the day of the Twelve to whom Jesus then spoke, but they are not to be troubled thereby; many things must yet transpire before the day of Jesus' return, and the end of all things is not for their day.

But when those of us who live in the day of restoration hear of wars; when voices of contention and conspiracy among us threaten to use the sword in this eventuality or that; when we hear reports and rumors about the use of atomic bombs, poisonous gases, and other weapons of unbelievable power and cruelty; when these things happen in our day, it is quite another thing. Such things are among the signs of the times, and the wars and desolations of our day will make the hostilities of the past seem like feeble skirmishes among childish combatants.

Ours is the dispensation of desolation and war that will be climaxed by a worldwide Armageddon of butchery and blood at the very hour of the coming of the Son of Man. Jesus speaks thus for the elect's sake; none others can read the signs of the times. Carnal men will consider war as a way of life and a norm of society, not as a scourge sent of God to cleanse the earth preparatory to the return of his Son.

Nor is war all we face; as the crusades of carnage increase, so will the plagues and pestilence. Famine and disease will stalk the earth. And for some reason, as yet undiscovered by modern geologists, earthquakes will increase in number and intensity. These are the last days, and the judgments of God are at hand.

All this shall be because iniquity abounds. Sin is the father of all the ills poured out upon mankind.

Gentile Fulness Ends Before the Second Coming
(Luke 21:24-28; JST, Luke 21:23-28; D&C 45:22-35)

As we have seen, Jerusalem, the Holy City, was to become a ghastly ruin; the pleasant home of the prophets was to be turned into a field of blood; its strong walls and magnificent Temple were to be as ashes and dust. And as we know, all that was promised came speedily to pass. Then, on the ancient site, there arose a Gentile Jerusalem, which remains unto this day. Of it Jesus now says:

And Jerusalem shall be trodden down of the Gentiles, until the times of the Gentiles be fulfilled.

He is here classifying all men as Jews or Gentiles. There are no others. Jews are the Israelites, no matter what their tribal ancestry (Paul, for instance, was of Benjamin), who in the meridian of time comprised the Israelite inhabitants of Palestine plus their kindred who had spread forth from them into Egypt and Greece and Rome and other nations where they dwelt as distinct groups. All other people are Gentiles, including Israelites who were not Jewish nationals as herein defined. In this sense Joseph Smith, a pure Ephraimite, was a Gentile, and the Book of Mormon came forth as promised by way of the Gentile. In this sense those of us of Ephraim and Manasseh and other tribes who are already gathered with latter-day Israel are Gentiles. The Gentiles are the non-Jews within the meaning of words as here used.

The times of the Gentiles is the period during which the gospel will be preached to the Gentiles in preference to the Jews, and the times of the Jews is the similar period when the Jewish nationals, so to speak, will again receive the message of salvation that is in Christ. We are living in the times of the Gentiles, but that era is drawing to its close, and the gospel will soon go to the Jews.

In the generation in which the times of the Gentiles shall be fulfilled, there shall be signs in the sun, and in the moon, and in the stars; and upon the earth distress of nations with perplexity, like the sea and the waves roaring. The earth also shall be troubled, and the waters of the great deep; Men's hearts failing them for fear, and for looking after those things which are coming on the earth: for the powers of heaven shall be shaken.

We see here, again, the perplexities and problems of nations and kingdoms, as wars and evil abound; we see men, subject to disease and pestilence, as their hearts fail them; and we see the geological changes out of which come earthquakes, tidal waves, and changes in the sea. In this respect, from the more amplified account of what Jesus said, we learn:

Ye say that ye know that the end of the world cometh; ye say also that ye know that the heavens and the earth shall pass away; And in this ye say truly, for so it is; but these things which I have told you shall not pass away until all shall be fulfilled.

Though there will be a new heaven and a new earth whereon dwelleth righteousness, such a millennial condition will not come into being until all the things of which Jesus is now speaking have been fulfilled.

And this I have told you concerning Jerusalem; and when that day shall come, shall a remnant be scattered among all nations; But they shall be gathered again; but they shall remain until the times of the Gentiles be fulfilled.

The scattered remnants of the ancient Jews are even now in all nations, where, in the main, they will remain until they accept their Messiah and believe in the true gospel. That stirrings within them are preparing the way for this day of conversion is seen from the religious-political movement that already has assembled some—still in their unbelief—back to the land of their ancestors. The identifying characteristics of the day when the Jews will begin to believe and come again into the true fold are described in these words:

And in that day shall be heard of wars and rumors of wars, and the whole earth shall be in commotion, and men's hearts shall fail them, and they shall say that Christ delayeth his coming until the end of the earth. And the love of men shall wax cold, and iniquity shall abound.

This is the description of the world in which we now live. Of this there can be no doubt. The signs of the times are being fulfilled, and the elect can discern their true meaning by the power of the Spirit.

And when these things begin to come to pass, then look up and lift up your heads, for the day of your redemption draweth nigh.

Such are our Lord's words as Luke has preserved them. The revealed account given in our day says:

And when the times of the Gentiles is come in, a light shall break forth among them that sit in darkness, and it shall be the fulness of my gospel; But they receive it not; for they perceive not the light, and they turn their

443

hearts from me because of the precepts of men. And in that generation shall the times of the Gentiles be fulfilled.

The time is at hand; the light has broken forth; it is the fulness of the everlasting gospel. So far the Jews have not received it, with isolated exceptions, because of the precepts of men. But soon the times of the Gentiles will be fulfilled, and the day of the Jews will commence.

And there shall be men standing in that generation, that shall not pass until they shall see an overflowing scourge; for a desolating sickness shall cover the land.

But my disciples shall stand in holy places, and shall not be moved; but among the wicked, men shall lift up their voices and curse God and die.

And there shall be earthquakes also in divers places, and many desolations; yet men will harden their hearts against me, and they will take up the sword, one against another, and they will kill one another.

That the disciples of old should have been sorely troubled by these words is almost self-evident. Hence Jesus said:

Be not troubled, for, when all these things shall come to pass, ye may know that the promises which have been made unto you shall be fulfilled.

That as modern disciples we should feel as our Lord counseled his ancient disciples is also self-evident. As the glorious conclusion of it all, Jesus said:

And then shall they see the Son of man coming in a cloud, with power and great glory.

NOTES

1. A perfect illustration of this religious turmoil is found in the religious revival that swept the frontier areas of America in the day of Joseph Smith. "It commenced with the Methodists," he said, "but soon became general among all the sects in that region of country. Indeed, the whole district of country seemed affected by it, and great multitudes united themselves to the different religious parties, which created no small stir and division amongst the people, some crying, 'Lo, here!' and others, 'Lo, there!' Some were contending for the Methodist faith, some for the Presbyterian, and some for the Baptist." (Joseph Smith—History 1:5.)

2. How glorious is the voice we hear, announcing the fulfillment of that which

John wrote. "I have sent forth mine angel flying through the midst of heaven," the voice says. "having the everlasting gospel. who hath appeared unto some and hath committed it unto man. who shall appear unto many that dwell on the earth. And this gospel shall be preached unto every nation. and kindred. and tongue. and people. And the servants of God shall go forth. saying with a loud voice: Fear God and give glory to him. for the hour of his judgment is come: And worship him that made heaven. and earth. and the sea. and the fountains of waters." (D&C 133:36-39.)

Chapter 92

THE OLIVET DISCOURSE: THE SECOND COMING

Prepare ye for the coming
of the Bridegroom;
go ye, go ye out to meet him.
(D&C 133:19-20.)
Behold, the day of the Lord cometh. . . .
And his feet shall stand in that day
upon the mount of Olives,
which is before Jerusalem on the east.
(Zech. 14:1, 4.)

The Abomination of Desolation at the Second Coming
(Matthew 24:29; 34-35; JST, Matthew 24:33-36; Mark 13:24-25, 30-31; JST, Mark 13:37-40; Luke 21:32-33; JST, Luke 23:32)

Titus crucified Jerusalem on a cross of Roman steel; desolation and death swept down the streets where apostles and prophets once taught; the spiritual capital of the world became the synagogue of Satan; the Holy City sank to the depths of Sodom and Egypt; and Jehovah's House was torn to bits—to rise no more. The Jewish Jerusalem made way for a Gentile Jerusalem that would continue until the day when the abomination of desolation would again pour its fury upon the place and the people.

In "the generation when the times of the Gentiles be fulfilled," this awesome scene will be reenacted. Jerusalem, this time besieged by the armies of the earth, shall be direly desolated. But this time there will be a different destiny. The Lord himself will come to fight her battles; a remnant of the people will be saved; and the Gentile Jerusalem will become again a Jewish Jerusalem. Sodomic influences will be consumed with devouring fire, and the New Jerusalem will become, in all her glory and magnificence, the spiritual capital of the world. Jehovah himself will come to the new temple, there to be constructed after the order of his new kingdom, and the saints shall worship in those sacred halls for a thousand years. And so, as Jesus continues the Olivet Discourse, we hear him say:

> *And again shall the abomination of desolation, spoken of by Daniel the prophet, be fulfilled. And immediately after the tribulation of those days, the sun shall be darkened, and the moon shall not give her light, and the stars shall fall from heaven, and the powers of heaven shall be shaken.*
>
> *Verily I say unto you, this generation, in which these things shall be shown forth, shall not pass away until all I have told you shall be fulfilled. Although the days will come that heaven and earth shall pass away, yet my word shall not pass away; but all shall be fulfilled.*

"I will gather all nations against Jerusalem to battle," the Lord says of this coming day, "and the city shall be taken, and the houses rifled, and the women ravished; and half of the city shall go forth into captivity, and the residue of the people shall not be cut off from the city." This is the dread day of Armageddon, the day when Satan shall be arrayed against freedom and light, the day when the armies of men shall number two hundred million men of arms. "Then shall the Lord go forth," the prophetic record says, "and fight against those nations, as when he fought in the day of battle. And his feet shall stand in that day upon the mount of Olives, which is before Jerusalem on the east. . . . And the

Lord my God shall come, and all the saints with thee. . . . And the Lord shall be king over all the earth: in that day shall there be one Lord, and his name one." (Zech. 14:2-5, 9.)

Be it noted that the Lord—who is the lowly Nazarene, and who is also a man of war—will come in his glory when war and desolation are sweeping the earth; when all nations are engaged in mortal combat; when the powers of earth are arrayed, ready for the burning destruction he will bring.

And be it also noted that it is "immediately after the tribulation of those days" that the heavenly manifestations incident to the Second Coming will shower their display before men, and that all this shall surely come to pass in the generation when the times of the Gentiles is fulfilled.

The Glories Attending Our Lord's Return
(Matthew 24:30-31; JST, Matthew 24:37-40; Mark 13:26-27; JST, Mark 13:41-44; D&C 45:39-55)

And as I said before, after the tribulation of those days, and the powers of the heavens shall be shaken, then shall appear the sign of the Son of Man in heaven; and then shall all the tribes of the earth mourn.

After the abomination of desolation sweeps Jerusalem in the last days; after the city is taken, its houses rifled, its women ravished, and half its inhabitants taken into captivity; after the sun and the moon refuse to give light and the stars fall from heaven—then will appear one grand sign of the Son of Man in heaven. At this time, the Lord in his wisdom has not seen fit to reveal the nature of this sign, though from what follows it is clear that the elect will recognize it as the heavenly portent given to announce the coming of their King.[1]

When the sign appears, there will be such mourning throughout the earth as has not before been known. As to the mourning in Israel, the prophetic word acclaims: "They shall mourn for him, as one mourneth for his only son, and shall be in bitterness for him, as one that is in bitterness for

448

his firstborn. In that day shall there be a great mourning in Jerusalem, . . . And the land shall mourn, every family apart." (Zech. 12:10-12.)

And they shall see the Son of Man coming in the clouds of heaven, with power and great glory;

And whoso treasureth up my word shall not be deceived.

For the Son of Man shall come; and he shall send his angels before him with the great sound of a trumpet, and they shall gather together the remainder of his elect from the four winds, from one end of heaven to the other.

Lo, he cometh; none can stay his hand, and all who remain on earth shall see him and know who he is. Once as the Suffering Servant he sat with his weary disciples on the Mount of Olives; now as Lord and Master that same mountain will cleave at his touch, and he shall be King over all the earth. And whereas the gathering of his people has heretofore been directed by fallible mortals, now the angels will direct the work, and none who deserve to be saved with chosen Israel shall be overlooked.

In the revealed account of the Olivet Discourse, the Lord gives us more of the words spoken on that sacred spot than have been preserved by the three Synoptists. From this latter-day record we take these additions and amplifications of the biblical accounts:

1. *Signs and Wonders Shall Precede the Second Coming.*

And it shall come to pass that he that feareth me shall be looking forth for the great day of the Lord to come, even for the signs of the coming of the Son of Man.

And they shall see signs and wonders, for they shall be shown forth in the heavens above, and in the earth beneath. And they shall behold blood, and fire, and vapors of smoke. And before the day of the Lord shall come, the sun shall be darkened, and the moon be turned into blood, and the stars fall from heaven.

Signs follow those who believe; signs are for people who have faith; signs reveal the handdealings of the Lord to those who treasure up his word. From the standpoint of the disciples, sitting with Jesus on Olivet, surely railroads and airplanes, radio and television, and satellites orbiting the earth would be signs and wonders on earth and in heaven. Vapors of smoke spray forth when atomic bombs are exploded; blood and fire are descriptive of modern warfare; and the sun, moon, and stars will yet speak forth their messages. When "the earth shall tremble and reel to and fro as a drunken man" (D&C 88:87) and "shall remove out of her place" (Isa. 13:10-13); when "the islands shall become one land" (D&C 133:23) and the whole face of the earth be changed, as a new heaven and a new earth is born, it will seem as though the very stars in the sidereal heavens are hurling themselves out of their places. These are signs that have been, signs that are, and signs that will yet herald the coming of the Promised One.

2. *The Jews Shall Gather at Jerusalem Before the Second Coming.*

And the remnant shall be gathered unto this place; And then they shall look for me, and, behold, I will come; and they shall see me in the clouds of heaven, clothed with power and great glory; with all the holy angels; and he that watches not for me shall be cut off.

These Jews, gathered at Jerusalem—pursuant to the command: "Let them who be of Judah flee unto Jerusalem, unto the mountains of the Lord's house" (D&C 133:13)—shall be members of The Church of Jesus Christ of Latter-day Saints. They will be Christians; they will believe in Christ; they will accept him as their Messiah; and they will be looking forward to his return. As Ezekiel prophesied, the Lord will make with them "a covenant of peace," they will receive his "everlasting covenant," and he will set his "sanctuary in the midst of them for evermore." (Ezek. 37:26-28.)[2]

3. *The Saints Shall Be Resurrected When the Lord Comes.*

All the faithful—their bodies in the grave, their spirits in paradise—shall come forth in glorious immortality; they shall rise in celestial splendor; they shall meet their gracious Lord and then return with him as part of his triumphal entourage. And the mortal saints, though they be scattered to the four quarters of the earth, shall be caught up to meet him and shall return to live and reign with him a thousand years. (D&C 88:95-98.)

But before the arm of the Lord shall fall, an angel shall sound his trump, and the saints that have slept shall come forth to meet me in the cloud.

Wherefore, if ye have slept in peace blessed are you; for as you now behold me and know that I am, even so shall ye come unto me and your souls shall live, and your redemption shall be perfected; and the saints shall come forth from the four quarters of the earth.

4. *Calamity and Mourning Shall Attend the Second Coming.*

Then shall the arm of the Lord fall upon the nations.

And then shall the Lord set his foot upon this mount, and it shall cleave in twain, and the earth shall tremble, and reel to and fro, and the heavens also shall shake.

And the Lord shall utter his voice, and all the ends of the earth shall hear it; and the nations of the earth shall mourn, and they that have laughed shall see their folly.

And calamity shall cover the mocker, and the scorner shall be consumed; and they that have watched for iniquity shall be hewn down and cast into the fire.

This is the day of vengeance which was in the heart of the Lord. It is the day when mourning and sorrow shall be universal; it is the day when all the nations of the earth shall weep because of the calamities that have befallen them; it is the day when rivers of blood shed in battle shall leave every family in deep anguish.

What of those who laughed at the upright and the godly, at those who would not stoop to live after the manner of the world? They shall see their folly, a folly that leaves them bound with the hellish chains of sin.

What of those who mocked the saints and derided the humble followers of Christ? The judgments of God will rest upon them; the calamities of nature will fall as hail and lightning from heaven.

What of the scorners, wise in their own worldly conceits, who belittle true believers for their creeds and doctrine? They shall be consumed by the glory of His presence.

And what of those who watched for iniquity? Would God they had watched and waited instead for the Lord, for they shall be hewn down, cast into the fire, and consigned to a burning endless hell.

5. *The Jewish Remnant Shall View Jesus' Wounds When He Returns.*

And then shall the Jews look upon me and say: What are these wounds in thine hands and in thy feet? Then shall they know that I am the Lord; for I will say unto them: These wounds are the wounds with which I was wounded in the house of my friends. I am he who was lifted up. I am Jesus that was crucified. I am the Son of God.

And then shall they weep because of their iniquities; then shall they lament because they persecuted their king.

The nail marks in his hands and in his feet, the gaping spear wound in his side—these are the signs of the cross; the signs of his crucifixion; the signs that he is the One who was lifted up that he might draw all men unto him on conditions of repentance. He manifests them in his resurrected flesh as and when occasion requires.

"And one shall say unto him," Zechariah prophesied, "What are these wounds in thine hands? Then shall he answer, Those with which I was wounded in the house of my friends." (Zech. 13:6.) Hearing the answer, the Jews will lament and mourn for their own iniquities—and on behalf of their fathers—because they persecuted and slew their King. Then shall the great conversion of the Jews take place; then shall be fulfilled that which the Lord spake by the mouth of Zechariah: "I will pour upon the house of David, and upon the inhabitants of Jerusalem, the spirit of grace and of supplications: and they shall look upon me whom they have pierced." (Zech. 12:10.)

6. *The Heathen Shall Be Redeemed and Satan Bound at the Second Coming.*

And then shall the heathen nations be redeemed, and they that knew no law shall have part in the first resurrection; and it shall be tolerable for them. And Satan shall be bound, that he shall have no place in the hearts of the children of men.

A gracious Lord offers to all men all that they are capable of receiving. Even the heathen who are without the law shall come forth in the afternoon of the first resurrection and be blessed with a terrestrial inheritance that shall be tolerable for them. And, finally, O glorious millennial reality, Satan shall be bound for a thousand years by "the righteousness" of men, and he shall have "no power over the hearts of the people, for they dwell in righteousness, and the Holy One of Israel reigneth." (1 Ne. 22:26.)

When Will the Son of Man Come?
(*Matthew 24:32-33, 36-39; JST, Matthew 24:41-45; Mark 13:28-29, 32; JST, Mark 13:45-49; Luke 17:26-30; 21:29-31; D&C 45:34-38*)

"What is the sign of thy coming, and of the end of the world, or the destruction of the wicked, which is the end of the world?" Such was the question propounded by the Twelve as they sat with their Lord on the pleasant slopes of the Mount of Olives. He has answered by naming the signs that will take place in the "generation" of his return. He will not particularize beyond this; indeed, he is about to decline to name the day and the hour. But first he will give the para-

453

ble of the fig tree. The disciples are troubled, as well they might be, at the desolations and sorrows that will yet befall men; at the bloodshed and wickedness that shall reign until the end comes; and over the many souls who shall be lost because men harden their hearts against the Holy One. Jesus says:

> *Be not troubled, for, when all these things shall come to pass, ye may know that the promises which have been made unto you shall be fulfilled.*

> *And when the light shall begin to break forth, it shall be with them like unto a parable which I will show you—*

> *Ye look and behold the fig-trees, and ye see them with your eyes, and ye say when they begin to shoot forth, and their leaves are yet tender, that summer is now nigh at hand; Even so it shall be in that day when they shall see all these things, then shall they know that the hour is nigh.*

As Matthew records it, Jesus said: "Mine elect, when they shall see all these things, they shall know that he is near, even at the doors."

Thus: "Jesus both reveals and keeps hidden the time of his coming. The parable is perfect for his purposes. It announces that he will most assuredly return in the 'season' when the promised signs are shown. But it refrains from specifying the day or the hour when the figs will be harvested, thus leaving men in a state of expectant hope, ever keeping themselves ready for the coming harvest. . . .

"This parable pertains to the latter days. The restoration of the gospel, with the light that thereby breaks forth in darkness, is the beginning of the shooting forth of the leaves of the fig tree." (*Commentary* 1:664.)

> *But of that day and hour no one knoweth; no, not the angels of God in heaven, but my Father only.*

> *But as it was in the days of Noah, so it shall be also at the coming of the Son of Man. For it shall be with*

*them as it was in the days which were before the flood;
for until the day that Noah entered into the ark, they
were eating and drinking, marrying and giving in marriage, and knew not until the flood came and took them
all away; so shall also the coming of the Son of Man
be.*

*Likewise also as it was in the days of Lot; they did
eat, they drank, they bought, they sold, they planted,
they builded; But the same day that Lot went out of
Sodom it rained fire and brimstone from heaven, and
destroyed them all. Even thus shall it be in the day
when the Son of man is revealed.*

The flood of Noah and the destruction of Sodom and
Gomorrah are types of the Second Coming. In Noah's day
the normal affairs of life continued until the flood came to
destroy the world that then was; in Lot's day, all went on, as
was common among men, until the Lord rained fire and
brimstone from heaven upon those wicked cities and
destroyed their world. So shall it be with the destruction of
the wicked, which is the end of the world. Such shall come
without warning, as a thief in the night, where the wicked
and ungodly are concerned. But with the elect of God, it is
quite another matter. Though even they do not know the
day or the hour, yet the season and the generation are clearly
revealed. It shall be the season and the generation in which
the signs of the times are manifest.

"Who May Abide the Day of His Coming?"
(*Matthew 24:40-41; JST, Matthew 24:46-48; JST, Mark 13:50-51;
Luke 17:34-37; JST, Luke 17:34-40*)

When the Lord comes—

*Then shall be fulfilled that which is written, That in
the last days, two shall be in the field, one shall be
taken and the other left. Two shall be grinding at the
mill: the one taken, and the other left.*

We have no present source for the scripture here quoted by Jesus relative to the last days. Malachi, however, in a Messianic passage of superlative power, says of the Second Coming: "The Lord, whom ye seek, shall suddenly come to his temple, . . . But who may abide the day of his coming? and who shall stand when he appeareth? for he is like a refiner's fire, and like fullers' soap. . . . For, behold, the day cometh, that shall burn as an oven; and all the proud, yea, and all that do wickedly, shall be stubble: and the day that cometh shall burn them up, saith the Lord of hosts, that it shall leave them neither root nor branch." In addition to "the proud, yea, and all that do wickedly," this passage also names sorcerers, adulterers, false swearers, those who oppress the hireling, the widow, and the fatherless in their wages, those who lead men away from the truth, and members of the true Church who do not pay an honest tithing—all these are named as among those who will not abide the day. (Mal. 3, 4.) Paul speaks of "them that know not God, and that obey not the gospel," as among those "who shall be punished with everlasting destruction from the presence of the Lord" at his Second Coming. (2 Thes. 1:7-9.) And our revelation proclaims that when he comes, "Every corruptible thing, both of man, or of the beasts of the field, or of the fowls of the heavens, or of the fish of the sea, that dwells upon all the face of the earth, shall be consumed." (D&C 101:24.)

Thus, when the Lord Jesus returns, he will destroy the wicked by the breath of his lips, the ungodly shall be burned as stubble, and the vineyard shall be cleansed of corruption. Though two, seemingly alike, work or walk or sleep or live together, one shall be destroyed by the brightness of his coming and the other preserved to enjoy the fruits of the millennial earth.

In an earlier day, in Galilee, after proclaiming this same doctrine, Jesus was asked: "Where, Lord, shall they be taken?" His answer:

Wheresoever the body is gathered; or, in other words, whithersoever the saints are gathered, thither will the eagles be gathered together.

Luke, our recorder of this prior teaching, writing by way of prophecy and revelation, then said: "This he spake, signifying the gathering of his saints; and of angels descending and gathering the remainder unto them; the one from the bed, the other from the grinding, and the other from the field, whithersoever he listeth. For verily there shall be new heavens, and a new earth, wherein dwelleth righteousness." Truly the angels shall complete the gathering of the elect. And as to those who are consumed and who abide not the day, Luke continues: "And there shall be no unclean thing; for the earth becoming old, even as a garment, having waxed in corruption, wherefore it vanisheth away, and the footstool remaineth sanctified, cleansed from all sin." Such is the new heaven and the new earth which shall come into being at the end of the world, which is the destruction of the wicked.

Watch, Pray, Take Heed, Be Ready!
(Matthew 24:42-51; JST, Matthew 24:49-50, 56; Mark 13:33-37; JST, Mark 13:52-61; Luke 12:35-48; 21:34-36; JST, Luke 12:38-57; 21:34, 36)

Prophetic preachments have a purpose; doctrines are not taught simply to entertain, or even to edify without more. Jesus has now taught the doctrine of the Second Coming of the Son of Man so that his disciples—and all future followers into whose hands the teachings come—may use them to prepare their own souls for salvation.

If there is to be a universal apostasy before the Lord returns, the elect must know this, lest they espouse false religions and lose their souls. If the gospel is to be restored and Israel gathered, let the chosen seed find the new gospel and learn where they should gather, lest they fail to gain the promised blessings. If the Gentile fulness is at hand and Jewish Israel is soon to be favored again, let this be known to

457

the Jews, lest they remain in darkness and be rejected with their fathers. If there are to be wars and calamities, desolations and signs, let the elect view these things in their eternal perspective, lest they remain as other men and reap the curses that shall be poured out without measure. If at our Lord's return the wicked will be as stubble and every corruptible thing shall be consumed by the brightness of his coming, how important it is to know how to escape the flames!

Thus, Jesus calls upon his disciples and all men to watch, pray, take heed, and be ready!

And what I say unto one, I say unto all men; Watch, therefore, for ye know not at what hour your Lord doth come. But know this, if the good man of the house had known in what watch the thief would come, he would have watched, and would not have suffered his house to have been broken up; but would have been ready.

Therefore be ye also ready: for in such an hour as ye think not, the Son of Man cometh.

The illustration is perfect; the application can never be forgotten. He will come as a thief in the night, unexpectedly and without warning, where the wicked and ungodly are concerned. And even as pertaining to his saints, it shall be at such an hour—though the generation is known!—which they think not.

Who then is a faithful and wise servant, whom his Lord hath made ruler over his household, to give them meat in due season? Blessed is that servant, whom his lord when he cometh shall find so doing. Verily I say unto you, That he shall make him ruler over all his goods.

But and if that evil servant shall say in his heart, My lord delayeth his coming; And shall begin to smite his fellowservants, and to eat and drink with the drunken; The lord of that servant shall come in a day when he looketh not for him, and in an hour that he is not aware

of, And shall cut him asunder, and appoint him his por-
tion with the hypocrites: there shall be weeping and
gnashing of teeth.

So the Lord purposes with reference to his own! His holy
apostles, all his disciples, the army of servants who hold his
holy priesthood—let them care for his earthly church. Their
reward? Rulership over all his house everlastingly. But those
servants who are overcome by the world, though they retain
their church title and power, shall be as the stubble of the
world. The blessed hour of his return overtaking them unawares, they shall be cast out to be damned with their ilk.

Both Mark and Luke, in recording the Olivet Discourse,
preserve for us some expressive verities not contained in the
Matthew version and not revealed anew in Doctrine and
Covenants, section 45. Mark tells us that Jesus said:

Take ye heed, watch and pray: for ye know not when
the time is. For the Son of man is as a man taking a far
journey, who left his house, and gave authority to his
servants, and to every man his work, and commanded
the porter to watch.

Watch ye therefore: for ye know not when the master
of the house cometh, at even, or at midnight, or at the
cockcrowing, or in the morning: Lest coming suddenly
he find you sleeping.

And what I say unto you I say unto all, Watch.

That is: Jesus leaves his church and journeys to his
Father; he gives his disciples authority to regulate his earthly
kingdom in his absence. They know not the time of his
return, whether in the darkness of the night or the dawning
of the day. They and all men must watch and be ready, lest
when he comes he find them indifferent to their Lord's business. Similar counsel, couched in different words, has been
preserved for us by Luke:

Let my disciples therefore take heed to themselves,
lest at any time their hearts be overcharged with surfeit-
ing, and drunkenness, and cares of this life, and that

day come upon them unawares. For as a snare shall it come on all them that dwell on the face of the whole earth.

And what I say unto one, I say unto all, Watch ye therefore, and pray always, and keep my commandments, that ye may be counted worthy to escape all these things which shall come to pass, and to stand before the Son of Man when he shall come clothed in the glory of his Father.

Three sins, common everywhere and among all peoples; three sins, which are scarcely deemed by men to be transgressions of the divine will; three sins, which are part of the common walk of almost all men—such are here named by Jesus; and the disciples are counseled to avoid them. They are:

1. *The sin of surfeiting*—the intemperate indulgence in food and drink, symbolical of setting one's heart and interests on carnal rather than spiritual things.

2. *The sin of drunkenness*—literally, the dulling of one's mental and spiritual faculties by alcohol; figuratively, the dulling of one's spiritual senses by imbibing the false doctrines and views of the world.

3. *The sin of being overcome by the cares of this life*—temporal pursuits, business dealings, civic and political positions, educational attainments, everything that detracts from putting first in one's life the things of God's kingdom.

These sins are a snare that entraps the whole earth. Only those who avoid them and who keep the commandments will be prepared to stand before the Son of Man when he comes again in glory.

Between four and six months before, at an unnamed place in Judea, perhaps in Jerusalem, Jesus taught some similar things that it is opportune for us to consider here:

Let your loins be girded about and have your lights burning; That ye yourselves may be like unto men who wait for their Lord, when he will return from the wed-

*ding; that, when he cometh and knocketh, they may
open unto him immediately.*

*Verily I say unto you, Blessed are those servants,
whom the Lord when he cometh shall find watching;
for he shall gird himself, and make them sit down to
meat, and will come forth and serve them.*

This is a sweet and lovely illustration, one that warns the
Twelve (and all disciples) to be ready for the Second Coming, which will come suddenly. The Lord leaves his servants
to care for his church while he ascends into heaven. Their
loins are girded for labor, for there is work to be done; there
are souls to be saved. Their lamps are lighted, for they must
enlighten a dark and sinful world; their words must shine
forth in celestial splendor, and their deeds must be beacons
of brightness to be seen by all men. The Lord's return from
the marriage feast is either his Second Advent or, as we shall
see, the judgment of each individual soul at death.

What blessed joy shall fill the hearts of those who watch
for his return! They will be in his presence and eat at his
table, where he himself will serve them. Having so taught,
Jesus then shows how the blessings of the Second Coming
will attend all faithful watchers, even though they do not live
at the day and the hour of his glorious return.

*For, behold, he cometh in the first watch of the night,
and he shall also come in the second watch, and again
he shall come in the third watch.*

*And verily I say unto you, He hath already come, as
it is written of him; and again when he shall come in
the second watch, or come in the third watch, blessed
are those servants when he cometh, that he shall find so
doing; For the Lord of those servants shall gird himself,
and make them to sit down to meat, and will come forth
and serve them.*

*And now, verily I say these things unto you, that ye
may know this, that the coming of the Lord is as a thief
in the night. And it is like unto a man who is an*

*householder, who, if he watcheth not his goods, the
thief cometh in an hour of which he is not aware, and
taketh his goods, and divideth them among his fellows.*

All men shall not be alive at the day of his coming, but
whenever they live, it will be as though the great and dreadful day of the Lord had come in their day. If his servants
have served faithfully in his earthly house—the Church and
kingdom of God on earth—his coming (to them) will be the
year of his redeemed. If they have eaten and drunken with
the wicked; if their lives have been overcharged with surfeiting and the cares of this life; if they have been proud and
evil and prone to wickedness—his coming (to them) will be
the day of vengeance which was in his heart.

And not only that—he hath come already! For those
then living, the Second Coming, as it were, was passed. The
Lord was there—at least their day of judgment had come—
and those who watched for righteousness were saved while
those who watched for iniquity were ready for the fire. He
was about to gird himself, wash the feet of the Twelve, and
serve them as they partook of the Passover meal. To them he
had already come as thief in the night. If they had watched,
their goods would not now be ready for the flames, for "the
fire shall try every man's work of what sort it is." (1 Cor.
3:12-15.)

Hearing and understanding all these things, the disciples
"said among themselves, If the good man of the house had
known what hour the thief would come, he would have
watched, and not have suffered his house to be broken
through and the loss of his goods." To this Jesus said:

*Verily I say unto you, be ye therefore ready also; for
the Son of Man cometh at an hour when ye think not.*

Peter, even then acting as a spokesman for the group,
asked: "Lord, speakest thou this parable unto us, or unto
all?" To this Jesus said: "I speak unto those whom the Lord
shall make rulers over his household, to give his children
their portion of meat in due season." The word is addressed
to the servants of the Lord! They are accountable for the

welfare of their brethren. Anxious to know their own state in this respect, they asked, "Who then is that faithful and wise servant?" Jesus replied:

It is that servant who watcheth, to impart his portion of meat in due season. Blessed be that servant whom his Lord shall find, when he cometh, so doing. Of a truth I say unto you, that he will make him ruler over all that he hath.

But the evil servant is he who is not found watching. And if that servant is not found watching, he will say in his heart, My Lord delayeth his coming; and shall begin to beat the menservants, and the maidens, and to eat, and drink, and to be drunken.

The Lord of that servant will come in a day he looketh not for, and at an hour when he is not aware, and will cut him down, and will appoint him his portion with the unbelievers.

And that servant who knew his Lord's will, and prepared not for his Lord's coming, neither did according to his will, shall be beaten with many stripes.

But he that knew not his Lord's will, and did commit things worthy of stripes, shall be beaten with few. For unto whomsoever much is given, of him shall much be required; and to whom the Lord has committed much, of him will men ask the more.[3]

NOTES

1. "But what will the world do," the Prophet Joseph Smith asked, when they see the sign of the Coming of the Son of Man? "They will say it is a planet, a comet,etc. But the Son of man will come as the sign of the coming of the Son of Man, which will be as the light of the morning cometh out of the east." (*Teachings,* p. 287.)

2. Joseph Smith said: "Judah must return, Jerusalem must be rebuilt, and the temple. . . .It will take some time to rebuild the walls of the city and the temple, etc.; and all this must be done before the Son of Man will make His appearance." (*Teachings,* p. 286.)

3. "For of him unto whom much is given much is required; and he who sins against the greater light shall receive the greater condemnation." (D&C 82:3.)

Chapter 93

THE OLIVET DISCOURSE: PARABLES AND THE JUDGMENT

In prison I saw him next, condemned
To meet a traitor's doom at morn;
The tide of lying tongues I stemmed,
And honored him 'mid shame and scorn.
My friendship's utmost zeal to try,
He asked if I for him would die;
The flesh was weak; my blood ran chill;
But the free spirit cried, "I will!"

Then in a moment to my view
The stranger started from disguise;
The tokens in his hands I knew;
The Savior stood before mine eyes.
He spake, and my poor name he named,
"Of me thou hast not been ashamed;
These deeds shall thy memorial be,
Fear not, thou didst them unto me."

(*Hymns,* no. 153.)

Parable of the Ten Virgins
(*Matthew 25:1-13; JST, Matthew 25:1, 8, 11*)

If the disciples of old, seated with Jesus on the gentle slopes of Olivet, desired to know when he would return, in all the glory of his Father's kingdom, how much more ought we who live in the generation when the promised signs, one by one, are making their appearance, how much more ought we to desire to know when the glorious day will be.

If those who, in that day, were destined to die for the name of Jesus and the testimony that was theirs, sought to read the signs of the times, how much more ought we, in this day, who are privileged to live to honor his name and testify of his goodness, how much more ought we to see and read the signs heralding his coming.

If the saints of former days who knew his coming would not be in their generation, were yet counseled to watch, pray, take heed, and be ready, how much more ought the saints of latter days, who know his coming will be in their generation (for the signs have now been given!), how much more ought they to make themselves ready.

"To impress yet more indelibly upon their minds the lessons of watchfulness and faithfulness, and to warn them yet more emphatically against the peril of the ungirdled loin and the smouldering lamp,[1] He told them the exquisite Parables—so beautiful, so simple, yet so rich in instruction—of the Ten Virgins and of the Talents; and drew for them a picture of that Great Day of Judgment on which the King should separate all nations from one another as the shepherd divideth his sheep from the goats." (Farrar, p. 584.)

All these things shall find fulfillment in this, the dispensation of the fulness of times, for the other signs have now been given and the time is at hand. He standeth at the door! In this setting, then, let us consider each of these events. First we must view this precious parable about the Bridegroom, the wedding feast, the virgins who attended the bride, and the lamps that lighted their way and gave a festive spirit to the marriage celebration.

And then, at that day, before the Son of Man comes, the kingdom of heaven shall be likened unto ten virgins, who took their lamps, and went forth to meet the bridegroom.

The Bridegroom, as he has before designated himself, is the Lord Jesus, returning from a far country, to attend the marriage feast when he will take the Church as his bride.[2] The ten virgins are the members of the Church; they are in the house of the Lord (which is the Church) awaiting his return and the great feast of good things of which the faithful will then partake. "The 'lamps'—not 'torches'—which the Ten Virgins carried, were of well-known construction. They bear in Talmudic writings commonly the name *Lappid,* but the Aramaised form of the Greek word in the New Testament also occurs as *Lampad* and *Lampadas.* The lamps consisted of a round receptacle for pitch or oil for the wick. This was placed in a hollow cup or deep saucer—the *Beth Shiqqua*—which was fastened by a pointed end into a long wooden pole, on which it was borne aloft. According to Jewish authorities, it was the custom in the East to carry in a bridal procession about ten such lamps. We have the less reason to doubt that such was also the case in Palestine, since, according to rubric, ten was the number required to be present at any office or ceremony, such as at the benedictions accompanying the marriage-ceremonies. And, in the peculiar circumstances supposed in the Parable, Ten Virgins are represented as going forth to meet the Bridegroom, each bearing her lamp." (Edersheim 2:455.)

And five of them were wise, and five were foolish. They that were foolish took their lamps, and took no oil with them: But the wise took oil in their vessels with their lamps.[3]

"And at that day, when I shall come in my glory," the Lord tells us in latter-day revelation, "shall the parable be fulfilled which I spake concerning the ten virgins. For they that are wise and have received the truth, and have taken the Holy Spirit for their guide, and have not been deceived— verily I say unto you, they shall not be hewn down and cast into the fire, but shall abide the day." As to their reward, the Great Judge continues: "And the earth shall be given unto them for an inheritance; and they shall multiply and wax strong, and their children shall grow up without sin unto salvation. For the Lord shall be in their midst, and his glory shall be upon them, and he will be their king and their lawgiver." (D&C 45:56-59.)

While the bridegroom tarried, they all slumbered and slept. And at midnight there was a cry made, Behold, the bridegroom cometh; go ye out to meet him.

The call is to the Church, to those who have forsaken the world, to those who are under covenant to wait for their Lord and to prepare themselves for his return. And now, almost two thousand years after he gave the parable, the call has gone forth. "O my people," saith the Lord, "sanctify yourselves; gather ye together, O ye people of my church. . . . Go ye out from Babylon. Be ye clean that bear the vessels of the Lord. Call your solemn assemblies, and speak often one to another. And let every man call upon the name of the Lord." Be ready; prepare yourselves; cleanse your souls; take the Holy Spirit as a guide; seek the Lord; keep his commandments. "Yea, let the cry go forth among all people: Awake and arise and go forth to meet the Bridegroom; behold and lo, the Bridegroom cometh; go ye out to meet him. Prepare yourselves for the great day of the Lord. Watch, therefore, for ye know neither the day nor the hour." (D&C 133:4-11.)

These are the last days—church members sleep; they are not watching on the towers of Zion; it is so long since the ascension; so many have waited in vain for his return; surely he will not come in our day. And then, at midnight, while the world sleeps—a most unlikely hour for a bridegroom to come and claim his bride—behold he cometh and his reward is with him.

Then all those virgins arose, and trimmed their lamps. And the foolish said unto the wise, Give us of your oil; for our lamps are gone out. But the wise answered, saying, Lest there be not enough for us and you, go ye rather to them that sell, and buy for yourselves.

> *And while they went to buy, the bridegroom came; and they that were ready went in with him to the marriage: and the door was shut.*
>
> *Afterward came also the other virgins, saying, Lord, Lord, open to us. But he answered and said, Verily I say unto you, ye know me not.*
>
> *Watch therefore, for ye know neither the day nor the hour wherein the Son of man cometh.*

Salvation is a personal matter. It comes only to those who keep the commandments and whose souls are filled with the Holy Spirit of God. No man can keep the commandments for and on behalf of another; no one can gain the sanctifying power of the Holy Spirit in his life and give or sell that holy oil to another. Every man must light his own lamp with the oil of righteousness which he buys at the market of obedience. Few doctrines are more evil and wicked than the false doctrine of supererogation, which is, that the saints, by doing more than is necessary for their own salvation, build up an immense treasure of merit in heaven, which can be dispensed and assigned to others so they too can be saved.

All that one person can do for the salvation of another is to preach, teach, expound, and exhort; all that one man can do for his fellows is to teach them the truth and guide their feet into paths of virtue and rectitude. All that the five wise virgins can do for the foolish is to tell them how to gain oil for themselves.

And the foolish virgins who do not come to know the Bridegroom by the power of the Spirit will not qualify to sit down with him at the marriage feast and there partake of the blessings reserved for the wise.

Parable of the Talents
(Matthew 25:14-30; JST, Matthew 25:13-14, 24-31)

There is an eternal principle that states: *Service is essential to salvation.* In the parable of the ten virgins, Jesus dramatized the truth that to gain salvation men must keep the commandments and be guided by the Holy Spirit. Thus, *Obedience is essential to salvation.* By now giving the parable of the talents, he completes the picture. Not only must mortals keep the commandments to gain an inheritance in the Father's kingdom, but they must also get outside themselves in service to their fellowmen. It is one thing to be virtuous and pay tithing; it is another to persuade others to walk in paths of purity and to make their means available for the building up of the Lord's earthly kingdom. The Lord will not be satisfied with the salvation of Moses alone; he expects that great lawgiver to guide all Israel to the summit of Sinai. Both obedience and service are essential to salvation.[4] And so Jesus says:

Now I will liken these things unto a parable. For it is like as a man travelling into a far country, who called his own servants, and delivered unto them his goods.

And unto one he gave five talents, to another two, and to another one; to every man according to his several ability; and straightway took his journey.

Jesus is speaking to the Twelve, who, in this as in all things, are made a pattern and a type of all disciples. In principle, thus, he is speaking to all of his servants and to all the members of his kingdom; and, for that matter, the same principle can be applied to all men in their varied walks, for all have talents and all will be accountable before the judgment bar for the use to which their talents are put. But the specific intent of the parable is to teach how the servants of the Lord must use their native endowments to further the work of Him who is now going on a long journey to a far-off heaven, there to be with his Father until that day when he shall return to live and reign on earth a thousand years.

Members of the Church in general and those called to ministerial service in particular are endowed with "spiritual gifts." All do not receive the same gift, and all are not endowed with the same talents. "There are diversities of gifts," Paul says, all of which come from "the same Spirit."

To one is given the gift of prophecy, to another the working of miracles, to yet another the gift of knowledge, or of wisdom, or of scriptural understanding, or any of the thousands of things that edify and uplift the souls of men. (1 Cor. 12.)

Further, all men, and the servants of the Lord in particular, acquired, in preexistence, by obedience to law, the specific talents and capacities with which they are endowed in this life. Men are not born equal; they come into mortality endowed with the abilities earned and developed in a long period of premortal schooling. And a just and equitable Being, who deals fairly and impartially with all his children, expects each of them to use the talents and abilities with which they are endowed and the gifts that are given them by a divine Providence.

Then he that had received the five talents went and traded with the same, and made them other five talents. And likewise he that had received two, he also gained other two. But he that had received one went and digged in the earth, and hid his lord's money.

Those who "embark in the service of God" are commanded to serve him with all their "heart, might, mind and strength." (D&C 4:2.) It is the will of Him who created us that "men should be anxiously engaged in a good cause, and do many things of their own free will, and bring to pass much righteousness." (D&C 58:27.) All those who are sent forth to preach the gospel are subject to the divine decree: "Thou shalt not idle away thy time, neither shalt thou bury thy talent that it may not be known." (D&C 60:13.) "Be not weary in well-doing," is the counsel to all, for "the Lord requireth the heart and a willing mind." (D&C 64:33-34.) The Lord expects his servants to be diligent; to be occupied till he comes; to labor on his errand with all the strength and power they possess.

After a long time the lord of those servants cometh, and reckoneth with them. And so he that had received five talents came and brought other five talents, saying,

Lord, thou deliveredst unto me five talents: behold, I have gained beside them five talents more.

His lord said unto him, Well done, thou good and faithful servant: thou hast been faithful over a few things, I will make thee ruler over many things: enter thou into the joy of thy lord.

The reward for faithful service is twofold:

1. *To be made ruler over many things.* This life is the probationary estate in which the Lord's servants learn how to rule their own houses—"For if a man know not how to rule his own house, how shall he take care of the church of God?" Paul asks (1 Tim. 3:5)—and how to rule some small part of the Lord's earthly kingdom. Men are called to rule a deacons quorum, an auxiliary organization, a Sunday School class, a ward or a stake, or whatever, all to gain experience for future eternal administration. Those who operate on true principles and succeed in this life will have power and ability to rule greater and larger kingdoms hereafter.

2. *To enter into the joy of the Lord.* Eternal life itself is to dwell in the presence of God, to receive, inherit, and possess as he does. The fulness of the joy of the Lord is to be like him, to be one with him, to have glory and exaltation forever as he does.

He also that had received two talents came and said, Lord, thou deliveredst unto me two talents: behold, I have gained two other talents beside them.

His lord said unto him, Well done, good and faithful servant; thou hast been faithful over a few things, I will make thee ruler over many things: enter thou into the joy of thy lord.

Again the reward is the same—to be ruler over many things and to enter into the joy of the Lord. No matter that one man serve with apostolic fervor in administering the worldwide kingdom of Him whose witness he is, while the other labor in a bishopric where the boundaries are scarcely a stone's throw in length—both gain the same reward. Truly, of those who reign in celestial splendor, it is written: "And he makes them equal in power, and in might, and in dominion." (D&C 76:95.) And also: "And the saints shall be filled with his glory, and receive their inheritance and be made equal with him." (D&C 88:107.)

Then he who had received the one talent came, and said, Lord, I knew thee that thou art a hard man, reaping where thou hast not sown, and gathering where thou hast not scattered. And I was afraid, and went and hid thy talent in the earth; and lo, here is thy talent; take it from me as thou hast from thine other servants, for it is thine.

This is idleness and indifference and more. It is also disobedience and dereliction; it is even defiance of him who is Master and Lord. The Lord's servants are under covenant, made in the waters of baptism, to love and serve him all their days. They have agreed to mourn with those that mourn, to weep with those that weep, and to bear the burdens of their brethren. Having put their hands to the plough, they must not look back lest they certify thereby that they are not fit for the kingdom of God. Hence:

His lord answered and said unto him, O wicked and slothful servant, thou knewest that I reap where I sowed not, and gather where I have not scattered. Having known this, therefore, thou oughtest to have put my money to the exchangers, and at my coming I should have received mine own with usury.

When the Lord's servants neglect and fail to do their Master's work, they are wicked!

I will take, therefore, the talent from you, and give it unto him who hath ten talents. For unto every one who hath obtained other talents, shall be given, and he shall have in abundance.

But from him that hath not obtained other talents, shall be taken away even that which he hath received.

And his lord shall say unto his servants, Cast ye the unprofitable servant into outer darkness; there shall be weeping and gnashing of teeth.

472

As arms that are never used wither; as legs that never walk shrivel; as eyes that are never opened become dull and blind—so the gifts of God that are unexercised soon fall away. As those who never walk lose the power of mobility, so those who bury their talents soon become as though they were never endowed with goodly gifts and glorious graces. The lot of the one is to be lame forever, of the other to die as pertaining to goodness and righteousness.

Christ Shall Sit in Judgment at His Coming
(*Matthew 25:31-46; JST, Matthew 25:33-34*)

As a crown of pure gold, signaling kingship and victory, so are these concluding words of the Olivet Discourse. Seldom—nay, never—has such a sweet and tender presentation been made relative to the coming of the Son of Man. Nothing shows more clearly the basis on which the disciples will then be judged.

Jesus has told the Twelve the things that will precede his coming; he has testified of the desolations and sorrows that will attend his return; his apostolic friends now know that the wicked will be as stubble and the vineyard will be cleansed by the brightness of his Presence.[5] Now he speaks of sitting with them in judgment on his saints, saints who in that day will be scattered—a few here and a small congregation there—in all the nations of the earth.

When the Son of man shall come in his glory, and all the holy angels with him, then shall he sit upon the throne of his glory: And before him shall be gathered all nations: and he shall separate them one from another, as a shepherd divideth his sheep from the goats: And he shall set the sheep on his right hand, but the goats on his left.

And he shall sit upon his throne, and the twelve apostles with him.

This is the day of judgment for the saints of the Most High. For them the judgment is set and the books are opened. Their eternal destiny is to be determined on the basis of their earthly works. This is the great day of division in the Church, the sheep being divided from the goats, the one group going to the right hand of honor, the other to the left hand of disgrace. It is the story of the ten virgins all over again—five wise, five foolish—half of whom entered the house and sat at the marriage feast and half of whom were locked out because they never knew the Bridegroom.

What feelings of wonderment and exultation must have filled the breasts of these humble Galileans—who served as his witnesses—to learn that they too would sit on thrones with their Lord and play a part in this glorious day of judgment.[6]

> *Then shall the King say unto them on his right hand, Come, ye blessed of my Father, inherit the kingdom prepared for you from the foundation of the world: For I was an hungred, and ye gave me meat: I was thirsty, and ye gave me drink: I was a stranger, and ye took me in: Naked, and ye clothed me: I was sick, and ye visited me: I was in prison, and ye came unto me.*

"From the foundation of the world," from the beginning, from all eternity—for such a length of time that no man can measure it—for just such a time has "the kingdom" been prepared for the faithful. And their inheritance therein is dependent upon their charitable works in mortality, upon how they give of themselves to serve their Lord and King.

> *Then shall the righteous answer him, saying, Lord, when saw we thee an hungred, and fed thee? or thirsty, and gave thee drink? When saw we thee a stranger, and took thee in? or naked, and clothed thee? Or when saw we thee sick, or in prison, and came unto thee?*
>
> *And the King shall answer and say unto them, Verily I say unto you, Inasmuch as ye have done it unto one of the least of these my brethren, ye have done it unto me.*

Such is the law of life. All men cannot feed and clothe and heal the Son of God; his mortal life was but for a moment in an appointed day; and his personal contacts were limited to the thousands who dwelt in the lands of his dwelling. But the billions of earth's inhabitants, everywhere and in all ages, are also the children of the Father of us all. And "when ye are in the service of your fellow beings ye are only in the service of your God." (Mosiah 2:17.) Or, as it is similarly expressed: "He that loveth not his brother whom he hath seen, how can he love God whom he hath not seen?" (1 Jn. 4:20.) Or, as he said it in our day, "He that receiveth my servants receiveth me." (D&C 84:36.)

Then shall he say also unto them on the left hand, Depart from me, ye cursed, into everlasting fire, prepared for the devil and his angels: For I was an hungred, and ye gave me no meat: I was thirsty, and ye gave me no drink: I was a stranger, and ye took me not in: naked, and ye clothed me not: sick, and in prison, and ye visited me not.

Then shall they also answer him, saying, Lord, when saw we thee an hungred, or athirst, or a stranger, or naked, or sick, or in prison, and did not minister unto thee?

Then shall he answer them, saying, Verily I say unto you, Inasmuch as ye did it not to one of the least of these, ye did it not to me.

And these shall go away into everlasting punishment: but the righteous into life eternal.

And thus, on this high note, ended the Olivet Discourse, as far as the written word attests; other things Jesus may have said on this memorable day—Tuesday, April 4, A.D. 30, the third day of the week of the atoning sacrifice—were for the ears of the disciples only. And so we leave them, for the moment, as the dusk of day spreads over the holy mount and as the setting sun of his life drops low in the western sky. The crucifixion is only three days away.

NOTES

1. Farrar gives as a translation of the phrase "our lamps *are gone out,*" as found in Matt. 25:8, "are smouldering," or, "are *being* quenched," which he, quite aptly, interprets

475

to mean that the light of God's Holy Spirit is dying away in the "earthen vessels" of their lives. (Farrar, p. 584, footnote 1.)

2. Of the millennial day, ushered in by the Second Coming, when there shall be "a new heaven and a new earth," the Beloved John says: "I . . . saw the holy city, new Jerusalem, coming down from God out of heaven, prepared as a bride adorned for her husband." (Rev. 21:1-2.) Thereafter an angelic ministrant said to him, "Come hither, I will shew thee the bride, the Lamb's wife." What he saw was "that great city, the holy Jerusalem, descending out of heaven from God." (Rev. 21:9-10.) Both the New Jerusalem, which will be set up on earth during the Millennium, and the Holy Jerusalem, which shall abide on this sphere when it becomes a celestial orb, are inhabited by the saints, the faithful members of the Lord's Church and kingdom. Hence the well-known expression in the text that the Church is the Lamb's bride.

3. "Not good and bad, not righteous and wicked, but *wise* and *foolish*. That is, all of them have accepted the invitation to meet the Bridegroom; all are members of the Church; the contrast is not between the wicked and the worthy. Instead, five are zealous and devoted, while five are inactive and lukewarm; ten have the testimony of Jesus, but only five are valiant therein. Hence, five shall enter into the house where Jesus is and five shall remain without—all of which raises the question: What portion of the Church shall be saved? Surely this parable is not intended to divide half the saints into one group and half into another. But it does teach, pointedly and plainly, that there are foolish saints who shall fail to gain the promised rewards." (*Commentary* 1:685.)

4. "The Parable of the Talents—their use and misuse—follows closely on the admonition to watch, in view of the sudden and certain Return of Christ, and the reward or punishment which will then be meted out. Only that, whereas in the Parable of the Ten Virgins the reference was to the *personal state,* in that of 'the Talents' it is to the *personal work* of the Disciples. In the former instance, they are portrayed as the bridal maidens who are to welcome His Return; in the latter, as the servants who are to give an account of their stewardship." (Edersheim 2:459.)

5. Of these same events, the Lord has told us in latter-day revelation: "For the hour is nigh and the day soon at hand when the earth is ripe; and all the proud and they that do wickedly shall be as stubble; and I will burn them up, saith the Lord of Hosts, that wickedness shall not be upon the earth; For the hour is nigh, and that which was spoken by mine apostles must be fulfilled; for as they spoke so shall it come to pass; For I will reveal myself from heaven with power and great glory, with all the hosts thereof, and dwell in righteousness with men on earth a thousand years, and the wicked shall not stand." (D&C 29:9-11.)

6. "Mine apostles, the Twelve which were with me in my ministry at Jerusalem, shall stand at my right hand at the day of my coming in a pillar of fire, being clothed with robes of righteousness, with crowns upon their heads, in glory even as I am, to judge the whole house of Israel, even as many as have loved me and kept my commandments, and none else." (D&C 29:12.)

INDEX

Abomination of desolation, 429-34, 447

Abraham: becoming seed of, 20 n. 2, 160, 162; Jews claimed lineage from, 158-59; God's covenant with, 161-62, righteous works of, 163; saw the day of Christ, 168, 170 n. 3; in parable of Lazarus and rich man, 262-63

Adultery: woman taken in, 140-44; penalty for, was death, 141; Jesus accuses Pharisees of, 259-60

Anarchy, religious, 331-32

Angels: different classes of, in Jewish tradition, 87; joy of, over repentant sinners, 247; ministering, 379; flying in the midst of heaven, 445 n. 2

Animals, caring for, on Sabbath, 230, 231

Anointing, 327; of Jesus, 335-37; was act of adoration, 343 n. 3

Antipas, Herod, 19-20, 35, 239

Apostasy, universal, 436-37

Apostles: chief, on Mount of Transfiguration, 55-56; questions of, concerning resurrection, 62-63. *See also* Twelve apostles

Aramaic, Jesus spoke, 15

Armageddon, 441, 447

Arrest of Jesus, Pharisees order, 130-31, 138

Ask and it shall be given, 188

Astoreth, 8

Atonement is for all men, 414

Authority: Jesus bestows, on Peter, 39-40; Nephi possessed, 41 n. 4; bestowed on apostles on Mount of Transfiguration, 57; bestowed upon Joseph Smith and Oliver Cowdery, 68 n. 5; of Jesus, 344-45, 357; of Jesus, Pharisees challenge, 352; formal teaching required, 353

Avenging of wrongs: God promises, 288-89; hope of, will nearly fade, 297 n. 1. *See also* Vengeance

Babes, things revealed to, that are hidden from wise, 173-74

Baptism: of blood, 314; of John, Jesus questions Pharisees concerning, 354-55

Barren fig tree: parable of, 195-96; Jesus curses, 345-47

Bartimeus, 315, 317-18

Bethany: Jesus' friends in, 181, 270, 333-34; Jesus spends his last Sabbath in, 333-37

Bethlehem, Christ was to come from, 137

Binding and loosing on earth and in heaven, 39-40; 91-93

Blasphemy, stoning Jesus for, 219-20

Blessings promised to Abraham's seed, 160

Blind man: healing of, by stages, 28-29; Jesus heals, on Sabbath, 198-201; reason for blindness of, 200; parents of, feared to acknowledge Jesus, 203-4; refused to recant testimony, 205-6; excommunication of, 207

Blindness, spiritual, 208

Bread, metaphor of, 26-27

Bridegroom, preparing to meet, 467

Caesar, paying tribute to, 370, 373

Caiaphas, 282

Called, many are, but few are chosen, 310

Capernaum, Jesus returns to, 75

Children: inherent holiness of, 79, 81; becoming as, to gain salvation, 81-82; are without sin, 83; fate of those who offend, 84; need no repentance, 245; brought by parents to Jesus, 299-300; are heirs of salvation, 300

Chosen people, 10-12

Christendom, modern: beware the sects

of, 30 n. 7, 437; gospel does not conform to, 115 n. 8

Chronology, difficulties of, 221 n. 1

Church: severing wicked from, 85; bringing offenders before, 90-91; organization of, in meridian of time, 93; membership in, is insufficient for salvation, 367; false, proselytizing for, 396

Circumcision, 127-28

Cities rejecting their God, fate of, 109-10

Cleanliness, inside and out, 398-99

Coin, lost, parable of, 247

Colt, Jesus rode, into Jerusalem, 338-39

Comforter, the Second, 61

Commandments: God requires men to keep, 266; keeping of, brings salvation, 302; greatest of all, 382-84, 387 n. 3

Controversy surrounding Jesus, 128-29, 137-38, 332-33

Cost, counting, before joining church, 240-41

Covetousness: Jesus counsels against, 191; of Pharisees, 258; among Jews, 266 n. 1; Jesus condemns Pharisees for, 395

Cross, taking up, 48, 240

Crucifixion, Jesus prophesies of, 313

Cursings upon those who reject gospel, 106, 394-402

David, son of, Pharisees named Jesus as, 385-86

Dead: let the dead bury their, 102-3; raising of Lazarus from, 269-80

Deaf and speech-impeded man, healing of, 14-15

Death: of Jesus, men plot for, 127, 153, 281-82; those who live gospel shall never see, 166-67; beliefs extend beyond, 263; state of men after, 267 n. 2; holds no sorrow for saints, 276

Debt, servant forgiven of, would not forgive another, 95-97

Decapolis, 13, 15-16, 20 n. 4-5

Deep doctrines, testing faith with, 44

Demoniac boy: disciples fail to heal 70-71; Jesus heals, 72-74

Desolation, abomination of, 429-34, 447

Devils, casting out, 172

Disciples of Jesus: failed to understand metaphor, 26-27, testimony meeting of, 31; must be willing to die for his cause, 47-49; 240; failure of, to heal demoniac boy, 70-71; jealousy among, 79-80; key to recognizing, 115 n. 3; becoming, 158; healed blind man joins with, 207-8; must be willing to forsake all, 240; Jesus blesses, for their adoration, 342; must watch for Second Coming, 458-60

Dissension, men who delight in, 176

Dives, rich man, 260-63

Divinity, Jesus proclaims his, 216-17

Divorce: is contrary to gospel, 292; Jewish laws concerning, 293-95; fornication was only justification for, 295

Doctrine: of the Father, Jesus preached, 126; new, rejection of, 242

Dogs, Gentiles equated with, 12

Drunkenness, sin of, 460

Earth: transfiguration of, seen in vision, 58; new, and new heaven, 457

Elect, deception of, 437-38

Eleventh hour, laborers called at, 309

Elias, some thought Jesus was, 35; Jewish tradition concerning, 64; John the Baptist as, 65-66; of the restoration, 66-67

Elijah, 14; conferred keys on Peter, James, and John, 57; called down fire from heaven, 114

Elisha, 14

Enemies of Jesus, punishment of, 321

Enoch, 58, 78 n. 2; city of, 52

Ephraim, Jesus retires to, 282

Eternal life, 50-51, 300-301; formula for gaining, 177, 302-3; comes by Jesus, 275; forsaking all to gain, 304-5; he that hath, is rich, 310 n. 1. See also Salvation

Eunuchs, 296

Evil, differing degrees of, 74

Exaltation, 253 n. 4

Excommunication, 91, 204-5; of blind man, 207

Faith: rituals may increase, 14-15; does not come from seeing signs, 24; testing, with deep doctrines, 44; power of, 72, 73-74, 93-94, 347; centers in Christ, not man, 85; sacrificing builds, 243 n. 1; as a grain of mustard seed, 264; definition of, 265

False doctrines: fate of preachers of, 85; beware of, 390-91

False prophets, 21-22, 212, 426

Family unit, eternal nature of, 292

Fear of men, 417-18

Feast, inviting poor to, 234-36

Feast of Tabernacles, 121-23, 134-36

Fig tree, barren: parable of, 195-96; Jesus curses, 345-47

Fig trees, parable of, 454

Fire: purging by, 86; calling down, from heaven, 113-14

First shall be last, 239

Fish, money in mouth of, 77

Food, temporal, vs. spiritual, 184

Foreordination, 312

Forgiveness: importance of, 89, 348; is required of man, 90; seventy times seven, 91; parable concerning, 95-98

Four thousand, feeling of, 16-19

Freedom, truth brings, 158

Friend at midnight, parable of, 187-89

Future, making provision for, 256-57

Galileans: most of the Seventy were, 171; accused of sin by Judeans, 194

Galilee: rejection of Jesus in, 107-8; fate of, 109-10; Jesus leaves, 111

Gates of hell, 42 n. 6

Gathering of Israel, 216, 439; keys of, 57

Gentile woman, Jesus heals daughter of, 9-13

Gentiles: equated with dogs, 12; harvest of, foreshadowed, 19; light unto, 147-48; some, shall be first, 239; extending of gospel to, 366-67, 411-15; Jerusalem to be trodden down of, 441; times of, to be fulfilled, 442

Geological changes in last days, 442

Gifts: good, from God, 189; spiritual, 469-70

Glory, seekers of, 127

Gnat, straining at, while swallowing camel, 398

God the Father: is an exalted man, 33, 41 n. 3, 416; literal son of, Jesus is, 36-37, 174; bore witness on Mount of Transfiguration, 54, 60-61; man's indebtedness to, 95-98; Jesus preached doctrine of, 126; Jesus would return to, 131, 153; is author of plan of salvation, 132 n. 2; Pharisees did not know, 151; was a witness of Christ, 152; covenant of, with Abraham, 161-62; Jesus' honor comes from, 167; you cannot serve mammon and, 257; saints' duty to, 265-66; is God of living, not dead, 380-81; love for, is first commandment, 383; words of, from heaven, 414-15

Godhood, attaining, 220, 221-22 n. 2

Good, addressing Jesus as, significance of, 301-2

Good Samaritan, parable of, 178-80

Good shepherd, Jesus is, 213-16

Gospel: Israel was entitled to receive, before Gentiles, 11-12, 365; of peace, 105; those who reject, shall be condemned, 106-7, 238; Jesus preached, wherever he went, 125; came from God the Father, 132 n. 2; power of, 172; understanding, requires revelation, 174; yoke of, 176; banquet of, was spurned by Jews, 235-36; all men shall hear, 238-39, 411; extending of, to Gentiles, 366-67, 411-15; restoration of, must precede Christ's Second Coming, 438-39; angel proclaiming, John's vision of, 445 n. 2

Grace, salvation by, 302

Gratitude, one of ten lepers expressed, 285

Great supper, parable of, 234-36

Greater light, sinning against, 209, 463 n. 3

Greatness: true, lies in service, 81; he who seeks, should be servant of all, 315, 393

Greeks sought to see Jesus, 411-13

Hallel, 368 n. 1

Hand, offensive, cutting off, 84

Healing: of Gentile woman's daughter,
9-13; formalities involved in, 14,
28-29; of deaf and dumb man, 14-15;
of multitudes in Decapolis, 15-16; may
inspire faith or persecution, 20 n. 5; of
blind man, by stages, 28-29; of
demoniac boy, disciples fail in, 70-71;
Jesus succeeds in, where disciples had
failed, 72-74; is sign of true church,
105; on Sabbath day, 127-28; of blind
man on Sabbath, 198-201; of woman
on Sabbath, 228-29; at Sabbath
banquet of Pharisees, 230-31;
spiritual, 269; of ten lepers, 284-85;
spiritual, of Zaccheus, 317; of blind
Bartimeus, 317-18

Heathen nations, redemption of, 453

Heaven, new, and new earth, 457

Hell, gates of, 42 n. 6

Hermon, Mount. *See* Mount of
Transfiguration

Herod Antipas, 19-20, 35, 239

Herodians, 370-72

Holy Ghost: is a revelator, 37; comes
with power, 172; apostles are to rely
on, 426

Hosanna Shout, 339

Humility: salvation depends on, 82;
greatness requires, 393

Husbandmen, wicked, parable of, 360-64

Husks fed to swine, 249

Hypocrisy: barren fig tree as symbol of,
346; Jesus condemns Pharisees for,
395

I Am, Jesus as the great, 168-69

Ignorance of Pharisees, 390

Immortality, Jesus inherited power of,
from his Father, 216-17

Ingratitude, sin of, 285-86

Inheritance, Jewish law of, 191, 196 n. 1,
248

Innocent: all men are, when born, 83;
should seek out guilty to restore peace,
90

Isaiah, 58, 184 n. 3

Israel: Jesus was sent only to, 10; house
of, is comprised of faithful from
preexistence, 11-12, 161; adoption into
house of, 13; gathering of, keys for,
57; punishment of, 115 n. 5; failure of,

to bear fruit, 196 n. 2; Nephites were
of, 216; gathering of, 216, 439;
received gospel first, 365. *See also* Jews

James, 55-58, 113-14, 313-14

Jealousy among disciples, 79-80

Jeremiah, some thought Jesus was, 35

Jericho, 315-16

Jerusalem: Jesus was destined to return
to, 45, 311; Peter counseled Jesus to
avoid, 46; Jesus' journey to, 111-13,
312; triumphal entry into, 338-40;
Jesus wept over, 340-41, 408;
destruction of, by Titus, 341; siege of,
433-34; Josephus' comments on, 435
n. 3; to be trodden down of Gentiles,
441; Jews to flee unto, in last days,
450; rebuilding of, 463 n. 2; the New,
476 n. 2

Jesus Christ: continuing Galilean
ministry of, 3-4; increasing opposition
to, 5-7; departed into Tyre and Sidon,
8; compassionate sighing of, 15, 20 n.
6; viewed by some as resurrected John
the Baptist, 19-20 n. 1, 35; salvation
comes through, 25, 214, 385; Pharisaic
view of, 26; as Son of Man, 32-33,
416; bears testimony of himself,
33-34; various men's views of, 34-36;
as Son of living God, 36-37, 174;
sufferings of, 43; had to lose his life,
45, 47; prayer of, on Mount of
Transfiguration, 55-56; God the
Father bore witness of, 61; prophesies
of his death and resurrection, 75-76,
155, 312-13; performing miracles in
name of, 82-83; voluntarily abased
himself, 88 n. 1; rejection of, in
Galilee, 107-8; leaves Galilee for
Jerusalem, 111; brethren of, challenge
him, 111-12; later Judean ministry of,
119-20; rumors of, preceded him into
Jerusalem, 123-24; taught in temple at
Tabernacle Time, 125-26; is accused
of having a devil, 127, 165-66; men
plot death of, 127, 153, 281-82;
controversy surrounding, 128-29,
137-38, 332-33; Pharisees order arrest
of, 130-31, 138; adulteress brought
before, 140-44; proclaims himself as
light of the world, 146, 149, 200,

417-48; bore record of himself,
151-52; preaches to multitude in
temple porch, 157; honor of, came
from God, 167; day of, Abraham saw,
168; affirms his divinity, 168-69; yoke
of, 176; is the good shepherd, 213-16;
had power to take up his life again,
216; works of, bear witness of him,
218; sheep of, hear his voice, 218-29;
Jews prepare to stone, for blasphemy,
219-20; escapes from Jews, 220-21;
Perean ministry of, 225-26; condemns
Pharisees, 259; tarries in Perea while
Lazarus is sick, 270-71; is resurrection
and life, 275; compassionate tears of,
277-78; journey of, to Jerusalem, 312;
was following foreordained course,
312; anointing of, by Mary, 335-37;
triumphal entry of, into Jerusalem,
338-40; weeps over Jerusalem, 340-41,
408; authority of, 344-45; cleanses his
house, the temple, 349; Pharisees
challenge authority of, 352; political
entrapment of, Pharisees attempt,
370-73; as son of David, 385-86;
speaks as Father directs, 419; wounds
of, Jews will recognize, 452
—miracles performed by: healing of
Gentile woman's daughter, 9-13;
healing of deaf and speech-impeded
man, 13-14; healing of multitudes in
Decapolis, 15-16; feeding of four
thousand, 16-19; each, was unique, 28;
healing of blind man by stages, 28-29;
healing of demoniac boy, 72-74;
healing of blind man on Sabbath,
198-201; healing of Perean woman on
Sabbath, 228-29; healing of man at
Pharisees' Sabbath banquet, 230-31;
raising of Lazarus, 269-80; cleansing
of ten lepers, 284-85; spiritual healing
of Zaccheus, 317; healing of blind
Bartimeus, 317-18; withering of
barren fig tree, 346
Jews: sects of, compared to modern
schools of thought, 30 n. 2; conflicting
views of, concerning resurrection,
62-63; marveled at Jesus' teachings,
126; symbolism of light among, 148;
Jesus condemns, 153-54; shall one day
know Christ, 155, 452; were
Abraham's seed literally but not
spiritually, 158-63; became children of
the devil, 163-64; did not know God,
167; practice of excommunication
among, 204-5; exhorted Jesus to speak
plainly, 217; had no excuse for
disbelief, 257-58; covetousness among,
266 n. 1; divorce laws of, 293-94;
rupture between Jesus and, becomes
complete, 407; could not understand
need for Messiah's death, 416;
desolation of, 425, 429-34; to flee unto
Jerusalem in last days, 450. *See also*
Israel
John, 55-58, 113-14, 313-14
John the Baptist: resurrected, some
thought Jesus was, 19-20 n. 1; as Elias,
65-66; Jesus questions Pharisees
concerning, 354-55; authority of,
357-58; belief in, implies belief in
Christ, 359
Jonah, sign of, 24-25
Joy of the Lord, entering into, 471-72
Judas, 336-37
Judean ministry, similarity of, to
Galilean ministry, 185, 189
Judge, unjust, parable of, 287-89
Judges, hierarchy of, 310 n. 2
Judgment: before hearing a man, 139;
condemning oneself through, 143-44;
belongs to Christ, 389-90; of
Pharisees, 390-91; day of, 473-75
Justice, rewards are meted out with, 323
n. 1

Keys: bestowal of, on apostles on Mount
of Transfiguration, 57; conferred upon
Joseph Smith and Oliver Cowdery, 68
n. 5; conferred upon twelve apostles,
92-93
King Follett sermon, 41 n. 3
Kingdom of God: Pharisees demanded
concerning, 286; had already come to
earth, 286-87; difficulty in entering,
for rich man, 304; to be taken from
Israel, and given to Gentiles, 363-64
Kingdom of heaven: keys of, 39-40, 57;
door to, will one day close, 238
King's son, marriage of, parable of,
364-68
Knock, and it shall be opened, 188
Knowledge, faith is born of, 265

Laborers in vineyard, parable of, 307-10
Last shall be first, 239
Lawyer who tempted Jesus, 177-78
Lazarus, 182; raising of, from dead, 269-80; sickness of, was for God's glory, 271; priests sought to kill, 385
Lazarus and rich man, parable of, 260-63
Least of brethren, deeds done to, 474-75
Leaven of Pharisees and Sadducees, 26-27
Lepers, ten, cleansing of, 284-85
Letter of law, 232
Levirate marriage, 275, 387 n. 1
Life: losing, to save it, 48, 413; eternal, 50-51; is more than food, 193, Jesus is, 275
Light, greater, sinning against, 209, 463 n. 3
Light of the world: Jesus was, 146-49, 200, 416-17; Pharisees rejected, 150
Living water, Jesus promises, to believers, 136
Loaves and fishes, multiplying of, 16-19
Lord's Prayer, the, 187
Lost coin, parable of, 247
Lost sheep, parable of, 245-46
Love of God and neighbor, 383-84

Magdala, rejection of Jesus in, 25-26
Mammon, ye cannot serve God and, 257
Man, Son of, significance of title of, 32-33
Marriage: varying laws concerning, 293; is ordained of God, 299; of king's son, parable of, 364-68; Mosaic law of, 375; celestial, 377; in resurrection, 377-78
Martha, 181-84; bade Jesus to ask Mary to help her, 183-84; expresses faith in Jesus' power, 274, 276
Martyrdom, era of, 427-29
Mary of Bethany, 276-77; sat at Jesus' feet to hear him, 182; anoints Jesus' feet, 335-37
Masks, wealth and poverty are, 267 n. 3
Master, call no man, 392-93
Masters, two, no man can serve, 257
Messiah: would give signs from heaven, 23; prophecies concerning, 129; was to bring light, 147; was to bring freedom from death, 167; temporal, Jesus was not, 218, 286-87; two ministries of,

scriptures indicate, 420 n. 3. *See also* Jesus Christ
Millennial prophecies, 132 n. 1
Ministering angels, 379
Ministers, true, vs. false, 391-92
Miracles: uniqueness of, 28; Rabbis attributed, to power of Satan, 32; man performing, disciples forbade, 82-83; controversy surrounding, 202; bear witness of Jesus' divinity, 207, 218; greatest among, 268-69. *See also* Jesus Christ, miracles performed by
Missionaries, Jesus' instructions to, 104-6. *See also* Seventies
Missionary work, 175
Missouri, judgments visited upon, 115 n. 6
Mite, widow's, 410-11
Mortality, cares of, 460
Moses, 67 n. 2-4; conferred keys on Peter, James, and John, 57; called seventy men to help bear his burden, 100; laws of, 127-28; disciples of, Pharisees claimed to be, 206; belief in, implies belief in Christ, 242; found straying sheep, 253 n. 1; law of marriage given by, 375; delineated curses of disobedience, 431
Mount of Olives, 424
Mount of Transfiguration: happenings on, are not fully revealed, 54; Peter, James, and John ascended, with Jesus, 55-56; Shekinah descended upon, 60-61; location of, 67 n. 1; was high point of Jesus' ministry, 69; descent from, into confusion, 70
Mountains, saints would flee to, 430
Mourning: accompanying Lazarus' death, 274; at time of Second Coming, 448-49
Multitude, feeding of, 16-19

Naaman, 14
Nazarene, Christ was to be called, 137, 145 n. 4
Neighbor: Jewish conception of, 178; parable defining, 178-80; love for, is second great commandment, 384
Nephites, 343 n. 1; Jesus refers to, as other sheep, 215-16
Nero, 427-28

New Jerusalem, 476 n. 2
Nicodemus, 139
Noah, days of, 454-55

Oaths, swearing with, 396-97
Obedience is essential to salvation, 469
Offenders: fate of, 84; aggrieved should seek out, to make peace, 90-91
Ointment, Mary anoints Jesus with 335-37
Olives, Mount of, 424
Oneness of God and Christ, 174-75, 219
Opposition to Jesus: increasing, 5-7; uniting of factions in, 23, 30 n. 6, 370-72; intensity of, 40; by deputation of religious leaders, 352
Ordination, authority bestowed by, 353
Other sheep, Jesus speaks of, 215-16

Parable: of unmerciful servant, 95-98; of good Samaritan, 178-80; of friend at midnight, 187-89; of rich fool, 191-93; of barren fig tree, 195-96; of wedding guests, 232-33; of great supper, 233-36; of lost sheep, 245-46; of lost coin, 247; of prodigal son, 248-53; of unjust steward, 254-57; of Lazarus and rich man, 260-63; of unprofitable servants, 265; of unjust judge, 287-89; of Pharisee and publican, 290-91; of laborers in vineyard,307-10; of the pounds, 319-22; of two sons, 358-59; of wicked husbandmen, 360-64; of marriage of king's son, 364-68; of fig trees, 454; of ten virgins, 465-68; of talents, 469-73
Passover, 331-32
Peace, missionaries preach gospel of, 105
Perean ministry of Jesus, 225-26
Persecution, Jesus warns apostles of, 426
Peter: bears testimony of Christ, 36; as son of Jonah, 38; testimony of, came through revelation, 38; blessings promised to, 44; counsels Jesus to avoid Jerusalem, 46; experiences of, on Mount of Transfiguration, 55-58; desired to build tabernacles for Moses and Elias, 59-60; pays temple tax with coin from fish's mouth, 77-78
Pharisee and publican, parable of, 290-91

Pharisees: demand arrest of Jesus, 130-31, 138; reject light of the world, 150; refuse to acknowledge Jesus' hand in miracle, 205-6; as robbers of sheepfold, 212; Sabbath banquet of, Jesus heals man at, 230-31; concern of, with rank, 233; covetousness of, 258; Jesus condemns, 259, 390-91; attempt to trap Jesus with question about divorce, 290-91; challenge Jesus' authority, 351-52; Jesus confounds, with question about baptism of John, 354-55; attempted to trap Jesus politically, 370-73; called Jesus the son of David, 385-86; ignorance of, 390; eight denunciations of woe upon, 394-402; parents' sins will fall upon, 404-5; seven classes of, 405-6 n. 1
Plough, putting hand to, and looking back, 103
Politics, Pharisees turned to, to trap Jesus, 370-73
Pounds, parable of, 319-22
Power: of faith, 72, 73-74, 93-94, 347; of gospel, 172
Prayer: of Jesus on Mount of Transfiguration, 55-56; in faith, 94; different types of, 186-87; the Lord's, 187; parables concerning, 287-91
Preexistence: faithful from, comprise house of Israel, 11-12, 161; allusion to, by Jesus, 88
Priesthood is power and authority from God, 345
Priests, craft of, was endangered by Jesus, 130-31. See also Pharisees
Prodigal son, parable of, 248-53
Prophets: false, 21-22, 212, 437; obedience to, Jewish views on, 209 n. 1; rejecting testimony of, 238, 400-402; persecution of, 361
Publican: and Pharisee, parable of, 290-91; chief, Jesus resides with, 316-17
Punishment, sufferings seen as, 194-95, 199
Purification, salt as symbol of, 87
Purse and scrip, traveling without, 105, 115 n. 2

Questioning: for questioning's sake, 176; of Pharisees, cessation of, 384

Rabbi Eliezer, signs given by, 30 n. 1
Rabbis, stature of, in Israel, 393
Rank, Pharisaic concern with, 233
Records kept in heaven, 184 n. 1
Regeneration, day of, 306
Rejection: of gospel, condemnation accompanying, 106-7; of living prophets, 400-402; of Jesus by majority of Jews, 417
Religion: letter vs. spirit in, 232; importance of sacrifice in, 243 n. 1; true, vs. false, 392; focusing on trifles of, 398; false, shall abound in last days, 437-38, 444 n. 1
Religious anarchy, 331-32
Remission of sins, 155 n. 3
Repentance: little children have no need of, 88, 245; leading men to, 249; belief in Jesus depends on, 358
Restoration: of all things, 65-66; era of, 438-39
Resurrection: of the just, 51, 234; conflicting views concerning, 62-63; miracle of, 268-69; and life, Jesus is, 275; day of, reward of apostles in, 305-6; Sadducees did not believe in, 374-75; Rabbis' statements on, 378-79; prophecies concerning, 380; at time of Second Coming, 451
Revelation: necessity of, in understanding God, 37, 174; Jesus' church is built on rock of, 38-39, 41-42 n. 5
Rich fool, parable of, 191-93
Riches: sharing, with others, 192; young man could not forsake, for gospel, 303-4
Righteous: state of, after death, 267 n. 2; rewards of, in resurrection, 306
Righteousness: of Abraham, 163; outward appearance of, 399-400
Roman invasion of Galilee, 109-10
Ruler over many things, becoming, 471

Sabbath: restrictions of, Jesus broke, 127-28, 198-202, 227-28; Jesus heals blind man on, 198-201; Rabbinical, 202; Jesus heals Perean woman on, 227-29; banquet of Pharisees on, Jesus heals man at, 230-31; Jesus spends his last, in Bethany, 333-37

Sacrifice: importance of, to religion, 243 n. 1; definition of, 306-7
Sadducees, 374-80
Saints: must be tried in all things, 86; duty of, to God, 265-66; persecution of, in meridian of time, 427-29; resurrection of, at Second Coming, 451; responsibilities of, in Christ's absence, 461
Salome, mother of James and John, 313-14
Salt: symbolism of, 87, 88 n. 2; with lost savor, 242
Salvation: comes through Christ, 25, 214, 385; Pharisaic view of, 26; becoming as children to gain, 82; is individual affair, 86, 367, 468; plan of, was created by God the Father, 132 n. 2; truth leads to, 158; plan of, Jews failed to understand, 220; gate of, is strait, 237; law of Moses is insufficient for, 242-43; greatness of gift of, 298; keeping commandments leads to, 302; closing door to, Pharisees condemned for, 394-95; obedience is essential to, 469
Samaritan: the good, parable of, 178-80; leprous, gave thanks for healing blessing, 285
Samaritans: refused to receive Jesus, 112-13; name of, as epithet, 165
Sanhedrin plot death of Jesus, 281-82
Satan: repeats his tactics throughout generations, 30 n. 2; Jesus' miracles attributed to, 32; quotes scripture for his own purposes, 137; children of, 163-64; was a liar from the beginning, 164-65; fall of, 172; seeks to destroy family unit, 292; shall have his day, 437; binding of, 453
Scriptures: Satan quotes, for his own purposes, 137; not knowing, the Sadducees erred in, 376; taking away fulness of, 403
Sealing power, 91-93; keys of, bestowed on Peter, James, and John, 57
Second Coming of Christ, 51, 436-63; signs of, 425, 449-50; restoration of gospel must precede, 438-49; grand sign of, 448, 463 n. 1; day of, who may abide, 455-56; saints are to watch for, 458; hour of, is nigh, 476 n. 5

Seed of Abraham, 20 n. 2, 158-63
Seek and ye shall find, 188
Sepulchres, whited, 399-400
Servants, unprofitable, men are, 265-66
Service: true greatness lies in, 81; is essential to salvation, 321; rewards for, 471-72
Seventies: calling and responsibility of, 99-101, 115 n. 1-4; appointed by Jesus, 101-2; commission of, 103-6; return of, from missions, 171-72; further power bestowed upon, 173
Seventy times seven, man should forgive, 91
Sheep: of Jesus hear his voice, 218-29; lost, parable of, 245-46; separating, from goats, 473
Shekinah, appearance of, on Mount of Transfiguration, 60-61
Shepherd: importance of, in Israel, 210-11; Jesus as, 213-16
Signs: seekers of, 22; demanding of, to damage Jesus' work, 22-23, 29 n. 1; do not produce faith, 24; of the times, 24, 30, 440-44; of Jonah, 24-25; given by Rabbi Eliezer, 30 n. 1; latter-day seeking of, 30 n. 4; Jesus' failure to show, weakened his influence, 32
Siloam, pool of, blind man washes in, 201
Sin: little children are free from, 82; against the greater light, 107, 463 n. 3; he who is without, to cast first stone, 142; remission of, 155 n. 3; freedom from, truth brings, 158; whoso committeth, is servant of, 159; physical punishment for, 199; of parents, Pharisees will bear, 404-5; three common types of, 460
Sinners: persons wronged should seek out, 90; Jesus eats with, 245; spiritual healing of, 269
Slothful servant, 320-21, 472
Smith, Joseph, 310 n. 3
Sodom and Gomorrah, 455
Son of Man, significance of title of, 32-33
Souls, worth of, 49-50
Spikenard, ointment of, Mary anoints Jesus with, 335-37
Spirit, gifts of, 469-70
Spiritual blindness, 208; healing of, 269
Steward, unjust, parable of, 254-57
Stone: rejected by builders, 363-64; one,

shall not be left upon another, 422, 423-24
Stoning of Jesus for blasphemy, Jews prepare for, 219-20
Suffering seen as punishment, 194-95, 199
Surfeiting, sin of, 460
Swine, Jewish contempt for, 249
Synagogue: being put out of, 204-5; ruler of, chastises Jesus for healing on Sabbath, 228-29

Tabernacles: Peter desired to build, 59-60; feast of, 121-23, 134-36
Talents, parable of, 469-73
Tax for temple services, 76-78
Teaching required authority, 353-54
Temple: tax of, 76-78; Jesus taught in, at Tabernacle Time, 125-26; Jesus cleanses, for a second time, 348-49; beauty of, 422-23; desolation of 423-24
Temporal deliverer: Jesus was not, 218, 286-87; Israel sought, 319
Temptation from friends, 46
Ten lepers, cleansing of, 284-85
Ten virgins, parable of, 465-68
Testimony: disciples meet to bear, 31; Jesus bears, of himself, 33-34; of Peter, 36; recording of, in heaven, 38; disciples were to keep secret, 40; relationship of, to forgiveness of sins, 40-41 n. 1; borne by Martha, 276
Thief in the night, coming of Lord as, 463, 464
Titus, destruction of Jerusalem by, 341-42, 424
Tomb: Lazarus was laid in, 273; Lazarus comes forth from, 279
Traditions, evil, Jesus decried, 6
Transfiguration: of prophets, 67 n. 3; of self-sacrifice, 312; See also Mount of Transfiguration
Translated beings, 52, 67 n. 4
Triumphal entry into Jerusalem, 338-40
Truth shall make you free, 158
Twelve apostles: received keys of kingdom of heaven, 92-93; reward of, in resurrection, 305-6; baptism of blood awaiting, 314; Jesus warns, of impending persecution, 426; role of, in judgment, 474, 476 n. 6

Two sons, parable of, 358-59
Tyre and Sidon, 8, 106-7

Unity, power in, 83-84
Unjust judge, parable of, 287-89
Unjust steward, parable of, 254-57
Unmerciful servant, parable of, 95-98
Unprofitable servants, men are, 265-66

Vengeance: is the Lord's, 389; day of,
    431, 451
Vineyard: laborers in, parable of, 307-10;
    that brought forth wild grapes, 362
Virgins, ten: parable of, 465-68;
    described as wise and foolish, 476 n. 3

Warnings, doctrines are given as, 457-58
Wars and rumors of wars, 440-41
Washings, ritualistic, 189
Water: symbolism of, 133-34, 145 n. 1-2;
    rituals involving, at Feast of
    Tabernacles, 134-36; living, Jesus
    promises, 136
Wealth: sharing, 192; is only a mask, 267
    n. 3

Wedding garment, man without, 367
Wedding guests, parable of, 232-33
Whited sepulchres, Pharisees likened to,
    399-400
Wicked: state of, after death, 267 n. 2; to
    be slain at Christ's coming, 321, 456;
    judgments upon, 452
Wicked husbandmen, parable of, 360-64
Widow's mite, 310-11
Wise, things hidden from, 173-74
Witnesses: of Christ, missionaries are,
    104; law of, 151-52
Woe, eight denunciations of, upon
    Pharisees, 394-402
Word of the Lord, 166
Works of Jesus: bear witness of him, 218;
    Jesus exhorts Jews to believe in, 220
Worldliness, 191
Wounds of Jesus, Jews shall recognize,
    452

Yoke of Rabbinism vs. yoke of gospel,
    175-76

Zaccheus, 315-17